The Allied Artists Checklist

McFarland Classics

Anderson. *Science Fiction Films of the Seventies*
Archer. *Willis O'Brien*
Benson. *Vintage Science Fiction Films, 1896–1949*
Bernardoni. *The New Hollywood*
Broughton. *Producers on Producing*
Byrge & Miller. *The Screwball Comedy Films*
Chesher. *"The End": Closing Lines...*
Cline. *In the Nick of Time*
Cline. *Serials-ly Speaking*
Darby & Du Bois. *American Film Music*
Derry. *The Suspense Thriller*
Douglas. *The Early Days of Radio Broadcasting*
Drew. *D.W. Griffith's* Intolerance
Ellrod. *Hollywood Greats of the Golden Years*
Erickson. *Religious Radio and Television in the U.S., 1921–1991*
Erickson. *Syndicated Television*
Frasier. *Russ Meyer—The Life and Films*
Fury. *Kings of the Jungle*
Galbraith. *Motor City Marquees*
Harris. *Children's Live-Action Musical Films*
Harris. *Film and Television Composers*
Hayes. *The Republic Chapterplays*
Hayes. *3-D Movies*
Hayes. *Trick Cinematography*
Hill. *Raymond Burr*
Hogan. *Dark Romance*
Holland. *B Western Actors Encyclopedia*
Horner. *Bad at the Bijou*
Jarlett. *Robert Ryan*
Kinnard. *Horror in Silent Films*
Langman & Gold. *Comedy Quotes from the Movies*
Levine. *The 247 Best Movie Scenes in Film History*
McGee. *Beyond Ballyhoo*
McGee. *The Rock & Roll Movie Encyclopedia of the 1950s*
McGee. *Roger Corman*
McGhee. *John Wayne*
Mank. *Hollywood Cauldron: Thirteen Horror Films*
Martin. *The Allied Artists Checklist*
Nollen. *The Boys: ...Laurel and Hardy*
Nowlan. *Cinema Sequels and Remakes, 1903–1987*
Okuda. *The Monogram Checklist*
Okuda & Watz. *The Columbia Comedy Shorts*
Parish. *Prison Pictures from Hollywood*
Pitts. *Western Movies*
Quarles. *Down and Dirty: Hollywood's Exploitation Filmmakers*
Selby. *Dark City: The Film Noir*
Sigoloff. *The Films of the Seventies*
Slide. *Nitrate Won't Wait*
Smith. *Famous Hollywood Locations*
Sturcken. *Live Television*
Tropp. *Images of Fear*
Tuska. *The Vanishing Legion: ...Mascot Pictures*
Von Gunden. *Alec Guinness*
Von Gunden. *Flights of Fancy*
Warren. *Keep Watching the Skies!*
Watson. *Television Horror Movie Hosts*
Watz. *Wheeler & Woolsey*
Weaver. *Poverty Row HORRORS!*
Weaver. *Return of the B Science Fiction and Horror Heroes*
West. *Television Westerns*

The Allied Artists Checklist

The Feature Films and Short Subjects of Allied Artists Pictures Corporation, 1947–1978

by
Len D. Martin

McFarland & Company, Inc., Publishers
Jefferson, North Carolina, and London

Len D. Martin is also the author of
The Columbia Checklist (McFarland, 1991); and
The Republic Pictures Checklist (McFarland, 1998)

The present work is a reprint of the library bound edition of The Allied Artists Checklist: The Feature Films and Short Subjects of Allied Artists Pictures Corporation, 1947–1978, *first published in 1993. McFarland Classics is an imprint of McFarland & Company, Inc., Publishers, Jefferson, North Carolina, who also published the original edition.*

Library of Congress Cataloguing-in-Publication Data
Martin, Len D., 1939–.
    The Allied Artists checklist : the feature films and short subjects of Allied Artists Pictures Corporation, 1947–1978 / by Len D. Martin.
       p.   cm.
    Includes bibliographical references and index.
    ISBN 0-7864-1113-9 (softcover : 50# alkaline paper) ∞
    1. Allied Artists Pictures Corporation—Catalogs. 2. Motion pictures—United States—Catalogs. I. Title.
PN1999.A4M37   2001   016.79143'75'0973—dc20   92-56665

British Library cataloguing data are available

©1993 Len D. Martin. All rights reserved

No part of this book may be reproduced or transmitted in any form or by any means, electronic or mechanical, including photocopying or recording, or by any information storage and retrieval system, without permission in writing from the publisher.

On the cover: A still from the 1959 film *The Giant Behemoth* (Courtesy Photofest)

Manufactured in the United States of America

McFarland & Company, Inc., Publishers
   Box 611, Jefferson, North Carolina 28640
     www.mcfarlandpub.com

Table of Contents

Preface	vii
Historical Overview	ix
Feature Films	1
Problem Films	153
Short Subjects	155
Appendix A: Film Titles by Release Date	157
Appendix B: Monogram/Allied Artists Movie Series	163
Appendix C: Westerns and Players Associated with Monogram/Allied Artists	166
Appendix D: Monogram/Allied Artists Academy Award Nominations	172
Bibliography	175
Name Index	177

Preface

This book is not intended to be an in-depth examination of Allied Artists Pictures Corporation or their product; rather it is intended as a handy reference guide to the output of a studio that started out as a B picture unit, Monogram Pictures Corporation, and eventually tried to graduate to an A picture unit.

Beginning with the decade of the sixties, Allied Artists concentrated their efforts on television sales and production and distributed films which were produced by independent producers and foreign-language studios with little domestically produced product. For the sake of completeness, these films are included in this work.

In doing research for this book, it was not uncommon to find different running times and release dates for certain titles along with different studio releases for the same title. I have tried to furnish the reader with information as accurate as possible.

Periodicals consulted were *The New York Times, The Los Angeles Times,* and *Variety.*

Abbreviations used in this book are as follows: *DIR* (director), *PRO* (producer), *SP* (screenplay), *B&W* (black & white), *SCOPE* (any of the wide screen processes: CinemaScope, TechniScope, VistaScope, SuperScope, TotalScope, etc.).

Len D. Martin
Houston, Texas
July, 1993

Historical Overview

Allied Artists Pictures Corporation had its beginnings in November of 1946 when Steve Broidy, president of Monogram Pictures Corporation,* formed Allied Artists Productions, Inc., as a wholly-owned subsidiary of Monogram Pictures Corporation, to exclusively handle production and distribution of high-budget motion pictures.

It was Steve Broidy's intention to distribute A quality pictures through Allied Artists and continue to let Monogram be the distributor for the B pictures. From 1947 to 1952, many of the pictures released by Allied Artists were top quality, such as *The Gangster, The Babe Ruth Story, Smart Woman, Southside 1–1000,* and *Flat Top.*

Although Allied Artists was treated as a separate entity at first, Monogram, wishing to change its image from a B picture unit to an A picture unit, began releasing its product at the beginning of 1953 through Allied Artists and, on November 12, 1953, the corporate name officially became Allied Artists Picture Corporation.

Stratford Pictures Corporation, organized in 1949 by Steve Broidy and George D. Burrows as president and vice-president respectively, distributed foreign language features, mostly from Britain, through Monogram and Allied exchanges until 1959, when Stratford Pictures Corporation ceased operation.

In 1951, Allied Artists engaged in the production of films for television and organized the Interstate Television Corporation, which later became Allied Artists Television Corporation and lasted until the seventies.

In 1965, Claude A. Giroux was elected president and chief executive officer to succeed Steve Broidy in a management realignment. It was during that period that Allied Artists moved away from the production of feature films and concentrated their efforts on television production. It is for this reason that many of the features released during this period were from foreign or independent producers.

*The history of Monogram Pictures Corporation and their films is to be found in The Monogram Checklist: The Films of Monogram Pictures Corporation, 1931–1952 *by Ted Okuda (McFarland, 1987).*

In 1968, Emanuel L. Wolf succeeded Claude Giroux as president and chief executive officer. It was through his leadership that Allied Artists resumed production of motion pictures. Many of the Allied Artists pictures, whether produced independently or by a studio, carried his personal inscription at the beginning of each film, "Emanuel L. Wolf presents."

Through the next ten years Allied Artists would produce box office hits such as *Cabaret, The Man Who Would Be King, The Betsy, The Wild Geese,* and *Papillon,* the highest grossing film in the studio's history.

On January 20, 1976, Allied Artists Pictures Corporation merged with Kalvex, Inc./PSP, Inc., into a new company, Allied Artists Industries Inc. In 1979 Allied Artists fell on hard times and, hoping to stay in business, filed for bankruptcy reorganization but could not make it. Finally, in 1980 Allied Artists was sold to Lorimar Productions.

And so, the company that began as Rayart Productions in 1924, Monogram Pictures Corporation in 1930, and finally, Allied Artists Pictures Corporation in 1953, had ceased to exist. But to those of us who remember their films, both good and bad, they will live on in our memories.

Feature Films
(1947-1978)

Following is a complete list of feature films produced and or distributed by Allied Artists Pictures Corporation and Stratford Pictures Corporation. Producer and screenwriter are given, where known.

Omitted from this listing are those Monogram features reissued under the Allied Artists logo. Also omitted from this listing is the 1954 release, *The Adventures of Hajji Baba*, which was produced by Allied Artists Pictures Corporation, but was released by 20th Century-Fox.

1. The Accursed (7/13/58) B&W – 78 mins. (Spy-Drama). *DIR/SP:* Michael McCarthy. *PRO:* E.J. Fancey. A Fantur Production. *CAST:* Donald Wolfit, Robert Bray, Jane Griffiths, Anton Diffring, Oscar Quitak, John Van Eyssen, Rupert Davies, Carl Jaffe, Frederick Schiller, Colin Croft, Christopher Lee, Karel Stepanek. *SYN:* At a reunion of former British underground agents, a Colonel (Wolfit) sets out to unmask one of the agents as a former Nazi who has been killing the surviving members of the group. *NOTES:* Released in Great Britain in 1957 at a running time of 88 mins. Re-released by Allied Artists in 1960 to profit by the popularity of Christopher Lee. [British title: *The Traitor*.]

2. Affair in Havana (10/1/57) B&W – 77 mins. (Crime-Drama). *DIR:* Laslo Benedek. *PRO:* Richard Goldstone. *SP:* Burton Lane, Maurice Zimm. Based on a story by Janet Green. *CAST:* John Cassavetes, Raymond Burr, Sara Shane, Lilia Lazo, Sergio Pena, Celia Cruz, Jose Antonio Rivero, Miguel Angel Blanco. *SYN:* A piano player (Cassavetes) falls for the wife (Shane) of a crippled plantation owner (Burr). He later learns from a servant (Pena) that she has murdered her husband to inherit his fortune. When she kills the servant and then is killed by the servant's wife (Lazo), he returns to his job. *NOTES:* Filmed in Cuba.

3. Affair in Monte Carlo (8/14/53) Technicolor – 75 mins. (Romance). *DIR:* Victor Saville. *PRO:* Ivan Foxwell. *SP:* Warren Chetham-Strode. Based on *Twenty-four Hours in a Woman's Life* by Stefan Zweig. An Associated British Picture-Pathé Production. *CAST:* Merle Oberon, Richard Todd, Leo Genn, Stephen Murray, Peter Reynolds, Joan Dowling, June Clyde, Peter Illing, Jacques Brunius, Isabel Dean, Peter Jones, Yvonne Furneaux, Mara Lane, Robert Ayres. *SYN:* A rich widow (Oberon) attempts to reform a compulsive gambler (Todd), offering him her love and fortune, to no avail. *NOTES:* Filmed in

Advertisement for *Affair in Monte Carlo* (1953).

Monte Carlo. Released in Great Britain in 1952 at a running time of 90 mins. [British title: *24 Hours in a Woman's Life*.]

4. Al Capone (4/5/59) B&W – 105 mins. (Biography-Crime). *DIR:* Richard Wilson. *PRO:* John H. Burrows, Leonard J. Ackerman. *SP:* Marvin Wald, Harry Greenburg. *CAST:* Rod Steiger, Fay Spain, James Gregory, Martin Balsam, Nehemiah Persoff, Murvyn Vye, Joe De Santis, Lewis Charles, Robert Gist, Sandy Kenyon, Raymond Bailey, Al Ruscio, Louis Quinn, Ron Soble, Steve Gravesi, Ben Ari, Peter Dane. *SYN:* Al Capone (Steiger), under the tutelage of Johnny Torrio (Persoff), rises from bar room bouncer, to crime lord of Chicago, and finally, Alcatraz convict. *NOTES:* This film has been rated by the critics as the definitive Capone picture.

Advertisement for *Al Capone* (1959).

5. Alice, Sweet Alice (5/78) Technicolor—108 mins. (Crime-Horror). *DIR:* Alfred Sole. *PRO:* Richard K. Rosenberg. *SP:* Alfred Sole, Rosemary Ritvo. *CAST:* Paula Sheppard, Brooke Shields, Linda Miller, Jane Lowry, Alphonso DeNoble, Rudolph Willrich, Mildred Clinton, Niles McMaster, Gary Allen, Michael Hardstack, Tom Signorelli, Louisa Horton, Antonino Rocco, Lillian Roth. *SYN:* Alice (Sheppard), a 12-year-old-girl, is suspected of killing her sister (Shields). As the police investigation continues, more people are killed and Alice appears to be the prime suspect. Or is she?? *NOTES:* The film debut of Brooke Shields. Originally released by Allied Artists in 1977 under the title *Communion*; re-released in 1978 by Allied Artists with the above re-renamed title. Re-released again by Dyna-Mite Entertainment in 1981 with the re-renamed title *Holy Terror*, at a running time of 96 mins. None of these titles helped; the film lost money all around. Filmed in Paterson, New Jersey.

6. Angel Baby (5/14/61) B&W—97 mins. (Drama). *DIR:* Paul Wendkos. *PRO:* Thomas F. Woods. *SP:* Orin Borsten, Paul Mason, Sam Roeca. Based on *Jenny Angel* by Elsie Oaks Barber. *CAST:* George Hamilton, Salome Jens, Mercedes McCambridge, Joan Blondell, Henry Jones, Burt Reynolds, Roger Clark, Dudley Remus, Victoria Adams, Harry Swoger, Barbara Biggart, Eddie Firestone. *SYN:* A faith healer (Hamilton) restores speech to a mute girl (Jens) and she, in turn, becomes a faith healer. The girl is exploited by an unscrupulous man (Reynolds) and is labelled a fake, but her faith is restored when she cures a lame child. *NOTES:* The film debuts of Salome Jens and Burt Reynolds.

Allied Artists' release of *Alice, Sweet Alice* played up the participation of Brooke Shields who only had a minor supporting role in the film (1978). *(Photo courtesy of Ted Okuda.)*

7. Angels One Five (4/30/54) B&W – 98 mins. (War-Drama). *DIR:* George More O'Ferrall. *PRO:* John Gossage, Derek Twist. *SP:* Derek Twist. Story by Pelham Groom. An Associated British Pathé-Templer Films Production. A Stratford Picture Presentation. *CAST:* Jack Hawkins, Michael Denison, Dulcie Gray, John Gregson, Cyril Raymond, Humphrey Lestocq, Andrew Osborn, Veronica Hurst, Harold Goodwin, Norman Pierce, Geoffrey Keen, Harry Locke, Philip Stanton, Vida Hope, Amy Veness, Ronald Adam, Colin Tapley, Peter Jones, Harry Fowler. *SYN:* In 1940 England, a volunteer reserve pilot (Gregson), always an individual, is at odds with his commanding officer (Hawkins). *NOTES:* Released in Great Britain in 1952.

8. An Annapolis Story (4/10/55) Technicolor – 81 mins. (War-Drama). *DIR:* Don Siegel. *PRO:* Walter Mirisch. *SP:* Daniel B. Ullman, Geoffrey Homes (Daniel Mainwaring). Story by Daniel B.

Ullman. *CAST:* John Derek, Diana Lynn, Kevin McCarthy, Alvy Moore, Pat Conway, L.Q. Jones, John Kirby, Don Haggerty, Barbara Brown, Betty Lou Gerson, Fran Bennett, Robert Osterloh, John Doucette, Don Kennedy, Tom Harmon. *SYN:* Two brothers (Derek, McCarthy) who go through Annapolis Naval Academy together become rivals when they both fall in love with the same girl (Lynn). Brotherhood wins out when, during the Korean War, one saves the other after he is shot down. [British title: *The Blue and the Gold.*]

9. The Anonymous Venetian (9/71) Eastmancolor — 91 mins. (Drama). *DIR:* Enrico Maria Salerno. *PRO:* Turi Vasile. *SP:* Enrico Maria Salerno, Giuseppe Berto. An Ultra Film Production. *CAST:* Tony Musante, Florinda Bolkan, Toti Cal Monte, Alessandro Grinfan, Brizio Montinaro, Giuseppe Bella. *SYN:* A man (Musante) dying of a brain tumor meets with his estranged wife (Bolkan) in Venice to discuss what went wrong with their relationship. [Original Italian title: *Anonimo Veneziano.*]

archy and mehitabel *see* **shinbone alley**

10. Armored Command (7/9/61) B&W — 99 mins. (War-Spy). *DIR:* Byron Haskin. *PRO/SP:* Ron W. Alcorn. *CAST:* Howard Keel, Tina Louise, Warner Anderson, Earl Holliman, Carleton Young, Burt Reynolds, James Dobson, Marty Ingels, Clem Harvey, Maurice Marsac, Thomas A. Ryan, Peter Capell, Charles Nolte, Branden Maggert. *SYN:* During World War II, a U.S. Army tank force is trapped in the Vosges Mountains of France. A colonel (Keel) devises a plan to defeat the advancing German unit while a sergeant (Holliman) exposes a German spy (Louise). *NOTES:* Thomas A. Ryan was also technical advisor on this film.

11. Arrow in the Dust (4/25/54) Technicolor — 80 mins. (Western). *DIR:* Lesley Selander. *PRO:* Hayes Goetz. *SP:* Don Martin. Based on *Road to San Jacinto* by L.L. Foreman. *CAST:* Sterling Hayden, Coleen Gray, Keith Larsen, Tom Tully, Jimmy Wakely, Tudor Owen, Lee Van Cleef, John Pickard, Carleton Young, Sheb Wooley, Iron Eyes Cody. *SYN:* A Cavalry soldier (Hayden) who deserted his unit assumes the identity of a dying officer and leads a wagon train to safety. *NOTES:* This film used stock footage from the 1951 United Artists film, *New Mexico.*

12. Arson for Hire (3/1/59) B&W — 67 mins. (Action-Crime). *DIR:* Thor Brooks. *PRO:* William F. Broidy. *SP:* Thomas G. Hubbard. *CAST:* Steve Brodie, Lyn Thomas, Frank Scannell, Anthony Carbone, John Merrick, Jason Johnson, Robert Riordan, Wendy Wilde, Walter Reed, Lari Lane, Reed Howes, Lyn Osborn, Frank Richards, Lester Dorr, Thomas G. Hubbard. *SYN:* An investigator (Brodie) for the fire department's arson squad sets out to find the gangsters who are setting fire to large buildings and then shaking down the owners for the insurance money they receive. *NOTES:* Double billed in some areas with *The Giant Behemoth.*

13. At Gunpoint (12/25/55) Technicolor/Scope — 81 mins. (Western). *DIR:* Alfred L. Werker. *PRO:* Vincent M. Fennelly. *SP:* Daniel B. Ullman. *CAST:* Fred MacMurray, Dorothy Malone, Walter Brennan, Tommy Rettig, Skip Homeier, John Qualen, Harry Shannon, Whit Bissell, Irving Bacon, Jack Lambert, Frank Ferguson, James Anderson, John Pickard, Anabel Shaw, Rick Vallin, Harry Lauter, Harry Strang, Kim Charney, Byron Foulger, Barbara Woodell, Gertrude Astor, Lyle Latell, Keith Richards, Stephen Wootten, James Griffith, Mimi Gibson, James Lilburn. *SYN:* A

Fred MacMurray in *At Gunpoint* (1955).

storekeeper (MacMurray) kills a robber in a hold-up and finds himself deserted by his friends when the man's brother (Homeier) vows revenge against him. NOTES: A reworking of the 1952 United Artists film, *High Noon*. [British title: *Gunpoint!*]

14. The Atomic Man (3/4/56) B&W – 76 mins. (Science Fiction-Spy). *DIR:* Ken Hughes. *PRO:* Alec C. Snowden. *SP:* Charles Eric Maine, Ken Hughes. Based on *The Isotope Man* by Charles Eric Maine. A Merton Park Production. *CAST:* Gene Nelson, Faith Domergue, Joseph Tomelty, Donald Gray, Vic Perry, Peter Arne, Launce Maraschal, Charles Hawtrey, Martin Wyldeck, Carl Jaffe, Barry Mackay. *SYN:* A reporter (Nelson) believes that an almost-dead man (Arne), fished out of the Thames River, is a double for an atomic scientist (Arne) who turns out to be a spy. The real scientist recovers but, because of exposure to radioactivity, his brain is 7½ seconds ahead of "real"

Joi Lansing and Arthur Franz in *The Atomic Submarine* (1959). *(Photo courtesy of Ted Okuda.)*

time. *NOTES:* Released in Great Britain in 1955 at a running time of 93 mins. Peter Arne plays a dual role in this film. Double billed in some areas with *Invasion of the Body Snatchers*. [British title: *Timeslip*.]

15. The Atomic Submarine (11/29/59) B&W – 72 mins. (Science Fiction). *DIR:* Spencer G. Bennet. *PRO:* Alex Gordon. *SP:* Orville H. Hampton. Story by Jack Rabin, Irving Block. A Gorham Production. *CAST:* Arthur Franz, Dick Foran, Brett Halsey, Tom Conway, Paul Dubov, Bob Steele, Victor Varconi, Joi Lansing, Selmer Jackson, Jack Mulhall, Jean Moorhead, Richard Tyler, Sid Melton, Ken Becker, Frank Watkins. Narrated by Pat Michaels. *SYN:* The commander (Franz) of a new atomic powered submarine is sent to the North Pole to investigate a series of mysterious sea disasters and encounters a flying saucer beneath the Arctic waters. *NOTES:* The special effects team consisted of Louis DeWitt and story writers Jack Rabin and Irving Block. Release date is also given as 2/12/60.

16. Attack of the Crab Monsters (2/10/57) B&W – 63 mins. (Science Fiction). *DIR/PRO:* Roger Corman. *SP:* Charles B. Griffith. A Los Altos Production. *CAST:* Richard Garland, Pamela Duncan, Russell Johnson, Leslie Brady, Mel Welles, Richard Cutting, Beech Dickerson, Tony Miller, Ed Nelson, Charles B. Griffith. *SYN:* Several scientists, stranded on a shrinking South Sea island, encounter giant brain eating crabs mutated by radiation from an atomic bomb test and try to devise a way

William Hudson and Allison Hayes in *Attack of the 50 Ft. Woman* (1958).

to destroy them. *NOTES:* Double billed in some areas with *Not of This Earth.*

17. Attack of the 50 Ft. Woman (5/18/58) B&W – 66 mins. (Science Fiction). *DIR:* Nathan Hertz (Nathan Juran). *PRO:* Bernard Woolner. *SP:* Mark Hanna. A Woolner Production. *CAST:* Allison Hayes, William Hudson, Yvette Vickers, Roy Gordon, George Douglas, Kenneth Terrell, Otto Waldis, Eileen Stevens, Michael Ross, Frank Chase, Dale Tate, Thomas Jackson. *SYN:* A woman (Hayes) grows to enormous height after encountering an alien and suffering ray burns. She wreaks vengeance on her unfaithful husband (Hudson) and his mistress (Vickers). *NOTES:* The TV version was released at a running time of 75 min., using hold frames and a long printed crawl at the beginning and end of the film. Working titles were *The Giant Woman* and *The Astounding Giant Woman.* Double billed in some areas with *War of the Satellites.*

18. The Babe Ruth Story (9/6/48) B&W – 106 mins. (Sports-Biography). *DIR:* Roy Del Ruth. *PRO:* Joe Kaufman. *SP:* Bob Considine, George Callahan. Based on *The Babe Ruth Story* by Babe Ruth as told to Bob Considine and serialized in *The Saturday Evening Post.* *CAST:* William Bendix, Claire Trevor, Charles Bickford, Sam Levene, William Frawley, Gertrude Niesen, Fred Lightner, Stanley Clements, Bobby Ellis, Lloyd Gough, Matt Briggs, Paul Cavanagh, Pat Flaherty, Richard Lane, Tony Taylor, Mark Koenig, Joseph Crehan, Harry Wismer, David Gorcey, Mel Allen, H. V. Kaltenborn. Narrated by Knox Manning. *SYN:* The biography of George Herman "Babe" Ruth (Bendix) who, as an orphan (Ellis) at St. Mary's Industrial School for Boys, was introduced to sand-

Jane Wyatt and Lloyd Nolan in *Bad Boy* (1949).

lot baseball by Brother Mathias (Bickford). The story then follows Ruth from pitcher with the Baltimore Orioles and Boston Red Sox to his career as a New York Yankee.

19. Bad Boy (1/22/49) B&W – 86 mins. (Crime-Drama). *DIR:* Kurt Neumann. *PRO:* Paul Short. *SP:* Robert D. Andrews, Karl Kamb. Story by Robert D. Andrews, Paul Short. Produced with the cooperation of Variety Clubs International. *CAST:* Lloyd Nolan, Jane Wyatt, Audie Murphy, James Gleason, Stanley Clements, Martha Vickers, Rhys Williams, James Lydon, Dickie Moore, Selena Royle, Tommy Cook, William Lester, Walter Sande, Stephen Chase, Charles Trowbridge, Francis Pierlot, Florence Auer, Barbara Woodell, George Beban, Bill Walker. *SYN:* A juvenile delinquent (Murphy) is sent to the Boy's Ranch at Copperas Cove, Texas, for rehabilitation. *NOTES:* Audie Murphy's first starring film role.

20. Bad Men of Tombstone (2/22/49) B&W – 74 mins. (Western). *DIR:* Kurt Neumann. *PRO:* Frank King, Maurice King. *SP:* Philip Yordan, Arthur Strawn. Based on *The Last of the Badmen* by Jay Monaghan. *CAST:* Barry Sullivan, Marjorie Reynolds, Broderick Crawford, Fortunio Bonanova, Guinn "Big Boy" Williams, John Kellogg, Mary Newton, Louis Jean Heydt, Virginia Carroll, Dick Wessel, Claire Carleton, Ted Hecht, Harry Cording, Lucien Littlefield, Harry Hayden, William Yip, Olin Howlin, Robert Barrat, Julie Gibson, Joseph Crehan, Ted Mapes, Rory Mallinson, Ted French, Douglas Fowley, Dennis Hoey, Morris Ankrum, Tom Fadden, Dick Foote, Billy Gray, Gerald Courtemarche, Bonnie Lou Donaldson, George Chesebro. *SYN:* Two ruthless gunfighters (Sullivan, Crawford) and their gang terrorize a western town.

21. The Badge of Marshal Brennan (4/14/57) B&W — 74 mins. (Western). *DIR/PRO:* Albert C. Gannaway. *SP:* Thomas G. Hubbard. *CAST:* Jim Davis, Arleen Whelan, Lee Van Cleef, Louis Jean Heydt, Carl Smith, Marty Robbins, Harry Lauter, Douglas Fowley, Lawrence Dobkin, Rick Vallin, Eddie Crandall, Darryl Guy, Edward Colemans. *SYN:* When Marshal Matt Brennan (Fowley) is ambushed and left for dead, an outlaw (Davis) finds him, assumes his identity when he dies, and helps a sheriff (Smith) thwart the local cattle baron (Heydt) and his son (Van Cleef). *NOTES:* Double billed in some areas with *Footsteps in the Night.*

The Barbarians *see* **The Pagans**

22. The Bashful Elephant (2/4/62) B&W — 82 mins. (Children). *DIR/PRO/SP:* Dorrell McGowan, Stuart E. McGowan. *CAST:* Molly Mack, Helmut Schmid, Kai Fischer, Buddy Baer, Fritz Weiss, Arnulf Schroeder, Hans Schumm, Hans Possenbacher, Gernot Duda, "Jeffrey" the dog, "Valle" the elephant. *SYN:* A 12-year-old orphan girl (Mack) and her dog escape from Hungary into Austria, pursued by the police. She joins a circus where she makes friends with one of the elephants. When the police locate her, she runs away, hides in an abandoned church, and is accidently knocked unconscious. Her friend the elephant rescues her and carries her back to the circus where she is adopted by the circus owner (Schmid) and his future wife (Fischer). *NOTES:* Filmed in Austria.

23. The Bat (8/9/59) B&W — 80 mins. (Mystery). *DIR/SP:* Crane Wilbur. *PRO:* C.J. Tevlin. Based on the book and play by Mary Roberts Rinehart and Avery Hopwood. A Liberty Production. *CAST:* Vincent Price, Agnes Moorehead, Gavin Gordon, John Sutton, Lenita Lane, Elaine Edwards, Darla Hood, John Bryant, Harvey Stephens, Mike Steele, Riza Royce, Robert B. Williams. *SYN:* A mystery writer (Moorehead) and her companion (Lane) rent a gloomy estate from a banker who has been murdered and has left a large sum of money hidden in the house. A mysterious figure known as "The Bat" begins his reign of terror and murder as he tries to find the money. *NOTES:* A remake of the 1926 United Artists film *The Bat* and the 1930 United Artists film *The Bat Whispers.* Darla Hood once played the role of "Darla" in the *Our Gang* shorts. Allied Artists' catchlines for this film were "When the Bat Flies...Someone Dies" or "When It Flies...Someone Dies." Double billed in some areas with *Face of Fire.*

24. Battle Flame (7/26/59) B&W — 78 mins. (War). *DIR:* R.G. Springsteen. *PRO:* Lester A. Sanson. *SP:* Elwood Ullman. Story by Elwood Ullman and Lester A. Sanson. *CAST:* Scott Brady, Elaine Edwards, Robert Blake, Wayne Heffley, Gordon Jones, Ken Miller, Arthur Walsh, Richard Harrison, Gary Kent, Peggy Moffitt, Jean Robbins, Richard Crane. *SYN:* A Marine (Brady) leads his men behind enemy lines to rescue a group of nurses held captive by North Korean soliders. *NOTES:* Double billed in some areas with *Surrender—Hell!*

25. The Battle of Algiers (9/21/67) B&W/Scope — 120 mins. (War). *DIR:* Gillo Pontecorvo. *PRO:* Antonio Musu, Yacef Saadi. *SP:* Gillo Pontecorvo, Franco Solinas. An Igor-Casbah Film Production. A Rizzoli Film Presentation. *CAST:* Yacef Saadi, Jean Martin, Brahim Haggiag, Tommaso Neri, Samia (Michele) Kerbash, Fawzia El-Kader, Mohamed Ben Kassen, Ugo Paletti. *SYN:* Told in semi-documentary style, this film traces the revolt of the Algerians against the French from 1954 to July 3, 1962, when

Algiers won its independence from France. *NOTES:* Filmed in Algiers in 1965. Released in Italy in 1966 at a running time of 135 mins. Allied Artists picked up U.S. distribution of this film. [Original Italian title: *La Battaglia di Algeri.*] [Original Algerian title: *Maarakat Alger.*]

26. Battle Zone (10/26/52) B&W — 81 mins. (War). *DIR:* Lesley Selander. *PRO:* Walter Wanger. *SP:* Steve Fisher. *CAST:* John Hodiak, Linda Christian, Stephen McNally, Martin Milner, Dave Willock, Jack Larson, Richard Emory, Philip Ahn, Carleton Young, John Fontaine, Todd Karns, Gil Stratton, Jr. *SYN:* During the Korean War, two military combat photographers (Hodiak, McNally), both in love with a Red Cross nurse (Christian), are at odds as they photograph military installations at the Yalu River.

27. Beast from Haunted Cave (3/14/60) B&W — 65 mins. (Horror). *DIR:* Monte Hellman. *PRO:* Gene Corman. *SP:* Charles B. Griffith. A Filmgroup Production. *CAST:* Michael Forest, Sheila Carol, Frank Wolff, Richard Sinatra, Wally Campo, Kay Jennings, Christopher (Chris) Robinson. *SYN:* A gangster (Wolff), his girl (Carol) and the rest of his gang are guided to the mountains by a ski instructor (Forest) after they rob a mine. During a snow storm, they seek shelter in a cave inhabited by a monster (Robinson) intent on killing off the group. *NOTES:* Director Monte Hellman's film debut. Executive Producer Roger Corman was uncredited. Running times for this film vary from 64 mins. to 75 mins. depending on area of country where it was distributed. This film was probably released independently by Filmgroup as early as 1959. The same cast appeared in *Ski Troop Attack* for Roger Corman. Double billed in some areas with *The Wasp Woman.*

28. The Beast of Budapest (2/23/58) B&W — 72 mins (War-Drama). *DIR:* Harmon C. Jones. *PRO:* Archie Mayo. *SP:* John McGreevey. Story by Louis Stevens. A Barlene Corporation Production. *CAST:* Gerald Milton, John Hoyt, Greta Thyssen, Michael Mills, Violet Rensing, John Mylong, Joseph Turkel, Booth Coleman, Svea Grunfeld, John Banner, Charles Brill, Kurt Katch, Robert Blake, Tommy Ivo, Collette Jackson. *SYN:* During the Hungarian Revolution of 1956, a father (Hoyt) and his son (Mills) differ over politics. When the father is killed, the son joins with "The Beast" (Milton) in opposing the Communist domination in their country.

Beatsville *see* **The Rebel Set**

The Beauty and the Brain *see* **Sex Kittens Go to College**

The Beauty and the Robot *see* **Sex Kittens Go to College**

29. Belle de Jour (Beauty of the Day) (4/10/68) Eastmancolor — 100 mins. (Drama). *DIR:* Luis Bunuel. *PRO:* Robert Hakim, Raymond Hakim. *SP:* Luis Bunuel, Jean-Claude Carriere. Based on the book by Joseph Kessel. A Paris Film–Five Films Production. *CAST:* Catherine Deneuve, Jean Sorel, Michel Piccoli, Genevieve Page, Pierre Clementi, Francisco Rabal, François Fabian, Maria Latour, Georges Marchal, Macha Meril, Muni, Iska Khan, D. deRoseville, Michel Charrel, Brigitte Parmentier, Francis Blanche, François Maistre, Dominique Dandrieux, Bernard Fresson. *SYN:* A bored housewife (Deneuve), unbeknownst to her husband (Sorel), works days in a Parisian brothel where she is known as "Belle de Jour." When one of her clients (Clementi), who wants her, learns her real identity, he shoots her husband, who is left paralyzed, and he, in turn, is killed by the police. She then feels remorse and leaves to care for her husband. *NOTES:*

Carole Mathews and Beverly Michaels cope with crowded prison conditions in *Betrayed Women* (1955). *(Photo courtesy of Ted Okuda.)*

Release date given is the general American release date. Released in France in April, 1967. Released in Italy in September, 1967. [Original Italian title: *Bella di Giorno*.]

30. Betrayed Women (7/17/55) B&W – 70 mins. (Crime). *DIR:* Edward L. Cahn. *PRO:* William F. Broidy. *SP:* Steve Fisher. Story by Paul Leslie Peil. *CAST:* Carole Mathews, Beverly Michaels, Peggy Knudson, Tom Drake, Sara Haden, John Dierkes, Esther Dale, Paul Savage, Darlene Fields, John Damler, G. Pat Collins, Burt Wenland, Pete Kellett. *SYN:* Two women inmates (Mathews, Michaels), fed up with the sadistic prison conditions and treatment by their guard (Haden), break out of prison with two hostages (Drake, Knudson), hoping to expose the conditions of the prison.

31. The Betsy (2/78)Technicolor – 125 mins. (Drama). *DIR:* Daniel Petrie.

PRO: Harold Robbins, Robert Weston. *SP:* Walter Bernstein, William Bast. Based on the book by Harold Robbins. *CAST:* Laurence Olivier, Robert Duvall, Katherine Ross, Tommy Lee Jones, Jane Alexander, Lesley-Anne Down, Joseph Wiseman, Kathleen Beller, Edward Herrmann, Paul Rudd, Roy Poole, Richard Venture, Titos Vandis, Clifford David, Inga Swenson, Whitney Blake, Carol Williard, Read Morgan, Charlie Fields. *SYN:* The multi-generational wheelings and dealings of an auto conglomerate family, the patriarch (Olivier), his son (Rudd), grandson (Duvall), their wives, and lovers. Problems arise when they are to unveil to the public their new auto, "The Betsy," named after the patriarch's great-granddaughter (Beller), an auto so perfect that it threatens the other auto companies.

32. Beyond Love and Evil (3/71) Eastmancolor – 90 mins. (Drama-Romance). *DIR:* Jacques Scandelari. *PRO:* Robert de Nesle. *SP:* Jean Stuart, Jean Pierre Deloux, Jacques Scandelari. Story by Jean Stuart. A Comptoir Français de Film Production. *CAST:* Souchka, Lucas de Chabanieux, Fred Saint-James, Marc Coutant, Sabry, Serge Halsdorf, Michel Lablais, Milarka Nervi, Dorsi Thon, Nicole Huc, Nadia Kempf, Ursula Pauly. *SYN:* An innocent young man (de Chabanieux) sets out to rescue his true love (Souchka) from the villain's (Saint-James) castle but succumbs to the pleasures within. *NOTES:* Another of the "soft-core" X-rated features distributed by Allied Artists in the seventies. [Original French title: *La Philosophie dans le Boudoir.*]

33. The Big Circus (7/5/59) Technicolor/Scope – 108 mins. (Adventure). *DIR:* Joseph M. Newman. *PRO:* Irwin Allen. *SP:* Irwin Allen, Charles Bennett, Irving Wallace. Story by Irwin Allen. A Saratoga–Vic Mature–Irwin Allen Production. *CAST:* Victor Mature, Red Buttons, Rhonda Fleming, Kathryn Grant, Vincent Price, Gilbert Roland, Peter Lorre, David Nelson, Adele Mara, Howard McNear, Charles Watts, Steve Allen, and the world's greatest circus acts. *SYN:* When the Whirling Circus is faced with bankruptcy after its split with the Borman Brothers, Hank Whirling (Mature) tries to get a bank loan to keep the circus. An accountant (Buttons) is sent to examine the workings of the circus before a loan can be given, but accidents and sabotage plague the circus as it begins its tour, threatening the loan.

34. The Big Combo (2/13/55) B&W – 89 mins. (Crime). *DIR:* Joseph Lewis. *PRO:* Sidney Harmon. *SP:* Philip Yordan. A Security-Theodora Production. *CAST:* Cornel Wilde, Richard Conte, Brian Donlevy, Jean Wallace, Robert Middleton, Lee Van Cleef, Earl Holliman, Helen Walker, Jay Adler, John Hoyt, Ted de Corsia, Helene Stanton, Roy Gordon, Whit Bissell, Philip Van Zandt, Steve Mitchell, Baynes Barron, Rita Gould, Tony Michaels, Bruce Sharpe, Michael Mark, Donna Drew. *SYN:* A police detective (Wilde), out to get evidence against a sadistic syndicate crime boss (Conte), receives the evidence he needs through his wife (Walker) and mistress (Wallace).

35. The Big Tip Off (3/20/55) B&W – 79 mins. (Crime-Drama). *DIR:* Frank McDonald. *PRO:* William F. Broidy. *SP:* Steve Fisher. *CAST:* Richard Conte, Constance Smith, Bruce Bennett, Cathy Downs, James Millican, Richard Benedict, Sam Flint, Mary Carroll, Murray Alper, Lela Bliss, Harry Guardino, G. Pat Collins, Frank Hanley, Virginia Carroll, Alan Wells, Pete Kellett, Tony DiMario, Cecil Elliott, Robert Carraher. *SYN:* A newspaper reporter (Conte) who refuses to divulge the source of his underworld information sets out to get the boss (Bennett) of a phony fund-raising telethon gang.

36. The Big Wave (4/29/62) B&W—73 mins. (Drama). *DIR/PRO:* Tad Danielewski. *SP:* Pearl S. Buck, Tad Danielewski. Based on the book by Pearl S. Buck. A Stratton-Toho Production. *CAST:* Sessue Hayakawa, Ichizo Itami, Mickey Curtis, Koji Shitara, Hiroyuki Ota, Rumiko Sasa, Juddy Onagg, Reiko Higa, Sachiko Atami, Henry Okawa, Chieko Murata, Tetsu Nakamura, Frank Tokunaga, Shigeru Nihonmatsu, Noriko Sengoku. *SYN:* A farmboy (Ota) and a fisherboy (Shitara), who survive a tidal wave as foretold by the Old Gentleman (Hayakawa) of their island village, grow up to be young men (Curtis, Itami) and decide to spend their lives there, knowing that the Old Gentleman will always warn them of tidal waves to come. *NOTES:* Limited theatrical release. Released in Japan at a running time of 98 mins.

37. Bikini Paradise (5/3/67) Eastmancolor—89 mins. (Comedy). *DIR:* Gregg Tallas. *PRO:* Lester A. Sansom, Bernard Glasser. *SP:* Howard Berk. Story by Howard Berk, Daniel Aubrey. A Philip Yordan Production. An A.C.E. Films–Security Pictures Presentation. *CAST:* Kieron Moore, Janette Scott, John Baer, Kay Walsh, Alexander Knox, Anna Brazzou, Sylvia Sorente, Margaret Nolan, Michele Mahaut, Francine Welch, Pilar Clemens, Aida Power, Robert Beatty, Shirley Faulls, Graham Summer. *SYN:* A Navy lieutenant (Moore) and his men search for a teacher (Walsh) and her female pupils who have been missing since escaping from the Japanese in World War II. When they locate them on a remote island, the women decide to make the lieutenant and his men their husbands and start an island paradise. *NOTES:* Filmed in the Canary Islands in 1964. Working title was *White Savage.* Limited theatrical release. [British title: *Mission to Paradise.*]

38. Billy Budd (11/12/62) B&W/Scope—112 mins. (Adventure-Drama). *DIR/PRO:* Peter Ustinov. *SP:* Peter Ustinov, DeWitt Bodeen. Based on *Billy Budd, Foretopman* by Herman Melville and the play by Robert Chapman and Louis O. Coxe. A Harvest Production. *CAST:* Robert Ryan, Peter Ustinov, Melvyn Douglas, Terence Stamp, John Neville, Ronald Lewis, David McCallum, Lee Montague, Paul Rogers, Niall McGinnis, Thomas Heathcoate, Cyril Luckham, Victor Brooks, Barry Keegan, John Meillon, Ray McAnally, Robert Brown. *SYN:* In 1797, an impressed seaman (Stamp) is hanged by the captain (Ustinov) of a man-of-war for accidently killing a sadistic master-at-arms (Ryan). *NOTES:* The American film debut of Terence Stamp. Screenwriter Robert Rossen was uncredited.

39. Bitter Creek (2/21/54) B&W—74 mins. (Western). *DIR:* Thomas Carr. *PRO:* Vincent M. Fennelly. *SP:* George Waggner. A Westwood Production. *CAST:* "Wild" Bill Elliott, Carleton Young, Beverly Garland, Veda Ann Borg, Claude Akins, Jim Hayward, John Harmon, John Pickard, Forrest Taylor, Mike Ragan (Holly Bane), Danny Mummert, Zon Murray, John Larch, Jane Easton, Florence Lake, Earle Hodgins, Joe Devlin, Stanley Price, Dabbs Greer. *SYN:* A cowboy (Elliott) goes to the town of Bitter Creek to find the man who murdered his rancher-brother. *NOTES:* Screenwriter George Waggner became a respected film and TV director and his credits always read "George WaGGner."

40. Black and White in Color (4/77) Eastmancolor—100 mins. (Satire). *DIR:* Jean-Jacques Arnaud. *PRO:* Arthur Cohn, Jacques Perrin, Giorgio Silagni. *SP:* Jean-Jacques Arnaud, Georges Conchon. *CAST:* Jean Carmet, Jacques Dufilho, Catherine Rouvel, Jacques Spiesser, Dora Doll, Maurice Barrier, Claude Legros, Jacques Monnet, Peter Berling, Marius Beugre

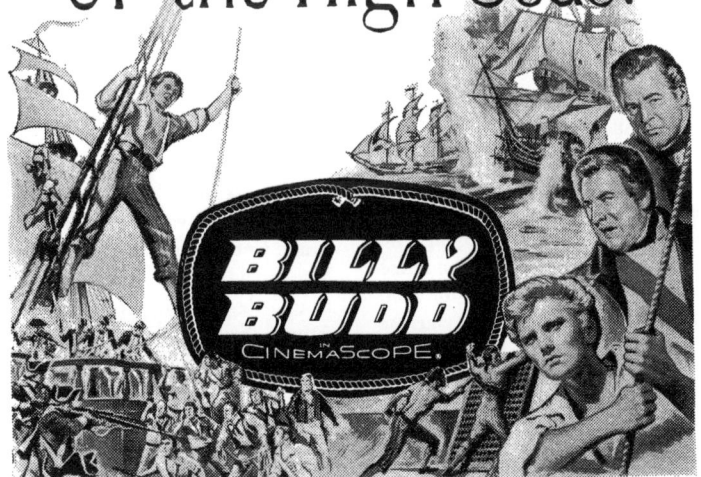

Advertisement for *Billy Budd* (1962).

Boignan, Dieter Schidor, Baye Macoumba Diop, Aboutbaker Toure, Marc Zuber, Klaus Huebel, Mamadou Coulibaly, Memel Atchori, Jean-Françoise Eyou N'Guessan, Natou Koly, Tanoh Kouao. *SYN:* In 1915 French Equatorial Africa, a geographer (Spiesser) leads a group of Frenchmen in attacking a neighboring fortress. *NOTES:* Director Jean-Jacques Arnaud's first feature film. Released in France in 1976. [Original French title: *La Victoire en Chantant.*] [Alternate French title: *Noir et Blancs en Couleur.*]

41. Black Gold (9/16/47) CineColor —92 mins. (Drama). *DIR:* Phil Karlson. *PRO:* Jeffrey Bernerd. *SP:* Agnes Christine Johnson. Story by Caryl Coleman. *CAST:* Anthony Quinn, Katherine DeMille, Elyse Knox, Kane Richmond, Ducky Louie, Raymond Hatton, Thurston Hall, Al Bridge, Moroni Olsen, H.T. Tsiang, Charles Trowbridge, Jonathan Hale, Jack Norman (Norman Willis), Darryl Hickman, Clem McCarthy, Joe Hernandez. *SYN:* An Indian (Quinn) and his wife (DeMille) adopt a Chinese boy (Louie). When oil is struck on his property, they name a new colt "Black Gold" and raise the colt into a championship horse. When the Indian is dying, he makes the boy promise to enter the horse in the Kentucky Derby and win for him. *NOTES:* Anthony Quinn's first starring role after appearing in 46 films as a costar.

Black Victory *see* **Black and White in Color**

42. Black Zoo (5/15/63) Eastmancolor—88 mins. (Horror). *DIR:* Robert Gordon. *PRO:* Herman Cohen. *SP:* Herman Cohen, Aben Kandel. *CAST:* Michael Gough, Jeanne Cooper, Rod Lauren, Virginia Grey, Jerome Cowan, Elisha Cook, Jr., Warene Ott, Marianna Hill, Oren Curtis, Eilene Janssen, Eric Stone, Dani Lynn, Susan Slavin, Edward Platt, Douglas Henderson, Jerry Douglas, Claudia Brack, Daniel Kurlick, Byron Morrow, Michael St. Angel. *SYN:* A madman (Gough), who belongs to a sect that worships animals and believes they take on human souls, operates a private zoo and uses his beasts to commit murder.

43. Blond Blackmailer (1/9/58) B&W—58 mins. (Crime-Drama). *DIR/PRO/SP:* Charles Deane. *CAST:* Richard Arlen, Susan Shaw, Constance Leigh, Vincent Ball, Andrea Malandrinos, Althea Siddons, Clive St. George, Patricia Salonika, Reginald Hearne, Howard Lang, John Dunbar, Sidney Bromley, Claudia Carr, Arnold Adrian. *SYN:* A man (Arlen), released from prison after serving time for the murder of a female blackmailer, a crime which he didn't commit, sets out to find the person who framed him. *NOTES:* Released in Great Britain in 1955 at a running time of 69 mins. [British title: *Stolen Time.*]

44. Blonde Sinner (11/18/56) B&W —73 mins. (Crime-Drama). *DIR:* J. Lee Thompson. *PRO:* Kenneth Harper. *SP:* Joan Henry, John Cresswell. Based on *Yield to the Night* by Joan Henry. *CAST:* Diana Dors, Yvonne Mitchell, Michael Craig, Geoffrey Keen, Olga Lindo, Mary Mackenzie, Joan Miller, Marie Ney, Liam Redmond, Marjorie Rhodes, Athene Seyler, Molly Urquhart, Harry Locke, Michael Ripper. *SYN:* On death row, a woman (Dors) recalls the events that led to her murdering the rich mistress of her pianist lover (Craig). *NOTES:* Released in Great Britain in 1955 at a running time of 99 mins. [British title: *Yield to the Night.*]

45. Blood and Black Lace (4/7/65) Technicolor—88 mins. (Horror). *DIR:* Mario Bava. *PRO:* Lou Moss. *SP:* Mario Bava, Marcel Fondat, Joe Borilla. A Wolner Bros. Picture Production. *CAST:* Cameron Mitchell, Eva Bartok, Thomas

Diana Dors in *Blonde Sinner* (1956).

Reiner, Arianna Gorini, Dante De Paolo, Mary Arden, Franco Ressel, Claude Dantes, Lea Krugher, Massimo Righi, Guiliano Raffaelli, Harriette White Medin. *SYN:* Fashion models are being murdered and suspicion falls on the fashion house owner (Bartok) and her drug addict boyfriend (Mitchell). *NOTES:* English version directed, produced, and written by Lou Moss. [Original Italian title: *Sei Donne per l'Assassino.*] [Original French title: *Six Femmes pour l'Assassin.*] [British title: *Fashion House of Death.*]

46. Blood on the Arrow (10/11/64) De-Luxe Color—91 mins. (Western). *DIR:* Sidney Salkow. *PRO:* Leon Fromkess, Sam Firks. *SP:* Robert E. Kent. Story by Robert E. Kent, Mark Hanna. *CAST:* Dale Robertson, Martha Hyer, Wendell Corey, Dandy Curran, Ted de Corsia, Paul Mantee, Elisha Cook, Jr., John Matthews, Tom Reese, Bloyce Wright, Michael Hammond, Leland Wainscott, Robert Carricart. *SYN:* An outlaw (Robertson), the only survivor of an Apache attack, takes refuge with a trading post couple (Hyer, Corey) and has to rescue their son (Curran) when he is taken hostage by Apaches demanding guns for his exchange.

47. The Blood Rose (10/70) Eastmancolor—87 mins. (Horror). *DIR:* Claude Mulot. *PRO:* Edgar Oppenheimer. *SP:* Claude Mulot, Edgar Oppenheimer, Jean Carriaga. A Transatlantic Production. *CAST:* Philippe Lemaire, Annie Duperey, Howard Vernon, Elisabeth Tessier, Olivia Robin, Michele Perello, Valerie Boisgel, Gerard Huart, Johnny Cacao. *SYN:* An artist (Lemaire) secures the services of a plastic surgeon (Vernon) to try and restore the facial features of his wife (Duperey) who was horribly burned in a fire. *NOTES:* Released in France in September, 1969, at a running time of 95

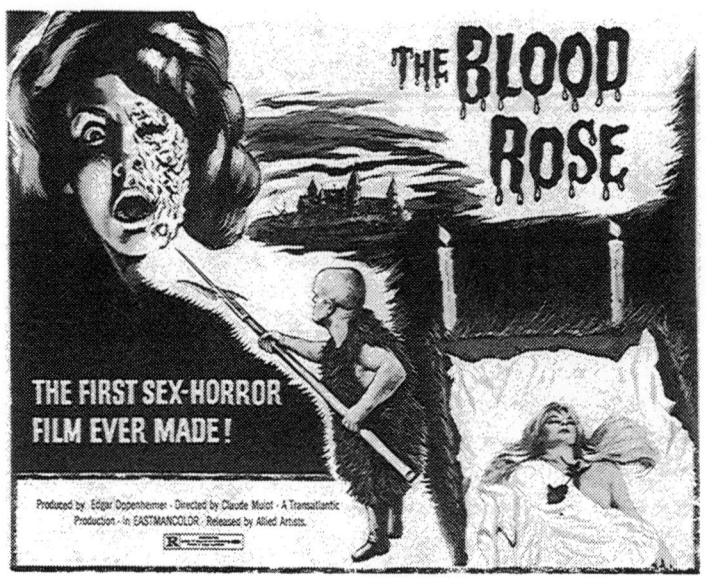

Advertisement for *The Blood Rose* (1970). *(Courtesy of Ted Okuda.)*

mins. Lesbian scenes were deleted for the American release, where it was billed as "the first sex-horror film." [Original French title: *La Rose Écorchée*.] [British title: *Ravaged*.]

48. The Bloody Brood (10/22/60) B&W – 68 mins. (Crime). *DIR/PRO:* Julian Roffman. *SP:* Elwood Ullman, Ben Kerner, Des Hardman. Story by Anne Howard Bailey. A Key Films–Sutton Production. *CAST:* Jack Betts, Barbara Lord, Peter Falk, Robert Christie, Ronald Hartmann, Anne Collins, William Brydon, George Sperdakos, Ronald Taylor, Michael Zenon, Billy Kowalchuk, Sammy Sales, Kenneth Wickes, Carol Starkman, Rolf Colstan. *SYN:* A man (Betts) goes after the leader (Falk) of a gang of beatniks and his men when they kill his brother for kicks. *NOTES:* Filmed in Canada in 1959. Released by Sutton Pictures in 1959. Picked up for distribution by Allied Artists in 1960. Released by Astor Pictures in 1962. Running times vary from 68 mins. to 80 mins. due to the violence being cut from the print in some areas of distribution.

49. Bluebeard's Ten Honeymoons (4/2/60) B&W – 93 mins. (Crime-Mystery). *DIR:* W. Lee Wilder. *PRO:* Roy Parkinson. *SP:* Myles Wilder. A Domino Pictures Production. *CAST:* George Sanders, Corinne Calvet, Jean Kent, Patricia Roc, Greta Gynt, Maxine Audley, Ingrid Hafner, Selma Caz Dias, Peter Illing, George Coulouris, Sheldon Lawrence. *SYN:* Henri Landru (Sanders), known as "Bluebeard," marries rich women and then murders them for their money.

50. The Bob Mathias Story (10/24/54) B&W – 79 mins. (Sports-Biography). *DIR:* Francis D. Lyon. *PRO:* William E. Selwyn. *SP:* Richard Collins. *CAST:* Bob Mathias, Ward Bond, Melba Mathias, Ann Doran, Howard Petrie, Diane Jergens. *SYN:* The biography of Bob Mathias, playing himself; his rise as

Feature Films

George Sanders and Corrine Calvet in *Bluebeard's Ten Honeymoons* (1960).

a star athlete with the training of his coach (Bond), his romance and eventual marriage, winning the Olympic Decathlon in 1948 and 1952, and his enlistment in the Marine Corps. [British title: *The Flaming Torch.*]

51. Bobby Ware Is Missing (10/23/55) B&W – 67 mins. (Crime-Mystery). *DIR:* Thomas Carr. *PRO:* Vincent M. Fennelly. *SP:* Daniel B. Ullman. *CAST:* Neville Brand, Arthur Franz, Jean Willes, Walter Reed, Paul Picerni, Kim Charney, Thorpe Whitman, Peter Leeds. *SYN:* When a boy turns up missing and a ransom note is found, police and parents go on an all night search for the missing boy and his abductors.

52. The Body Stealers (4/69) Eastmancolor – 91 mins. (Science Fiction). *DIR:* Gerry Levy. *PRO:* Tony Tenser. *SP:* Michael St. Clair, Peter Marcus. A Tigon British–Sagittarius Production. *CAST:* George Sanders, Maurice Evans, Patrick Allen, Nel Connery, Hilary Dwyer, Robert Flemyng, Lorna Wilde, Allan Cuthbertson, Michael Culver, Sally Faulkner, Shelagh Fraser, Jan Miller, Carl Rigg, Carol Ann Hawkins. *SYN:* When several parachutists disappear as they pass through a red mist while testing a new type of parachute, a U.S. Air Force investigator (Sanders) and two British investigators (Connery, Allen) find a top secret space research laboratory where aliens have taken over the bodies of the men who disappeared. *NOTES:* Working title was *Invasion of the Body Stealers.*

53. Bond Street (3/29/50) B&W – 109 mins. (Drama). *DIR:* Gordon Parry. *PRO:* Anatole de Grunwald. *SP:* Anatole de Grunwald, Terence Rattigan, Rodney Ackland. Based on an idea by J.G. Brown. An Associated British Pictures–World Screenplays Production. A Stratford Picture Presentation. *CAST:* Jean Kent, Roland Young, Kathleen Harrison, Derek Farr, Hazel Court, Ronald Howard, Paula Valenska, Patricia Plunkett, Robert Flemyng, Adrianne Allen, Kenneth Griffith, Joan Dowling, Charles Goldner, James McKechnie, Leslie Dwyer, Mary Jerrold, Marian Spencer. *SYN:* Twenty-four hours in the life of London's Bond Street as told through four episodes, linked by a bride's (Court) wedding dress, pearls, veil, and flowers. *NOTES:* Released in Great Britain in 1948.

54. Border City Rustlers (11/15/53) B&W – 54 mins. (Western). *DIR:* Frank McDonald. *PRO:* Wesley E. Barry. *SP:* William Raynor. A Newhall Production. *CAST:* Guy Madison, Andy Devine, Gloria Talbott, Isabel Randolph, George J. Lewis, George Eldredge, Steve Pendleton, Murray Alper, Robert Bice, Don Turner. *SYN:* Compiled from two episodes of the *Wild Bill Hickok* television series: "Border City" and one untitled episode.

55. The Bowery Boys Meet the Monsters (6/6/54) B&W – 66 mins. (Comedy). *DIR:* Edward Bernds. *PRO:* Ben Schwalb. *SP:* Elwood Ullman, Edward Bernds. *CAST:* Leo Gorcey, Huntz Hall, David Condon, Bennie Bartlett, Bernard Gorcey, John Dehner, Lloyd Corrigan, Paul Wexler, Ellen Corby, Laura Mason, Norman Bishop, Steve Calvert, Rudy Lee, Paul Bryar, Pat Flaherty, Jack Diamond. *SYN:* The Bowery Boys, hunting for a place for the local kids to play baseball, encounter a strange family (Dehner, Corby, Corrigan, Mason) who want Sach (Hall) and Slip (Leo Gorcey) for their experiments. *NOTES:* This film was the series's highest grossing film.

56. Bowery to Baghdad (1/2/55) B&W – 64 mins. (Comedy). *DIR:* Edward Bernds. *PRO:* Ben Schwalb. *SP:* Elwood Ullman, Edward Bernds. *CAST:* Leo Gorcey, Huntz Hall, David Condon, Bennie Bartlett, Bernard Gorcey, Joan Swawlee, Eric Blore, Robert Bice, Dick Wessel, Rayford Barnes, Michael Ross, Rick Vallin, Paul Marion, Jean Willes, Charlie Lung, Leon Burbank. *SYN:* Slip (Leo Gorcey) and Sach (Hall) get mixed up with gangsters when they acquire a magic lamp with a genie (Blore) and end up in Baghdad. *NOTES:* Released in Great Britain in October, 1954.

57. Brainwashed (6/25/61) B&W – 102 mins. (Drama). *DIR:* Gerd Oswald. *PRO:* Luggi Waldleitner. *SP:* Harold Medford, Gerd Oswald, Herbert Reinecker. Based on *The Royal Game* by Stefan Zweig. A Roxy Film Production. *CAST:* Curt Jurgens, Claire Bloom, Hansjorg Felmy, Mario Adorf, Albert Lieven, Alan Gifford, Dietmar Schonherr, Karel Stepanek, Wolfgang Wahl, Rudolf Forster, Albert Bessler, Jan Hendriks, Harald Maresch, Dorothea Wieck, Susanne Korber, Hans Sohnker, Ryk De Gooyer. *SYN:* An Austrian aristocrat (Jurgens) is captured by the Nazis and is to be interrogated for vital secrets. He attempts to retain his sanity and clear his mind by concentrating on the complex moves of chess. [Original German title: *Schachnovelle.*] [British title: *Three Moves to Freedom.*]

58. The Bride and the Beast (2/23/58) B&W – 78 mins. (Horror). *DIR/PRO:* Adrian Weiss. *SP:* Edward D. Wood, Jr. A Weiss Production. *CAST:* Charlotte Austin, Lance Fuller, Johnny Roth, Steve Calvert, William Justine, Jeanne Gerson, Gil Frye, Slick Slavin, Jean Ann Lewis, Bhogwan Singh. *SYN:* A big-game huner (Fuller) sets out to rescue his bride (Austin), who believes she was a gorilla in a former life, when she is kidnapped by a huge gorilla. *NOTES:* Executive produce was Louis Weiss. Jungle footage is from the documentary feature, *Man-Eater of Kumaon.*

59. The Bridge (5/1/61) B&W – 102 mins. (Drama). *DIR:* Bernhard Wicki. *PRO:* Dr. Herman Schwerin. *SP:* Karl-Wilhelm Vivier, Michael Mansfield. Based on the book by Manfred Gregor. *CAST:* Volker Bohnet, Fritz Wepper, Michael Heinz, Frank Glaubrecht, Karl Michael Balzer, Volker Lechtenbrink, Guenther Hoffman, Cordula Trantow, Wolfgang Stumph, Gunther Pfitzmann, Siegfried Schurenberg, Ruth

Guy Madison in his role as Wild Bill Hickok in *Border City Rustlers* (1953). Allied Artists carried on this series, compiled from episodes of the popular *Wild Bill Hickok* television series started by Monogram, for 12 more features.

Hausmeister, Eva Vaitl, Edith Schulze-Westrum, Hans Elvenspoeck, Trudy Brietschopf, Kalus Hellmold, Inge Benz, Edeltraut Elsner. *SYN:* During the closing days of World War II, seven German school boys are drafted into the German Army and must defend an unimportant bridge from the Allied invasion, even if it means their deaths. *NOTES:* Released as a German language version with

Advertisement for *The Bridge* (1961).

subtitles. Re-released in 1963 dubbed in English. [Original German title: *Die Brucke*.]

60. A Brief Vacation (2/75) Eastmancolor – 106 mins. (Drama). *DIR:* Vittorio De Sica. *PRO:* Marina Cicogna, Arthur Cohn. *SP:* Cesare Zavattini. Story by Rodolfo Sonego. *CAST:* Florinda Bolkan, Renato Salvatori, Daniel Quenaud, Jose Maria Prada, Teresa Gimpera, Hugo Blanco, Julia Pena, Miranda Campa, Angela Cardile, Anna Carena, Monica Guerritore, Maria Mizar, Allesandro Romanazzi, Adriana Asti. *SYN:* A factory worker (Bolkan) barely

Rhonda Fleming and Guy Madison in *Bullwhip* (1958).

able to take care of her family is diagnosed as tubercular and is sent to a mountainside spa to recuperate. While there she thrives physically and spiritually and finds new life. When she is cured, she must return to her family and empty life. [Original Italian title: *Una Breva Vacanza*.]

61. Bruce Lee – Super Dragon (7/76) Eastmancolor/Scope – 90 mins. (Martial Arts). *DIR/PRO:* Chang Yeuh Hua. *SP:* No credits available. *CAST:* Lee Shaio Lung, Jimmy Wang Yu. *SYN:* Bruce Lee (Lung) learns how to fight, comes to America and achives stardom, then comes home to Hong Kong to battle bullies. *NOTES:* Interspersed with footage from various kung fu movies, this is another of the many attempts to recreate Bruce Lee's life story. (See also *The Dragon Dies Hard*).

62. Bullwhip (5/25/58) Deluxe Color/Scope – 80 mins. (Western-Comedy). *DIR:* Harmon C. Jones. *PRO:* Helen Ainsworth. *SP:* Adele Buffington. A Romsom-Broidy Production. *CAST:* Guy Madison, Rhonda Fleming, James Griffith, Don Beddoe, Peter Adams, Dan Sheridan, Burt Nelson, Al Terry, Tim Graham, Hank Worden, Wayne Mallory, Barbara Woodell, Rhys Williams, Don Shelton, Jack Reynolds, Frank Griffin, J.W. Cody, Jack Carr, Rick Vallin, Saul Gorss. *SYN:* A cowboy (Madison) is forced to marry a woman (Fleming) or hang for a false murder charge. *NOTES:* Executive producer was William F. Broidy. Remade by Paramount in 1978 as *Goin' South*.

63. Cabaret (2/72) Technicolor – 124 mins. (Musical-Drama). *DIR:* Bob Fosse. *PRO:* Cy Feuer. *SP:* Jay Allen. Based on the musical play by Joe Masteroff, the play *I Am a Camera* by John Van Druten, and the book *Goodbye to Berlin* by Christopher Isherwood. An

Allied Artists—ABC Pictures Production. *CAST:* Liza Minelli, Michael York, Helmut Griem, Joel Grey, Fritz Wepper, Marisa Berenson, Elisabeth Neumann-Viertel, Sigrid Von Richthofen, Helen Vita, Gerd Vespermann, Ralf Wolter, Georg Hartmann, Ricky Renee, Estrongo Nachama. *SYN:* The lives of several people—an American girl (Minnelli), a writer (York), a Jewish heiress (Berenson) and her lover (Wepper), a wealthy playboy (Griem), and the Master of Ceremonies (Grey)—are caught up in the phony glitter of pre-war Berlin at the Kit-Kat Club.

Liza Minelli in her Award-winning role as Sally Bowles in *Cabaret* (1972).

64. Calling Homicide (9/30/56) B&W—61 mins. (Crime-Mystery). *DIR/SP:* Edward Bernds. *PRO:* Ben Schwalb. *CAST:* Bill Elliott, Don Haggerty, Kathleen Case, Myron Healey, Jeanne Cooper, Thomas Browne Henry, Lyle Talbot, Almira Sessions, Herb Vigran, James Best, John Dennis, Mel Wells, Stanley Adams, Jack Mulhall, Harry Strang, Jack Sparks. *SYN:* Lt. Doyle (Elliott) and Sgt. Duncan (Haggerty), investigating the murder of a policeman, learn that the murder of a woman (Cooper) who owned a modeling studio may be linked to the policeman's murder.

65. Caltiki, the Immortal Monster (9/20/60) B&W—76 mins. (Horror). *DIR:* Robert Hamton (Ricardo Freda). *PRO:* Bruno Vailati. *PRO-U.S.:* Samuel Schneider. *SP:* Philip Just (Filippano Sanjust). Based on a Mexican legend. A Galatea Film—Lux Film—Climax Pictures Production. *CAST:* John Merivale, Didi Sullivan (Didi Perego), Gerald Haerter, Gay Pearl, Daniella Rocca, Daniele Pitani, Victor Andree, G.R. Stuart (Giacomo Rossi Stuart), Arthur Domick (Arturo Dominci). *SYN:* A scientist (Merivale) uncovers a blob-like creature in a Mayan tomb. The creature is sealed in the tomb, but not before it attacks one of the other scientists (Haerter). The scientist is taken to the hospital where he soon goes mad, and a portion of blob is removed from him and taken to a laboratory where it begins to grow to

Caltiki, the Immortal Monster: an Italian science fiction thriller photographed by Mario Bava (1960). *(Photo courtesy of Ted Okuda.)*

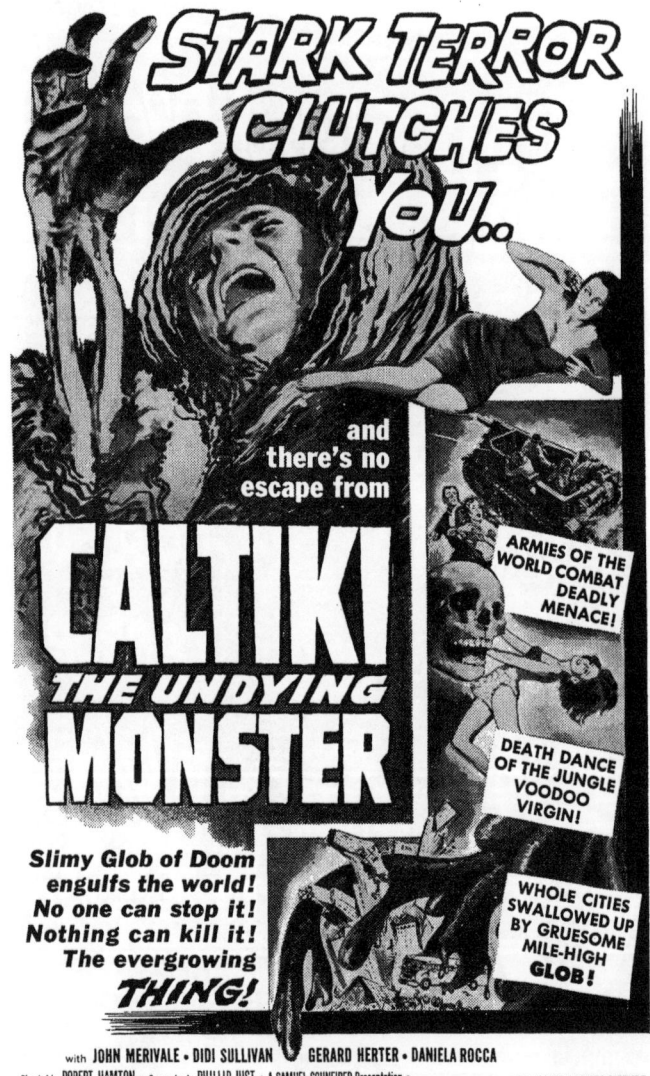

Another advertisement for *Caltiki*, this time as *The Undying Monster* (1960).

gigantic size and soon begins wreaking havoc on the countryside. *NOTES:* Cinematographer John Foam was Mario Bava, who was also uncredited as co-director. Possibly released independently in 1959 before being picked up for distribution by Allied Artists. Double billed in some areas with *Tormented*. [Original Italian title: *Caltiki, Il Mostro Immortale*.] [British title: *The Immortal Monster*.]

Caltiki, the Undying Monster see **Caltiki, the Immortal Monster**

George Montgomery and Marcia Henderson in *Canyon River* (1956).

66. Calypso Joe (6/9/57) B&W – 74 mins. (Musical). *DIR:* Edward Dein. *PRO:* William F. Broidy. *SP:* Edward Dein, Mildred Dein. *CAST:* Herb Jeffries, Angie Dickinson, Ed Kemmer, Stephen Bekassy, Laurie Mitchell, Claudia Drake, Murray Alper, Linda Terrace, Charles R. Keans, Genie Stone, Robert Sherman, Lord Flea and His Calypsonians, the Lester Horton Dancers, Duke of Iron, Herb Jeffries' Calypsomaniacs, the Easy Riders, Lady T. *SYN:* An airline stewardess (Dickinson) heads to South America to see her television star boyfriend (Kemmer), but she is pursued by her former sweetheart (Bekassy). *NOTES:* Double billed in some areas with *Hot Rod Rumble*.

67. The Candy Man (7/69) Eastmancolor – 97 mins. (Crime). *DIR/PRO/SP:* Herbert J. Leder. Story by Francis Swann. A Sagittarius Production. *CAST:* George Sanders, Leslie Parrish, Manolo Fabregas, Gina Romand, Carlos Cortez, Pedro Galvan, Pixie Hopkins, Nancy Rodman, Chuck Anderson, Felix Gonzalez, Lupita Ferrat. *SYN:* A British drug pusher (Sanders), known as the "Candy Man," plans to kidnap the daughter of a visiting American actress (Parrish) with the help of an addict (Cortez) and his girlfriend (Romand). *NOTES:* Filmed in Mexico City.

68. Canyon River (8/5/56) DeLuxe Color/Scope – 80 mins. (Western). *DIR:* Harmon C. Jones. *PRO:* Richard Heermance. *SP:* Daniel B. Ullman. *CAST:* George Montgomery, Peter Graves, Marcia Henderson, Richard Eyer, Walter Sande, Robert J. Wilke, Alan Hale, Jr., John Harmon, Jack Lambert, William Fawcett, Bud Osborne, Lee Roberts. *SYN:* A rancher (Montgomery) driving his herd of cattle from Oregon to Wyoming is unaware that his foreman (Graves) has made a deal with a rival rancher (Sande) to steal his herd. *NOTES:* Executive producer was Scott R. Dunlap.

69. Case of the Red Monkey (6/19/55) B&W – 74 mins. (Spy-Drama). *DIR:* Ken Hughes. *PRO:* Alec C. Snowden. *SP:* James Eastwood, Ken Hughes. Based on the story and British TV serial *Little Red Monkey* by Eric Maschwitz. A Todon–Merton Park Production. *CAST:* Richard Conte, Rona Anderson, Russell Napier, Colin Gordon, Arnold Marle, Sylva Langova, Donald Bissett, John King-Kelly, Bernard Rebel, Noel Johnson, John Horsley, Colin Tapley. *SYN:* A U.S. State Department agent (Conte) and a British special agent (Napier) investigate the murders of top British nuclear scientists. Their only clue is a little red monkey that was seen at every murder. *NOTES:* Released in Great Britain in January, 1955. Double billed in some areas with *Fingerman*. [British title: *Little Red Monkey*.]

70. Castle in the Air (12/26/52) B&W – 92 mins. (Comedy). *DIR:* Henry Cass. *PRO:* Edward Dryhurst, Ernest Gartside. *SP:* Alan Melville, Edward Dryhurst. Based on the play by Alan Melville. An Associated British Picture–Hallmark Production. A Stratford Picture Presentation. *CAST:* David Tomlinson, Helen Cherry, Margaret Rutherford, Barbara Kelly, A.E. Matthews, Patricia Dainton, Brian Oulton, Ewan Roberts, Clive Morton, Gordon Jackson, Russell Waters. *SYN:* A penniless Scottish Earl (Tomlinson) takes in an assortment of boarders in an effort to keep his castle. *NOTES:* Released in Great Britain in June, 1952.

71. Chain of Evidence (1/6/57) B&W – 64 mins. (Crime-Mystery). *DIR:* Paul Landres. *PRO:* Ben Schwalb. *SP:* Elwood Ullman. *CAST:* Bill Elliott, Don Haggerty, James Lydon, Claudia Barrett, Tina Carver, Ross Elliott, Meg Randall, Timothy Carey, John Bleifer, Dabbs Greer, John Close, Hugh Sanders, Paul Bryar, Francis McDonald, John Damler, Murray Alper, Ralph Gamble. *SYN:* A young man (Lydon), released from the Honor Farm, gets beaten up by an old enemy (Carey) and suffers amnesia. When he is befriended by a man (Sanders) who is later murdered, Lt. Doyle (Bill Elliott) and Sgt. Duncan (Haggerty) help to clear him of the murder.

Cid, El see **El Cid**

72. City of Fear (9/8/65) B&W – 90 mins. (Spy-Drama). *DIR:* Peter Bezencenet. *PRO:* Sandy Howard, Arthur Steloff, Harry Alan Towers. *SP:* Peter Welbeck (Harry Alan Towers), Max Bourne. Story by Peter Welbeck (Harry Alan Towers). A Towers of London–Javelin Production. *CAST:* Paul Maxwell, Terry Moore, Marisa Mell, Albert Lieven, Pinkas Braun, Zsu Zsu Banki, Brigit Heiberg, Marie Rohm, Maria Takacs, Helga Lehner. *SYN:* A newsman (Maxwell) en route to Hungary finds himself in grave danger when he is asked by a man (Braun) to deliver a package to his sister in Hungary. The package contains two passports for a scientist (Lieven) and an American fashion expert (Moore) who wish to escape to freedom in Austria. *NOTES:* Released in Great Britain in 1966 at a running time of 75 mins. Filmed in Austria and Hungary.

73. Clipped Wings (8/14/53) B&W – 65 mins. (Spy-Comedy). *DIR:* Edward Bernds. *PRO:* Ben Schwalb. *SP:* Charles R. Marion, Elwood Ullman. Story by Charles R. Marion. *CAST:* Leo Gorcey, Huntz Hall, David Condon, Bennie Bartlett, Bernard Gorcey, Todd Karns, June Vincent, Fay Roope, Philip Van Zandt, Renie Riano, Mary Treen, Frank Richards, Michael Ross, Elaine Riley, Jeanne Dean, Anne Kimbell, Henry Kulky, Lyle Talbot, Ray Walker, Arthur Space, Lou Nova, Conrad Brooks. *SYN:* Slip (Leo Gorcey) and Sach (Hall) mistakenly join the Air Force as they try to

Feature Films 29

Advertisement for *Cole Younger, Gunfighter* (1958).

locate their friend Dave (Karns), and they get mixed up with a spy ring.

74. Cocktails in the Kitchen (6/20/55) Eastmancolor—84 mins. (Comedy-Romance). *DIR:* J. Lee Thompson. *PRO:* Kenneth Harper. *SP:* J. Lee Thompson, Peter Myers, Alec Grahame. Based on the play by Arthur Watkyn. An Associated British Picture–Kenwood Production. A Stratford Picture Presentation. *CAST:* Dirk Bogarde, Susan Stephen, Cecil Parker, Eileen Herlie, Athene Seyler, Pia Terri, Dennis Price, James Hayter, Thora Hird, Charles Victor, Sidney James, George Woodbridge, Peter Jones, Robin Bailey, Digby Wolfe, Edwin Styles. *SYN:* A young married couple (Bogarde, Stephen) go through a number of trials and tribulations as their marriage progresses. *NOTES:* Released in Great Britain in 1954. [British title: *For Better, For Worse.*]

75. Cole Younger, Gunfighter (3/30/58) DeLuxe Color/Scope—78 mins. (Western). *DIR:* R.G. Springsteen. *PRO:* Ben Schwalb. *SP:* Daniel Mainwaring. Based on a story by Clifton Adams. *CAST:* Frank Lovejoy, James Best, Abby

Dalton, Jan Merlin, Douglas Spencer, Ainslie Pryor, Frank Ferguson, Myron Healey, George Keymas, Dan Sheridan, John Mitchum. *SYN:* In 1873 Texas, a man (Best) teams with Cole Younger (Lovejoy) to wage war against the corrupt lawmen occupying his town. When he is accused of murder, Younger comes to his aid and reveals the real killer (Merlin). *NOTES:* Frank Lovejoy's last film.

76. The Come-On (4/16/56) B&W — 82 mins. (Drama). *DIR:* Russell Birdwell. *PRO:* Lindsley Parsons. *SP:* Warren Douglas, Whitman Chambers. Based on the book by Whitman Chambers. *CAST:* Anne Baxter, Sterling Hayden, John Hoyt, Jesse White, Walter (Wally) Cassell, Lee Turnbull, Alex Gerry, Paul Picerni, Karolee Kelly, Theodore Newton, Tyler McVey. *SYN:* In Mexico, a down-and-out wanderer (Hayden) falls for a woman (Baxter) he sees on the beach, and she tries to persuade him to aid her in killing her overbearing husband (Hoyt). *NOTES:* This film is vaguely reminiscent of the 1948 Columbia film *The Lady from Shanghai.*

77. Cometogether (9/71) Eastmancolor — 91 mins. (Drama). *DIR:* Saul Swimmer. *PRO/SP:* Saul Swimmer, Tony Anthony. An ABKCO–William Cash Production. *CAST:* Tony Anthony, Luciana Paluzzi, Rosemary Dexter. *SYN:* An American (Anthony) working as an actor in Italy has a love relationship with two women (Paluzzi, Dexter).

Communion see **Alice, Sweet Alice**

78. Conduct Unbecoming (8/75) Technicolor — 107 mins. (Drama). *DIR:* Michael Anderson. *PRO:* Michel Deeley, Barry Spikings, Andrew Donally. *SP:* Robert Enders. Based on the play by Barry England. A British Lion Production. *CAST:* Michael York, Richard Attenborough, Trevor Howard, Stacy Keach, Christopher Plummer, Susannah York, James Faulkner, Michael Culver, James Donald, Rafiq Anwar, Helen Cherry, Michael Fleming, David Robb, David Purcell, Andrew Lodge, David Neville, Persis Khambatta, Michael Byrne. *SYN:* In 1890 India, a British officer (Faulkner) accused of molesting the widow (Susannah York) of an officer, is secretly tried for the crime by his fellow British officers.

79. Confessions of an Opium Eater (6/20/62) B&W — 86 mins. (Drama). *DIR/PRO:* Albert Zugsmith. *SP:* Robert Hill, Seton I. Miller. Based on *Confessions of an English Opium-eater* by Thomas DeQuincey. A Photoplay Associated Incorporated Production. *CAST:* Vincent Price, Linda Ho, Richard Loo, June Kim, Philip Ahn, Yvonne Moray, Caroline Kido, Terence DeMarney, Gerald Jann, Vivianne Manku, Miel Saan, Jo Anne Miya, Geri Hoo, John Mamo, Keiko, Victor Sen Yung, Ralph Ahn, Arthur Wong, Alicia Li, Carol Russell, Vincent Barbi. *SYN:* In 1800s San Francisco, Thomas DeQuincey (Price) becomes involved in the Chinatown Tong Wars and helps a newspaper publisher (Loo) in his crusade to rid the city of the Oriental auction rooms where young girls are sold into marriage. *NOTES:* Re-released by Allied Artists as *Secrets of a Soul.* [TV title: *Souls for Sale.*] [British title: *Evils of Chinatown.*]

80. The Constant Husband (7/25/57) Technicolor — 87 mins. (Comedy). *DIR:* Sidney Gillat. *PRO:* Frank Launder, Sidney Gillat. *SP:* Sidney Gillat, Val Valentine. A British Lion-Individual Production. A Stratford Picture Presentation. *CAST:* Rex Harrison, Margaret Leighton, Kay Kendall, Cecil Parker, Nicole Maurey, George Cole, Raymond Huntley, Michael Hordern, Robert Coote, Eric Pohlmann, Marie Burke, Valerie French, Jill Adams, Muriel Young, John Robinson. *SYN:* A man (Harrison) recovers from amnesia

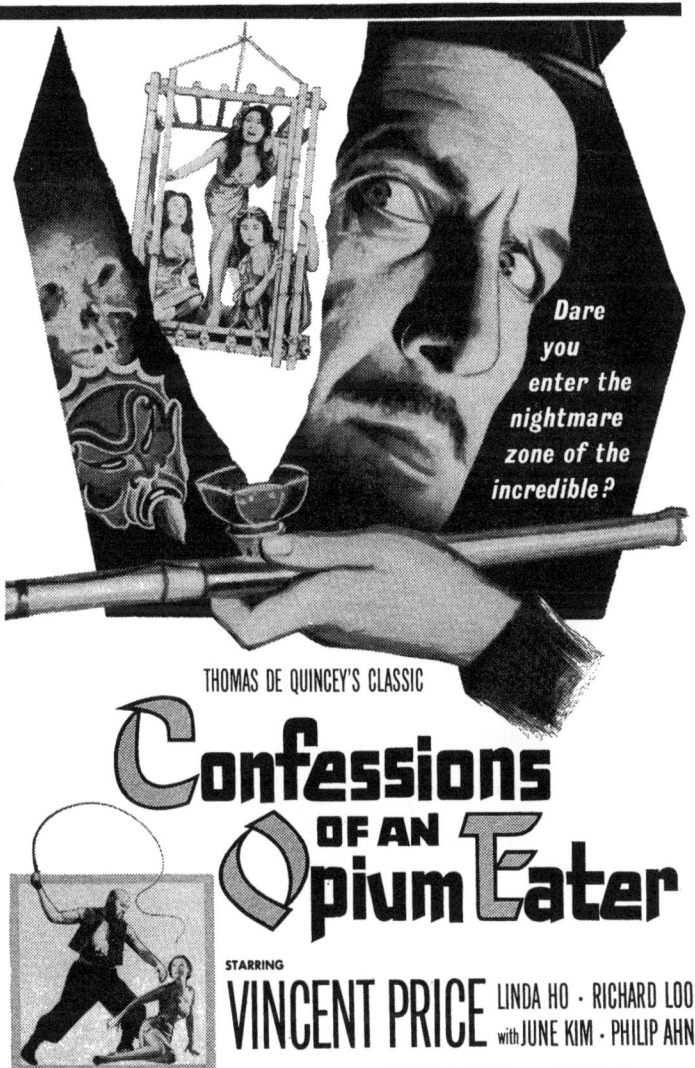

Advertisement for *Confessions of an Opium Eater* (1962).

and discovers he has seven wives. While on trial for bigamy, his lawyer (Leighton) falls for him too. He chooses to go to jail rather than face the wrath of seven wives. When he is released from prison, he succeeds in evading his seven wives, but not his lawyer. *NOTES:* Released in Great Britain in 1955.

81. Contraband Spain (4/10/58) Eastmancolor – 82 mins. (Crime-Mystery). *DIR/SP:* Lawrence Huntington. *PRO:* Ernest Gartside. An Associated British Picture–Diadem Production. A Stratford Picture Presentation. *CAST:* Richard Greene, Anouk Aimée, Michael Denison, Jose Nieto, John Warwick, Philip Saville, Alfonso Estella, G.H. Mulcaster, Robert Ayres, Olive Milbourne, Arnold Bell, Cornado San Martin, Antonio Almoros. *SYN:* An FBI agent (Greene) enlists the aid of his girlfriend (Aimée) and a customs agent (Denison) in tracking down the smugglers who murdered his brother. *NOTES:* Released in Great Britain in 1955.

82. Convicts 4 (9/15/62) B&W – 106 mins. (Prison Drama). *DIR/SP:* Millard Kaufman. *PRO:* A. Ronald Lubin. Based on *Reprieve* by John Resko. A Kaufman-Lubin Production. *CAST:* Ben Gazzara, Stuart Whitman, Ray Walston, Vincent Price, Rod Steiger, Broderick Crawford, Dodie Stevens, Jack Kruschen, Sammy Davis, Jr., Naomi Stevens, Carmen Phillips, Susan Silo, Timothy Carey, Tom Gilson, Arthur Malet, Lee Krieger, Myron Healey, Josip Elric, Jack Albertson, Robert H. Harris, John Kellogg, Adam Williams, Andy Albin, Burt Lange, Robert Christopher, Warren Kemmerling, Kreg Martin, John Close, Billy Varga, Reggie Nalder, John Dennis. *SYN:* After killing a storekeeper, John Resko (Gazzara) is sentenced to prison for life where, during his rehabilitation, his talent as an artist emerges and with the help of an art critic (Price), he receives a parole. *NOTES:* Based on the true story of John Resko. [British title: *Repreive!*]

83. The Cosmic Man (2/17/59) B&W – 72 mins. (Science Fiction). *DIR:* Herbert Greene. *PRO:* Robert A. Terry. *SP:* Arthur C. Pierce. A Futura Pictures Production. *CAST:* Bruce Bennett, John Carradine, Angela Greene, Paul Langton, Scott Morrow, Lyn Osborn, Walter Maslow, Herbert Lytton, Ken Clayton, Alan Wells, Harry Fleer, Hal Torey, John Erman, Dwight Brooks. *SYN:* An alien (Carradine) arrives on Earth bearing a message of interplanetary peace. *NOTES:* Double billed in some areas with *House on Haunted Hill.*

84. Cow Country (4/26/53) B&W – 82 mins. (Western). *DIR:* Lesley Selander. *PRO:* Scott R. Dunlap. *SP:* Adele Buffington. Adapted by Tom W. Blackburn. Based on *Shadow Range* by Curtis Bishop. *CAST:* Edmond O'Brien, Helen Westcott, Robert Lowery, Barton MacLane, Peggie Castle, Robert Barrat, James Millican, Don Beddoe, Robert J. Wilke, Raymond Hatton, Chuck Courtney, Steve Clark, Rory Mallinson, Marshall Reed, Brett Houston, Tom Tyler, Sam Flint, Jack Ingram, George J. Lewis, Lane Chandler, Lee Roberts, Chuck Roberson, Ray Jones. *SYN:* In 1875 Texas, a freight operator (O'Brien) sets out to stop a crooked banker (MacLane) and rancher (Lowery) from driving the other ranchers off their land.

85. Crashing Las Vegas (4/22/56) B&W – 62 mins. (Comedy). *DIR:* Jean Yarbrough. *PRO:* Ben Schwalb. *SP:* Jack Townley. *CAST:* Leo Gorcey, Huntz Hall, David Condon, Jimmy Murphy, Mary Castle, Nicky Blair, Mort Mills, Don Haggerty, Doris Kemper, Jack Rice, Bob Hopkins, John Bleifer, Emil Sitka, Dick Foote, Don Marlowe, Jack Grinnage, Terry Frost, Minerva Urecal, Frank Scannell, Joey Ray, Jack Chefe, Frank

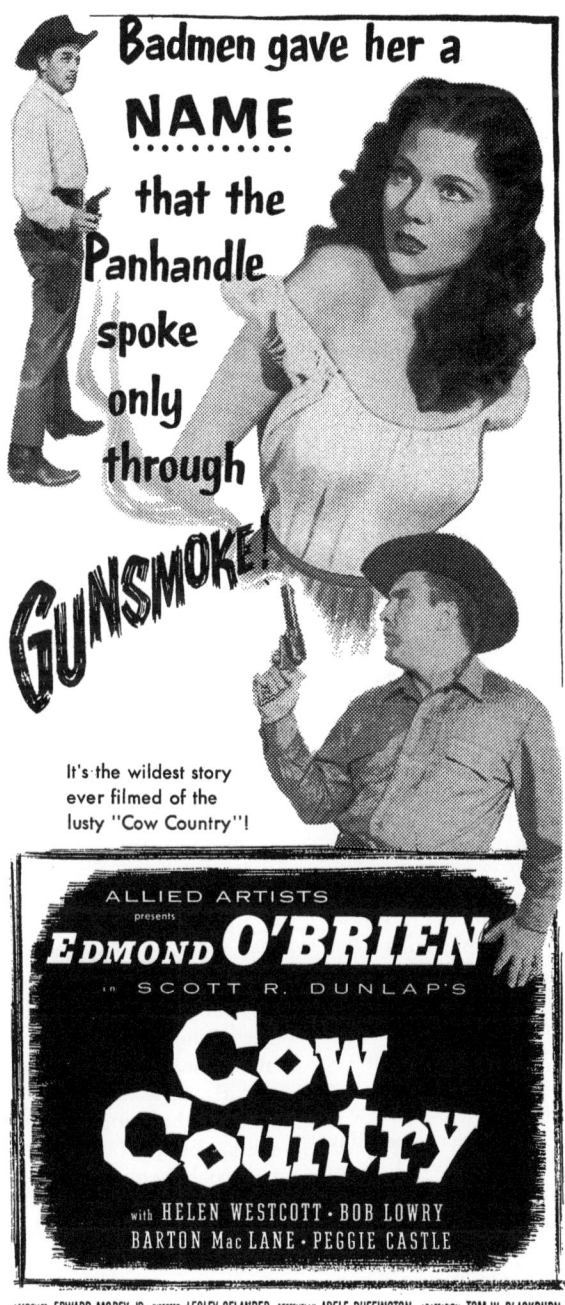

Advertisement for *Cow Country* (1953). *(Photo courtesy of Ted Okuda.)*

Hagney. *SYN:* After receiving an electric shock, Sach (Hall) learns he is able to predict numbers. He wins a trip to Las Vegas on a game show where he, Slip (Gorcey) and the rest of the Bowery Boys (Condon, Murphy) get mixed up with gangsters. *NOTES:* The first "Bowery Boys" film since 1948 without Bernard Gorcey, and Leo Gorcey's last "Bowery Boys" film after 10 years of "Leo Gorcey and the Bowery Boys in . . . ."

Crazy Paradise *see* **Once Upon an Island**

86. Crime and Punishment, U.S.A. (11/1/59) B&W – 78 mins. (Crime-Drama). *DIR:* Denis Sanders. *PRO:* Terry Sanders. *SP:* Walter Newman. Based on *Crime and Punishment* by Feodor Dostoyevsky. A Sanders Associates Production. *CAST:* George Hamilton, Mary Murphy, Frank Silvera, Marian Seldes, John Harding, Wayne Heffley, Toni Merrill, Lew Brown, Barry Atwater, Sidney Clute, Ken Drake, Jim Hyland, Len Lesser, Eve McVeagh, Magda Harout, George Saris. *SYN:* A law student (Hamilton) murders a pawnbroker and is hounded by the policeman (Silvera) who believes him guilty of the crime. *NOTES:* The film debut of George Hamilton.

87. Crime in the Streets (6/10/56) B&W – 91 mins. (Crime). *DIR:* Don Siegel. *PRO:* Vincent M. Fennelly. *SP:* Reginald Rose. Based on the television play by Reginald Rose. A Lindbrook Production. *CAST:* James Whitmore, John Cassavetes, Sal Mineo, Mark Rydell, Denise Alexander, Malcolm Atterbury, Peter Votrian, Virginia Gregg, Ray Stricklyn, Dan Terranova, Will Kuluva, Peter Miller, Steve Rowland, James Ogg, Robert Alexander, Duke Mitchell, Richard Curtis, Doyle Baker. *SYN:* A social worker (Whitmore) tries to change the lives of three hoodlums—Frankie Dane (Cassavetes), Lou Macklin (Rydell), and Baby Gioia (Mineo)—but when they plan to murder a man who humiliated Frankie, it is Frankie's younger brother (Votrian) who intervenes and keeps them from killing. *NOTES:* John Cassavetes, Sal Mineo, and Mark Rydell repeated their roles from the television play. John Cassavetes' first starring role. Mark Rydell became a director and directed *The Rose* and *On Golden Pond.*

88. The Cruel Tower (10/28/56) B&W – 79 mins. (Drama). *DIR:* Lew Landers. *PRO:* Lindsley Parsons. *SP:* Warren Douglas. Based on the book by William B. Hartley. *CAST:* John Ericson, Mari Blanchard, Charles McGraw, Steve Brodie, Peter Whitney, Alan Hale, Jr., Diana Darrin, Carol Kelly, Barbara Bel Wright. *SYN:* The friendship between two steeplejacks (Ericson, McGraw) becomes strained when they fall in love with the same woman (Blanchard).

89. Cry Baby Killer (8/17/58) B&W – 62 mins. (Crime-Drama). *DIR:* Jus Addiss. *PRO:* David Kramarsky, David March. *SP:* Leo Gordon, Melvin Levy. Story by Leo Gordon. *CAST:* Jack Nicholson, Harry Lauter, Carolyn Mitchell, Brett Halsey, Lynn Cartwright, Ralph Reed, Barbara Knudson, Jordan [Robert] "Smoki" Whitfield, John Shay, Claude Stroud, Ruth Swanson, William A. Forester, John Weed, Frank Richards, Bill Erwin, James Fillmore, Ed Nelson, Mitzi McCall, Leo Gordon, Roger Corman. *SYN:* A juvenile delinquent (Nicholson) panics when he kills two men and barricades himself in a storeroom of a nearby drive-in with three hostages—a janitor (Whitfield), a woman (Knudson), and her baby. *NOTES:* The film debut of Jack Nicholson; executive producer was Roger Corman. Some TV prints run 60 mins. Double billed in some areas with *Hot Car Girl.*

90. Cry of Battle (10/9/63) B&W – 99 mins. (War). *DIR:* Irving Lerner. *PRO:* Joe Steinberg. *SP:* Bernard Gordon.

Based on *Fortress in the Rice* by Benjamin Appel. *CAST:* Van Heflin, Rita Moreno, James MacArthur, Leopoldo Salcedo, Sidney Clute, Marilou Munoz, Oscar Roncal, Liza Moreno, Michael Parsons, Claude Wilson, Vic Salyin, Oscar Keese. *SYN:* At the beginning of World War II, a young boy (MacArthur), an ex-skipper (Heflin), and a Filipino girl (Rita Moreno) join a band of Filipino guerillas to help fight the Japanese. [British title: *To Be a Man*.]

91. Cry Vengeance (11/21/54) B&W —83 mins. (Crime-Drama). *DIR:* Mark Stevens. *PRO:* Lindsley Parsons. *SP:* Warren Douglas, George Bricker. *CAST:* Mark Stevens, Martha Hyer, Skip Homeier, Joan Vohs, Douglas Kennedy, Don Haggerty, Cheryl Callaway, Warren Douglas, Mort Mills, John Doucette, Lewis Martin, Dorothy Kennedy. *SYN:* Framed and sent to prison for a crime he didn't commit, a man (Stevens) sets out to get the gangsters who framed him and killed his wife and child.

92. Curse of the Voodoo (9/22/65) B&W—77 mins. (Drama). *DIR:* Lindsay Shonteff. *PRO:* Kenneth Rive. *SP:* Tony O'Grady, Leigh Vance. A Galaworld–Gordon Films Production. A Futurama Entertainment Corporation Presentation. *CAST:* Bryant Halliday, Dennis Price, Lisa Daniely, Mary Kerridge, Ronald Leigh Hunt, Jean Lodge, Dennis Alaba Peters, Tony Thawnton, Michael Nightingale, Andy Meyers, Louis Majoney, Jimmy Felgate, Nigel Feyistan, Chief M'Gobo, Beryl Cunningham, Bobby Breen Quintet. *SYN:* A big game hunter (Halliday) on African safari kills a sacred lion and is cursed by the tribal chief (Chief M'Gobo). He returns to London and suffers fever, wounds, hallucinations, and mental anguish. Through the advice of an African expert (Majoney), he must return to Africa and kill the tribal chief in order to lift the curse. *NOTES:* Released in Great Britain in 1965 at a running time of 61 mins. Double billed in some areas with *Frankenstein Meets the Space Monster*. [British title: *Curse of Simba*.]

93. The Cyclops (7/28/57) B&W—75 mins. (Science Fiction). *DIR/PRO/SP:* Bert I. Gordon. A B&H Production. *CAST:* Gloria Talbott, James Craig, Lon Chaney, Jr., Tom Drake, Dean Parkin. *SYN:* A woman (Talbott) organizes an expedition to Mexico with a pilot (Craig) and two others (Drake, Chaney) to find her missing fiancé (Parkin), who has mutated into a scarred one-eyed giant because of exposure to high radiation in the area. *NOTES:* Released in Great Britain at a running time of 65 mins. Originally scheduled to be released by RKO Radio Pictures, distribution went to Allied Artists. Part of Bert I. Gordon's "Colossal Man" series of films in which man, mutated by science, becomes a rampaging giant. The other two features were AIP's *The Amazing Colossal Man* and *War of the Colossal Beast*, which also starred Dean Parkin in the same makeup as this film. Double billed in some areas with *Daughter of Dr. Jekyll*.

94. The Dancing Years (8/23/50) Technicolor—98 mins. (Musical-Drama). *DIR:* Harold French. *PRO:* Warwick Ward. *SP:* Warwick Ward, Jack Wittingham. Based on the play by Ivor Novello. An Associated British Pathé Production. A Stratford Picture Presentation. *CAST:* Dennis Price, Giselle Preville, Patricia Dainton, Anthony Nicholls, Olive Gilbert, Grey Blake, Muriel George, Jeremy Spenser, Gerald Case, Carl Jaffe, Moyra Frazer, Pamela Foster, Barry Ashton. *SYN:* In 1910 Vienna, a young composer (Price) loses the love of his life (Preville) to a prince (Nicholls). *NOTES:* Released in Great Britain in 1949.

95. Daughter of Dr. Jekyll (7/28/57) B&W—67 mins. (Horror). *DIR:* Edgar G. Ulmer. *PRO/SP:* Jack Pollexfen.

Nicole Maurey, Janina Faye, and Howard Keel take time out from fighting Triffids to pose for a publicity photo for *Day of the Triffids* (1963).

A Film Venturers Production. *CAST:* John Agar, Gloria Talbott, Arthur Shields, John Dierkes, Martha Wentworth, Mollie McCart. *SYN:* A woman (Talbott) and her fiancé (Agar) arrive in England to claim her father's inheritance. She is informed that her father was a werewolf named Hyde, and when several people are presumably killed by a werewolf, she believes she has inherited her father's curse and is to blame. *NOTES:* Double billed in some areas with *The Cyclops.*

96. David and Goliath (5/28/60) Eastmancolor/Scope—95 mins. (Biblical). *DIR:* Richard Pottier, Ferdinando Baldi. *PRO:* Emimmo Salvi. *SP:* Umberto Scarpelli, Gino Mangini, Ambrogio Molteni, Emimmo Salvi. An Ansa Cinematografica Production. A Beaver–Champion Attractions Presentation. *CAST:* Orson Welles, Ivo Payer, Edward Hilton, Massimo Serato, Eleonora Rossi-Drago, Giulia Rubini, Pierre Cressoy, Furio Meniconi, Kronos, Dante Maggio, Luigi Tosi, Umberto Fiz, Ugo Sasso, Carlo D'Angelo, Gabriele Tinti, Ileana Danelli, Carla Foscari, Fabrizio Capucci, Roberto Miali, Renato Terra. *SYN:* David (Payer) defeats the Philistine giant Goliath (Kronos), finds favor with King Saul (Welles) and wins the hand of Saul's daughter, Merab (Rossi-Drago). *NOTES:* Released in Italy in 1959 at a running time of 110 mins. [Original Italian title: *David e Golia.*]

97. Day of the Triffids (4/27/63) Eastmancolor/Scope—94 mins. (Science Fiction). *DIR:* Steve Sekely. *PRO:* George Pitcher. *SP:* Philip Yordan. Based on the book by John Wyndham. A Philip Yordan Production. *CAST:* Howard Keel, Nicole Maurey, Janette Scott, Kieron Moore, Mervyn Johns, Janina Faye,

Alison Leggatt, Ewan Roberts, Colette Wilde, Carole Ann Ford, Geoffrey Matthews, Gilgi Hauser, Katya Douglas, Victor Brooks, Thomas Gallagher, Sidney Vivian, Gary Hope, John Simpson. *SYN:* A meteor shower, carrying alien spores, causes most of the Earth's population to go blind. The spores grow to seven-foot tall plants attacking and killing the Earth's population. A naval officer (Keel), woman (Maurey), and child (Faye), spared from blindness, make their way to the coast, while in a lighthouse a marine biologist (Moore) and his wife (Scott) try to find a way to destroy the plants. *NOTES:* Executive producer was Philip Yordan. Co-director Freddie Francis went uncredited. Howard Keel rewrote most of his own dialog as he was displeased with Yordan's screenwriting dialog.

98. The Deadliest Sin (1/29/56) B&W – 77 mins. (Crime). *DIR/SP:* Ken Hughes. *PRO:* Alec C. Snowden. Based on the play *Confession* by Don Martin. An Anglo-Guild Production. *CAST:* Sydney Chaplin, Audrey Dalton, John Bentley, Peter Hammond, John Welsh, Jefferson Clifford, Patrick Allen, Pat McGrath, Robert Raglan, Betty Wolfe, Richard Huggett, Eddie Stafford, Alan Robinson, Edward Dane, Sheila Allen, Hugh Munroe, Dorinda Stevens, Percy Herbert. *SYN:* A British thief, Mike Nelson (Chaplin), returns to England after ditching his partner, Corey (Allen). Corey follows him to England where he is shot by Nelson's brother-in-law, Alan (Hammond). Alan, feeling remorse for the crime, goes to confess his crime to a priest, but is shot by Nelson. Before Nelson can kill the priest, he is cornered in the church and is killed by the police. *NOTES:* Released in Great Britain in 1955 at a running time of 90 mins. [British title: *Confession.*]

99. Death in Small Doses (9/15/57) B&W – 78 mins. (Drama). *DIR:* Joseph M. Newman. *PRO:* Richard Heermance. *SP:* John McGreevey. Based on a magazine article by Arthur L. Davis. *CAST:* Peter Graves, Mala Powers, Chuck Connors, Merry Anders, Roy Engel, Robert B. Williams, Harry Lauter, Pete Kooy, Robert Christopher. *SYN:* An investigator (Graves) for the Food and Drug Administration poses as a truck driver in order to crack a drug ring that has been supplying the truck drivers with amphetamines ("bennies").

100. The Desert Raven (10/27/65) B&W – 90 mins. (Crime). *DIR:* Alan S. Lee. *PRO:* Cal Dunn. *SP:* Rachel Romen, Alan S. Lee. A Cal Dunn Studios Production. *CAST:* Rachel Romen, Rosalind C. Roberts, Robert A. Terry, Robert Ward, Bea Silvern, Rance Howard, Paul L'Amoreaux, Edward Schaff, Stuart Walsh, Bill Lloyd, Joe Slattery, Gregg Donavan. *SYN:* A gang of killers flee to the desert after killing and robbing a wealthy old woman. They seek refuge in a cabin and force an Indian woman (Silvern) and her daughter (Romen) to hide them. The daughter falls in love with one of the gang (Howard) and together they plan to escape, expose the gang and return the stolen money. *NOTES:* Assistant director and production manager was Vernon Keays. Filmed in the Mojave Desert. Working title was *Fly, Raven, Fly.*

101. The Desperado (6/20/54) B&W – 79 mins. (Western). *DIR:* Thomas Carr. *PRO:* Vincent M. Fennelly. *SP:* Geoffrey Homes (Daniel Mainwaring). Based on the book by Clifton Adams. A Silvermine Production. *CAST:* Wayne Morris, James Lydon, Beverly Garland, Rayford Barnes, Dabbs Greer, Lee Van Cleef, Nestor Paiva, Roy Barcroft, John Dierkes, Richard Shackelton, I. Stanford Jolley, Charles Garland, Florence Lake, Reed Howes, Stanley Price, William Fawcett, Robert Shayne, Lyle Talbot. *SYN:* In 1870 Texas, a young Texan (Lydon), framed for murder by his friend (Barnes), teams with a gunfighter (Morris) to prove his innocence and to oppose the Carpetbagger government. *NOTES:* Lee Van Cleef plays a dual role in this film.

102. Destination 60,000 (5/12/57) B&W – 66 mins. (Drama). *DIR / SP:* George Waggner. *PRO:* Jack J. Gross, Philip N. Krasne. *CAST:* Preston Foster, Pat Conway, Jeff Donnell, Coleen Gray, Bobby Clark, Denver Pyle, Russell Thorsen, Ann Barton. *SYN:* An aircraft manufacturer (Foster) conducts tests on his new jet aircraft.

103. Dial Red "O" (3/13/55) B&W – 63 mins. (Crime-Mystery). *DIR / SP:* Daniel B. Ullman. *PRO:* Vincent M. Fennelly. *CAST:* Bill Elliott, Keith Larsen, Helene Stanley, Paul Picerni, Jack Kruschen, Elaine Riley, Robert Bice, Rick Vallin, George Eldredge, John Phillips, Regina Gleason, Rankin Mansfield, William Tannen, Mort Mills, John Hart, Mike Ragan (Holly Bane), Sam Peckinpah, Larry

Advertisement for *Destination 60,000* (1957).

Blake, Lee Roberts. *SYN:* An ex-G.I. (Larsen) escapes from a psychiatric ward of a veteran's hospital to find his wife (Stanley) who divorced him. When she is found murdered, Lt. Flynn (Elliott) must find the real killer and prevent the ex-G.I. from finding him and becoming a murderer.

104. Diary of a Schizophrenic Girl (4/70) Eastmancolor – 94 mins. (Drama). *DIR:* Nelo Risi. *PRO:* Gian Vittorio Baldi. *SP:* Nelo Risi, Fabio Carpi. Based on *Journal d'une Schizophrène* by Renee and Marguerite Andree Sechehaye. An Idi Cinematografica Production. *CAST:* Ghislaine d'Orsay, Umbato Raho, Marija Tocinowsky, Margarita Lozano, Gabriella Mulachie, Manilo Busoni, Giuseppe Liuzzi, Sara Ridolfi. *SYN:* A psychiatrist (Lozano) attempts to treat a schizophrenic 17-year-old girl (d'Orsay) bent on committing suicide. [Original Italian title: *Diario di una Schizofrenica*.]

105. Dig That Uranium (1/8/56) B&W – 61 mins. (Western-Comedy). *DIR:* Edward Bernds. *PRO:* Ben Schwalb. *SP:* Elwood Ullman, Bert Lawrence. *CAST:* Leo Gorcey, Huntz Hall, David Condon, Bennie Bartlett, Bernard Gorcey, Mary Beth Hughes, Raymond Hatton, Harry Lauter, Myron Healey, Richard Powers (Tom Keene), Paul Fierro, Francis McDonald, Frank Jenks, Don C. Harvey, Carl "Alfalfa" Switzer. *SYN:* The Bowery Boys find themselves at odds with crooks when they buy a uranium mine in Nevada. *NOTES:* This film contains a "dream sequence" where the Boys imagine themselves in the old West. This is the last screen appearance of Bennie Bartlett; he left Hollywood and never made another

Advertisement for *Dig That Uranium* (1956).

Advertisement for *Dino* (1957). (Photo courtesy of Ted Okuda.)

film. It was the last film of Bernard Gorcey. He died in September, 1955, after completing work on this film, from injuries received in an auto accident.

106. Dino (7/21/57) B&W – 93 mins. (Drama). *DIR:* Thomas Carr. *PRO:* Bernice Block. *SP:* Reginald Rose. Based on the television play by Reginald Rose. *CAST:* Sal Mineo, Brian Keith, Susan Kohner, Frank Faylen, Joe De Santis, Penny Santon, Pat DeSimone, Richard Bakalyan, Mollie McCart, Cindy Robbins, Rafael Campos, Don C. Harvey, Michael Mineo, Ken Miller, Joel Collins, Kip King, Byron Foulger. *SYN:* A juvenile delinquent (Sal Mineo) recently released from reform school is befriended by a young girl (Kohner) and a social worker (Keith). *NOTES:* Sal Mineo repeated his role from the television play. [British title: *Killer Dino.*]

107. Dirty Money (1/77) Eastmancolor – 100 mins. (Crime). *DIR/SP:* Jean-Pierre Melville. *PRO:* Robert Dorfmann. A Corona–Oceania–Paris Production. *CAST:* Alain Delon, Catherine Deneuve,

Richard Crenna, Riccardo Cucciolla, Michael Conrad, Andre Pousse, Paul Crauchet, Simone Valere, Jean Desailly. *SYN:* A cop (Delon), intent on smashing a drug smuggling operation, gets a lead to the gang through a bank robbery in a seaside town. Arriving there, he has an affair with a woman (Deneuve) who turns out to be the mistress of the gang leader (Crenna). *NOTES:* Released in France in 1972. [Original French title: *Un Flic*.]

108. Disc Jockey (9/30/51) B&W – 77 mins. (Musical). *DIR:* Will Jason. *PRO:* Maurice Duke. *SP:* Clark E. Reynolds. *CAST:* Ginny Simms, Tom Drake, Jane Nigh, Michael O'Shea, Lenny Kent, Jerome Cowan, Tommy Dorsey, George Shearing, Sarah Vaughn, Herb Jeffries, Nick Lucas, the Weavers, Jack Fina, Vito Musso, Red Nichols, Red Norvo, Ben Pollack, Joe Venuti, Foy Willing and the Riders of the Purple Sage, Russ Morgan, Martin Block, Joe Adams, Joe Allison, Bill Anson, Doug Arthur, Don Bell, Paul Brenner, Bob Clayton, Paul Dixon, Ed Gallaher, Dick Gilbert, Bill Gordon, Maurice Hart, Bruce Hayes, Eddie Hubbard, Bea Kalmus, Les Malloy, Paul Masterson, Ed McKenzie, Tom Mercein, Gill Newsome, Gene Norman, Art Pallans, Bob Poole, Norman Prescott, Fred Robbins, Ernie Simon, Larry Wilson. *SYN:* A disc jockey promoter (O'Shea) claims that he can turn an unknown singer (Simms) into a star with the aid of radio exposure.

109. The Disembodied (8/25/57) B&W – 65 mins. (Horror). *DIR:* Walter Grauman. *PRO:* Ben Schwalb. *SP:* Jack Townley. *CAST:* Paul Burke, Allison Hayes, John E. Wengraf, Eugenia Paul, Joel Marston, Robert Christopher, Norman Fredric, A.E. Ukonu, Paul Thompson, Otis Greene. *SYN:* In the wilds of a jungle, Tonda (Hayes), the wife of a doctor (Wengraf), resorts to voodoo rituals to carry out her evil deeds. *NOTES:* Double billed in some areas with *From Hell It Came.*

110. Disk-O-Tek Holiday (6/1/66) Eastmancolor – 72 mins. (Musical-Documentary). *DIR:* Douglas Hickok. *PRO:* Jacques De Lane Lea. *DIR:*/U.S.: Vince Scarza. *PRO/U.S.* Frank C. Slay. *SP:* David Edwards. From an idea by Douglas Hickok, Jacques De Lane Lea. A Delmore-Canterbury Production. *CAST:* Peter and Gordon, the Chiffons, a Band of Angels, the Bachelors, Freddy Cannon, the Vagrants, Casey Paxton, Louise Cordet, the Merseybeats, Caroline Lee, Roy Sone, Judy Jason, Johnny B. Great, the Applejacks, the Rockin' Ramrods, the Orchids, Freddie and the Dreamers, Jackie and the Raindrops, Millie Small, Al Saxon, Douglas Sheldon, Mark Wynter, the Warriors. *SYN:* A series of rock performances given in London and the United States. *NOTES:* Released in Great Britain in 1964 at a running time of 64 mins. In the English version, English disc jockey Sam Costa introduced the British acts. For the American version, some of the British performers were cut and replaced with American performers and were introduced by disc jockeys Arnie Ginsburg of Boston, Hy Lit of Philadelphia, and Bob Foster of Baltimore and Boston. [British title: *Just for You*.]

111. Dondi (3/26/61) B&W – 100 mins. (Drama-Children). *DIR:* Albert Zugsmith. *PRO/SP:* Albert Zugsmith, Gus Edson. Based on the comic strip created by Gus Edson and Irwin Hasen. A Photoplay Associates Production. *CAST:* David Janssen, Patti Page, Walter Winchell, David Kory, Mickey Shaughnessy, Robert Strauss, Arnold Stang, Louis Quinn, Gale Gordon, Dick Patterson, Susan Kelly, John Melfi, Bonnie Scott, William Wellman, Jr., Nola Thorp, Joan Staley. *SYN:* A five-year-old homeless Italian war refugee, Dondi (Kory) is befriended by a group of American GIs.

He stows away on their troop ship and journeys to America where he has several adventures before being reunited with his soldier buddy (Janssen) and his girlfriend (Page). With the help of Walter Winchell, he is awarded American citizenship.

The Double Agents *see* **Night Encounter**

112. Double Confession (11/4/51) B&W – 86 mins. (Crime-Mystery). *DIR:* Ken Annakin. *PRO:* Harry Reynolds. *SP:* William Templeton, Ralph Keene. Based on *All on a Summer's Day* by John Garden. An Associated British Picture–Reynolds Production. A Stratford Picture Presentation. *CAST:* Derek Farr, Joan Hopkins, Peter Lorre, William Hartnell, Naunton Wayne, Ronald Howard, Kathleen Harrison, Leslie Dwyer, Edward Rigby, George Woodbridge, Henry Edwards, Vida Hope, Esma Cannon, Mona Washbourne. *SYN:* A disillusioned war veteran (Farr) returns home to find the body of his wife and another man at the bottom of a cliff. He confronts the wife's lover (Hartnell) and tells him that he killed them and he is going to frame the lover for the crime. *NOTES:* Released in Great Britain in 1950.

113. The Dragon Dies Hard (4/75) Eastmancolor/Scope – 90mins. (Martial Arts). *DIR/SP:* Kong Hung. *PRO:* Shaw Pau Wau. A Hallmark Presentation. *CAST:* Chung Nick, Nam Kung Fen. *SYN:* Bruce Lee (Nick) goes from Kung Fu teacher and television star in Los Angeles to director and super star in Hong Kong. *NOTES:* Still another of the many attempts to recreate Bruce Lee's life story. (See also: *Bruce Lee–Super Dragon*).

114. Dragonfly Squadron (3/21/54) B&W – 82 mins. (War). *DIR:* Lesley Selander. *PRO/SP:* John C. Champion. *CAST:* John Hodiak, Barbara Britton, Bruce Bennett, Jess Barker, Gerald Mohr, Chuck Connors, Harry Lauter, Pamela Duncan, Adam Williams, John Lupton, Benson Fong, John Hedloe, Fess Parker, Gene Wesson. *SYN:* An Air Force major (Hodiak), in South Korea to get the local air force ready for battle, finds time to renew a romance with a Red Cross worker (Britton). *NOTES:* Although filmed in 3-D, this film was released flat only.

115. Dragoon Wells Massacre (4/28/57) Deluxe Color/Scope – 88 mins. (Western). *DIR:* Harold Schuster. *PRO:* Lindsley Parsons. *SP:* Warren Douglas. Story by Oliver Drake. *CAST:* Barry Sullivan, Mona Freeman, Dennis O'Keefe, Katy Jurado, Jack Elam, Sebastian Cabot, Casey Adams, Trevor Bardette, Jon Shepodd, Hank Worden, Warren Douglas, Judy Stranges, Alma Beltran, John War Eagle. *SYN:* A Cavalry captain (O'Keefe) and a convict (Sullivan) lead a group of people back to civilization through Indian territory.

116. The Dude Goes West (5/30/48) B&W – 86 mins. (Western-Comedy). *DIR:* Kurt Neumann. *PRO:* Frank King, Maurice King. *SP:* Richard Sale, Mary Loos. *CAST:* Eddie Albert, Gale Storm, James Gleason, Gilbert Roland, Binnie Barnes, Barton MacLane, Douglas Fowley, Tom Tyler, Harry Hayden, Chief Yowlachie, Sarah Padden, Catherine Doucet, Edward Gargan, Frank Yaconelli, Olin Howlin, Charles Williams, Francis Pierlot, Dick Elliot, Lee "Lasses" White, Si Jenks, Tom Fadden, George Meeker, Ben Welden. *SYN:* A gunsmith (Albert) from New York heads west to Arsenic City, Arizona, where he figures to relocate his business and make a fortune since everyone there owns a gun. *NOTES:* Working title was *The Tenderfoot.*

117. El Cid (12/15/61) Technicolor/ Super Technirama 70 – 184 mins. (Ad-

Eddie Albert signals for peace much to the concern of Gale Storm in *The Dude Goes West* (1948).

venture-Historical). *DIR:* Anthony Mann. *PRO:* Samuel Bronston. Anthony Mann. *SP:* Philip Yordan, Fredric M. Frank. A Samuel Bronston–Rank Production. *CAST:* Charlton Heston, Sophia Loren, John Fraser, Raf Vallone, Genevieve Page, Gary Raymond, Herbert Lom, Massimo Serato, Douglas Wilmer, Frank Thring, Hurd Hatfield, Ralph Truman, Andrew Cruickshank, Michael Hordern, Carlo Giustini, Christopher Rhodes, Gerard Tichy, Fausto Tozzi, Tullio Carminati, Barbara Everest. *SYN:* In 11th century Spain, Rodrigo Diaz de Bivar (Heston), dubbed "El Cid" because of his nobility, courage, and spirituality, defends Spain against the invading Moors. With the death of King Ferdinand (Truman) and the further division of his kingdom by his warring children (Fraser, Page, Raymond), El Cid lays seige to Valencia, the last outpost of the Moorish usurpers. *NOTES:* Roadshow engagements were shown in Super Technirama 70. Scope prints were released for regular showings in 1962.

118. The Eleanor Roosevelt Story (11/18/65) B&W – 90 mins. (Documentary) *DIR:* Richard Kaplan. *PRO:* Sidney Glazier. *SP:* Archibald MacLeish. A Landau/Unger Releasing Organization Presentation. *CAST:* Narrated by Eric Sevareid, Archibald MacLeish, Mrs. Francis Cole. *SYN:* A documentary biography of Eleanor Roosevelt told through still photographs and newsreel footage, from her early years to her later years as a significant figure on the world scene. *NOTES:* This film, originally released by Allied Artists, was later released by American-International.

119. End of the Road (2/70) Eastmancolor—111 mins. (Drama). *DIR:* Aram Avakian. *PRO:* Terry Southern, Stephen F. Kesten. *SP:* Dennis McGuire, Terry Southern, Aram Avakian. Based on *The End of the Road* by John Barth. *CAST:* Stacy Keach, Harris Yulin, Dorothy Tristan, James Earl Jones, Grayson Hall, Ray Brock, James Coco, Oliver Clark, June Hutchinson, Graham Jarvis, Maeve McGuire, Joel Oppenheimer, John Picchette, Norman Simpson, Joel Wolfe, M. Emmet Walsh, Gail Gibson, Aram Avakian. *SYN:* An unstable English instructor (Keach), discharged from a sanitarium, accepts a teaching position at a local university and becomes friends with a gun enthusiast (Yulin) and his wife (Tristan), who involve him in adultery, abortion, and death. *NOTES:* Another of the "softcore" X-rated features distributed by Allied Artists in the seventies. By today's standards, this film would be rated R.

120. Escape by Night (8/29/64) B&W—75 mins. (Crime-Drama). *DIR:* Montgomery Tully. *PRO:* Maurice J. Wilson. *SP:* Maurice J. Wilson, Montgomery Tully. Based on *Clash by Night* by Rupert Croft-Cooke. An Eternal Films Production. *CAST:* Terence Longdon, Jennifer Jayne, Harry Fowler, Peter Sallis, Alan Wheatley, Vanda Godsell, Arthur Lovegrove, Hilda Fenemore, Mark Dignam, John Arnatt, Richard Carpenter, Stanley Meadows, Robert Brown, Tom Bowman, Ray Austen. *SYN:* A gang of crooks hijack a busload of convicts in order to free one of the prisoners (Bowman). The crooks imprison the convicts in a deserted barn, and threaten to burn down the barn if they try to escape. *NOTES:* Released in Great Britain in 1963. [British title: *Clash by Night*.]

121. Face of Fire (8/9/59) B&W— 83 mins. (Drama). *DIR:* Albert Band. *PRO:* Albert Band, Louis Garfinkle. *SP:* Louis Garfinkle. Based on *The Monster* by Stephen Crane. A Mardi Gras Production. *CAST:* Cameron Mitchell, James Whitmore, Bettye Ackerman, Royal Dano, Miko Oscard, Robert F. Simon, Richard Erdman, Howard Smith, Lois Maxwell, Jill Donahue. *SYN:* A handyman (Whitmore), once adored by the local townspeople, is shunned when he is horribly disfigured in a fire while rescuing a young boy (Oscard). *NOTES:* Filmed in Sweden. Although promoted as a horror film by Allied Artists, this film was more drama than horror. Double billed in some areas with *The Bat*.

The Faceless Monsters *see* **Nightmare Castle**

122. Fangs of the Arctic (1/18/53) B&W—63 mins. (Western). *DIR:* Rex Bailey. *PRO:* Lindsley Parsons. *SP:* William Raynor, Warren Douglas. Based on a story by James Oliver Curwood. *CAST:* Kirby Grant, Lorna Hansen, Warren Douglas, Leonard Penn, Richard Avonde, Robert Sherman, John Close, Phil Tead, Roy Gordon, Kit Carson, "Chinook," the dog. *SYN:* A Mountie (Grant) goes after crooks engaged in illegal fur trapping.

Fascination *see* **Love in the Afternoon**

123. Father's Doing Fine (4/22/53) Technicolor—83 mins. (Comedy). *DIR:* Henry Cass. *PRO:* Victor Skutezky. *SP:* Anne Burnaby. Based on the play *Little Lambs Eat Ivy* by Noel Langley. An Associated British Picture–Marble Arch Production. A Stratford Picture Presentation. *CAST:* Richard Attenborough, Heather Thatcher, Noel Purcell, George Thorpe, Diane Hart, Susan Stephen, Mary Germaine, Virginia McKenna, Jack Watling, Peter Hammond, Brian Worth, Sidney James, Ambrosine Phillpotts, Harry Locke, Jonathan Field. *SYN:* A scatterbrained widow (Thatcher) with four equally scatterbrained daughters (Hart, Stephen, Germaine, McKenna)

Joy Page and Sterling Hayden take time out for a tender moment in *Fighter Attack* (1953).

must contend with a variety of problems including one daughter's husband (Attenborough) who is nervous about becoming a father. *NOTES:* Released in Great Britain in 1952.

123a. La Femme Infidele (The Unfaithful Wife) (11/69) Eastmancolor—98 mins. (Crime-Drama). *DIR/SP:* Claude Chabrol. *PRO:* Andre Genoves. A Les Films de Boetie-Cinégay Production. *CAST:* Stephane Audran, Michel Bouquet, Maurice Ronet, Serge Bento, Michel Duchaussoy, Guy Marly, Stephane Di Napoli, Louise Chevalier, Louise Rioton, Henri Marteau, François Moro-Giafferi, Dominique Zardi, Michel Charrel, Henri Attal, Jean-Marie Arnoux, Donatella Turri. *SYN:* When a man (Bouquet) suspects that his wife (Audran) is unfaithful, he travels to Paris, confronts her lover (Ronet) and kills him. When he returns home, she finds evidence that he has killed the lover and tries to protect him from the police. *NOTES:* Opened in Paris in January, 1969, at a running time of 105 mins.

124. 55 Days at Peking (6/26/63) Technicolor/Super Technirama 70—150 mins. (Historical-War). *DIR:* Nicholas Ray. *PRO:* Samuel Bronston. *SP:* Philip Yordan, Bernard Gordon, Robert Hamer. A Samuel Bronston Production. *CAST:* Charlton Heston, Ava Gardner, David Niven, Flora Robson, John Ireland, Harry Andrews, Leo Genn, Kurt Kasznar, Paul Lukas, Jerone Thor, Elizabeth Sellars, Jacques Sernas, Walter Gotell, Geoffrey Bayldon, Eric Pohlmann, Mervyn Johns, Massimo Serato, Robert Helpmann, Ichizo Itami, Philippe Leroy, Lynne Sue Moon, Joseph Furst, Alfred Lynch, Martin Miller, Alfredo Mayo, Conchita Montes, Jose Nieto, Aram Stephan, Robert Urquhart, Felix Defauce, Andre Esterhazy, Carlos Casaravilla, Fernando Sancho, Michael Chow, Mitchell Kowal, Ronald Brittain, Nicholas Ray. *SYN:* In 1900 Peking, China, eleven nations under the command of U.S. Marine Major Matt Lewis (Heston) and the British Ambassador (Niven) take a stand in their international compound and defend themselves against the Society of the Righteous and Harmonious Fists, the "Boxers," until reinforcements can arrive. *NOTES:* Second unit director Andrew Marton, who was uncredited, took over directing the battle sequences when director Nicholas Ray became ill. The first of Samuel Bronston's Spanish-made epics to lose money. Roadshow prints were shown in Super Technirama 70; scope prints were released for regular showings in late 1963. Reissued by Allied Artists in 1967.

125. Fighter Attack (11/29/53) CineColor—80 mins. (War). *DIR:* Lesley Selander. *PRO:* William Calihan. *SP:* Simon Wincelberg. *CAST:* Sterling Hayden, J. Carrol Naish, Joy Page, Kenneth Tobey, Anthony Caruso, Frank DeKova, Paul Fierro, Maurice Jara, Tony Dante, David Leonard, James Flavin, Harry Lauter, John Fontaine, David Bond, Louis Lettieri, Joel Marston. *SYN:* During World War II, an American fighter pilot (Hayden) is shot down while trying to destroy a Nazi supply dump. He is rescued by a band of guerrillas and together, with the help of the other pilots, they succeed in destroying the dump.

126. The Fighting Lawman (9/20/53) B&W—71 mins. (Western). *DIR:* Thomas Carr. *PRO:* Vincent M. Fennelly. *SP:* Daniel B. Ullman. A Westwood Production. *CAST:* Wayne Morris, Virginia Grey, John Kellogg, Harry Lauter, John Pickard, Rick Vallin, Myron Healey, Dick Rich. *SYN:* A deputy marshal (Morris) goes after bank robbers and becomes involved with a woman (Grey) who wants the stolen money.

127. Fighting Trouble (9/16/56) B&W—61 mins. (Comedy). *DIR:* George Blair. *PRO:* Ben Schwalb. *SP:* Elwood Ullman. *CAST:* Huntz Hall, Stanley Clements, David Gorcey, Danny Welton, Adele Jergens, Thomas Browne Henry, William Boyett, Joseph Downing, Tim Ryan, Queenie Smith, John Bleifer, Laurie Mitchell, Charles Williams, Clegg Hoty, Michael Ross, Benny Burt, Rick Vallin, Ann Griffith. *SYN:* Sach (Hall) and Duke (Clements) try to get a photo of a notorious gangster (Henry) but Sach ruins the film. Sach then poses as a gangster to gain entrance to the gangster's nightclub and get his picture. *NOTES:* Beginning with this film, the billings were to read "Huntz Hall and The Bowery Boys in . . . ." Working title was *Chasing Trouble.*

128. Finger on the Trigger (5/26/65) Technicolor/Scope—87 mins. (Western). *DIR/PRO:* Sidney Pink. *SP:* Sidney Pink, Luis De Los Arcos. A Comet Production. *CAST:* Rory Calhoun, James Philbrook, Todd Martin, Silvia Solar, Brad Talbot, Leo Anchoriz, Jorge Rigaud, Eric Chapman, Beny Deus, Axel Anderson, Tito Garcia, John Clarke, Willy P. Elie, Antonio Molino Rojo, Jose Antonio Peral, German Grech, Fernando Bilboa, Sebastian Cavalier. *SYN:* After the Civil War, a group of ex-Union soldiers head for New Mexico to homestead. They encounter renegade Confederate troops awaiting a gold shipment. Finding the gold in a ghost town, the rival forces unite to fight off an Indian attack. [Original Spanish title: *El Dedo en el Gatillo.*]

129. Fingerman (6/19/55) B&W—81 mins. (Crime). *DIR:* Harold Schuster. *PRO:* Lindsley Parsons. *SP:* Warren Douglas. Story by Morris Lipsius, John Lardner. *CAST:* Frank Lovejoy, Forrest Tucker, Peggie Castle, Timothy Carey, John Cliff, William Leicester, Glenn Gordon, John Close, Hugh Sanders, Evelynne Eaton, Charles Maxwell, Lewis Charles, Henry Kulky, Joi Lansing. *SYN:* Told in semi-documentary style, a four-time loser (Lovejoy) agrees to be a fingerman for the Bureau of Internal Revenue to gain evidence against a notorious mobster (Tucker). *NOTES:* Double billed in some areas with *Case of the Red Monkey.*

Sterling Hayden and Richard Carlson in *Flat Top* (1952).

130. The First Texan (6/29/56) Technicolor/Scope—82 mins. (Western). *DIR:* Byron Haskin. *PRO:* Walter Mirish. *SP:* Daniel B. Ullman. *CAST:* Joel McCrea, Felicia Farr, Jeff Morrow, Wallace Ford, Abraham Sofaer, Jody McCrea, Chubby Johnson, Dayton Lummis, Rodolfo Hoyos, William Hopper, Roy Roberts, David Silva, Frank Puglia, James Griffith, Nelson Leigh, Carl Benton Reid, William Phipps, Scott Douglas, Lane Chandler, Myron Healey, William Tannen, Salvador Baguez. *SYN:* Sam Houston (Joel McCrea), a lawyer who wants no part of the fight for Texas independence, is urged by President Jackson (Reid) to take the lead in helping Texas free itself of Mexican rule.

131. Flat Top (10/26/52) CineColor—83 mins. (War). *DIR:* Lesley Selander. *PRO:* Walter Mirisch. *SP:* Steve Fisher. *CAST:* Sterling Hayden, Richard Carlson, John Bromfield, William Phipps, Keith Larsen, William Schallert, Todd Karns, Walter Coy, Dave Willock, Phyllis Coates. *SYN:* Told in flashback and using actual combat footage. It is 1944 aboard the *USS Princeton* and the hard-as-nails commanding officer (Hayden) of a carrier air group is at odds with the new air group commander (Carlson) who is friendly with his men and never pushes them. *NOTES:* Associate producer was Richard Heermance. [British title: *Eagles of the Fleet.*]

132. The Fool Killer (4/28/65) B&W—99 mins. (Drama). *DIR:* Servando Gonzalez. *PRO:* David Friedkin. *SP:* Morton Fine, David Friedkin. Based on the book by Helen Eustis. A Jack J.

Dreyfus, Jr.–Landau/Unger Releasing Organization Presentation. CAST: Anthony Perkins, Edward Albert, Jr., Dana Elcar, Henry Hull, Salome Jens, Charlotte Jones, Arnold Moss, Sindee Anne Richards, Francis Garr, Wendell Phillips. SYN: After the Civil War, a twelve-year-old orphan (Albert) runs away from his foster home and meets an old man (Hull) who relates to him the legend of the "fool killer," an axe murderer who rids the world of fools. The boy then moves in with a kindly couple (Elcar, Jens) and when a preacher (Moss) is found murdered, suspicion falls on an ex-soldier (Perkins). NOTES: The film debut of Edward Albert, Jr. Filmed in 1963 in Knoxville, Tennessee. Publicity title for this film was *The Legend of the Fool Killer*. In 1968, Jack J. Dreyfus, Jr., purchased the exclusive rights to this film and then re-edited and rereleased it independently as *Violent Journey*.

133. Footsteps in the Night (4/14/57) B&W – 62 mins. (Crime). DIR: Jean Yarbrough. PRO: Ben Schwalb. SP: Elwood Ullman, Albert Band. Story by Albert Band. CAST: Bill Elliott, Don Haggerty, Eleanore Tanin, Douglas Dick, Robert Shayne, James Flavin, Gregg Palmer, Harry Tyler, Ann Griffith, John Close, Zena Marshall, Forrest Taylor, Minerva Urecal, John Bleifer, Ralph Sanford. SYN: Lt. Doyle (Elliott) and Sgt. Duncan (Haggerty), called in to investigate a murder, suspect the murdered man's friend (Dick) who was the last to see him. After careful investigation, they find that the man is innocent and they set a trap for the real murderer, using a decoy (Flavin) who strongly resembles the murdered man. NOTES: Bill Elliott's last feature film after a career spanning 32 years. Double billed in some areas with *The Badge of Marshal Brennan*.

134. For Them That Trespass (7/6//50) B&W – 95 mins. (Crime). DIR: Cavalcanti. PRO: Victor Skutezky. SP: J. Lee Thompson, William Douglas Home. Based on the book by Ernest Raymond. An Associated British Picture Production. A Stratford Picture Presentation. CAST: Stephen Murray, Richard Todd, Patricia Plunkett, Rosalyn Boulter, Michael Laurence, Mary Merrall, Joan Dowling, Frederick Leister, Helen Cherry, Michael Medwin, Vida Hope, Harry Fowler, Irene Handl, James Hayter, George Curzon, Valentine Dyall, Harcourt Williams. SYN: A writer, Christopher Drew (Murray), seeking to gather firsthand information for his book, travels to the dangerous side of town and witnesses a murder of a local prostitute (Boulter). Not wishing to get involved, he lets an innocent man, Herb Logan (Todd), go to prison for the crime. Years later, when Logan is released, he extracts a deathbed confession from the real killer (Laurence) and then tricks Drew into revealing the true facts of the crime that will clear his name. NOTES: Released in Great Britain in 1949.

135. Fort Vengeance (3/29/53) CineColor – 75 mins. (Western). DIR: Lesley Selander. PRO: Walter Wanger. SP: Daniel B. Ullman. CAST: James Craig, Rita Moreno, Keith Larsen, Reginald Denny, Charles Irwin, Morris Ankrum, Guy Kingsford, Michael Granger, Patrick Whyte, Paul Marion, Emory Parnell, Jack Ingram, William Forrest. SYN: Two men (Craig, Larsen), one wanted by the law, cross the border to Canada and join the Mounties where they get involved with fur thieves and try to stop Sitting Bull (Granger) and his Sioux braves from inciting the local Indian chief, Crowfoot (Ankrum), and his people to start an Indian war.

136. The Forty-Niners (5/4/54) B&W – 71 mins. (Western). DIR: Thomas Carr. PRO: Vincent M. Fennelly. SP: Daniel B. Ullman. A Westwood Production. CAST: "Wild" Bill Elliott, Virginia

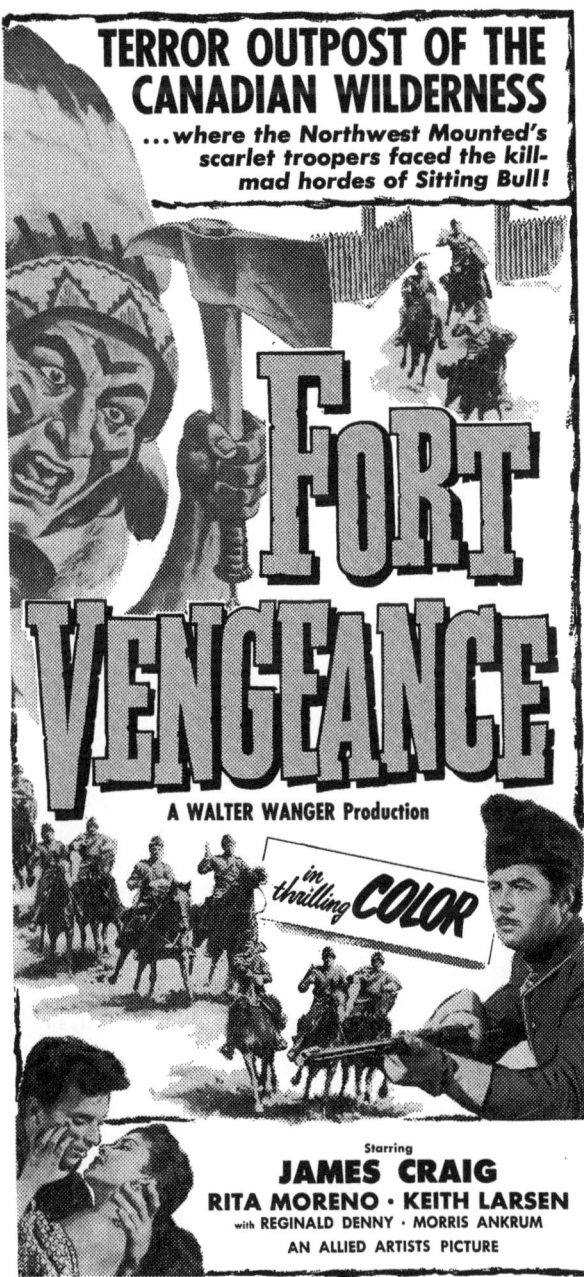

Advertisement for *Fort Vengeance* (1953).

Grey, Henry (Harry) Morgan, John Doucette, Lane Bradford, I. Stanford Jolley, Gregg Barton, Ralph Sanford, Harry Lauter, Earle Hodgins, Dean Cromer, Stanley Price, Jack O'Shea. *SYN:* A U.S. Marshal (Elliott) poses as a gunman to learn the identity of the killers of a federal marshal. He becomes friends with a card sharp (Morgan) in the hopes that he will lead him to the killers (Doucette, Bradford). *NOTES:* This was Bill Elliott's last starring role in a western. After almost 26 years of playing western roles at the studios of Columbia, Republic, Monogram, and Allied Artists, Bill hung up his guns. He would make five detective features, four of them as the character "Lt. Doyle," for Allied Artists before retiring from films.

137. The Franchise Affair (4/28/52) B&W – 95 mins. (Crime). *DIR:* Lawrence Huntington. *PRO:* Robert Hall. *SP:* Lawrence Huntington, Robert Hall. An Associated British Picture Production. A Stratford Picture Presentation. *CAST:* Michael Denison, Dulcie Gray, Anthony Nicholls, Marjorie Fielding, Athene Seyler, Ann Stephens, Hy Hazell, Kenneth More, John Bailey, John Warwick, Avice Landone, Moultrie Kelsall, Maureen Glynne, Peter Jones, Martin Boddey, Victor Maddern, Patrick Troughton, Ambrosine Phillpotts. *SYN:* A mother (Fielding) and daughter (Gray) live a reclusive life in their large house, The Franchise. When a young teenage girl (Stephens) accuses them of kidnapping and abusing her, they are put on trial. Evidence mounts against them until their lawyer (Denison) breaks down the girl's story and she admits it was all a lie to hide her own misdeeds. *NOTES:* Released in Great Britain in 1951 at a running time of 88 mins.

Frankenstein Meets the Spacemen *see* **Frankenstein Meets the Space Monster**

138. Frankenstein Meets the Space Monster (9/22/65) B&W – 75 mins. (Science Fiction). *DIR:* Robert Gaffney. *PRO:* Robert McCarty. *SP:* George Garrett. Story by John Rodenbeck, R.H.W. Dillard. A Futurama Entertainment Corporation presentation of a Vernon Films–Seneca Production. *CAST:* Robert Reilly, James Karen, David Kerman, Nancy Marshall, Marilyn Hanold, Lou Cutell. *SYN:* An android astronaut (Reilly) has his craft shot down by aliens and lands in Puerto Rico. An alien princess (Hanold) and dwarf (Cutell) land to bring back females to repopulate their dying planet. The android goes mad when his face is disfigured and his brain is short circuited. He is found and repaired by two scientists (Karen, Marshall) in time to destroy the aliens and their ship. *NOTES:* This film, considered to be one of the worst science fiction films ever made, has nothing to do with Mary Shelley's Frankenstein monster. To get people into the theatre to see this film, Allied Artists encouraged theatre owners to supply their patrons with "Space Shield Eye Protectors" to protect against the "high intensity cobalt rays that glow from the screen and to prevent your abduction into Outer Space." Double billed in some areas with *Curse of the Voodoo* [Original Puerto Rican title: *Marte Invade a Puerto Rico.*] [British title: *Duel of the Space Monsters.*]

139. Frankenstein–1970 (7/20/58) B&W/Scope – 83 mins. (Horror). *DIR:* Howard W. Koch. *PRO:* Aubrey Schenck. *SP:* Richard Landau, George Worthing Yates. Story by Aubrey Schenck, Charles A. Moses. Based on characters created by Mary Shelley. An A-Z Production. *CAST:* Boris Karloff, Tom Duggan, Jana Lund, Donald "Red" Barry, Charlotte Austin, Irwin Berke, Rudolph Anders, John Dennis, Norbert Schiller, Mike Lane, Jack Kenny, Franz Roehn, Joe Ploski. *SYN:* Set in 1970,

Advertisement for *Friendly Persuasion* (1956), Allied Artists' first real attempt to produce a big-budget, prestige picture.

Baron Victor von Frankenstein (Karloff), a descendent of Victor Frankenstein, and who has been disfigured by the Nazis, permits a television crew to film the story of his ancestor and his infamous creation while secretly working on his own monster in the basement. *NOTES:* Working titles were *Frankenstein–1960* and *Frankenstein–1975*. Double billed in some areas with *Queen of Outer Space*.

Fresh from Paris *see* **Paris Follies of 1956**

140. Friendly Persuasion (11/25/56) DeLuxe Color/Scope – 139 mins. (Western-Drama). *DIR/PRO:* William Wyler. *SP:* Uncredited (see notes). Based on *Friendly Persuasion* by Jessamyn West. *CAST:* Gary Cooper, Dorothy McGuire, Anthony Perkins, Marjorie Main, Richard Eyer, Robert Middleton, Phyllis Love, [Peter] Mark Richman, Walter Catlett, Richard Hale, Joel Fluellen, Theodore Newton, John Smith, Mary Carr, Russell Simpson, Charles Halton, Everett Glass, Richard Garland, James Dobson, James Seay, Diane Jergens, Ralph Sanford, Nelson Leigh, William Schallert, John Craven, Frank Jenks, Frank Hagney, Edna Skinner, Marjorie Durant, Frances Farwell, John Compton, Jean Inness, Helen Klebb, Marty Jackson. *SYN:* In 1862, a Southern Indiana Quaker family (Cooper, McGuire, Perkins, Eyer, Love) have their lives changed when the Civil War descends on their community. *NOTES:* Screenwriter Michael Wilson, who invoked the Fifth Amendment when summoned as a witness by the House Committee on un-American Activities in 1951, had his name withheld from the credits because Allied Artists chose to "deny credit to a writer revealed to be a member of the Communist Party or one who refused to answer charges of Communist affiliations." When his script was nominated for an Academy Award for Best Adapted Screenplay, he was rendered ineligible by Academy bylaws since his name was removed from the credits. Remade by Allied Artists as a TV movie in 1978 starring Richard Kiley, Shirley Knight and Michael O'Keefe.

141. Fright (6/30/56) B&W – 68 mins. (Drama). *DIR/PRO:* W. Lee Wilder. *SP:* Myles Wilder. An Exploitation Production. *CAST:* Eric Fleming, Nancy Malone, Frank Marth, Humphrey Davis, Dean L. Almquist, Elizabeth Watts, Amelia Conley, Walter Klaven, Ned Glass, Norman Burton, Tom Reynolds, Robert Gardett, Norman MacKaye, Don Douglas, Philip Kenneally, Sid Raymond, Chris Bohn, Alney Alba. *SYN:* A psychiatrist (Fleming) probes the mind of a young woman (Malone) who believes she was the lover of Austria's Crown Prince Rudolph and died with him in a suicide pact in 1889. She is shocked back to reality when the psychiatrist hypnotizes a psychotic criminal (Marth) to impersonate the long dead Crown Prince and to commence the suicide pact. *NOTES:* This film was released independently as *Spell of the Hypnotist* and has since had many distributors with both titles.

142. Fright (5/72) Eastmancolor – 87 mins. (Suspense). *DIR:* Peter Collinson. *PRO:* Harry Fine, Michael Style. *SP:* Tudor Gates. A British Lion International Film Production. *CAST:* Susan George, Honor Blackman, Ian Bannen, John Gregson George Cole, Dennis Waterman, Tara Collinson, Maurice Kaufmann, Michael Brennan, Roger Lloyd Pack. *SYN:* A babysitter (George) hired by a woman (Blackman) to watch her son is unaware that the woman's husband (Bannen), who has just escaped from a mental hospital, is hiding in the house and will kill anyone to get his son. *NOTES:* Released in Great Britain in 1971.

143. The Frightened City (7/20/62) B&W – 86 mins. (Crime). *DIR:*

John Lemont. *PRO:* John Lemont, Leigh Vance. *SP:* Leigh Vance. Story by Leigh Vance, John Lemont. A Zodiac–Anglo Amalgamated Production. *CAST:* Herbert Lom, John Gregson, Sean Connery, Alfred Marks, Yvonne Romain, Olive McFarland, David Davies, Kenneth Griffith, Frederick Piper, John Stone, Robert Cawdron, Tom Bowman, Patrick Jordan, George Pastell, Patrick Holt, Bruce Seton, Robert Percival, Joan Haythorne, Arnold Diamond, Jack Stewart, Douglas Robinson, Marianne Stone. *SYN:* An unscrupulous accountant (Lom) decides to organize the six gangs operating separately in London into an organization with the help of a gang leader (Marks) and one of his henchmen (Connery). When one of the gang leaders (Davies) decides to quit the organization, he is murdered and then the downfall of the organization begins. *NOTES:* Released in Great Britain in 1961 at a running time of 97 mins.

144. From Hell It Came (8/25/57) B&W – 73 mins. (Horror). *DIR:* Dan Milner. *PRO:* Jack Milner. *SP:* Richard Bernstein. Story by Richard Bernstein, Jack Milner. A Milner Bros. Production. *CAST:* Tod Andrews, Tina Carver, Suzanne Ridgway, Gregg Palmer, Robert Swan, Baynes Barron, Linda Watkins, John McNamara, Mark Sheeler, Lee Rhodes, Grace Matthews, Tani Marsh, Chester Hayes, Lenmana Guerin. *SYN:* On a south sea ialand, a native prince (Palmer) is murdered by the witch doctor (Swan) for helping scientists (Andrews, Carver) on the island investigate radiation residue from an atom bomb blast. Before he dies, he vows to come back from the dead and seek his revenge, which he does, as a walking tree stump! *NOTES:* Released in Great Britain at a running time of 70 mins. Double billed in some areas with *The Disembodied*.

145. The Gangster (11/22/47) B&W – 84 mins. (Crime). *DIR:* Gordon Wiles. *PRO:* Maurice King, Frank King. *SP:* Daniel Fuchs. Based on the book *Low Company* by Daniel Fuchs. *CAST:* Barry Sullivan, Belita, Joan Lorring, Akim Tamiroff, Henry (Harry) Morgan, John Ireland, Sheldon Leonard, Elisha Cook, Jr., Fifi D'Orsay, Leif Erickson, Virginia Christine, Charles McGraw, John Kellogg, Ted Hecht, Jeff Corey, Peter Whitney, Clancy Cooper, Murray Alper, Shelley Winters, Edwin Maxwell, Ruth Allen, Billy Gray, Dewey Robinson, Sid Melton, Don Haggerty, Griff Barnett, Michael Vallon, Greta Granstedt. *SYN:* The rise and fall of a gangster (Sullivan) from a petty thief to crime lord to his eventual murder by a rival gangster (Leonard).

146. The Gentle Rain (2/10/66) Eastmancolor – 110 mins. (Drama). *DIR/PRO:* Burt Balaban. *SP:* Robert Crean. A Comet Film Production. *CAST:* Christopher George, Lynda Day, Fay Spain, Maria Helena Dias, Lon Clark, Barbara Williams, Herbert Moss, Roberto Assumpaco, Nadyr Fernandes. *SYN:* A woman (Day) on the rebound from a bad marriage travels to Rio de Janeiro and meets a mute (George) whom she tries to help. *NOTES:* Filmed in 1965 in Brazil. Also released at a running time of 94 mins. Released by Comet Film Distributors in 1965 before being picked up for distribution by Allied Artists.

147. The George Raft Story (11/22/61) B&W – 105 mins. (Biography). *DIR:* Joseph M. Newman. *PRO:* Ben Schwalb. *SP:* Crane Wilbur. *CAST:* Ray Danton, Jayne Mansfield, Julie London, Barrie Chase, Frank Gorshin, Barbara Nichols, Brad Dexter, Robert Strauss, Herschel Bernardi, Margo Moore, Neville Brand, Joe De Santis, Argentina Brunetti, John Bleifer, Jack Lambert, Tol Avery, Robert H. Harris,

Jayne Mansfield and Ray Danton in *The George Raft Story* (1961).

Jack Albertson, Murvyn Vye, Myron Healey. *SYN:* This film traces the life of George Raft (Danton) from his beginning as an exhibition dancer at the Dreamland Casino in New York and his association with bootleggers and gangsters, such as Bugsy Siegel (Dexter). But eventually his career fades and he has to give up his lavish lifestyle. He then goes to Havana to participate in a hotel/casino venture, but as he arrives, the Castro revolution breaks out and he has to flee. The film ends as he makes his film comeback in 1959's *Some Like It Hot. NOTES:* Filmed while George Raft was still alive. Neville Brand makes a cameo appearance as Al Capone. [British title: *Spin of a Coin.*]

148. The Giant Behemoth (3/1/59) B&W – 79 mins. (Science Fiction). *DIR:* Douglas Hickox, Eugene Lourie. *PRO:* David Diamond. *SP:* Eugene Lourie. Story by Robert Abel, Allen Adler. An Artistes Alliance–Eros Production. *CAST:* Gene Evans, Andre Morell, Leigh Madison, Henry Vidon, John Turner, Jack McGowran, Maurice Kaufmann, Leonard Sachs, Georgina Ward, Neal Arden. *SYN:* An American scientist (Evans) in London fights to destroy a prehistoric dinosaur resurrected by an atomic explosion. *NOTES:* Screenwriter Daniel Hyatt was uncredited. Stop-motion animation scenes were designed and directed by Willis O'Brien and Louis DeWitt. Released in Great Britain at a running time of 72 mins. Working title was *The Behemoth.* Double billed in some areas with *Arson for Hire.* [British title: *Behemoth, the Sea Monster.*]

149. Gold (10/74) Technicolor/Panavision – 118 mins. (Drama). *DIR:* Peter

Advertisement for *The Giant Behemoth* (1959).

Hunt. *PRO:* Michael Klinger. *SP:* Wilbur Smith, Stanley Price. Based on *Goldmine* by Wilbur Smith. *CAST:* Roger Moore, Susannah York, Ray Milland, Bradford Dillman, John Gielgud, Simon Sabela, Tony Beckley, Bernard Horsfall, Marc Smith, John Hussey, Norman Coombes, George Jackson, Michael McGovern, Andre Maranne, John Bay, Paul Hansard. *SYN:* A mine foreman (Moore) is used by an unscrupulous mine owner (Dillman) in a plot to flood the gold mines of South Africa, thereby raising gold prices around the world. *NOTES:* In 1975, this film was double billed in some areas with *Mitchell.*

150. The Golden Idol (1/10/54) B&W – 71 mins. (Jungle-Adventure). *DIR/PRO/SP:* Ford Beebe. Based on characters in the *Bomba* books by Roy Rockwood. *CAST:* Johnny Sheffield, Anne Kimbell, Lane Bradford, Paul Guilfoyle, Leonard Mudie, Robert "Smoki" Whitfield, Roy Glenn, Rick Vallin, James Adamson, William Tannen, Don C. Harvey. *SYN:* Bomba (Sheffield) helps an African tribe get back their treasured golden idol from an Arab chieftain (Guilfoyle).

151. The Golden Madonna (9/15/49) B&W – 88 mins. (Drama). *DIR:* Ladislas Vajda. *PRO:* John Stafford. *SP:* Akos Stolnay. An Independent Film Producers Production. A Stratford Picture Presentation. *CAST:* Phyllis Calvert, Michael Rennie, Tullio Carminati, David Greene, Aldo Silvani, Francesca Bondi, Claudio Ermeli, Franco Coop, Pippe Benucci. *SYN:* A British woman (Calvert) inherits a villa in Italy and accidently throws away a painting that symbolizes prosperity to the villagers. With the help of an art collector (Rennie), she retrieves the painting from a black marketeer (Carminati) and returns it to the village. *NOTES:* Released in Great Britain in May, 1949. Re-released in 1953 by Warner Bros.

152. The Good Beginning (11/28/54) B&W – 64 mins. (Crime-Drama). *DIR:* Gilbert Gunn. *PRO:* Robert Hall. *SP:* Robert Hall, Gilbert Gunn, Janet Green. Story by Janet Green. An Associated British Pathé Production. A Stratford Picture Presentation. *CAST:* John Fraser, Eileen Moore, Peter Reynolds, Lana Morris, Humphrey Lestocq, Hugh Pryse, Ann Stephens, Peter Jones, Robert Raglan, David Kossoff, Victor Maddern, Roland Curram, Virginia Clay, Oliver Johnston, Lou Jacobi, Ronnie Harries, Barbara Cavan, Rosemary Whitfield, Eddie Vitch, Alma Cookson. *SYN:* A man (Fraser) desiring to keep up with his neighbors (Reynolds, Morris) buys his wife (Moore) a fur coat. Eventually, he gets deeper in debt and is forced to sell the coat when he cannot keep up the payments. *NOTES:* Released in Great Britain in 1953.

153. The Good Companions (5/1/58) Technicolor/Scope – 104 mns. (Musical). *DIR:* J. Lee Thompson. *PRO:* Hamilton G. Inglis. *SP:* T.J. Morrison, J.L. Hodgson, John Whiting. Based on the book and play by J.B. Priestley. An Associated British Pathé Production. A Stratford Picture Presentation. *CAST:* Eric Portman, Celia Johnson, Hugh Griffith, Janette Scott, John Fraser, Joyce Grenfell, Bobby Howes, Rachel Roberts, Thora Hird, Mona Washbourne, John Salew, Paddy Stone, Beatrice Varley, Alec McCowen, Fabia Drake, John Le Mesurier, Anthony Newley. *SYN:* A spinster (Johnson), a schoolteacher-composer (Fraser) and a dissatisfied Yorkshireman (Portman) inject money into a dying charity show and help two chorus people (Scott, Stone) rise to the top. *NOTES:* Released in Great Britain in 1957. A remake of the 1933 British film.

Goodbye to the Hill *see* **Paddy**

154. Guilt Is My Shadow (7/8/51) B&W – 86 mins. (Crime). *DIR:* Roy Kellino. *PRO:* Ivan Foxwell. *SP:* Ivan Foxwell, Roy Kellino, John Gilling. Based on *You're Best Alone* by Peter Curtis. An Associated British Pathe Production. A Stratford Picture Presentation. *CAST:* Patrick Holt, Elizabeth Sellars, Lana Morris, Peter Reynolds, Lawrence O'Madden, Avice Landone, Esma Cannon, Wensley Pithey. *SYN:* A young wife

(Sellars) accidently kills her husband (Reynolds), a wanted bank robber, in a fight. With the help of the husband's uncle (Holt), she hides the body. Plagued by nightmares and guilt, the wife and uncle confess to the crime. *NOTES:* Released in Great Britain in 1950.

155. Gun Battle at Monterey (10/27/57) B&W – 67 mins. (Western). *DIR:* Carl K. Hittleman, Sidney A. Franklin, Jr. *PRO:* Carl K. Hittleman. *SP:* Jack Leonard, Lawrence Resner. Story by Frank Fenton, Jack Leonard, Lawrence Resner. *CAST:* Sterling Hayden, Pamela Duncan, Ted de Corsia, Mary Beth Hughes, Lee Van Cleef, Charles Cane, Pat Comiskey, Byron Foulger, Mauritz Hugo, Fred Sherman, I. Stanford Jolley, George Baxter, Michael Vallon, John Damler. *SYN:* An outlaw (Hayden) seeks revenge against his partner (de Corsia) who shot him and left him for dead. *NOTES:* Working title was *Gun Battle of Monterey*. The title of this film is misleading as no gun battle takes place at Monterey.

156. The Gun Hawk (8/28/63) DeLuxe Color – 92 mins. (Western). *DIR:*

Advertisement for *Gunfight at Comanche Creek* (1963).

Edward Ludwig. *PRO:* Richard Bernstein. *SP:* Jo Heims. Story by Richard Bernstein, Max Steeber. *CAST:* Rory Calhoun, Rod Cameron, Ruta Lee, Rod Lauren, Morgan Woodward, Robert J. Wilke, John Litel, Rodolfo Hoyos, Lane Bradford, Glenn

Stensel, Joan Conners, Ron Whelan, Lee Bradley, Greg Barton, Jody Daniels, Frank Gardner, Harry Fleer. *SYN:* An aging gunfighter (Calhoun) tries to prevent a younger gunfighter (Lauren) from continuing his life of crime.

Gun Point *see* **At Gunpoint**

157. Gunfight at Comanche Creek (11/6/63) DeLuxe Color/Panavision – 90 mins. (Western). *DIR:* Frank McDonald. *PRO:* Ben Schwalb. *SP:* Edward Bernds. *CAST:* Audie Murphy, Ben Cooper, Colleen Miller, DeForrest Kelley, Jan Merlin, John Hubbard, Damian O'Flynn, Susan Seaforth, Adam Williams, Mort Mills, Douglas Kennedy, Thomas Browne Henry, William Wellman, Jr., Eddie Quillan, Laurie Mitchell, Tim Graham, Michael Mikler. *SYN:* A detective (Murphy), out to stop an outlaw gang from freeing convicts, making them participate in further crimes and then killing them for the reward money, becomes a member of the gang to learn the identity of their leader. *NOTES:* A remake of the 1953 Allied Artists film *Star of Texas.* Working title was *The Great Gunfighter.*

158. Gunmen of the Rio Grande (6/23/65) Eastmancolor/Scope — 86 mins. (Western). *DIR:* Tulio Demicheli. *PRO:* Ike Zingarmann (Italo Zingarelli). *SP:* Gene Luotto, Giovanni Simonell, Italo Zangarelli, Natividad Zaro, Tulio Demicheli, Guy Lionel. Story by Chen Morrison. A West Film–Flora Film–Llama Film–S.N. Pathé Cinema Co-Production. *CAST:* Guy Madison, Madeleine Lebeau, Gerard Tichy, Fernando Sancho, Carolyn Davys, Olivier Hussenot, Massimo Serato, Beny Deus, Dario Michaelis, Natividad Zaro, Alvaro de Luna, Xan Das Bolas, Juan Majan, E. Marn, H. Morrow. *SYN:* Marshal Wyatt Earp (Madison), in disguise as a gunfighter, travels south to Mexico to aid a woman (Lebeau) in saving her mine from an unscrupulous land baron (Tichy). [Original Italian title: *Sieda a Rio Bravo.*] [Original French title: *Duel à Rio Bravo.*] [Original Spanish title: *Desafío en Rio Bravo.*] [Alternate Spanish title #1: *Jenne Lees a una Nuova Pistola.*] [Alternate Spanish title #2: *El Sheriff del O.K. Corral.*]

159. Gunsmoke in Tucson (12/7/58) DeLuxe Color/Scope – 80 mins. (Western). *DIR:* Thomas Carr. *PRO:* Herbert Kaufman. *SP:* Paul Leslie Peil, Robert Joseph. Story by Paul Leslie Peil. *CAST:* Mark Stevens, Forrest Tucker, Gale Robbins, Vaughn Taylor, John Ward, Kevin Hagen, Bill Henry, Richard Reeves, John Cliff, Gail Kobe, George Keymas, Zon Murray, Paul Engle, Anthony Sydes, Terry Frost, I. Stanford Jolley. *SYN:* A lawman (Tucker) persuades his outlaw brother (Stevens) to join forces and help the local farmers fight cattlemen set on taking their land. *NOTES:* Working title was *Tucson.*

160. Hands of a Stranger (4/22/62) B&W – 86 mins. (Horror). *DIR/SP:* Newton Arnold. *PRO:* Newton Arnold, Michael duPont. Based on *Les Mains d'Orlac (The Hands of Orlac)* by Maurice Renard. A Glenwood-Neve Production. *CAST:* James Stapleton, Paul Lukather, Joan Harvey, Michael duPont, Sally Kellerman, Barry Gordon, Irish McCalla, Ted Otis, Michael Rye, Larry Haddon, Elaine Martone, George Sawaya, David Kramer. *SYN:* A concert pianist (Stapleton) loses his hands in an accident and has the hands of a murderer grated onto his arms by a famous surgeon (Lukather). Soon the hands begin to control him, and going insane, he goes on a murderous rampage. *NOTES:* Filmed in 1960. Running time is also listed at 95 mins. The only film directed by Newton Arnold. Working title was *The Answer!* Filmed in 1925 by Pan Film of Austria as *Orlacs Haende*, in 1935 by MGM as *Mad Love* and in 1960 by Riviera Pendennis as *The Hands of Orlac* (U.S. *Hands of a Strangler*).

Jeffrey Hunter, as Guy Gabaldon, says goodbye to his adopted Japanese-American mother, Tsuru Aoki Hayakawa, in *Hell to Eternity* (1960).

Happy Ever After see Tonight's the Night

161. The Head of the Family (7/70) Eastmancolor—105 mins. (Drama). *DIR:* Nanni Loy. *PRO:* Turi Vasile. *SP:* Nanni Loy, Ruggero Maccari. Story by Nanni Loy, Ruggero Maccari, Giorgio Arlorio. An Ultra Film—MN Produzione—Cinematografica—CFC—Marianne Production. An Alpha Film Associates Presentation. *CAST:* Leslie Caron, Nino Manfredi, Claudine Auger, Ugo Tognazzi, Evi Maltagliati, Sergio Tofano, Mario Carotenuto, Elsa Vazzoler, Adolfo Celi, Antonella Della Porta, Marisa Solinas. *SYN:* In post-World War II Rome, two architecture students (Caron, Manfredi) fall in love and marry. With the arrival of a family, she gives up her career and their home becomes a haven for friends and relatives. When she neglects her appearance, he takes a mistress (Auger), but his wife wins him back and he renews his career. *NOTES:* Limited theatrical release. Released in Italy at a running time of 115 mins, and in France at a running time of 111 mins. [Original Italian title: *Il Padre di Famiglia.*] [Original French title: *Jeux d'Adultes.*]

162. Hell to Eternity (9/30/60) B&W—132 mins. (War-Biography). *DIR:* Phil Karlson. *PRO:* Irving H. Levin. *SP:* Ted Sherdeman, Walter Roeber Schmidt. Story by Gil Doud. An Atlantic Pictures Corporation Production. *CAST:* Jeffrey Hunter, David Janssen, Vic Damone, Patricia Owens, Richard Eyer, John Larch, Bill Williams, Miiko Taka, Sessue Hayakawa, Tsuru Aoki Hayakawa, Michi

Kobi, George Shibata, Reiko Sato, Richard Gardner, Bob Okazaki, George Matsui, Nicky Blair, George Takai. *SYN:* Based on the true life story of Guy Gabaldon (Hunter) who as a boy (Eyer) was raised by Japanese parents. When World War II breaks out and he is shipped overseas, he struggles with his identity as an American or Japanese. Later, he proves his heroism when he convinces a Japanese general (Sessue Hayakawa) that as a human being he must let his soldiers and the people of Saipan live. *NOTES:* Filmed on the island of Okinawa.

163. Hell's Five Hours (4/13/58) B&W – 73 mins. (Thriller). *DIR/PRO/SP:* Jack L. Copeland. A Muriel Corporation Production. *CAST:* Stephen McNally, Coleen Gray, Vic Morrow, Maurice Manson, Robert Foulk, Dan Sheridan, Will J. White, Robert Christopher, Charles J. Conrad, Ray Ferrel. *SP:* When an employee (Morrow) of a missile depot goes berserk, holds several hostages, and threatens to blow up the depot, the manager (McNally) of the depot tries to dissuade him from carrying out his threat.

164. Her Panelled Door (7/3051) B&W – 84 mins. (Drama). *DIR:* Ladislas Vajda, George More O'Ferrall. *PRO:* John Stafford. *SP:* Ladislas Vajda, Guy Morgan. Based on *Happy Now I Go* by Theresa Charles. An Associated British Picture Production. A Stratford Picture Presentation. *CAST:* Phyllis Calvert, Edward Underdown, Helen Cherry, Richard Burton, Anthony Nicholls, James Hayter, Betty Ann Davies, Amy Veness, Andrew Osborn, Patrick Troughton, Olive Milbourne, June Bardsley, Will Ambro, Harold Scott, Willoughby Gray, Vi Stevens, David Keir, Kathleen Boutall, Irlin Hall, Leslie Phillips, Terence Alexander. *SYN:* In 1940, a woman (Calvert) suffers amnesia during the London blitz. She marries the Norwegian officer (Burton) who saved her but he is later killed on a mission. Later, she learns she has an estranged husband (Underdown) and a half-sister (Cherry) who is out to destroy her. *NOTES:* Released in Great Britain in 1950. [British title: *The Woman with No Name.*]

165. Herod the Great (12/5/60) Eastmancolor/Scope – 93 mins. (Biblical). *DIR:* Arnaldo Genoino. *PRO:* W. Tourjansky. *SP:* Damiano Damiani, Federico Zardi, Fernando Cerchio, W. Tourjansky. Story by Damiano Damiani, Tullio Pinelli. A Gian Paolo Bigazzi Production. *CAST:* Edmund Purdom, Sylvia Lopez, Sandra Milo, Alberto Lupo, Massimo Girotti, Elena Zareschi, Renato Baldini, Corrado Pani. *SYN:* Based on the life of Herod (Purdom) and his reign, from his defeat in alliance with Antony (Baldini) at the hands of Rome, to his insane demise following the birth of Christ. *NOTES:* Released in Italy in 1959. [Original Italian title: *Erode Il Grande.*]

166. Heroes Die Young (5/22/60) B&W – 76 mins. (War). *DIR/SP:* Gerald S. Shepard. *PRO:* Gerald S. Shepard, Frank Russell. *CAST:* James Strother, Erika Peters, Scott Borland, Robert Getz, Bill Browne, Malcolm Smith, Donald Joslyn, Arthur Tennen, Chick Bilyeu, Jack Card. *SYN:* During World War II, a group of American soldiers are led behind enemy lines by a partisan (Peters) to set bombing flares for the attack on the Ploesti oil fields. *NOTES:* Based on a true story of the Ploesti raid. The American film debut of European actress Erika Peters.

167. Hiawatha (12/28/52) CineColor – 79 mins. (Western). *DIR:* Kurt Neumann. *PRO:* Walter Mirisch. *SP:* Arthur Strawn, Daniel B. Ullman. Based on the poem *Song of Hiawatha* by Henry Wadsworth Longfellow. *CAST:* Vince Edwards, Yvette Dugay, Keith Larsen, Morris Ankrum, Eugene Iglesias, Ian MacDonald, Stuart Randall, Katherine

Emery, Stephen Chase, Armando Silvestre, Michael Tolan, Richard Bartlett, Michael Granger, Robert Bice, Gene Peterson, Henry Corden. *SYN:* The chief of an Indian tribe (Edwards) tries to bring peace between his tribe and another.

168. High Society (4/17/55) B&W—61 mins. (Comedy). *DIR:* William Beaudine. *PRO:* Ben Schwalb. *SP:* Bert Lawrence, Jerome S. Gottler. Story by Elwood Ullman, Edward Bernds. *CAST:* Leo Gorcey, Huntz Hall, David Condon, Bennie Bartlett, Bernard Gorcey, Ronald Keith, Dayton Lummis, Amanda Blake, Gavin Gordon, Addison Richards, Kem Dibbs, Paul Harvey, Dave Barry. *SYN:* When it is learned that Sach (Hall) is heir to the Jones fortune, Slip (Leo Gorcey), Louie (Bernard Gorcey), and Sach go to the Jones mansion and encounter the real heir (Keith) and a pair of schemers (Lummis, Blake) who are after the fortune. *NOTES:* This was the only "Bowery Boys" film to be nominated, and withdrawn, for an Academy Award (Best Original Motion Picture Story). It was the following year, 1956, that MGM released its blockbuster of the same title. When ballots were sent to Academy voters, the ballots listed only the title and studio (AA instead of MGM), ignoring the writers. Many of the Academy voters paid no attention to the studio and thought they were voting for the MGM picture. Writer Edward Bernds caught the mistake, notified the Academy, and had the film withdrawn from competition. Bernds and Ullman were allowed to keep their nomination plaques.

169. The High Terrace (12/9/56) B&W—77 mins. (Mystery). *DIR:* Henry Cass. *PRO:* Robert S. Baker, Monty Berman. *SP:* Alfred Shaughnessey, Norman Hudis, Brock Williams. Story by A.T. Weisman. A Cipa Production. *CAST:* Dale Robertson, Lois Maxwell, Derek Bond, Eric Pohlmann, Mary Laura Wood, Lionel Jeffries, Jameson Clark, Carl Bernard, Garard Green, Olwen Brookes, Benita Lydal, Marianne Stone, Frederick Treves, Jonathan Field, Gretchen Franklin, Alan Robinson, Jack Cunningham. *SYN:* When a stage producer (Pohlmann) is found murdered by an actress (Maxwell), an American playwright (Robertson), believing she was set up for the murder, helps her hide the body and begins an investigation to find the real murderer. *NOTES:* Released in Great Britain at a running time of 82 mins. This film, originally scheduled to be released in the U.S. by RKO Radio Pictures, was released by Allied Artists when RKO ceased production.

170. Highway Dragnet (2/7/54) B&W—70 mins. (Crime-Drama). *DIR:* Nathan Juran. *PRO:* William F. Broidy, Jack Jungmeyer, Jr. *SP:* Herb Meadow, Jerome Odlum, Thomas G. Hubbard, Fred Eggers. Story by U.S. Anderson, Roger Corman. A William F. Broidy Picture Production. *CAST:* Richard Conte, Joan Bennett, Wanda Hendrix, Reed Hadley, Mary Beth Hughes, Iris Adrian, Harry Harvey, Thomas G. Hubbard, Frank Jenks, Murray Alper, Zon Murray, House Peters, Jr., Joseph Crehan, Tony Hughes, Bill Hale, Fred Gabourie. *SYN:* An ex–Marine (Conte), suspected of killing an ex–Las Vegas model (Hughes) with whom he had an argument, escapes the police and while hitchiking is picked up by two women (Bennett, Hendrix) who believe him guilty of the crime. *NOTES:* Co-producers were Roger Corman and A. Robert Nunes. The original title of Corman's story was *The House in the City.* It was rewritten by U.S. Anderson, and Allied Artists changed the title to *Highway Dragnet* since the "Dragnet" television series was popular.

171. The Highwayman (8/12/51) CineColor—82 mins. (Adventure). *DIR:* Lesley Selander. *PRO:* Hal E. Chester. *SP:* Jan Jeffries. Based on the poem *The Highwayman* by Alfred Noyes. Story by

Philip Friend and Wanda Hendrix in *The Highwayman* (1951).

Jack DeWitt and Renault Duncan (Duncan Renaldo). A Jack Dietz Production. *CAST:* Charles Coburn, Wanda Hendrix, Philip Friend, Cecil Kellaway, Victor Jory, Scott Forbes, Virginia Huston, Dan O'Herlihy, Henry (Harry) Morgan, Albert Sharpe, Lowell Gilmore, Alan Napier. *SYN:* In 18th century England, a nobleman (Friend) poses as a Quaker and leads his gang (Hendrix, Kellaway, O'Herlihy) in midnight rides robbing the rich to help the poor. When they try to stop a couple of noblemen (Coburn, Jory) from kidnapping free men and selling them as slaves to the Colonies, they are killed in an ambush.

172. Hitler (3/21/62) B&W –107 mins. (Drama). *DIR:* Stuart Heisler. *PRO:* E. Charles Straus. *SP:* Sam Neuman. A Three Crown Production. *CAST:* Richard Basehart, Cordula Trantow,

Huntz Hall and Jane Nigh in *Hold That Hypnotist* (1957).

Maria Emo, Martin Kosleck, John Banner, Martin Brandt, John E. Wengraf, William Sargent, Narda Onyx, Gregory Gay, Theo Marcuse, Berry Kroeger, Rick Traeger, Lester Fletcher, Celia Lovsky, John Mitchum, Albert Szabo, G. Stanley Jones, Walter Kohler, Carl Esmond, Norbert Schiller, Ted Knight, Willy Kaufman, Sirry Steffen, John Siegfried, Otto Reichow. *SYN:* This film deals with Hitler's (Basehart) rise to power and the destruction his madness brought to the world; a subplot suggests his impotence with women, particularly his young niece (Trantow) and Eva Braun (Emo). *NOTES:* Martin Kosleck played Josef Goebbels in this film and also in the 1944 Paramount film, *The Hitler Gang*.

173. Hold Back the Night (7/29/56) B&W – 80 mins. (War-Drama). *DIR:* Allan Dwan. *PRO:* Hayes Goetz. *SP:* John C. Higgins, Walter A. Doniger. Based on the book by Pat Frank. A Hayes Goetz Production. *CAST:* John Payne, Mona Freeman, Peter Graves, Chuck Connors, Audrey Dalton, Robert Nichols, John Wilder, Bob Easton, Stanley Cha, Nicky Blair, John Craven, Nelson Leigh. *SYN:* During the Korean War, a Marine captain (Payne), ordered to retreat his men to protect the main division, tells in flashback of a bottle of scotch he always carries with him.

174. Hold That Hypnotist (3/10/57) B&W – 61 mins. (Comedy). *DIR:* Austen Jewell. *PRO:* Ben Schwalb. *SP:* Dan Pepper. *CAST:* Huntz Hall, Stanley Clements, David Gorcey, Jimmy Murphy, Jane Nigh, Robert Foulk, Queenie Smith, James Flavin, Murray Alper, Dick Elliott, Mary Treen, Mel Welles. *SYN:* The Bowery Boys (Hall, Clements, Gorcey, Murphy) set out to expose a hypnotist (Foulk) as a "quack," but when he hypnotizes Sach (Hall) and

Sach reveals he had hidden a treasure in his former life, the hypnotist, his assistant (Flavin), and the Bowery Boys go after the treasure. *NOTES:* The directorial debut of Austen Jewell.

Holy Terror *see* **Alice, Sweet Alice**

175. The Homesteaders (3/22/53) Sepiatone—62 mins. (Western). *DIR:* Lewis D. Collins. *PRO:* Vincent M. Fennelly. *SP:* Sol Theil, Milton Raison. A Silvermine Production. *CAST:* "Wild" Bill Elliott, Barbara Allen, Robert Lowery, Emmett Lynn, George Wallace, Robert "Buzz" Henry, Stanley Price, Rick Vallin, William Fawcett, James Seay, Tom Monroe, Ray Walker, Barbara Woodell. *SYN:* Two Oregon homesteaders (Elliott, Lowery) are transporting a load of dynamite from an Army post to clear land. An unscrupulous landgrabber (Seay) tries to highjack the shipment for his own gain. After fighting off the highjackers and an Indian raid, the two men continue on their way.

176. Hong Kong Affair (5/11/58) B&W—79 mins. (Crime). *DIR:* Paul F. Heard. *PRO:* Paul F. Heard, J. Raymond Friedgen. *SP:* Herman G. Luft, Paul F. Heard, J. Raymond Friedgen, Helene Turner. A Claremont Pictures Production. *CAST:* Jack Kelly, May Wynn, Richard Loo, Lo Lita Shek, Gerald Young, Michael Bulmer, James Hudson. *SYN:* A plantation owner (Kelly) travels to Hong Kong to learn why he is not showing a profit in shipments of tea. With the help of a secretary (Wynn), he discovers that an attorney (Young) is keeping the profits and using the tea shipments to smuggle opium.

177. The Hooked Generation (11/13/68) Eastmancolor—92 mins. (Crime). *DIR/PRO:* William Grefe. *SP:* William Grefe, Quinn Morrison, Ray Preston. Story by William Grefe. A Film Artists International Production. *CAST:* Jeremy Slate, Steve Alaimo, John Davis Chandler, Willie Pastrano, Cece Stone, Socrates Ballis, Walter Philbin, Milton Smith, Lee Warren, William Kerwin, Dete Parson, Stuart Merrill, Marilyn Nordman, Curtis Perdue, Burt Huttinger, Terry Smith, Clinton Nye, Michael De Beausset, Gay Perkins, Emil Deaton. *SYN:* A young couple (Alaimo, Stone) are taken hostage by a drug dealer (Slate) and his men (Chandler, Pastrano) when they witness them murdering their Cuban suppliers and Coast Guardsmen. *NOTES:* Filmed in Florida. Working title was *The Pushers*.

Horrors of the Black Zoo *see* **Black Zoo**

178. Hot Car Girl (8/17/58) B&W—71 mins. (Drama). *DIR:* Bernard L. Kowalski. *PRO:* Gene Corman. *SP:* Leo Gordon. A Santa Cruz Production. *CAST:* Richard Bakalyan, June Kenney, John Brinkley, Robert Knapp, Jana Lund, Sheila McKay, Bruno Ve Sota, George Albertson, Jack Lambert, Ed Nelson, Hal Smith, Howard Culver, Tyler McVey. *SYN:* A juvenile delinquent (Bakalyan) gets involved in an auto theft ring, causes the death of another teenager (Lund) during a game of "chicken," and flees with his girl (Kenney) only to be gunned down by the police. *NOTES:* Executive producer was Roger Corman. Not to be confused with *Hot Car Girl* (1956), an alternate title to AIP's *Hot Rod Girl* (1956). Double billed in some areas with *Cry Baby Killer*.

179. Hot News (10/11/53) B&W—68 mins. (Crime). *DIR:* Edward Bernds. *PRO:* Ben Schwalb. *SP:* Charles R. Marion, Elwood Ullman. *CAST:* Stanley Clements, Gloria Henry, Ted de Corsia, Veda Ann Borg, Scotty Beckett, Carl Milletaire, James Flavin, Hal Baylor, Paul Bryar, Myron Healey, Mario Siletti. *SYN:* A former boxer (Clements), now a sports columnist, goes on a one man crusade to stop a gambling ring after they arrange a mismatched fight and a boxer (Healey) is killed.

180. Hot Rod Hullabaloo (11/1/66) B&W – 81 mins. (Action-Drama). *DIR:* William T. Naud. *PRO:* Martin L. Low, William T. Naud. *SP:* Stanley Schneider. A Silvercliff Pictures Production. *CAST:* John Arnold, Arlen Dean Snyder, Kendra Kerr, Ron Cummins, Val Bisoglio, Marsha Mason, William Hunter, Gene Bau, Robert Paget. *SYN:* A student (Arnold) enters a demolition derby to earn money for his college education, unaware that his chief rival intends to kill anyone who gets in his way. *NOTES:* The film debut of Marsha Mason. Filmed in Washington, D.C.

181. Hot Rod Rumble (6/9/57) B&W – 79 mins. (Crime-Drama). *DIR:* Leslie Martinson. *PRO:* Norman T. Herman. *SP:* Meyer Dolinsky. A Nacirema Production. *CAST:* Leigh Snowden, Richard Hartunian, Brett Halsey, Wright King, Joey Forman, Larry Dolgin, John Brinkley, Chuck Webster, Ned Glass, Phil Adams, Joe Mell. *SYN:* A young hot-rodder (Hartunian), blamed for a rival's (Dolgin) death, must try to clear his name before the big race. *NOTES:* Double billed in some areas with *Calypso Joe*.

182. Hot Shots (12/23/56) B&W – 61 mins. (Comedy). *DIR:* Jean Yarbrough. *PRO:* Ben Schwalb. *SP:* Elwood Ullman, Jack Townley. Story by Jack Townley. *CAST:* Huntz Hall, Stanley Clements, David Gorcey, Jimmy Murphy, Philip Phillips, Queenie Smith, Mark Dana, Joi Lansing, Robert Shayne, Henry Rowland, Dennis Moore, Isabel Randolph, Frank Marlowe, Joe Kirk, Ray Walker. *SYN:* Sach (Hall) and Duke (Clements) are hired to handle a temperamental child television star (Phillips) and end up rescuing him when he is kidnapped.

183. House of Intrigue (11/15/59) Eastmancolor/Scope – 94 mins. (Spy-Drama). *DIR/PRO:* Duilio Coletti. *SP:* Duilio Coletti, Ennio De Concini, Giuseppe Scoponi, Massimo Mida. Based on *London Calling North Pole* by H.J. Giskes. *CAST:* Curt Jurgens, Dawn Addams, Folco Lulli, Dario Michaelis, Philippe Hersent, Rene Deltgen, Albert Lieven, Jack Stuart (Giacomo Rossi Stuart), Matteo Spinola, Ludovico Ceriana, Adriano Uriani, Alphonse Mathis, Chris Hofer, Edith Jost, Stephen Garrett. *SYN:* During World War II, a British secret agent is captured in Amsterdam. A high-ranking German intelligence officer (Jurgens) learns that the agent was to radio information to London each day, so the broadcasts continue with false information leading to the capture of other British agents. *NOTES:* Based on a true incident. [Original Italian title: *Londra Chiama Polo Nord*.]

184. The House of the Arrow (8/1/54) B&W – 73 mins. (Crime). *DIR:* Michael Anderson. *PRO:* Vaughan M. Dean. *SP:* Edward Dryhurst. Based on the book and play by A.E.W. Mason. An Associated British Pathé Production. A Stratford Picture Presentation. *CAST:* Oscar Homolka, Yvonne Furneaux, Robert Urquhart, Anthony Nicholls, Josephine Griffin, Pierre le Fevre, Andrea Lea, Harold Kasket, Jeanne Pali, Jacques Cey, Pierre Chaminade, Keith Pyott, Ruth Lodge, Rene Leplat, Colette Wilde, Rene Poirier. *SYN:* Inspector Hanaud (Homolka) is assigned to investigate the mysterious death of a wealthy French widow (Pali). *NOTES:* Released in Great Britain in 1953. A remake of the 1930 and 1940 British films. The 1940 film version was released in the U.S. as *Castle of Crimes*.

185. House on Haunted Hill (2/17/59) B&W – 75 mins. (Horror). *DIR/PRO:* William Castle. *SP:* Robb White. *CAST:* Vincent Price, Carol Ohmart, Richard Long, Alan Marshal, Carolyn Craig, Elisha Cook, Jr., Julie

House on Haunted Hill (1959): a typically sensational William Castle ad campaign. *(Photo courtesy of Ted Okuda.)*

Mitchum, Leona Anderson, Howard Hoffman. *SYN:* Frederick Loren (Price) and his wife (Ohmart) rent a haunted mansion, the scene of several grisley murders, for a party for their guests (Long, Marshal, Craig, Cook, Jr., Mitchum). Loren offers each guest $10,000, if they are able to spend the entire night without going mad or getting killed. For their protection he offers his guests handguns in little coffins. If they do not survive, the money goes to their heirs. *NOTES:* Director Castle's gimmick for this film was "Emergo," in which at a crucial point in the film, theatre owners would release a luminous skeleton on an invisible wire that would fly over the audience's heads. This worked fine for a first showing, but when the audience got wise and started pelting the skeleton with concession items, "Emergo" was stopped by the theatre owners. Double billed in some areas with *The Cosmic Man.*

186. The Human Duplicators (3/3/65) Eastmancolor–82 mins. (Science Fiction). *DIR:* Hugo Grimaldi. *PRO:* Hugo Grimaldi, Arthur C. Pierce. *SP:* Arthur C. Pierce. A Crest–Woolner Bros. Production. *CAST:* George Nader, Barbara Nichols, George Macready, Dolores Faith, Richard Kiel, Hugh Beaumont, Richard Arlen, Ted Durant, Tommy Leonetti, Lonnie Sattin, John Indrisano. *SYN:* An alien (Kiel) arrives on Earth to make duplicates of the world's leaders so that the invasion by his planet will be easy, but his plans are thwarted by a government agent (Nader). *NOTES:* Double billed in some areas with *Mutiny in Outer Space.*

187. The Human Jungle (10/3/54) B&W–82 mins. (Crime-Drama). *DIR:* Joseph M. Newman. *PRO:* Hayes Goetz. *SP:* William Sackheim, Daniel Fuchs. Story by William Sackheim. *CAST:* Gary Merrill, Jan Sterling, Paula Raymond, Emile Meyer, Regis Toomey, Chuck Connors, Patrick Waltz, George Wallace, Chubby Johnson, Don Keefer, Rankin Mansfield, Lamont Johnson, Leo Cleary, Florenz Ames, Claude Akins, Hugh Boswell, James Westerfield. *SYN:* A police captain (Merrill) meets opposition from the criminal element and corrupt police officers when he is assigned to clean up a new district.

188. The Hunchback of Notre Dame (11/3/57) Technicolor/Scope–110 mins. (Drama). *DIR:* Jean Delannoy. *PRO:* Robert Hakim. *SP:* Jacques Prevert, Jean Aurenche, Based on the book by Victor Hugo. A Paris Film Production. *CAST:* Anthony Quinn, Gina Lollobrigida, Jean Danet, Alain Cuny, Philippe Clay, Danielle Dumont, Robert Hirsch, Valentine Tessier, Jacques Hilling, Jacques Dufilho, Roger Blin, Marianne Oswald, Pieral, Robert Lombard, Albert Remy, Hubert de Lapparent, Boris Vian, Paul Bonifas, Madeleine Barbulee, Albert Michel, Daniel Emilfork. *SYN:* Quasimodo (Quinn), the hunchback bellringer of Paris's Notre Dame Cathedral, falls hopelessly in love with Esmeralda (Lollobrigida), the gypsy. *NOTES:* Considered to be the weakest film version of Victor Hugo's novel. Working title was to be *The Hunchback of Paris* since producers Robert and Raymond Hakim could not secure title rights from RKO Pictures. When RKO suddenly decided to release its copyright to the title, the film was released with the above title. A remake of the 1939 RKO film. Remade in 1977 and 1982 as television movies. [Original French title: *Notre Dame de Paris.*]

189. The Hunted (4/3/48) B&W–88 mins. (Mystery). *DIR:* Jack Bernhard. *PRO:* Scott R. Dunlap. *SP:* Steve Fisher. *CAST:* Preston Foster, Belita, Pierre Watkin, Edna Holland, Russell Hicks, Frank Ferguson, Joseph Crehan, Larry Blake, Cathy Carter, Thomas Jackson, Charles McGraw, Tristram Coffin. *SYN:* The fiancée (Belita) of a police detective

(Foster) is framed for a bank robbery and sent to prison. Released on parole, she finds herself framed again, this time for murder. *NOTES:* Running time is also given as 67 mins.

190. The Hypnotic Eye (2/27/60) B&W – 77 mins. (Horror). *DIR:* George Blair. *PRO:* Charles B. Bloch. *SP:* Gitta Woodfield, William Read Woodfield. Story by Charles B. Bloch. A Penguin Production. *CAST:* Jacques Bergerac, Allison Hayes, Marcia Henderson, Merry Anders, Joe Patridge, Guy Prescott, James Lydon, Phyllis Cole, Carol Thurston, Holly Harris, Mary Foran, Lawrence Lipton, Eva Lynd, Eric "Big Daddy" Nord, Ferdinand W. "Fred" Demara. *SYN:* The Great Desmond (Bergerac) hypnotizes women who then go home and mutilate themselves while under his spell. A detective (Patridge) figures out that the person responsible is Desmond's wife/assistant (Hayes) who was disfigured herself and takes her revenge on beautiful, innocent women. *NOTES:* Release date is also given as 1959 by some sources. Producer Bloch, taking a cue from director William Castle, came up with the gimmick "HypnoMagic" to promote his film. Just before the film ends, Jacques Bergerac would look into the camera, ask that the house lights be turned up, and pretend to hypnotize the audience by having

Advertisement for *I Passed for White* (1960). (Photo courtesy of Ted Okuda.)

them stamp their feet, clap their hands, and lift balloons, which were handed out by the theatre owners. This film was later re-released by Allied Artists in the late 60's under the title *The Torturer!, Master of "The Hypnotic Eye,"* using the gimmick of Touch-O-Vision. Associate producer was Ben Schwalb. Ferdinand W. "Fred" Demara, who impersonates an actor impersonating a doctor, is the same Ferdinand Waldo Demara whose life story was made by Universal Pictures in 1960 as *The Great Imposter.*

I Lived a Lie see **I Passed for White**

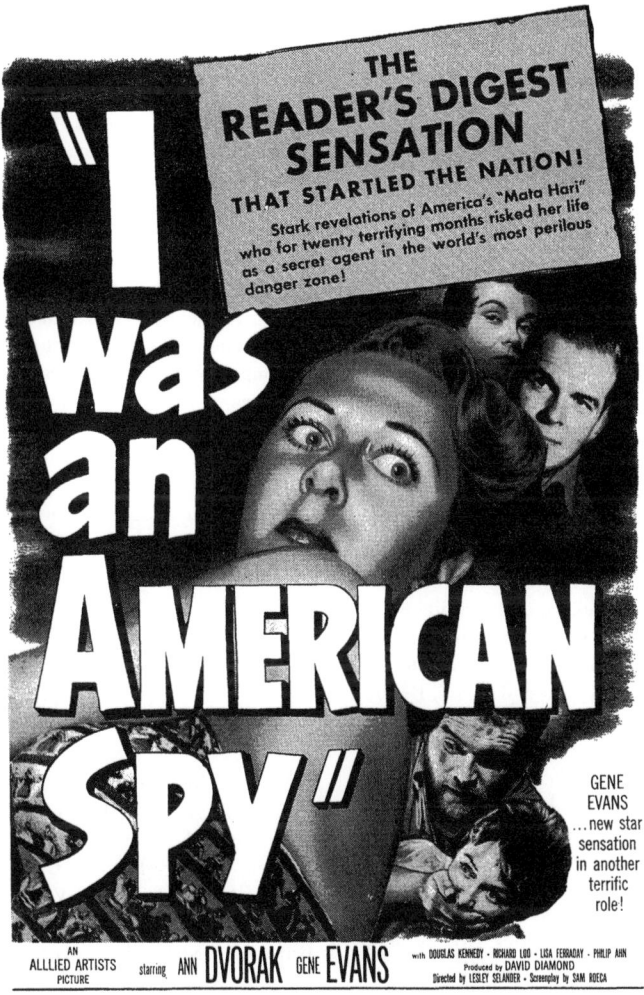

Advertisement for *I Was an American Spy* (1951). (Photo courtesy of Scott MacGillivray.)

191. I Passed for White (3/18/60) B&W – 93 mins. (Drama). *DIR/PRO/SP:* Fred M. Wilcox. Based on the book by Mary H. Bradley as told by Reba Lee. *CAST:* Sonya Wilde, James Franciscus, Pat Michon, Elizabeth Council, Isabelle Cooley, James Lydon, Thomas Browne Henry, Max Mellinger, Phyllis Cox, Calvin Jackson, Temple Hatton, Freita Shaw, Lon Ballantyne, Ed Shashe, Ray Kellogg, Elizabeth Harrower. *SYN:* A light-skinned black girl (Wilde) leaves her black community and pretends she is white. She marries a rich white man (Franciscus) without revealing her heritage and creates a whole new set of problems. Eventually she leaves her husband when the strain becomes too great to cope with. *NOTES:* Re-released as *I Lived a Lie*.

192. I Was an American Spy (4/14/51) B&W – 84 mins. (War-Drama). *DIR:* Lesley Selander. *PRO:* David Diamond. *SP:* Sam Roeca. Based on *Manila Espionage* by Claire Phillips and Myron B. Goldsmith. *CAST:* Ann Dvorak, Gene Evans, Douglas Kennedy, Richard Loo, Leon Lontac, Chabing, Philip Ahn, Marya Marco, Nadene Ashdown, Lisa Ferraday, Howard Chuman, Freddie Revelala, James Leong, Leo Abbey, Escolastico Baucin, Celeste Madamba, Andres Lucas, Frank Jenks, Gil Herman, George Fields, Dennis Moore, Richard Bartlett, Riley Hill, Brett Hamilton, Lane Bradford, John Damler, Jack Reynolds, Angel Crux, William Tannen. *SYN:* Based on the true story of Claire Phillips (Dvorak), who, during World War II, loses her husband (Kennedy) in the Bataan death march. She then poses as an Italian national and operates a nightclub in Manila where she obtains information from the Japanese and forwards it to the leader (Evans) of a guerrilla band. Before she can be killed by the Japanese, who learn of her activities, she is rescued by the guerrillas and taken to safety. *NOTES:* Prologue by Gen. Mark W. Clark. Mrs. Phillips was awarded the Freedom Medal for her espionage activities.

193. In the Money (2/16/58) B&W – 61 mins. (Comedy). *DIR:* William Beaudine. *PRO:* Richard Heermance. *SP:* Elwood Ullman, Al Martin. Story by Al Martin. *CAST:* Huntz Hall, Stanley Clements, David Gorcey, Eddie LeRoy, John Dodsworth, Patricia Donahue, Leonard Penn, Paul Cavanagh, Leslie Denison, Dick Elliott, Owen McGiveney, Norma Varden, Ashley Cowan, Ralph Gamble, Patrick O'Moore, Pamela Light, Snub Pollard. *SYN:* When Sach (Hall) is duped by diamond smugglers into escorting a pedigree poodle to London, not knowing that diamonds are hidden in its coat, the rest of the Bowery Boys (Clements, Gorcey, LeRoy) tag along. *NOTES:* Working title was *On the Make.* After 12 years (1946–1958), this was the last film in the "Bowery Boys" series.

194. The Inbetween Age (8/3/58) B&W – 78 mins. (Musical). *DIR:* Don Sharp. *PRO:* W.G. Chalmers. *SP:* Don Sharp, Don Nicholl. Story by Gee Nicholl. A Butcher Film Production. *CAST:* Lee Patterson, Mary Steele, Terry Dene, Linda Gray, Ronald Adam, Peter Dyneley, David Jacobs, David Williams, Richard Turner, Marianne Stone, Olive Milbourne, Dennis Lotis, Nancy Whiskey, Les Hobeaux, Murray Campbell, Sheila Buxton, Phil Seamon Jazz Group, Sonny Stewart's Skiffle Kings, Teddy Kennedy Group, Don Rendell's Six. *SYN:* A young couple (Patterson, Steele) turn a café into a coffee bar and record production company and find a star singer (Dene) in their handyman. They are threatened with a takeover by the company that presses their discs, but a merger with an American company solves their problems. [British title: *The Golden Disc.*]

195. The Indestructible Man (3/25/56) B&W – 70 mins. (Horror). *DIR/PRO:* Jack Pollexfen. *SP:* Vy Russell, Sue Bradford. A CGK Production. *CAST:* Lon Chaney, Jr., Casey Adams, Marian Carr, Ross Elliott, Stuart Randall, Kenneth Terrell, Robert Shayne, Marvin Ellis. *SYN:* A convict (Chaney) is brought back to life with electricity after being executed and seeks revenge against those who double-crossed him and sent him to prison. *NOTES:* Double billed in some areas with *World Without End.*

196. The Internecine Project (9/74) Eastmancolor – 89 mins. (Thriller). *DIR:* Ken Hughes. *PRO:* Barry Levinson. *SP:* Barry Levinson, Jonathan Lynn. Based on *Internecine* by Mort W. Elkind. A Lion International–Hemisphere Production. *CAST:* James Coburn, Lee

Grant, Harry Andrews, Ian Hendry, Michael Jayston, Keenan Wynn, Christiane Kruger, Terence Alexander, Philip Anthony, David Swift, Julian Glover, Kevin Scott, Ray Callaghan, Geoffrey Burridge, Robert Tayman, Judy Robinson, John Savident, Richard Cornish. *SYN:* A businessman (Coburn) on his way to becoming key advisor to the U.S. President arranges for four individuals (Andrews, Kruger, Jayston, Hendry) who know about his shady past to kill each other.

197. Invasion of the Body Snatchers (2/5/56) B&W/Scope—80 mins. (Science Fiction). *DIR:* Don Siegel. *PRO:* Walter Wanger. *SP:* Daniel Mainwaring. Based on *The Body Snatchers* by Jack Finney as serialized in *Collier's Magazine*. *CAST:* Kevin McCarthy, Dana Wynter, King Donovan, Carolyn Jones, Larry Gates, Ralph Dumke, Jean Willes, Virginia Christine, Tom Fadden, Kenneth Patterson, Gay Way, Bobby Clark, Eileen Stevens, Beatrice Maude, Jean Andrew, Everett Glass, Dabbs Greer, Pat O'Malley, Guy Rennie, Marie Selland, Sam Peckinpah, Harry J. Vejar, Whit Bissell, Richard Deacon, Robert Osterloh. *SYN:* A doctor (McCarthy) returns to his home town after attending a medical convention and learns that the town has been taken over by pods from outer space which take on the form of a person and then take over the victim completely while they sleep. *NOTES:* Working titles were *They Came from Another World*, *Sleep No More*, *I Am a Pod*, and *The Body Snatchers*. The original ending of this film had Kevin McCarthy standing in traffic yelling "You're next!" The studio heads at Allied Artists thought this ending was too depressing so Siegel shot an opening prologue and epilogue where McCarthy is in a hospital and relates the story of the invasion in flashback. It is probable that portions of this film had rewrites by Sam Peckinpah. When this film was remade by United Artists in 1978, director Don Siegel had a role as a cab driver, and Kevin McCarthy was seen standing in traffic yelling "You're next!" as in the original film. Double billed in some areas with *The Atomic Man*.

198. Island of the Doomed (11/15/67) Technicolor/Scope—88 mins. (Horror). *DIR:* Mel Welles. *PRO:* George Ferrer. *SP:* Stephen Schmidt. Story by Ira Meltcher, Ernst Ritter von Theumer. An Orbita–Tefi Films Production. *CAST:* Cameron Mitchell, Elisa Montes, George Martin, Kai Fischer, Rolf von Naukoff, Hermann Nehlsen, Matilde Sampedro-Munoz, Ricardo Valle, Mike Brendel. *SYN:* When a group of tourists arrive at an island off the Italian coast, a mad botanist (Mitchell), who has created a carnivorous tree that uses its branches to ensnare its victims and drain their blood, kills the tourists to feed his creation. *NOTES:* Released in West Germany in September 1967 and in Spain in 1968. Director Mel Welles played Gravis Mushnik in Roger Corman's film *Little Shop of Horrors*. [Original Spanish title: *La Isla de la Muerte*.] [Original German title: *Das Geheimnis der Todesinsel*.] [British title: *Bloodsuckers*.]

199. Isn't Life Wonderful (11/10/54) Technicolor—83 mins. (Comedy). *DIR:* Harold French. *PRO:* Patrick Ward. *SP:* Brock Williams. Based on *Uncle Willie and the Bicycle Shop* by Brock Williams. An Associated British Picture Production. A Stratford Picture Presentation. *CAST:* Eileen Herlie, Cecil Parker, Donald Wolfit, Robert Urquhart, Eleanor Summerfield, Dianne Foster, Peter Asher, Cecil Trouncer, Russell Waters, Edwin Styles, Fabia Drake, Arthur Young, Viola Lyel. *SYN:* The black sheep (Wolfit) of a stuffy Victorian family is set up with a bicycle shop to impress the American fiancée (Foster) of his nephew (Urquhart). *NOTES:* Released in Great Britain in 1953.

Don DeFore and Gale Storm in *It Happened on Fifth Avenue* (1947). (Photo courtesy of Scott MacGillivray.)

200. It Happened on Fifth Avenue (4/19/47) B&W—116 mins. (Comedy-Musical). *DIR/PRO:* Roy Del Ruth. *SP:* Everett Freeman, Vick Knight. Story by Herbert Clyde Lewis, Frederick Stephani. *CAST:* Don DeFore, Ann Harding, Charlie Ruggles, Victor Moore, Gale Storm, Grant Mitchell, Edward Brophy, Cathy Carter, Edward Ryan, Jr., Dorothea Kent, Arthur Hohl, Anthony Sydes, Linda Lee Solomon, Alan Hale, Jr., Garry Owen, George Lloyd, George Meader, John Hamilton, Johnny Arthur, Chester Clute, Florence Auer, Charles Lane, James Cardwell, James Flavin, Edward Gargan, Max Willenz, Leon Belasco, Pat Goldin, Eddie Marr, Dudley Dickerson, Abe Reynolds, Joan Andren, the Kings Men. *SYN:* A millionaire (Ruggles) lets a vagabond (Moore) live in his

5th Avenue penthouse while he vacations in South Carolina. The vagabond befriends an ex–GI (DeFore), and before he knows it, the penthouse is full of people, including the millionaire and his daughter (Storm), both in disguise. *NOTES:* The first feature film release of Allied Artists.

201. It's Never Too Late (9/2/58) Eastmancolor – 95 mins. (Comedy). *DIR:* Michael McCarthy. *PRO:* George Pitcher. *SP:* Edward Dryhurst. Based on the play by Felicity Douglas. An Associated British Picture–Park Lane Films Production. A Stratford Picture Presentation. *CAST:* Phyllis Calvert, Guy Rolfe, Patrick Barr, Susan Stephen, Sarah Lawson, Delphi Lawrence, Peter Hammond, Richard Leech, Jean Taylor Smith, Robert Ayres, Irene Handl, Peter Illing, Stanley Maxted, Barbara Calvin. *SYN:* A housewife (Calvert), who is a part-time writer, leaves the turmoil of her family and heads to Hollywood to work on a script. She finds the life of California too sedate and tame and returns home where she can work properly, amidst the family turmoil. *NOTES:* Released in Great Britain in 1956. Re-released by 7 Arts in 1963.

202. Jack Slade (11/8/53) B&W – 89 mins. (Western). *DIR:* Harold Schuster. *PRO:* Lindsley Parsons. *SP:* Warren Douglas. *CAST:* Mark Stevens, Dorothy Malone, Barton MacLane, John Litel, Paul Langton, Harry Shannon, John Harmon, Jim Bannon, Lee Van Cleef, David Day, Ron Hargrave, Sammy Ogg, Nelson Leigh, John Halloran, Robert Reeves, Dorothy Kennedy, Duane Thorsen, Harry Landers, Ann Navarro, Steve Darrell, Hank Patterson. *SYN:* A young man (Stevens) grows up and becomes a notorious gunfighter and outlaw, spurning those who love and care for him. [British title: *Slade*.]

203. Jail Busters (9/18/55) B&W – 61 mins. (Comedy) *DIR:* William Beaudine. *PRO:* Ben Schwalb. *SP:* Elwood Ullman. *CAST:* Leo Gorcey, Huntz Hall, David Condon, Bennie Bartlett, Bernard Gorcey, Percy Helton, Barton MacLane, Anthony Caruso, Murray Alper, Michael Ross, Fritz Feld, Lyle Talbot, Henry Kulky, Emit Sitka, John Harmon, Henry Tyler. *SYN:* When Chuck (Condon) gets beaten up while on undercover assignment in prison, the Bowery Boys (Leo Gorcey, Hall, Bartlett) get sent to prison to help Chuck expose a scam – prisoners paying off guards to live the easy life. *NOTES:* Working title was *Doing Time.* The only film in the "Bowery Boys" series with an all male cast.

204. Jalopy (2/15/53) B&W – 62 mins. (Comedy). *DIR:* William Beaudine. *PRO:* Ben Schwalb. *SP:* Tim Ryan, Jack Crutcher, Edmond Seward, Jr., Bert Lawrence. Story by Tim Ryan, Jack Crutcher. *CAST:* Leo Gorcey, Huntz Hall, David Condon, Bennie Bartlett, Bernard Gorcey, Robert Lowery, Jane Easton, Leon Belasco, Richard Benedict, Murray Alper, Tom Hanlon, Mona Knox, Conrad Brooks. *SYN:* The Bowery Boys enter their car in a big race when Sach (Hall) invents a super fuel that makes their car go at lightning speed and they get mixed up with gangsters who want the formula. *NOTES:* The first "Bowery Boys" film to be produced by Ben Schwalb. It was Schwalb who decided to instill pure slapstick comedy into the series. This film used leftover racing footage from Allied Artists' *Roar of the Crowd.*

205. Jennifer (10/25/53) B&W – 73 mins. (Crime-Drama). *DIR:* Joel Newton. *PRO:* Berman Swarttz. *SP:* Virginia Meyers. *CAST:* Ida Lupino, Howard Duff, Robert Nichols, Mary Shipp, Matt Dennis, Ned Glass, Kitty McHugh, Russ Conway, Lorna Thayer. *SYN:* A woman (Lupino) takes a job as caretaker at an eerie mansion and believes she has

Advertisement for *Johnny Rocco* (1958). (Photo courtesy of Ted Okuda.)

stumbled on a murder that happened there years ago.

206. Johnny Rocco (12/21/58) B&W – 84 mins. (Crime). *DIR:* Paul Landres. *PRO:* Scott R. Dunlap. *SP:* James O'Hanlon, Sam Roeca. Story by Richard Carlson. *CAST:* Richard Eyer, Stephen McNally, Coleen Gray, Russ Conway, Leslie Bradley, James Flavin, M.G. (Matty) Fain, John Mitchum, Frank Wilcox, Harry Loftin, Bob Mitchel, the Mitchell Boy's Choir. *SYN:* Johnny Rocco (Eyer), the son of an important gangster (McNally), becomes the target of the mob when he witnesses a killing. His father also becomes a target when he tries to protect his son.

207. Joy Ride (11/23/58) B&W – 65 mins. (Crime). *DIR:* Edward Bernds. *PRO:* Ben Schwalb. *SP:* Christopher Knopf. Story by C.B. Gilford. *CAST:* Rad Fulton, Ann Doran, Regis Toomey, Nicholas King, Robert Levin, Jim Bridges, Roy Engel, Robert Colbert, Robert Anderson. *SYN:* A teenage gang of hoodlums (Fulton, King, Levin, Bridges) launch a campaign of terror against a middle-aged couple (Toomey, Doran) when they mistake kindness for fear. *NOTES:* Double billed in some areas with *Unwed Mother*.

208. Jungle Giants (9/5/54) B&W – (Comedy). Dir. Edward Bernds. *PRO:* Ben Schwalb. *SP:* Elwood Ullman, Edward Bernds. *CAST:* Leo Gorcey, Huntz Hall, David Condon, Bennie Bartlett, Bernard Gorcey, Patrick O'Moore, Rudolph Anders, Laurette Luez, Harry Cording, Eric Snowden, Woody Strode, Joel Fluellen, Murray Alper, Emory Parnell, Jett Norman (Clint Walker), Emil Sitka, Roy Glenn, John Harmon, Pat Flaherty. *SYN:* When it is learned that Sach (Hall) can sniff out diamonds, the Bowery Boys head to Africa where they expose a fake spirit scaring the natives. *NOTES:* This film was shot indoors on the "Bomba, the Jungle Boy" sets, and was the weakest of the "Bowery Boys" series.

209. Kansas Pacific (2/22/53) CineColor – 73 mins. (Western). *DIR:* Ray Nazarro. *PRO:* Walter Wanger. *SP:* Daniel B. Ullman. *CAST:* Sterling Hayden, Eve Miller, Barton MacLane, Harry Shannon, Reed Hadley, Tom Fadden, Douglas Fowley, Robert Keys, Irving Bacon, Myron Healey, James Griffith, Clayton Moore, Jonathan Hale, I. Stanford Jolley, Riley Hill, Carol Henry, Lee Roberts, Fred Graham, Lane Bradford. *SYN:* In 1860, an Army engineer (Hayden) is sent to speed the building of the Kansas Pacific Railroad, much to the opposition of Southern sympathizers who do not want the railroad completed to the West as it might spell disaster for the South should war be declared. *NOTES:* Assistant director was Andrew V. McLaglen.

210. Karate, the Hand of Death (8/9/61) B&W/Scope – 80 mins. (Martial Arts) *DIR/PRO:* Joel Holt. *SP:* David Hill. A Joseph Brenner Production. *CAST:* Joel Holt, Frank Blaine, Akira Shiga, Joe Hirakawa, Reiko Okada, Ken Noyle, Fujio Ito, Bob Markworth, Maurice Gruel, Tom Moore. *SYN:* A karate expert (Holt), visiting Japan, learns that a mysterious coin holds the secret to a fortune in platinum smuggled from Germany.

211. Killer Leopard (8/22/54) B&W – 70 mins. (Jungle-Adventure). *DIR:* Ford Beebe. *PRO:* Ford Beebe, Edward Morey, Jr. *SP:* Ford Beebe. Based on characters in the *Bomba* books by Roy Rockwood. *CAST:* Johnny Sheffield, Russ Conway, Beverly Garland, Bill Walker, Milton Wood, Barry Bernard, Donald Murphy, Robert "Smoki" Whitfield, Rory Mallinson, Leonard Mudie, Harry Cording, Guy Kingsford, Roy Glenn, Charles Stevens. *SYN:* Bomba (Sheffield) is menaced by a killer leopard as he tries to help an American movie actress (Garland) search the jungle for her missing husband.

212. King and Country (11/30/65) B&W – 86 mins. (War). *DIR:* Joseph Losey. *PRO:* Joseph Losey, Norman Priggen. *SP:* Evan Jones. Based on the play *Hamp* by John Wilson and *Return to the Wood* by James Lansdale Hodson. A British Home Entertainment Production. A Landau/Unger Releasing Organization Presentation. *CAST:* Dirk Bogarde, Tom Courtenay, Leo McKern, Barry Foster, Peter Copley, James Villiers, Jeremy Spenser, Barry Justice, Vivian Matalon, Keith Buckley, James Hunter, Jonah Seymour, Larry Taylor, David Cook, Richard Arthur, Derek Partridge, Brian

Tipping. *SYN:* A British private (Courtenay), court-martialled for desertion when he walks away from battle during World War I, is defended by a British captain (Bogarde) who is sympathetic to his story. *NOTES:* Released independently in 1964; released by Allied Artists in 1965 and released by American-International in 1966. Working title was *Hamp.*

213. King of the Coral Sea (6/24/56) B&W – 74 mins. (Adventure-Crime). *DIR:* Lee Robinson. *PRO:* Chips Rafferty. *SP:* Chips Rafferty, Lee Robinson. A Southern International Film Production. *CAST:* Chips Rafferty, Charles Tingwell, Ilma Adley, Rod Taylor, Lloyd Berrell, Reginald Lye, Frances Chin Soon, Salapata Sagigi. *SYN:* A gang of smugglers try to bring illegal Asian immigrants into Australia via Thursday Island, the main pearl diving area. *NOTES:* Underwater director was Noel Monkman. Released in Australia in 1954. This was one of Australian stage actor Rod Taylor's two films that were made in Australia before he came to Hollywood and became a major star.

214. King of the Roaring 20's – The Story of Arnold Rothstein (6/11/61) B&W – 106 mins. (Crime-Drama). *DIR:* Joseph M. Newman. *PRO:* Samuel Bischoff, David Diamond. *SP:* Jo Swerling. Based on *The Big Bankroll* by Leo Katcher. *CAST:* David Janssen,

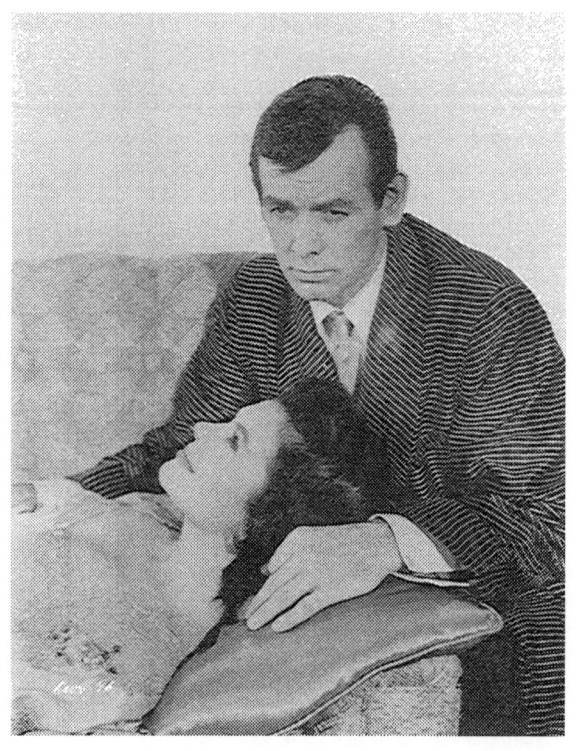

David Janssen and Diane Foster in *King of the Roaring 20's – The Story of Arnold Rothstein* (1961).

Diane Foster, Mickey Rooney, Jack Carson, Diana Dors, Dan O'Herlihy, Mickey Shaughnessy, Keenan Wynn, Joseph Schildkraut, William Demarest, Murvyn Vye, Regis Toomey, Robert Ellenstein, Teri Janssen, Jim Baird, Tim Rooney. *SYN:* The life of Arnold Rothstein (Janssen), a mathematical whiz with a fascination for the easy dollar who strives to become gambling czar of New York's lower East Side. His double dealings eventually lead to his downfall and he is gunned down in a hotel room while playing poker (holding a royal flush). [British title: *The Big Bankroll.*]

215/216. King of the Wild Stallions (5/17/59) DeLuxe Color/Scope – 76

Advertisement for *King of the Wild Stallions* (1959).

mins. (Western). *DIR:* R.G. Springsteen. *PRO:* Ben Schwalb. *SP:* Ford Beebe. *CAST:* George Montgomery, Diane Brewster, Edgar Buchanan, Emile Meyer, Jerry Hartleben, Byron Foulger, Denver Pyle, Dan Sheridan, Rory Mallinson. *SYN:* A widow (Brewster) and her son (Hartleben), with the help of a drifter (Montgomery), fight to save their ranch from an unscrupulous rancher (Meyer) who also wants the wild stallion the boy secretly captured.

217. Landfall (5/11/53) B&W – 88 mins. (War). *DIR:* Ken Annakin. *PRO:* Victor Skutezky. *SP:* Talbot Jennings, Gilbert Gunn, Anne Burnaby. Based on the book by Nevil Shute. An Associated British Picture Production. A Stratford Picture Presentation. *CAST:* Michael Denison, Patricia Plunkett, Kathleen Harrison, David Tomlinson, Joan Dowling, Maurice Denham, A.E. Matthews, Denis O'Dea, Margaretta Scott, Sebastian Shaw, Nora Swinburne, Charles Victor, Laurence Harvey, Paul Carpenter, Frederick Leister, Hubert Gregg, Walter Hudd, Margaret Barton. *SYN:* In 1940, an RAF pilot (Denison) believes he has sunk a German U-boat in the English Channel. A court of inquiry, suspecting it was actually a British sub, relieves him of duty. His girlfriend (Plunkett), a barmaid, gathers information to clear him by proving that the sub was indeed a German U-boat disguised as a British sub. *NOTES:* Released in Great Britain in 1949.

218. Las Vegas Shakedown (5/15/55) B&W – 79 mins. (Drama). *DIR:* Sidney Salkow. *PRO:* William F. Broidy. *SP:* Steve Fisher. *CAST:* Dennis O'Keefe, Coleen Gray, Charles Winninger, Thomas Gomez, Dorothy Patrick, Mary Beth Hughes, Elizabeth Patterson, James Millican, Robert Armstrong, Joseph Downing, Lewis Martin, Mara McAfee, Charles Fredericks, Regina Gleason, Murray Alper, Jim Alexander, Frank Hanley, Allen Mathews. *SYN:* Amidst a variety of gamblers who come to Las Vegas to win, a casino owner (O'Keefe) fights to keep his casino from falling into the hands of a gangster (Gomez).

219. Last Holiday (11/13/50) B&W – 88 mins. (Comedy). *DIR:* Henry Cass. *PRO:* Stephen Mitchell, A.D. Peters, J.B. Priestley. *SP:* J.B. Priestley. An Associated British Picture–Watergate Production. A Stratford Picture Presentation. *CAST:* Alec Guinness, Beatrice Campbell, Kay Walsh, Bernard Lee, Wilfrid Hyde-White, Muriel George, Helen Cherry, Jean Colin, Brian Worth, Sidney James, Coco Aslan, Ernest Thesiger, David McCallum, Esma Cannon, Ronald Simpson, Peter Jones, Meier Tzeiniker. *SYN:* When a man (Guinness) learns that he has an incurable disease, he withdraws his savings and moves to a fashionable seaside hotel where he helps people in trouble and receives several job offers. When the diagnosis proves wrong he is overjoyed and as he heads for home, he swerves his car to avoid an accident and is killed. *NOTES:* Released in Great Britain in May, 1950.

220. Last of the Badmen (2/17/57) DeLuxe Color/Scope – 79 mins. (Western). *DIR:* Paul Landres. *PRO:* Vincent M. Fennelly. *SP:* Daniel B. Ullman, David Chantler. Story by Daniel B. Ullman. *CAST:* George Montgomery, Keith Larsen, James Best, Douglas Kennedy, Robert Foulk, Tom Greenway, Meg Randall, Willis Bouchey, Michael Ansara, Addison Richards, John Doucette, John Damler, Harlan Warde, Walter Reed. *SYN:* A gang of outlaws are freeing prisoners and then killing them to claim the reward on their heads. A Chicago detective (Montgomery) infiltrates the

**Last summer was too beautiful to forget.
And too painful to remember.**

FRANK PERRY'S

LAST SUMMER

with BARBARA HERSHEY, RICHARD THOMAS, BRUCE DAVISON and CATHY BURNS
Screenplay by ELEANOR PERRY From the novel by EVAN HUNTER Produced by ALFRED W CROWN
and SIDNEY BECKERMAN Associate Producer JOEL GLICKMAN Directed by FRANK PERRY In EASTMAN COLOR

Advertisement for *Last Summer* (1969).

221. Last Summer (10/69) Eastmancolor—97 mins. (Drama). *DIR:* Frank Perry. *PRO:* Alfred W. Crown, Sidney Beckerman. *SP:* Eleanor Perry. Based on the book by Evan Hunter. An Alsid-Francis Production. *CAST:* Barbara Hershey, Richard Thomas, Bruce Davison, Cathy Burns, Ernesto Gonzales, Peter Turgeon, Ralph Waite, Conrad Bain, Eileen Letchworth, Maeve McGuire, Lou Gary, Andrew Krance, Wayne Meyer, Ed Stevlingson. *SYN:* Three teens (Hershey, Thomas, Davison) spend their summer on Fire Island boating, swimming, smoking marijuana, and experimenting with sex. When another teen (Burns) arrives and tries to join their group, tragedy results. *NOTES:* Cathy Burns is now a writer. Originally released at 100 mins. This film received an R rating after 3 mins. were cut. Working title was *Love in Our Time*.

gang to learn the identity of their leader. *NOTES:* A loose remake of the 1953 Allied Artists film *Star of Texas*.

222. Laughter in Paradise (11/11/51) B&W—93 mins. (Comedy) *DIR/PRO:* Mario Zampi. *SP:* Michael Pertwee, Jack Davies. An Associated British Picture–Transocean Production. A Stratford Picture Presentation. *CAST:* Alastair Sim, Fay Compton, Beatrice Campbell, Veronica Hurst, Guy Middleton, George Cole, A.E. Matthews, Joyce Grenfell, Anthony Steel, John Laurie, Eleanor Summerfield, Ronald Adam, Leslie Dwyer, Ernest Thesiger, Hugh Griffith, Michael Pertwee, Audrey Hepburn. *SYN:* A practical joker (Griffith) leaves each of his four relatives a large sum of money on the condition they follow certain specific instructions. His sister (Compton) must work as a maid for a month; a cousin (Middleton) must marry the first girl he meets; a timid bank clerk (Cole) must pretend to hold up his bank, and an ex-army officer/novelist (Sim) must commit a petty theft and spend time in jail. *NOTES:* Released in Great Britain in April, 1951. Audrey Hepburn appears in a minor role as a cigarette girl.

223. The Leather Boys (11/8/65) B&W/Scope–108 mins. (Drama). *DIR:* Sidney J. Furie. *PRO:* Raymond Stross. *SP:* Gillian Freeman. Based on the book by Eliot George (Gillian Freeman). An RLP Picture Production. An R. Lee Platt Presentation. *CAST:* Rita Tushingham, Colin Campbell, Dudley Sutton, Gladys Henson, Avice Landone, Lockwood West, Betty Marsden, Martin Mathews, Johnny Briggs, James Chase, Geoffrey Dunn, Dandy Nichols, Valerie Varnam, Jill Meredith. *SYN:* Two London teenagers (Campbell, Tushingham) marry and immediately begin having trouble when she refuses to give up her childlike ways and he seeks out his friends at the local motorcycle club. *NOTES:* Released in Great Britain in January, 1964, at a running time of 105 mins.

224. Legion of the Doomed (9/21/58) B&W–75 mins. (Adventure). *DIR:* Thor Brooks. *PRO:* William F. Broidy. *SP:* Thomas G. Hubbard, Fred Eggers. *CAST:* Bill Williams, Dawn Richard, Anthony Caruso, Kurt Krueger, Thomas G. Hubbard, John Damler, Rush Williams, George Baxter, Saul Gorss, Joseph Abdullah, Hal Gerard, Peter Bourne, Richard Farnsworth, Zeev Bufman, James Bronte, Rick Vallin, Darlene Fields, Bud Wolfe, Gary Kent, Vicki Bakken, George Offerman, Yvonne de Lavallade, Spiros Casimis. *SYN:* An American officer (Williams) in the French Foreign Legion learns that his commanding officer (Krueger) is a traitor who has formed an alliance with the desert tribes.

225. Lemonade Joe (11/25/67) B&W/Scope–90 mins. (Western). *DIR:* Oldrich Lipsky. *PRO:* Jaroslav Jilovec. *SP:* Jiri Bredecka, Oldrich Lipsky. Based on the book and play by Jiri Bredecka. A Barrandov-Ceskoslovensky Production. A Tele-Net International Film Presentation. *CAST:* Karel Fiala, Olga Schoberova, Kveta Fialova, Milos Kopecky, Rudolf Deyl, Josef Hlinomaz, Bohus Zahorsky, Karel Effa, Waldemar Matuska, Eman Fiala, Jiri Steimar, Oldrich Lukes, Viktor Ocasek. *SYN:* A father (Zahorsky) and daughter (Schoberova), saved by a gunfighter (Fiala) who gets his strength drinking Kolaloka lemonade, team with him to drum whiskey out of the West and open lemonade saloons. [Original Czech title: *Limonadovy Joe.*] [Alternate Czech title: *Konska Opera.*]

226. Let's Be Happy (5/26/57) Technicolor/Scope–93 mins. (Musical-Comedy). *DIR:* Henry Levin. *PRO:* Marcel Hellman. *SP:* Diana Morgan, Dorothy Cooper. Based on the play *Jeannie* by Aimee Stuart. An ABE-Pathé Production. *CAST:* Vera-Ellen, Tony Martin, Robert Flemyng, Zena Marshall, Helen Horton, Beckett Bould, Alfred Burke, Vernon Greeves, Richard Molinas, Eugene Deckers, Russell Waters, Paul Young, Peter Sinclair, Magda Miller, Brian Oulton, Guy Middleton, Katherine Kath, Charles Carson, Jock McKay, Michael Anthony, Jean Cadell, Gordon Jackson, Carl Duering, Molly Weir, Jameson Clark, Ewan Roberts. *SYN:* An American girl (Vera-Ellen) receives a small inheritance and visits Scotland where she is courted by a washing machine salesman (Martin) and a Scottish Lord (Flemyng), who thinks she's wealthy. When her money runs out, the lord has nothing more to do with her, and

Advertisement for *Legion of the Doomed* (1958).

she returns to America where she finds the salesman waiting for her. NOTES: Released in Great Britain at a running time of 107 mins. A musical remake of the 1941 British film *Jeannie*, which was released in the U.S. as *Girl in Distress*.

227. Let's Talk About Men (8/76) B&W – 93 mins. (Drama-Comedy-Romance). *DIR/SP:* Lina Wertmuller. *PRO:* Pietro Notorianni. *CAST:* Nino Manfredi, Luciana Paluzzi, Milena Vukotic, Margaret Lee, Patrizia de Clara. *SYN:* A series of four vignettes showing different ways men abuse women. In the first, a businessman (Manfredi), whose deals turn sour, makes use of his wife's (Paluzzi) kleptomania; in the second, an aging knife thrower (Manfredi), needing glasses, fails to heed the pleas of his wife (Vukotic), who is also his target; in the third, a man's (Manfredi) treatment of his wife (Lee) leads her to mutiny, which he tries to quell by plotting to kill her; in the fourth, a man (Manfredi) returns home drunk after a day's work and demands his marital rights of his wife (de Clara). NOTES: Originally filmed in 1965. [Original Italian title: *Questa Volta Parliamo di Uomini*.]

228. Life in Danger (2/1/64) B&W—63 mins. (Crime). *DIR:* Terry Bishop. *PRO:* Jack Parsons. *SP:* Malcolm Hulke, Eric Paice. A Parroch Films Production. *CAST:* Derren Nesbitt, Julie Hopkins, Howard Marion Crawford, Victor Brooks, Jack Allen, Christopher Witty, Carmel McSharry, Mary Mason, Bruce Seton, Peter Swanwick, Bryan Coleman, Humphrey Lestocq, Richard Pearson, Celia Hewitt, Brian Rawlinson. *SYN:* When a young man (Nesbitt) stops at a house for food and rest he is befriended by the young woman (Hopkins) living there. When they retreat to a nearby barn to talk, she is assumed missing and a major (Crawford) leads the townspeople to find the man whom they suspect as being an escaped child murderer. *NOTES:* Released in Great Britain in 1959.

229. Life Upside Down (8/17/65) B&W—92 mins. (Drama). *DIR/SP:* Alain Jessua. *PRO:* Michel Peynet. An A.J. Films Production. A Landau/Unger Releasing Organization Presentation. *CAST:* Charles Denner, Anna Gaylor, Guy Saint-Jean, Nicole Gueden, Jean Yanne, Yvonne Clech, Robert Bousquet, Françoise Moncey, Jean Dewever, Gilbert Meunier, Andre Thorent, Bernard Sury, Jenny Orleans, Nane Germon. *SYN:* A man (Denner) withdraws from the world around him causing him to lose his job and fiancée (Gaylor) and finally ends up being committed to an asylum. *NOTES:* Released in France in 1964. Released at the New York Film Festival in April, 1965. [Original French title: *La Vie à l'Envers*.] [New York Film Festival title: *Inside Out*.]

230. The Littlest Hobo (7/6/58) B&W—77 mins. (Children). *DIR:* Charles R. Rondeau. *PRO:* Hugh M. Hooker. *SP:* Dorrell McGowan. *CAST:* Buddy Hart, Wendy Stuart, Carlyle Mitchell, Howard Hoffman, Robert Kline, Pat Bradley, Bill Coontz, Dorothy Johnson, William Marks, Pauline Moore, Larry Thor, Norman Bartold, "London," the dog, "Fleecie," the lamb. *SYN:* The littlest Hobo (London) rides into town on a freight train and rescues a lamb (Fleecie) from a slaughter house. Both wander onto the governor's (Mitchell) estate inspiring his paralyzed daughter (Stuart) to walk.

231. Look in Any Window (1/29/61) B&W—87 mins. (Drama). *DIR:* William Alland. *PRO:* William Alland, Laurence E. Mascott. *SP:* Laurence E. Mascott. A New Films Company Production. *CAST:* Paul Anka, Ruth Roman, Alex Nicol, Gigi Perreau, Carole Mathews, George Dolenz, Jack Cassidy, Robert Sampson, Dan Grayam, Jacqueline Kruger, Norman Winston. *SYN:* A teenager (Anka), unhappy and mixed up because his father (Nicol) is an alcoholic and his mother (Roman) runs around with other men, becomes a peeping Tom, spying on his neighbors and almost causing the death of a teenage girl (Perreau) through his actions.

232. Looking for Danger (10/6/57) B&W—62 mins. (Spy-Comedy). *DIR:* Austen Jewell. *PRO:* Ben Schwalb. *SP:* Elwood Ullman, Edward Bernds. *CAST:* Huntz Hall, Stanley Clements, David Gorcey, Jimmy Murphy, Eddie LeRoy, Lili Kardell, Richard Avonde, Michael Granger, Peter Mamakos, Otto Reichow, Dick Elliott, John Harmon, Joan Bradshaw, Harry Strang, Paul Bryar, George Khoury, Henry Rowland, Jane Burgess, Michael Vallon. *SYN:* In flashback, Duke (Clements) relates the story of how he and the rest of the Bowery Boys were sent on a mission to North Africa in World War II to locate a member of the North African underground called "The Hawk." *NOTES:* The last "Bowery Boys" film to be produced by Ben Schwalb.

233. Loophole (3/28/54) B&W—79 mins. (Crime-Drama). *DIR:* Harold

Advertisement for *Look in Any Window* (1961).

Schuster. *PRO:* Lindsley Parsons. *SP:* Warren Douglas. Story by George Bricker, Dwight V. Babcock. *CAST:* Barry Sullivan, Charles McGraw, Dorothy Malone, Don Haggerty, Mary Beth Hughes, Don Beddoe, Dayton Lummis, Joanne Jordan, John Eldredge, Richard Reeves. *SYN:* A bank teller (Sullivan) accused of stealing $50,000 from his bank sets out to locate the real culprit (Beddoe) while being hounded by a private detective (McGraw) who believes him guilty.

234. Loose in London (5/24/53) B&W – 62 mins. (Comedy). *DIR:* Edward Bernds. *PRO:* Ben Schwalb. *SP:* Elwood Ullman, Edward Bernds. *CAST:* Leo Gorcey, Huntz Hall, David Condon, Bennie Bartlett, Bernard Gorcey, Walter Kingsford, Norma Varden, Angela Greene, William Cottrell, Rex Evans, James Logan, Alex Fraser, Clyde Cook, Joan Shawlee, James Fairfax, Wilbur Mack, Charles Keane, Teddy Mangean, Gertrude Astor, Matthew Boulton, Charles Wagenheim. *SYN:* The Bowery Boys head to London when it is discovered that Sach (Hall) is a distant relative to a dying British Earl (Kingsford). *NOTES:* The first "Bowery Boys" film to be directed by Edward Bernds. Walter Kingsford played a dual role in this film. Working titles were *Bowery Knights* and *Knights of the Square Table.*

235. Lord of the Jungle (6/12/55) B&W – 69 mins. (Jungle-Adventure). *DIR/PRO/SP:* Ford Beebe. Based on characters in the *Bomba* books by Roy Lockwood. *CAST:* Johnny Sheffield, Wayne Morris, Nancy Hale, Paul Picerni, William Phipps, Robert "Smoki" Whitfield, Leonard Mudie, James Adamson, Harry Lauter, Joel Fluellen, Juanita Moore. *SYN:* Bomba (Sheffield) sets out to destroy the leader of a group of rogue elephants that have been terrorizing the natives. *NOTES:* The last of the "Bomba, the Jungle Boy" features. Johnny Sheffield retired from acting and went into the real estate business.

236. Love in a Four Letter World (3/70) Eastmancolor – 93 mins.

Advertisement for *Love in the Afternoon* (1957).

(Drama). *DIR:* John Stone. *PRO:* Arthur Voronka. *SP:* John Stone, Arthur Voronka. A Multivision-Multiplex Production. *CAST:* Michael Kane, Andre Lawrence, Kayle Chernin, Helen Whyte, Candy Greene, Pierre Letourneau, Monique Mercure. *SYN:* A group of people try to live in a disillusioned society. *NOTES:* Limited theatrical release. Financed by the Canadian Film Development Corporation. Another of the "soft core" X-rated features distributed by Allied Artists in the seventies. [Original Canadian-French title: *Viens Mon Amour.*] [British title: *Sex Isn't Sin.*]

237. Love in the Afternoon (6/30/57) B&W – 130 mins. (Comedy-Drama). *DIR/PRO:* Billy Wilder. *SP:* Billy Wilder, I.A.L. Diamond. Based on *Ariane* by Claude Anet. *CAST:* Gary Cooper, Audrey Hepburn, Maurice Chevalier, John McGiver, Lise Bourdin, Paul Bonifas, Audrey Wilder, the Four Gypsies (Gyula Kokas, Michael Kokas, George Cocos, Victor Gazzoli), Olga Valery, Leila Croft, Valerie Croft, Charles Bouillard, Minerva Pious, Andre Priez. *SYN:* The daughter (Hepburn) of a Parisien detective (Chevalier) falls in love with an American playboy (Cooper) and pretends to be a woman of mystery as she cons him with her imaginary tales of lovers. *NOTES:* Filmed in Paris. Re-released by Allied Artists in 1961 as *Fascination* with a running time of 125 mins. Billy Wilder's and I.A.L. Diamond's first co-written script. Gary Cooper's first film on foreign soil. Minerva Pious played the role of "Mrs. Nussbaum" on the Fred Allen radio show "Allen's Alley."

Lovers from Beyond the Tomb *see* **Nightmare Castle**

238. The Lucky Mascot (10/11/51) B&W – 84 mins. (Comedy-Thriller). *DIR:* Thornton Freeland. *PRO:* Nat A. Bronsten, David Copelan. *SP:* Alec Coppel, Thornton Freeland, C. Dennis Freeman. Story by Alec Coppel. A Diadem-Alliance Production. *CAST:* Carole Landis, Carroll Levis, Herbert Lom, Avril Angers, Ernest Thesiger, Henry Edwards, Edward Underdown, Gwyneth Vaughn, Jack McNaughton, Gus McNaughton, John Salew, Carole

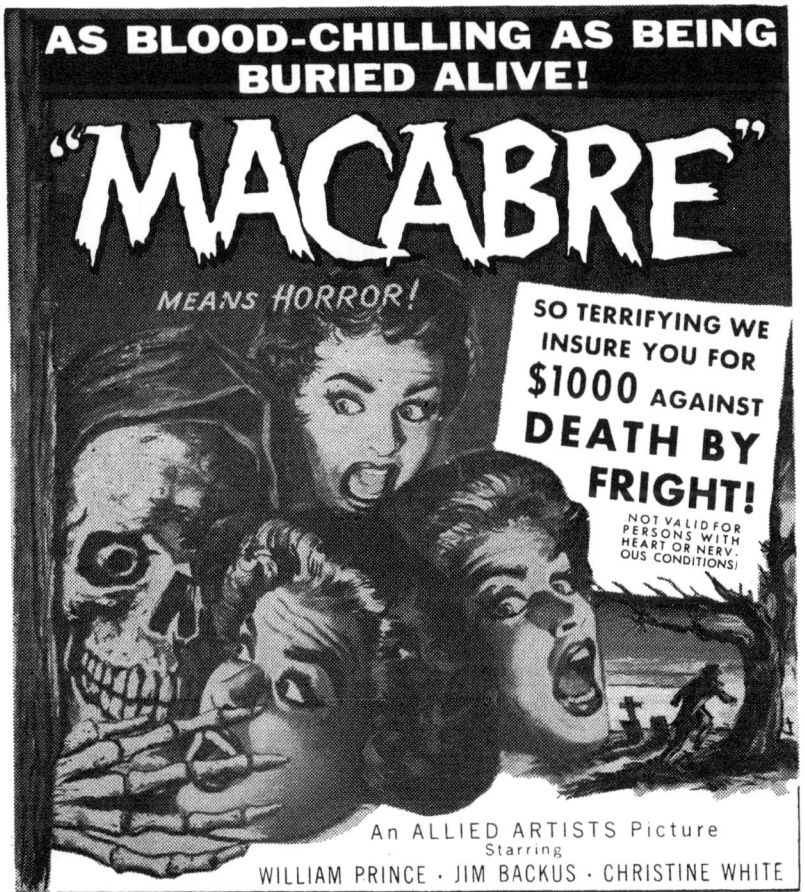

Advertisement for *Macabre* (1958). Did anyone ever collect the $1,000 insurance money offered by William Castle and Allied Artists?

Lesley, Terry-Thomas, Albert Ward, Les Ward, Leslie "Hutch" Hutchinson, Carroll Levis's Discoveries. *SYN:* A radio personality (Levis) and his "Discoveries" become involved with a connoisseur (Lom) of Buddist art who will stop at nothing to secure a rare brass monkey artifact. *NOTES:* Released in Great Britain in 1948. [British title: *The Brass Monkey*.]

239. Macabre (3/9/58) B&W – 73 mins. (Horror). *DIR/PRO:* William Castle. *SP:* Robb White. Based on *The Marble Forest* by Theo Durrant. A William Castle–Robb White Production. *CAST:* William Prince, Jim Backus, Christine White, Jacqueline Scott, Susan Morrow, Philip Tonge, Johnathan Kidd, Dorothy Morris, Howard Hoffman, Ellen Corby, Linda Guderman, Voltaire Perkins, Robert Colbert. *SYN:* A small town doctor (Prince) receives a mysterious phone call that his young daughter (Guderman) has been kidnapped and buried alive in a small coffin. When he, his father-in-law (Tonge), and nurse (Scott) locate the coffin in a graveyard, the father-in-law suffers a heart attack at seeing the dead body of his granddaughter. It is later revealed that the doctor had hidden his daughter and had perpetrated the hoax to kill his father-in-law in order to gain the family inheritance. *NOTES:* Director William Castle's horror film debut after 15 years of directing B pictures. He would continue directing and or producing in this genre until his death in 1977. He also started his series of gimmicks beginning with this film. His gimmick here was to insure each filmgoer with a Lloyds of London insurance policy for $1,000 against "death by fright" while viewing this film. He also had fake nurses and hearses at select theatre premiers. Theo Durant is a pseudonym for the 12 California men and women, members of the Mystery Writers of America, who wrote the book, *The Marble Forest*, chapter by chapter.

240. The Magic Weaver (9/22/65) Eastmancolor—87 mins. (Fantasy). *DIR:* Aleksandr Rou. *PRO:* Gorky Film Studio. *SP:* Yevgeniy Shvarts. Based on Russian folk tales. A Gorky Film Studio Production. *CAST:* Mikhail Kuznetsov, Ninel Myshkova, Vitya Perevalov, Anatoliy Kubatskiy, Olya Khachapuridze, Georgiy Millyar, Vera Altayskaya, L. Troitskiy, Aleksandr Khvylya. *SYN:* A soldier (Kuznetsov) returning home after many years meets a boy (Perevalov) whose mother (Myshkova) has been imprisoned by the water czar (Kubatskiy). They enter the underwater kingdom and, with the help of the czar's granddaughter (Khachapuridze), rescue her. *NOTES:* Released in the U.S.S.R. in March, 1960, at a running time of 78 mins. [Original Russian title: *Marya-Iskusnitsa*.]

241. Magnificent Roughnecks (7/22/56) B&W—73 mins. (Drama-Romance). *DIR:* Sherman A. Rose. *PRO:* Herman Cohen. *SP:* Stephen Kandel. *CAST:* Jack Carson, Mickey Rooney, Nancy Gates, Jeff Donnell, Myron Healey, Willis Bouchey, Eric Feldary, Alan Wells, Frank Gerstle, Larry Carr, M.G. (Matty) Fain, Joe Locke. *SYN:* Two oil well drillers (Rooney, Carson) in South America must contend with a female oil expert (Gates) who is sent out by their company to replace one of the men.

242. A Man and a Woman (8/5/66) Eastmancolor—102 mins. (Drama). *DIR/PRO:* Claude Lelouch. *SP:* Pierre Uytterhoeven, Claude Lelouch. Story by Claude Lelouch. A Les Films 13 Production. *CAST:* Anouk Aimée, Jean-Louis Trintignant, Pierre Barouh, Valerie Lagrange, Simone Paris, Antoine Sire, Souad Amidou, Yane Barry, Paqul le Person, Henri Chemin, Gerard Sire. *SYN:* Friendship and then love develops between a widow (Aimée) and widower (Trintignant) when they meet during a visit to their respective children at a boarding school. *NOTES:* Remade as a western in 1977 by Claude Lelouch as *Another Man, Another Chance* and released by United Artists. A sequel, *A Man and a Woman: 20 Years Later*, was released in 1986 by Warner Bros. with the same director and two leading stars. [Original French title: *Un Homme et Une Femme*.]

Man Eater of Hydra *see* **Island of the Doomed**

243. Man from God's Country (2/9/58) DeLuxe Color/Scope—72 mins. (Western). *DIR:* Paul Landres. *PRO:* Scott R. Dunlap. *SP:* George Waggner. *CAST:* George Montgomery, Randy Stuart, James Griffith, House Peters, Jr., Susan Cummings, Kim Charney, Frank Wilcox, Gregg Barton, Philip Terry, Al Wyatt, Kenneth MacDonald, I. Stanford Jolley, Frank Sully, Kermit Maynard, Ted Mapes, Byron Foulger. *SYN:* A sheriff (Montgomery), asked to resign his post because of his blazing guns, travels to the town of Sundown where he and his

George Montgomery is ready to deal out justice in *Man from God's Country* (1958).

Civil War buddy (Peters, Jr.) join forces to clean up the lawless town. *NOTES:* Working title was *New Day at Sundown*.

The Man in the Steel Mask *see* **Who?**

244. Man on the Run (8/29/51) B&W – 82 mins. (Crime). *DIR/PRO/SP:* Lawrence Huntington. An Associated British Picture Production. A Stratford Picture Presentation. *CAST:* Derek Farr, Joan Hopkins, Edward Chapman, Laurence Harvey, John Bailey, John Stuart, Edward Underdown, Leslie Perrins, Kenneth More, Martyn Miller, Eleanor Summerfield, Anthony Nicholls. *SYN:* While trying to sell his revolver, an army deserter (Farr) becomes indirectly involved in a robbery and is arrested as part of the gang. With the help of a woman (Hopkins) he escapes, trails the crooks, and is eventually captured by them. The woman leads the police to their hideout where he is held and the crooks are captured. He then returns to the army. *NOTES:* Released in Great Britain in 1949.

245. The Man Outside (6/20/68) Technicolor/Scope—97 mins. (Spy-Drama). *DIR:* Samuel Gallu. *PRO:* William Gell. *SP:* Samuel Gallu, Julian Bond, Roger Marshall. Based on *Double Agent* by Gene Stackleborg. A Trio Films–Group W Films Production. A London Independent Producers Presentation. *CAST:* Van Heflin, Heidelinde Weis, Pinkas Braun, Peter Vaughn, Charles Gray, Paul Maxwell, Ronnie Barker, Linda Marlowe, Gary Cockrell, Bill Nagy, Larry Cross, Archie Duncan, Willoughby Gray, Christopher Denham, Carole Ann Ford, Carmel McSharry, John Sterland, Alex Marchevsky, Paul Armstrong, Hugh Elton, Derek Baker, Roy Stone. *SYN:* An ex-CIA agent (Heflin) is framed for murder and hunted by the Russians when he refuses to turn over a Russian defector (Braun). He eventually succeeds in bringing the defector to safety and exposes a double agent (Gray). *NOTES:* Released in Great Britain in 1968.

246. The Man Who Would Be King (12/75) Technicolor/Panavision—129 mins. (Drama-Adventure). *DIR:* John Huston. *PRO:* John Foreman. *SP:* John Huston, Gladys Hill. Based on the story by Rudyard Kipling. A Persky-Bright Devon Picture. An Allied Artists-Columbia Pictures Production. *CAST:* Sean Connery, Michael Caine, Christopher Plummer, Saeed Jaffrey, Karroum Ben Bouih, Jack May, Doghmi Larbi, Shakira Caine, Mohammed Shamsi, Paul Antrim, Albert Moses. *SYN:* Rudyard Kipling (Plummer) listens to a tale told by Peachy Carnehan (Michael Caine) of how he and his friend, Danny Dravot (Connery), traveled to the city of Sikandergul where Danny is revered as the reincarnation of Alexander the Great and is declared their god. Things go well until Danny decides to take a wife (Shakira Caine). She is terrified at being married to a god and scratches his face and draws blood. The natives know that gods do not bleed; they pursue them out of the city where they kill Danny and crucify Peachy, leaving him for dead. Peachy survives, and as proof of the tale, shows Kipling Danny's decomposed head, still wearing its crown. *NOTES:* John Huston had wanted to film this story in the fifties with Clark Gable and Humphrey Bogart as leads, but other commitments prevailed, and when Bogart died, the project was shelved. In the late sixties he resurrected the idea hoping to get Richard Burton and Peter O'Toole as leads, but financing proved a problem and the project was shelved again. It wasn't until producer John Foreman secured joint financing from Allied Artists and Columbia Pictures that the project was finally realized. Shakira Caine was then the wife of Michael Caine. Released in the United States by Allied Artists; released to the European market by Columbia Pictures.

247. Mara of the Wilderness (1/20/65) DeLuxe Color—90 mins. (Adventure). *DIR:* Frank McDonald. *PRO:* Brice Mack, Lindsley Parsons. *SP:* Tom W. Blackburn. Story by Rod Scott. A Unicorn Production. *CAST:* Adam West, Linda Saunders, Theo Marcuse, Denver Pyle, Sean McClory, Eve Brent, Roberto Contreras, Ed Kemmer, Stuart Walsh, Lelia Walsh. *SYN:* After her parents (McClory, Brent) are killed by a bear in the Alaskan wilderness, a seven-year-old girl (Lelia Walsh) is taken in and raised by wolves. When she reaches adulthood, the girl (Saunders) is befriended by an anthropologist (West) who wants to bring her back to civilization.

Advertisement for *The Man Who Would Be King* (1975). Note the new Allied Artists logo for the '70s.

Maria, the Wonderful Weaver see **The Magic Weaver**

248. The Marksman (4/12/53) B&W – 62 mins. (Western). *DIR:* Lewis D. Collins. *PRO:* Vincent M. Fennelly. *SP:* Daniel B. Ullman. A Westwood Production. *CAST:* Wayne Morris, Elena Verdugo, Frank Ferguson, Rick Vallin, Tom Powers, I. Stanford Jolley, Robert Bice, Stanley Price, Russ Whiteman, Brad Johnson, William Fawcett, Jack Rice, Tim Ryan. *SYN:* Because he is an expert marksman with a telescopic rifle, a man (Morris) is hired as a deputy marshal to stop a gang of outlaws and rustlers.

249. Marry Me! Marry Me! (11/69) DeLuxe Color – 87 mins. (Comedy). *DIR/PRO/SP:* Claude Berri. A Renn–Parafrance Films–Madeleine Films Production. *CAST:* Claude Berri, Elisabeth Wiener, Regine, Louisa Colpeyn, Gregoire Aslan, Prudence Harrington, Betsy Blair, Gabriel Jabbour, Estera Galion. *SYN:* A Jewish encyclopedia salesman (Berri) in Paris, falls in love with a Belgian girl (Wiener) and must go to Belgium to meet her parents before they marry. Before leaving, he decides to take English lessons and falls in love with his tutor (Harrington). He goes to Belgium to meet the parents but returns to Paris to see his tutor. He learns the tutor is to marry someone else, so he returns to Belgium and marriage. *NOTES:* Released in France in 1968 at a running time of 90 mins. [Original French title: *Mazel Tov où le Mariage.*]

Mars Invades Puerto Rico see **Frankenstein Meets the Space Monster**

250. Marshals in Disguise (12/26/54) B&W – 54 mins. (Western). *DIR:* Frank McDonald. *PRO:* Wesley E. Barry. *SP:* William Raynor, Maurice Tombragel. A Newhall Production. *CAST:* Guy Madison, Andy Devine, Norma Eberhardt, Leonard Penn, Tristram Coffin, Fred Kelsey, John Merton, Pat Mitchell, Rick Vallin, Bill Hale, David Sharpe, Don Turner, Anthony Sydes, Guy Beach, John Eldredge, James Bush, Bud Osborne. *SYN:* Compiled from two episodes of the *Wild Bill Hickok* television series: "The Lost Indian Mine" and "Civilian Clothes."

251. Massacre River (6/26/49) B&W – 77 mins. (Western). *DIR:* John Rawlins. *PRO:* Julian Lesser, Frank Melford. *SP:* Louis Stevens. Based on the book by Harold Bell Wright. A Windsor Pictures Production. *CAST:* Guy Madison, Rory Calhoun, Carole Mathews, Cathy Downs, Johnny Sands, Steve Brodie, Art Baker, Iron Eyes Cody, Emory Parnell, Queenie Smith, Eddy Waller, James Bush, John Holland, Douglas Fowley, Harry Brown, Kermit Maynard, Gregg Barton. *SYN:* When three cavalry officers (Madison, Calhoun, Sands) are assigned West after the Civil War, two of them (Madison, Calhoun) jeopardize their careers and friendship over a colonel's daughter (Downs) and a gambling establishment. *NOTES:* Guy Madison's second starring western.

252. Master Spy (8/19/64) B&W – 71 mins. (Drama). *DIR:* Montgomery Tully. *PRO:* Maurice J. Wilson. *SP:* Maurice J. Wilson, Montgomery Tully. Based on *They Also Serve* by Gerald Anstruther and Paul White. An Eternal Films Production. *CAST:* Stephen Murray, June Thorburn, Alan Wheatley, John Carson, John Brown, Jack Watson, Ernest Clark, Peter Gilmore, Marne Maitland, Ellen Pollock, Hugh Morton, Basil Dignam, Victor Beaumont, Derek Francis. *SYN:* A Russian physicist (Murray), secretly working for British Intelligence, attends a conference in London and seeks political asylum. He goes to work at a nuclear laboratory and passes secrets to a fellow Russian (Wheatley).

Convicted of spying, he is sent back to Russia where he continues his work for the British Government. *NOTES:* Released in Great Britain in 1963 at a running time of 73 mins.

253. The Match-Making Marshal (5/8/55) B&W – 54 mins. (Western). *DIR:* Frank McDonald. *PRO:* Wesley E. Barry. A Newhall Production. *CAST:* Guy Madison, Andy Devine. *SYN:* Compiled from two episodes of the *Wild Bill Hickok* television series: titles unknown.

254. The Maverick (12/14/52) Sepiatone – 71 mins. (Western). *DIR:* Thomas Carr. *PRO:* Vincent M. Fennelly. *SP:* Sid Theil. A Silvermine Production. *CAST:* "Wild" Bill Elliott, Phyllis Coates, Myron Healey, Richard Reeves, Terry Frost, Rand Brooks, Russell Hicks, Robert Bray, Denver Pyle, Florence Lake, Gregg Barton, Robert J. Wilke, Gene Roth, Joel Allen. *SYN:* Lt. Pete Devlin (Elliott) and his men (Bray, Healey) are taking four prisoners to Fort Jeffrey. The prisoners manage to win over one of the men (Healey) and Devlin has to make him a prisoner also. When an outlaw band tries to free the prisoners, a gun battle ensues with the Army winning and Devlin continuing on with his prisoners.

255. The Maze (7/26/53) B&W/ 3-D – 81 mins. (Horror). *DIR:* William Cameron Menzies. *PRO:* Richard Heermance. *SP:* Daniel B. Ullman. Based on the book by Maurice Sandoz. *CAST:* Richard Carlson, Veronica Hurst, Katherine Emery, Michael Pate, Hillary Brooke, John Dodsworth, Lillian Bond, Robin Hughes, Stanley Fraser, Owen McGiveney, Clyde Cook. *SYN:* On the eve of his engagement, a Scotsman (Carlson) is summoned to his ancestral castle following the death of his uncle. When he fails to return, his fiancée (Hurst), her aunt (Emery), and a group of friends decide to visit him at his castle. When they arrive, they find him much older and are determined to find out the castle's secret. *NOTES:* Executive producer was Walter Mirisch. This was Allied Artists' first and only 3-D film release. Reissued in 1982 by StereoVision International in single strip anaglyphic duo-color format as *Creature of the Maze* in StereoVision 3-D.

256. Men Are Children Twice (6/21/54) B&W – 74 mins. (Comedy). *DIR:* Gilbert Gunn. *PRO:* Vaughan N. Dean. *SP:* Cliff Gordon, Phil Park. Based on the radio play *Choir Practice* by Cliff Gordon. An Associated British Picture Production. A Stratford Picture Presentation. *CAST:* Mervyn Johns, Clifford Evans, Maureen Swanson, John Fraser, Rachel Thomas, Betty Cooper, Rachel Roberts, Hugh Pryse, Edward Evans, Kenneth Williams, Alun Owen. *SYN:* The choirmaster (Evans) of a small Welsh village creates havoc between two families when he agrees to let Mrs. Davies (Cooper) sing the lead in Handel's "Messiah" which Mrs. Lloyd (Swanson) has sung for the past fifteen years. To bring peace between the two families, he decides to let both women sing the lead. *NOTES:* Released in Great Britain in 1953. [British title: *Valley of Song*.]

257. Mexican Manhunt (9/13/53) B&W – 71 mins. (Mystery). *DIR:* Rex Bailey. *PRO:* Lindsley Parsons. *SP:* George Bricker. *CAST:* George Brent, Hillary Brooke, Morris Ankrum, Karen Sharpe, Marjorie Lord, Douglas Kennedy, Alberto Morin, Carleton Young, Stuart Randall, Marvin Press. *SYN:* While in Mexico, a novelist (Brent) turns detective to solve a fifteen-year-old murder mystery. *NOTES:* After appearing in this film, George Brent retired from acting, except for a bit part in the 1956 RKO film, *Death of a Scoundrel*, and a small featured role in the 1978 Avco-Embassy film, *Born Again*.

258. Mission Mars (7/26/68) Berkley Color—87 mins. (Science Fiction). *DIR:* Nicholas Webster. *PRO:* Everett Rosenthal. *SP:* Michael St. Clair. Story by Aubrey Wisberg. A Red Ram–Sagittarius Production. *CAST:* Darrin McGavin, Nick Adams, George De Vries, Heather Hewitt, Michael De Beausset, Shirley Parker, Bill Kelly, Chuck Zink, Ralph Miller, Art Barker, Monroe Myers. *SYN:* Three astronauts (McGavin, Adams, De Vries) encounter dangers when they make man's first flight to Mars and find a Russian cosmonaut (Kelly) on the planet in a state of suspended animation. *NOTES:* This film was copyrighted at a running time of 95 mins. This was the first feature to be filmed at Miami's Studio City Complex.

259. Mr. Potts Goes to Moscow (9/3/53) B&W—94 mins. (Comedy). *DIR/PRO:* Mario Zampi. *SP:* Jack Davies, Michael Pertwee. An Associated British Pathé–Transocean Production. A Stratford Picture Presentation. *CAST:* George Cole, Oscar Homolka, Nadia Gray, Frederick Valk, Geoffrey Sumner, Wilfrid Hyde-White, Ronald Adam, Edwin Styles, Kynaston Reeves, Ernest Jay, Richard Wattis, Michael Medwin, Frederick Leister, Henry Hewitt, Walter Horsbrugh, Anthony Shaw, Tim Turner, Michael Balfour, David Hurst, Charles Goldner, Irene Handl, Gerard Heinz, Olaf Pooley, Eleanor Summerfield, Phyllis Morris, Ronnie Stevens, Victor Maddern, Willoughby Gray, Christopher Lee. *SYN:* A sanitary engineer (Cole) gets involved in espionage when he picks up the wrong briefcase containing atomic secrets and gets whisked off to Moscow. He thinks the Russians are interested in his design for a new type of toilet. Eventually, he gets out of Russia with the help of an interpreter (Gray). *NOTES:* Released in Great Britain in 1952. Re-released under the Allied Artists logo in 1954. [British title: *Top Secret*.]

260. Mitchell (6/75) Technicolor—97 mins. (Crime). *DIR:* Andrew V. McLaglen. *PRO:* R. Ben Efraim. *SP:* Ian Kennedy Martin. An Essex Enterprises Limited Production. *CAST:* Joe Don Baker, Linda Evans, Martin Balsam, John Saxon, Merlin Olsen, Morgan Paull, Harold J. Stone, Robert Phillips, Buck Young, Rayford Barnes, Sidney Clute, Duffy Hambleton, Vicky Peters, Carole Estes, Bill Sullivan, Jim B. Smith, Charles Glover. *SYN:* A hard-nosed Los Angeles detective (Baker), disliked by his colleagues because of his stubborn pursuit of justice as a loner, goes after the leaders (Balsam, Saxon) of a drug ring to locate a cache of heroin. *NOTES:* In 1975, this film was double billed in some areas with *Gold*.

261. Moonwolf (5/11/66) B&W—74 mins. (Drama). *DIR:* Martin Nosseck, George Freedland. *PRO:* Martin Nosseck, Wolf Brauner. *SP:* George Freedland. An Alfa Film–Suomen Filmiteollisuus Production. *CAST:* Carl Mohner, Ann Savo, Helmut Schmid, Paul Dahlke, Richard Haussler, Ingrid Lutz, Horst Janson, Ake Lindman. *SYN:* A zoologist (Mohner) allows his dog to be used in a space project. When the capsule lands in the Arctic terrain, he goes there on a recovery mission and is reunited with his love (Savo). *NOTES:* Also reviewed at a running time of 85 mins. Filmed in the Arctic regions. Released in West Germany in 1959 at running times of 83 and 91 mins. [Original West German title: *...Und Immer Ruft das Herz*.]

262. Mrs. Fitzherbert (5/10/50) B&W—103 mins. (Historical). *DIR/SP:* Montgomery Tully. *PRO:* Louis H. Jackson. Based on *Princess Fitz* by Winifred Carter. A British National–Pathé Production. A Stratford Picture Presentation. *CAST:* Peter Graves, Joyce Howard, Leslie Banks, Margaretta Scott, Wanda Rotha, Mary Clare, Frederick

Barbara Payton and Paul Langton in *Murder Is My Beat* (1955).

Valk, Ralph Truman, John Stuart, Helen Haye, Chili Boucher, Lily Kann, Lawrence O'Madden, Frederick Leister, Julian Dallas, Barry Morse. *SYN:* In 1783, the prince regent (Graves) falls in love with a Catholic widow, Maria Fitzherbert (Howard). She spurns his advances, so he feigns suicide. Later, they secretly marry. Called before King George III (Valk), he denies the marriage, and Maria runs away leaving the prince to marry Princess Caroline of Brunswick (Rotha). *NOTES:* Released in Great Britain in 1948 at a running time of 99 mins.

263. Murder Is My Beat (2/27/55) B&W—77 mins. (Mystery). *DIR:* Edgar G. Ulmer. *PRO:* Aubrey Wisberg, Ilse Lahn. *SP:* Aubrey Wisberg. Story by Aubrey Wisberg, Martin Field. *CAST:* Paul Langton, Barbara Payton, Robert Shayne, Selena Royle, Roy Gordon, Tracey Roberts, Kate McKenna, Henry A. Harvey, Sr., Jay Adler. *SYN:* A nightclub singer (Payton) proclaims her innocence when she is convicted of murder. On her way to prison, she sees the man she is supposed to have killed and convinces the police detective (Langton) escorting her to help her find him and prove her innocence. *NOTES:* Working title was *The Long Chance*.

264. Murder Without Crime (4/27/51) B&W—76 mins. (Crime). *DIR/SP:* J. Lee Thompson. *PRO:* Victor Skutezky. Based on the play *Double Error* by J. Lee Thompson. An Associated British Picture Production. A Stratford Picture Presentation. *CAST:* Dennis Price, Derek Farr, Patricia Plunkett, Joan Dowling. *SYN:* An author (Farr) quarrels with his wife (Plunkett), who leaves him. Later, he goes to a pub, meets a girl (Dowling), and brings her home. They have a fight and he hits her.

He thinks he has killed her, and his landlord (Price) tries to blackmail him, knowing that the girl is still alive. *NOTES:* Released in Great Britain in 1950.

265. Murder Without Tears (6/14/53) B&W – 64 mins. (Crime). *DIR:* William Beaudine. *PRO:* William F. Broidy. *SP:* Jo Pagano, William Raynor. Based on *Double Jeopardy* by Jo Pagano. *CAST:* Craig Stevens, Joyce Holden, Richard Benedict, Edward Norris, Clair Regis, Thomas G. Hubbard, Murray Alper, Robert Carson, Paul Murray, Edith Angold, Leonard Penn, Hal Gerard, Burt Wenland, Fred Kelsey, Gregg Sanders, Charles Victor, Jack George. *SYN:* When a man (Norris) arranges for his wife's (Regis) murder and has a bank clerk (Holden) give him an alibi, a police detective (Stevens) becomes suspicious and investigates deeper into the crime.

266. Mutiny in Outer Space (3/3/65) B&W – 80 mins. (Science Fiction). *DIR:* Hugo Grimaldi. *PRO:* Hugo Grimaldi, Arthur C. Pierce. *SP:* Arthur C. Pierce. Story by Arthur C. Pierce, Hugo Grimaldi. A Woolner Bros. Production. *CAST:* William Leslie, Dolores Faith, Pamela Curran, Richard Garland, Carl Crow, Harold Lloyd, Jr., James Dobson, Glenn Langan, Ron Stokes, Robert Palmer, Gabriel Curtis. *SYN:* Two astronauts (Leslie, Crow) return to their space station after an exploration of lunar ice caves, unaware that they have brought back with them a creeping fungus that threatens to take over the space station. *NOTES:* Working titles were *Space Station X* and *Invasion from the Moon*. Released in 1964 by Crest Pictures before being picked up for distribution by Allied Artists. Double billed in some areas with *The Human Duplicators*. [Original Italian title: *Ammutinamento nello Spazio*.] [British title: *Invasion from the Moon*.]

267. My Brother Jonathan (6/29/49) B&W – 102 mins. (Drama). *DIR:* Harold French. *PRO:* Warwick Ward. *SP:* Leslie L. Landau, Adrian Arlington. Based on the book by Francis Brett Young. An Associated British Picture Production. *CAST:* Michael Denison, Dulcie Gray, Ronald Howard, Stephen Murray, Mary Clare, Finlay Currie, Beatrice Campbell, Arthur Young, James Robertson Justice, James Hayter, Peter Murray, Jessica Spencer, Desmond Newling, Alan Goodwin, R. Stuart Lindsell, Avice Landone, Hildy Bayley, Wylie Watson, Josephine Stuart, Fred Groves, Wilfrid Hyde-White, Beatrice Varley, Eric Messiter, Peter Hobbes, David Ward, Jack Melford, Paul Farrell, Derek Farge, John Salew, George Woodbridge, Leslie Weston, Merle Tottenham. *SYN:* Told in flashback, a doctor (Denison) loses his girl (Campbell) to his brother (Howard), so he buries himself in a mining town to forget. When his brother is killed during World War I, he marries the girl but she dies in childbirth. Eventually he marries the nurse (Gray) who stands by him and they raise his son. *NOTES:* Released in Great Britain in 1948.

268. My Friends (7/76) Eastmancolor – 113 mins. (Comedy). *DIR:* Mario Monicelli. *PRO:* Carlo Nebiolo. *SP:* Pietro Germi, Pietro de Barnardi, Leo Benvenuti, Tullio Pinelli. A Rizzoli Films Production. *CAST:* Ugo Tognazzi, Gastone Moschin, Philippe Noiret, Duilio Del Prete, Adolfo Celi, Bernard Blier, Olga Karlatos, Milena Vukotic, Angela Goodwin. *SYN:* Four middle-aged men (Tognazzi, Moschin, Noiret, Del Prete) spend an evening playing practical jokes on the populace of the town. *NOTES:* This film, begun by Pietro Germi, was completed by Mario Monicelli after Germi's death. [Original Italian title: *Amici Miei*.]

269. The Naked Hills (6/17/56) Pathé Color – 73 mins. (Western). *DIR/PRO/SP:* Josef Shaftel. Story by Helen S.

Bilkie. A LaSalle Production. *CAST:* David Wayne, Keenan Wynn, James Barton, Jim Backus, Marcia Henderson, Denver Pyle, Myrna Dell, Lewis Russell, Frank Fenton, Fuzzy Knight, Jim Hayward, Chris Olsen, Steve Terrell. *SYN:* In 1849, an Indiana farmer (Wayne) gets "gold fever," deserts his family, and heads west to spend the next forty years prospecting for gold.

270. Naked in the Sun (9/29/57) Eastmancolor—78 mins. (Western). *DIR/ PRO:* R. John Hugh. *SP:* John Cresswell. Based on *The Warrior* by Frank G. Slaughter. An Empire Production. *CAST:* James Craig, Lita Milan, Barton MacLane, Robert Wark, Jim Boles, Tony Hunter, Douglas Wilson, Dennis Cross, Peter Dearing, Mike Recco. *SYN:* In Florida, the Osceola and Seminole Indian tribes unite to fight an evil slave trader (MacLane).

271. The Naked Kiss (5/4/64) B&W — 93 mins. (Drama). *DIR/PRO/SP:* Samuel Fuller. A Leon Fromkess–Sam Firks Presentation. *CAST:* Constance Towers, Anthony Eisley, Michael Dante, Virginia Grey, Patsy Kelly, Betty Bronson, Marie Devereux, Karen Conrad, Linda Francis, Bill Sampson, Sheila Mintz, Patricia Gayle, Gerald Michenaud, George Spell, Barbara Perry, Walter Mathews, Betty Robinson, Chris-

Constance Towers and Michael Dante in *The Naked Kiss* (1964).

topher Barry, Patty Robinson, Neyle Morrow, Monte Mansfield, Fletcher Fist, Gerald Milton, Breena Howard, Sally Mills, Edy Williams, Michael Barrere. *SYN:* An ex-prostitute (Towers) arrives in a small town and tries to make a new start, but because of her past, she has trouble with the police chief (Eisley). Later, when she discovers her fiancé (Dante) molesting a little girl, she kills him and has to prove her innocence. *NOTES:* Working title was *The Iron Kiss.*

272. Navy Wife (5/20/56) B&W — 83 mins. (Comedy). *DIR:* Edward Bernds. *PRO:* Walter Wanger. *SP:* Kay Lenard. Based on *Mother, Sir* by Tats Blain. *CAST:* Joan Bennett, Gary Merrill,

Judy Nugent, Maurice Manson, Teru Shimada, Tom Komuro, Shizue Nakamura, Robert Nichols, Carol Veazie, John Craven, Shirley Yamaguchi, Arnold Ishii, Maudie Prickett, Phil Arnold, Ziro Tenkai, Kyoko Kamo, Julia Katayama, Karie Shindo, Micko Shintani, Tauenko Takahashi, Richard Tyler, Morgan Jones, Jack Bradford. *SYN:* A Navy wife (Bennett) joins her husband (Merrill) in Japan and creates chaos as she dominates her husband. Japanese housewives, known for their obedience, try to copy her Western ways and do the same to their husbands. [British title: *Mother, Sir!*]

273. Never Love a Stranger (6/22/58) B&W—91 mins. (Drama). *DIR:* Robert Stevens. *PRO/SP:* Harold Robbins, Richard Day. Based on the book by Harold Robbins. *CAST:* John Drew Barrymore, Lita Milan, Robert Bray, Steve McQueen, Salem Ludwig, R.G. Armstrong, Douglas Rodgers, Felice Orlandi, Augusta Merighi, Abe Simon, Dolores Vitina, Walter Burke, Joseph Leberman, Robert O'Connell, Michael O'Dowd, John Dalz, Dort Clark, Gino Ardito, Joseph Costa. *SYN:* A young hoodlum (Barrymore) becomes head of the entire New York–New Jersey crime syndicate. *NOTES:* Steve McQueen's second film and first featured role.

274. Never Put It in Writing (4/28/64) B&W—93 mins. (Comedy). *DIR/SP:* Andrew L. Stone. *PRO:* Andrew L. Stone, Virginia Stone. A Seven Arts Production. *CAST:* Pat Boone, Milo O'Shea, Fidelma Murphy, Reginald Beckwith, Harry Brogan, Nuala Moiselle, John Le Mesurier, Sarah Ballantine, John Gardiner, Colin Blakely, Ed Devereaux, Derry Power, Bill Foley, Polly Adams, Julia Nelson, John Dunbar, Susan Richards, Liz Lanchbury. *SYN:* When a London insurance executive (Boone), on business in Ireland, learns that he has been passed over for promotion, he writes a letter of resignation to his company. When he is later informed that he has been made vice president and junior partner, he secures the help of a postal clerk (Murphy) and the race is on to retrieve the letter. *NOTES:* Released in Great Britain in July, 1964, at a running time of 90 mins.

275. New Orleans After Dark (6/15/58) B&W—69 mins. (Crime). *DIR:* John Sledge. *PRO:* Eric Sayers. *SP:* Frank Phares. Based on official records from the New Orleans Police Department. *CAST:* Stacy Harris, Capt. Louis Sirgo, Ellen Moore, Tommy Pelle, Wilson Bourg, Harry Wood, Johnny Aladdin, Jeanine Thomas, Leo Zinser, Kathryn Copponex, Bob Samuels, Steve Lord, Louis Gurvich, Frank Fiasconaro, Allan Binkley, Claude Evans, Bill Matthews, La Vergne Smith. *SYN:* Told in semi-documentary style, lieutenants Beaujac (Harris) and Conroy (Sirgo) are on the trail of a murderer which leads them to a dope smuggling operation. *NOTES:* Based on the 1956 syndicated television series *N.O.P.D.*, which also starred Stacy Harris as Lt. Beaujac and Louis Sirgo as Lt. Conroy. Louis Sirgo was an actual detective with the New Orleans Police Department and was granted leave to do the television series and this film. In 1962, director Sledge reunited the two stars for the MPA Feature Film, *Four for the Morgue*.

276. The Next Man (11/76) Technicolor—108 mins. (Spy-Drama-Romance). *DIR:* Richard C. Sarafian. *PRO:* Martin Bregman. *SP:* Morton Fine, Alan Trustman, David M. Wolf, Richard C. Sarafian. Story by Martin Bregman, Alan Trustman. An Artists Entertainment Production. *CAST:* Sean Connery, Cornelia Sharpe, Albert Paulsen, Adolfo Celi, Marco St. John, Ted Beniades, Charles Cioffi, Salem Ludwig, Tom Klunis, Jaime Sanchez, Stephen D. Newman, Holland Taylor, Peggy Feury, Patrick Bedford, Roger Omar Serbagi,

Armand Dahan, Charles Randall, Ian Collier, Michael Storm, Lance Henrickson. *SYN:* Arab terrorists hire an international hit lady (Sharpe) to kill a United Nations representative to Saudi Arabia (Connery), who is attempting to arrange a peace settlement with the Israelis. *NOTES:* Action takes place in New York, Bavaria, Germany, London, and Morocco. Released on video with the above title and also as *Double Hit* and *The Arab Conspiracy.*

277. Night Encounter (12/28/62) B&W – 80 mins. (Spy-Drama). *DIR/PRO:* Robert Hossein. *SP:* Robert Hossein, Louis Martin, Alain Poire. Story by Robert Hossein. A SNE Gaumont–Film Constellazione Production. *CAST:* Robert Hossein, Marina Vlady, Robert Le Beal, Roger Crouzet, Clement Harari, George Vitaly, Michel Etcheverry. *SYN:* During World War II, two spies (Hossein, Vlady) cross paths and neither knows whether the other is a double agent or not. *NOTES:* Briefly released in some areas by Allied Artists. Released by Shawn International Films in 1963. [Original French title: *La Nuit des Espions.*] [Original Italian title: *La Notte della Spie.*] [TV title: *The Double Agents.*]

278. Night Freight (8/28/55) B&W – 79 mins. (Drama). *DIR:* Jean Yarbrough. *PRO:* Ace Herman. *SP:* Steve Fisher. A William F. Broidy Production. *CAST:* Forrest Tucker, Barbara Britton, Keith Larsen, Thomas Gomez, Michael Ross, Myrna Dell, Lewis Martin, G. Pat Collins, Sam Flint, Ralph Sanford, Joe Kirk, Jim Alexander, Charles Fredericks, Guy Rennie, Michael Dale. *SYN:* Two brothers (Tucker, Larsen) who own a short line railroad, fight a trucking operator (Gomez) who wants to put them out of business.

Night Legs *see* **Fright (142)**

279. Nightmare Castle (7/5/66) B&W – 90 mins. (Horror–Science Fiction). *DIR:* Mario Caiano (Allen Grunewald). *PRO:* Carlo Caiano. *SP:* Mario Caiano, Fabio de Agostini. A Produzione Cinematografica Emmeci Production. *CAST:* Barbara Steele, Paul Miller, Helga Line, Lawrence Clift, Rik Battaglia, John McDouglas (Giuseppe Addobbati). *SYN:* A scientist (Miller) kills his wife (Steele) and her lover (Battaglia) and places their hearts in an urn. He uses their blood to rejuvenate his faithful and aged servant (Line), making her youthful again. When he marries the wife's sister (Steele) to get her fortune, her doctor (Clift) sees through the scheme, and breaks the urn, releasing the ghosts of the wife and lover who seek their revenge on the scientist and servant. *NOTES:* Barbara Steele plays a dual role in this film. [Original Italian Title: *Amanti D'Oltretomba.*] [British title: *Night of the Doomed.*]

280. No Place for Jennifer (3/30/51) B&W – 90 mins. (Drama). *DIR:* Henry Cass. *PRO:* Hamilton G. Inglis. *SP:* J. Lee Thompson. Based on *No Difference to Me* by Phyllis Hambledon. An Associated British Picture Production. A Stratford Picture Presentation. *CAST:* Leo Genn, Rosamund John, Beatrice Campbell, Guy Middleton, Janette Scott, Anthony Nicholls, Jean Cadell, Megs Jenkins, Edith Sharpe, Ann Codrington, Brian Smith, Andre Morell, Macdonald Hobley, Harold Scott. *SYN:* A young girl (Janette Scott), nearly driven to suicide by her parents (Genn, Campbell) when they divorce and remarry, runs away and finds happiness with a caring couple. *NOTES:* Released in Great Britain in 1949.

281. No Place to Hide (8/28/56) DeLuxe Color – 71 mins. (Drama). *DIR/PRO:* Josef Shaftel. *SP:* Norman Corwin. Story by Josef Shaftel. A Shaftel–LVN Pictures Production. *CAST:* David Brian, Marsha Hunt, Hugh Corcoran, Ike Jarlego, Jr., Celia Flor, Eddie Infante, Manuelk Silos, Lou Salvador, Pianing

Vidal, Alfonzo Carvajal, Vicenta Advincula. *SYN:* An American doctor (Brian) in the Philippines frantically searches through the streets of Manila for his son (Corcoran), who has in his possession deadly virus capsules that he had mistaken for marbles.

282. No Room at the Inn (1/10/50) B&W – 83 mins. (Drama). *DIR:* Dan Birt. *PRO:* Ivan Foxwell. *SP:* Ivan Foxwell, Dylan Thomas. Based on the play by Joan Temple. A British National–Pathé Production. A Stratford Picture Presentation. *CAST:* Freda Jackson, Joy Shelton, Hermione Baddeley, Joan Dowling, Harcourt Williams, Niall McGinnis, Sydney Tafler, Ann Stephens, Frank Pettingell, Robin Netscher, Betty Blacker, Jill Gibbs, Wylie Watson, Beatrice Varley, Cyril Smith, Dora Bryan. *SYN:* Wartime evacuee children and orphans suffer in the hands of an alcoholic landlady (Jackson) who denies them their basic comforts and treats them like filth. *NOTES:* Released in Great Britain in 1948.

283. Northern Patrol (7/12/53) B&W – 63 mins. (Western). *DIR:* Rex Bailey. *PRO:* Lindsley Parsons. *SP:* Warren Douglas. Based on *Nomads of the North: A Story of Romance and Adventure Under the Open Stars* by James Oliver Curwood. *CAST:* Kirby Grant, Marian Carr, Emmett Lynn, William Phipps, Claudia Drake, Frank Sully, Dale Van Sickel, Gloria Talbott, Richard Walsh, Frank Lackteen, "Chinook" the dog. *SYN:* A Mountie (Grant) finds the body of a dead trapper and uncovers a plot by a gang of crooks planning to plunder an Indian burial ground for buried treasure.

284. Not of This Earth (2/10/57) B&W – 67 mins. (Horror). *DIR/PRO:* Roger Corman. *SP:* Charles B. Griffith, Mark Hanna. A Los Altos Production. *CAST:* Paul Birch, Beverly Garland, Morgan Jones, William Roerick, Jonathan Haze, Dick Miller, Anne Carroll, Tamar Cooper, Roy Engel, Pat Flynn, Gail Ganley, Ralph Reed, Harold Fong. *SYN:* A vampire alien (Birch) arrives on Earth in search of blood for himself and his planet. He "matter-transforms" humans back to his planet to be drained of blood while he remains on Earth. Eventually he is discovered and killed, but another alien arrives to take his place. *NOTES:* Released in Italy as *Il Vampiro del Planeta Rosso.* Double billed in some areas with *Attack of the Crab Monsters.* Remade in 1988 by Concorde Films.

285. Now and Forever (6/21/58) Technicolor – 91 mins. (Romance). *DIR/PRO:* Mario Zampi. *SP:* R.F. Delderfield, Michael Pertwee. Based on the play *The Orchard Walls* by R.F. Delderfield. An Associated British Pathé–Anglofilm Production. A Stratford Picture Presentation. *CAST:* Janette Scott, Vernon Gray, Kay Walsh, Jack Warner, Pamela Brown, David Kossoff, Wilfrid Lawson, Ronald Squire, Sonia Dresdel, Guy Middleton, Charles Victor, Marjorie Rhodes, Bryan Forbes, Michael Pertwee. *SYN:* Two teenagers (Scott, Gray) fall in love and wish to get married but their parents object. When she fails to commit suicide, they try to elope but are stopped by the police at the Scottish border. Seeing that they are truly in love, their parents consent to the marriage. *NOTES:* Released in Great Britain in 1956. Janette Scott's first adult role after a career as a child star in Britain.

286. Oh! Those Most Secret Agents (3/25/66) Eastmancolor – 83 mins. (Comedy). *DIR:* Lucio Fulci. *PRO:* Antonio Colantuoni. *SP:* Lucio Fulci, Vittorio Metz, Amedeo Sollazzo, Mario Guerra, Vittorio Vighi. Story by Vittorio Metz. A Mega Film–Sherpix Production. *CAST:* Franco Franchi, Ciccio Ingrassia, Ingrid Schoeller, Aroldo Tieri, Anne Gorassini, Carla Calo, Poldo Bendandi, Luca Sportelli, Enzo Andronico, Nando

Angelini, Connie Jorgenson, Francesco Torrisi. *SYN:* A pair of thieves (Franchi, Ingrassia), who have in their possession a formula for a secret weapon, get mistaken for spies and are chased all over the French Riviera by agents from around the world. *NOTES:* Released in Italy in 1964 at a running time of 90 mins. Released in 1965 by Sherpix Pictures as *00-2 Most Secret Agents.* [Original Italian title: *002 Agenti Segretissimi.*]

287. The Oklahoman (5/19/57) DeLuxe Color/Scope – 81 mins. (Western). *DIR:* Francis D. Lyon. *PRO:* Walter Mirisch. *SP:* Daniel B. Ullman. *CAST:* Joel McCrea, Barbara Hale, Brad Dexter, Gloria Talbott, Michael Pate, Verna Felton, Douglas Dick, Anthony Caruso, Esther Dale, Adam Williams, Ray Teal, Peter Votrian, John Pickard, Diane Brewster, Sheb Wooley, Harry Lauter, Mimi Gibson, I. Stanford Jolley, Don Marlowe, Robert Hinkle, Doris Kemper, Dorothy Neumann, Gertrude Astor, Wheaton Chambers, Earle Hodgins, Rankin Mansfield, Laurie Mitchell, Jennifer Lea, Scotty Beckett, Al Kramer, Kermit Maynard, Bill Foster. *SYN:* A doctor (McCrea) comes to the aid of an Indian (Pate) when he is cheated out of his land by a couple of cattle barons (Dexter, Dick).

O'Leary Night *see* **Tonight's the Night**

288. Once Upon an Island (6/15/66) Eastmancolor – 95 mins. (Comedy). *DIR:* Gabriel Axel. *PRO:* John Hilbard. *SP:* Gabriel Axel, Robert Ramsing. Based on *Det Tossede Paradis* by Ole Juul. A Palladium Production. *CAST:* Dirch Passer, Hans W. Petersen, Ghita Norby, Paul Hagen, Bodil Steen, Karl Stegger, Lone Hertz. *SYN:* When the Danish island of Trang declares its independence from Denmark, the foreign minister (Steen) is sent to investigate. She falls under the spell of the island's patriarch (Petersen) who eats aphrodisiac eggs to maintain his virility. He returns with her to the mainland leaving his son (Passer) to carry on as patriarch of the island. *NOTES:* Limited theatrical release. In Danish with English subtitles. Opened in Copenhagen in 1962 at a running time of 104 mins. Released in 1965 by Sherpix Pictures as *Crazy Paradise.* [Original Danish title: *Det Tossede Paradis.*]

289. Operation C.I.A. (9/8/65) B&W – 90 mins. (Spy-Action). *DIR:* Christian Nyby. *PRO:* Peer J. Oppenheimer. *SP:* Peer J. Oppenheimer, Bill S. Ballinger. Story by Peer J. Oppenheimer. A Hei-Ra-Matt–Peer J. Oppenheimer Production. *CAST:* Burt Reynolds, Kieu Chinh, Danielle Aubry, John Hoyt, Cyril Collick, Victor Diaz, William Catching, Marsh Thomson, Frank Estes, John Laughinghouse, Michael Schwiner, Robert Gulbranson, Janet Russell. *SYN:* A C.I.A. agent (Reynolds), sent to Saigon to investigate the death of a fellow agent, learns from his contact (Chinh) that terrorists plan to assassinate the American ambassador. *NOTES:* Working title was *Last Message from Saigon.*

290. Operation Eichmann (3/15/61) B&W – 92 mins. (Spy-Drama). *DIR:* R.G. Springsteen. *PRO:* Samuel Bischoff, David Diamond. *SP:* Lewis Copley. A Bischoff-Diamond Production. *CAST:* Werner Klemperer, Ruta Lee, Donald Buka, Barbara Turner, John Banner, Hanna Landy, Lester Fletcher, Steve Gravers, Jim Baird, Debbie Cannon, Jackie Russo, Paul Thierry, Rodolfo Hoyos, Norbert Schiller, Luis Van Rooten, Oscar Beregi, Jr., Theo Marcuse, Otto Reichow, Walter Linden, Hans Hermann, Hans Gudegast (Eric (Braeden), Robert Christopher, Carla Lucerne, Austin Green, Robert H. Harris. *SYN:* Two Israeli agents (Buka, Gravers), survivors of the holocaust, are

Advertisement for *Oregon Passage* (1957).

assigned to arrest Adolf Eichmann (Klemperer). They track him from Barcelona to Kuwait and finally Argentina where they kidnap him and take him to Israel to stand trial for his crimes against humanity. *NOTES:* This film was padded with World War II newsreel footage and concentration camp footage. It was released while the real Eichmann was awaiting trial in Israel.

291. Oregon Passage (12/29/57) DeLuxe Color/Scope–82 mins. (Western). *DIR:* Paul Landres. *PRO:* Lindsley Parsons. *SP:* Jack DeWitt. Story by Gordon D. Shirreffs. *CAST:* John Ericson, Lola Albright, Toni Gerry, Edward Platt, Judith Ames, H.M. Wynant, Jon Shepodd, Walter Barnes, Paul Fierro, Harvey Stephens. *SYN:* A cavalry officer (Ericson) incurs the wrath of Shoshone Indian chief, Black Eagle (Wynant), when he raids an Indian camp and rescues his intended bride, Little Deer (Gerry), from a tribal ceremony. *NOTES:* Release date is also given as 1/12/58.

Our Man in Marrakesh *see* **That Man George**

292. Outlaw's Son (12/26/54) B&W–54 mins. (Western). *DIR:* Frank McDonald. *PRO:* Wesley E. Barry. *SP:* Maurice Tombragel. A Newhall Production. *CAST:* Guy Madison, Andy Devine, Anne Kimbell. *SYN:* Compiled from two episodes of the *Wild Bill Hickok* television series: titles unknown.

293. Paddy (4/70) Eastmancolor–97 mins. (Drama). *DIR:* Daniel Haller. *PRO:* Tamara Asseyev. *SP:* Lee Dunne. Based on *Goodbye to the Hill* by Lee Dunne. A Dun Laoghaire Production. *CAST:* Milo O'Shea, Des Cave, Dearbhla Molloy, Maureen Toal, Peggy Cass, Judy Cornwell, Donal LeBlanc, Lillian Rappel, Desmond Perry, Marie O'Donnell, Vincent Smith, Ita Darcy, Dominic Roche, Clive Geraghty, Mary Larkin, Pat Layde, John Kananagh, John Molloy, William Foley, Brendan Dunne, Mary Jo Kennedy, Mark Mulholland. *SYN:* In Ireland, a butcher boy (Cave) helps to support his family, but spends his nights with his pub companion (O'Shea) as they drink and romance the women. He later takes a job as a mail clerk and falls in love with a secretary (Molloy). When she suggests marriage and announces she is pregnant, he refuses to accept his responsibility, quits his job and resumes his carefree life. NOTES: Filmed in Ireland and released there in January, 1970, at a running time of 87 mins.

294. The Pagans (6/1/58) B&W – 80 mins. (Drama). DIR: Ferrucio Cerio. PRO: Mario Francisci. SP: Giuseppe Mangione, Alessandro Ferrau, Mario Francisci. English version directed by Richard Heinz. Dialogue by Joe Weiner. A William M. Pizor Production. CAST: Pierre Cressoy, Helene Remy, Vittorio Sanipoli, Luigi Tosi, Franco Fabrizi, Annamaria Bugliari, Mario Ferrari. SYN: Massimo Colonna (Cressoy), accused of murdering the father of his sweetheart, Angela Orsini (Remy), flees Rome. When the Spanish attack Rome, he returns, helping to repel the invaders and proving himself innocent of the murder of Angela's father. NOTES: Based on the sacking of Rome by Emperor Charles I of Spain in the 16th Century. [Original Italian title: *Il Sacco di Roma*.]

295. Panhandle (2/22/48) Sepiatone – 85 mins. (Western). DIR: Lesley Selander. PRO/SP: John C. Champion, Blake Edwards. CAST: Rod Cameron, Cathy Downs, Reed Hadley, Anne Gwynne, Blake Edwards, Dick Crockett, Rory Mallinson, Charles Judels, Alex Gerry, Francis McDonald, J. Farrell MacDonald, Henry Hall, Stanley Andrews, Jeff York, James Harrison, Charles LaTorre, Frank Dae, Bud Osborne, John C. Champion. SYN: An ex-lawman (Cameron), now a gunfighter, goes after the saloon owner (Hadley) who killed his brother. NOTES: Remade by Lesley Selander and John C. Champion in 1966 for Columbia Pictures as *The Texican*.

296. Papillon (12/73) Technicolor/Panavision – 150 mins. (Biography-Drama). DIR: Franklin J. Schaffner. PRO: Franklin J. Schaffner, Robert Dorfmann. SP: Dalton Trumbo, Lorenzo Semple, Jr. Based on the book by Henri Charriere. A Corona-General Production. CAST: Steve McQueen, Dustin Hoffman, Victor Jory, Don Gordon, Anthony Zerbe, Robert Deman, Woodrow Parfrey, Bill Mumy, George Coulouris, Ratna Assan, William Smithers, Gregory Sierra, Vic Tayback, Barbara Morrison, Allen Moss, Don Hanmer, Dalton Trumbo. SYN: Based on the life of Henri Charriere (McQueen), also known as "Papillon – the butterfly" because of the butterfly tattoo on his chest. In the 1930s, he is sentenced to the penal colony of Cayenne in French Guiana for the crime of murder. He later escapes and lives for awhile with the native Indians until they depart, leaving him alone. He makes his way to civilization and is later recaptured and sent to the "inescapable" Devil's Island, from which he successfully escapes. NOTES: The only film released by Allied Artists in 1973. Originally given a R rating by the MPAA for its extreme violence, Allied Artists argued against the rating and won a PG rating. Henri Charriere died in July, 1973, before filming was complete and never saw the completed epic of his life.

297. Paris Follies of 1956 (11/27/55) DeLuxe Color – 73 mins. (Musical). DIR: Leslie Goodwins. PRO: Bernard Tabakin. SP: Miklos Lazarus. An Ohio Films Incorporated–Mercury International Production. CAST: Forrest Tucker, Margaret Whiting, Dick Wesson, Lloyd Corrigan, Martha Hyer, Barbara Whiting, Walter (Wally) Cassell, Fluff Charlton, James Ferris, Bill Henry, Frank Parker, the Sportsmen. SYN: When a producer (Tucker) decides to open a theatre-restaurant in Hollywood, he suddenly learns that his wealthy backer (Corrigan) is a looney who has no money, so he has to scramble to get the cash to open his theatre-restaurant.

Margaret Whiting and Martha Hyer in *Paris Follies of 1956* (1955).

NOTES: Shot on location at the famed "Moulin Rouge" in Hollywood. [British title: *Showtime*.]

298. Paris Playboys (3/7/54) B&W—65 mins. (Spy-Comedy). *DIR:* William Beaudine. *PRO:* Ben Schwalb. *SP:* Elwood Ullman, Edward Bernds. *CAST:* Leo Gorcey, Huntz Hall, David Condon, Bennie Bartlett, Bernard Gorcey, Veola Vonn, Steven Geray, John E. Wengraf, Fritz Feld, Marianne Lynn, Alphonse Martell, Gordon Clark. *SYN:* Sach (Hall) is mistaken for a French scientist and he, Slip (Leo Gorcey), and Louie (Bernard Gorcey) go to Paris to bring the real scientist out of hiding. While there, Sach invents a rocket formula which spies try to steal, but they are routed by Sach, Slip, and the real scientist (Hall). *NOTES:* Huntz Hall plays a dual role in this film.

299. The Party's Over (3/23/66) B&W—94 mins. (Drama). *DIR:* Guy Hamilton. *PRO:* Anthony Perry. *SP:*

Marc Behm. A Tricastle Films Production. *CAST:* Oliver Reed, Clifford David, Catherine Woodville, Ann Lynn, Louise Sorel, Eddie Albert, Mike Pratt, Maurice Browning, Jonathan Burn, Roddy Maude-Roxby, Annette Robertson, Mildred Mayne, Alison Seebohm, Barbara Lott. *SYN:* An American industrialist (Albert) sends his daughter's (Sorel) fiancé (David) to England to find her and bring her back. When he arrives, he learns that she had joined "The Pack," a group of depraved beatniks, and has since been missing. Later, when the father arrives, they learn from the leader of the beatniks (Reed) that the girl had been killed in an auto accident and they prepare to send her body back home to America. *NOTES:* Executive producers were Jack Hawkins and Jules Buck. Filmed in Great Britain in 1962 but not released there until 1965 due to censorship problems.

300. The Pawnbroker (4/20/65) B&W—114 mins. (Drama). *DIR:* Sidney Lumet. *PRO:* Roger Lewis, Philip Langer. *SP:* David Friedkin, Morton Fine. Based on the book by Edward Lewis Wallant. A Pawnbroker Co. Production. A Landau/Unger Releasing Organization Presentation. *CAST:* Rod Steiger, Geraldine Fitzgerald, Brock Peters, Jaime Sanchez, Thelma Oliver, Marketa Kimbrell, Baruch Lumet, Juano Hernandez, Linda Geiser, Nancy R. Pollack, Raymond St. Jacques, John McCurry, Charles Dierkop, Eusebia Cosme, Warren Finnerty, Jack Adler, E.M. Margolese, Marianne Kanter, Ed Morehouse, Marc Alexander. *SYN:* A Jewish pawnbroker (Steiger) in Harlem lives in a sheltered world with memories of past horrors inflicted on his family by the Nazis. He refuses to be friends with anyone, including his assistant (Sanchez) and a social worker (Fitzgerald). When his assistant takes a bullet meant for him in an attempted holdup, he finally shows some tenderness as the boy dies. In frustration, he impales his hand on the metal receipt spindle and wanders into the street. *NOTES:* This film, originally released by Allied Artists, was later released by American International. Filmed on location in New York City. Controversy surrounded this film from the moment of its release; Jewish groups felt it was anti–Semitic; black groups hated the portrayal of Brock Peters as a gangster; and the Catholic Legion of Decency condemned the movie because of a scene in which Thelma Oliver bared her breasts.

301. Pay or Die (7/27/60) B&W—111 mins. (Crime-Drama). *DIR/PRO:* Richard Wilson. *SP:* Richard Collins, Bertram Millhauser. Based on *Pay Off in Sicily* by Burnett Hershey and the life of Lt. Joseph Petrosino. *CAST:* Ernest Borgnine, Zohra Lampert, Alan Austin, Renata Vanni, Bruno Della Santina, Franco Corsaro, Robert F. Simon, Robert Ellenstein, Howard Caine, John Duke, John Marley, Mario Siletti, Mimi Doyle, Mary Carver, Paul Birch, Vito Scotti, Nick Pawl, Vincent Barbi, Sherry Alberoni, Sal Armetta, Carlo Tricoli, Bart Bradley, Joseph D. Sargent, Sam Capuano, Judy Strangis, David Poleri (voice). *SYN:* Based on true incidents in the life of Lt. Joseph Petrosino (Borgnine), who with his band of loyal officers set about to reduce Mafia crimes in New York's Little Italy between 1906 and 1909. When he travels to Palermo, Sicily, to obtain evidence against the Mafia, he is assassinated by unknown killers. *NOTES:* The film debut of Zohra Lambert. This film was very reminiscent of the 1950 MGM film, *The Black Hand.*

302. Payroll (5/20/62) B&W—94 mins. (Crime). *DIR:* Sidney Hayers. *PRO:* Norman Priggen. *SP:* George Baxt. Based on the book by Derek Bickerton. A Lynx Films–Independent Artists Production. *CAST:* Michael Craig, Françoise

Prevost, Billie Whitelaw, William Lucas, Kenneth Griffith, Tom Bell, Barry Keegan, Edward Cast, Andrew Faulds, William Peacock, Glyn Houston, Joan Rice, Vanda Godsell, Stanley Meadows, Brian McDermott, Hugh Morton, Keith Faulkner, Bruce Beeby, Murray Evans, Kevin Bennett. *SYN:* When a gang member is killed during a payroll robbery, his wife (Whitelaw) goes after the inside man (Lucas) on the job by threatening him with anonymous letters and phone calls in an attempt to get at the gang's leader (Craig). She eventually locates him and exacts her revenge. *NOTES:* Also released at a running time of 80 mins. Released in Great Britain in 1961 at a running time of 105 mins. Working title was *I Promise to Pay.*

303. The Persuader (5/5/57) B&W – 72 mins. (Western). *DIR/PRO:* Dick Ross. *SP:* Curtis Kenyon, Dick Ross. A World Wide Pictures Production. *CAST:* William Talman, James Craig, Kristine Miller, Darryl Hickman, Georgia Lee, Alvy Moore, Rhoda Williams, Gregory Walcott, Paul Engle, Jason Johnson, Nolan Leary, John Milford, Frank Richards, Joyce Compton, Leilani Sorenson, Wendy Stuart. *SYN:* When a preacher (Talman) learns that his brother was killed by a town boss (Craig), he uses the word of the Lord to spur the townspeople to stand up to the boss and bring him to justice.

304. Phantom Trails (5/8/55) B&W – 54 mins. (Western). *DIR:* Frank McDonald. *PRO:* Wesley E. Barry. A Newhall Production. *CAST:* Guy Madison, Andy Devine. *SYN:* Compiled from two episodes of the *Wild Bill Hickok* television series: titles unknown.

305. The Phenix City Story (8/14/55) B&W – 100 mins. (Crime). *DIR:* Phil Karlson. *PRO:* Samuel Bischoff, David Diamond. *SP:* Crane Wilbur, Daniel Mainwaring. Documented in Phenix City by Crane Wilbur. A Bischoff Enterprises Production. *CAST:* John McIntire, Richard Kiley, Kathryn Grant, Edward Andrews, Lenka Peterson, Biff McGuire, Truman Smith, Jean Carson, Meg Myles, Katherine Marlow, John Larch, Allen Nourse, James Edwards, Helen Martin, Otto Hulett, George Mitchell, James Ed Seymour, Ma Beachie. *SYN:* Albert Patterson (McIntire), district attorney of Phenix City, Alabama, and candidate for attorney general of Alabama, is murdered in his fight to clean up "the wickedest city in the U.S." His son, John (Kiley), accepts the post of attorney general and begins his fight to clean up Phenix City. *NOTES:* Theatre exhibitors had the option of showing a thirteen minute prologue featuring Clete Roberts interviewing citizens of Phenix City, Alabama, including James Ed Seymour and Ma Beachie, who were associated with this story and the principals. Many exhibitors chose to run the film without the prologue.

Philosophy of the Bedroom *see* **Beyond Love and Evil**

Phoenix City Story *see* **The Phenix City Story**

Pie in the Sky *see* **Terror in the City**

306. Play It Cool (5/29/63) B&W – 74 mins. (Drama-Musical). *DIR:* Michael Winner. *PRO:* Leslie Parkyn, Julian Wintle. *SP:* Jack Henry. An Independent Artists–Coronado–Lynx Films Production. *CAST:* Billy Fury, Michael Anderson, Jr., Dennis Price, Richard Wattis, Anna Palk, Keith Hamshere, Ray Brooks, Jeremy Bulloch, Maurice Kaufmann, Peter Barkworth, Max Bacon, Felicity Young, Bernie Winters, Monty Landis, Helen Shapiro, Bobby Vee, Danny Williams, Shane Fenton and the Fentones, Jimmy Crawford, Lionel Blair and His Dancers. *SYN:* Stranded in London when fog grounds her plane, a girl (Palk) takes a nightclub tour of the city with a rock idol (Fury) and his band. *NOTES:* Released in Great Britain in 1962 at a running time of 82 mins. This film provides a glimpse of pre-Beatlemania English pop rock stars.

307. The Plunderers (11/15/60) B&W – 94 mins. (Western). *DIR/PRO:* Joseph Pevney. *SP:* Bob Barbash. An August Productions Picture. *CAST:* Jeff Chandler, John Saxon, Dolores Hart, Marsha Hunt, Ray Stricklyn, J.C. Flippen, James Westerfield, Dee Pollack, Roger Torrey, Harvey Stephens, Vaughn Taylor, Joseph Hamilton, Ray Ferrell, William Challee, Kenneth Patterson, Ella Ethridge. *SYN:* A one-armed Civil War veteran (Chandler) stands up to a quartet of hoodlums (Saxon, Stricklyn, Pollack, Torrey) as they take over a town. *NOTES:* Executive producer was Scott R. Dunlap. This film has been likened to 1954 Columbia film *The Wild One*, but with a western setting.

308. Port of Hell (12/5/54) B&W – 80 mins. (Spy-Drama). *DIR:* Harold Schuster. *PRO:* William F. Broidy, A. Robert Nunes. *SP:* Thomas G. Hubbard, Gil Doud, Fred Eggers. Story by Gil Doud, D.D. Beauchamp. *CAST:* Dane Clark, Carole Mathews, Wayne Morris, Marshall Thompson, Harold Peary, Marjorie Lord, Otto Waldis, Thomas G. Hubbard, Charles Fredericks, Jim Alexander, Victor Sen Yung, Gene Roth. *SYN:* A Los Angeles Harbor port warden (Clark) and his partner (Thompson) set out to stop enemy agents from detonating an atomic bomb on a freighter docked there.

309. Portland Exposé (8/11/57) B&W – 72 mins. (Crime). *DIR:* Harold Schuster. *PRO:* Lindsley Parsons. *SP:* Jack DeWitt. Based on *Portland Exposé* by Bernard Victor Dryer. *CAST:* Edward Binns, Carolyn Craig, Virginia Gregg, Russ Conway, Lawrence Dobkin, Frank Gorshin, Joe Marr, Rusty Lane, Dickie Bellis, Lea Penman, Jeanne Carmen, Stanley Farrar, Larry Thor, Francis De Sales, Kort Falkenberg, Joe Flynn. *SYN:* In Portland, Oregon, a saloon keeper (Binns), forced by gangsters to let the syndicate use his establishment, becomes an undercover agent for a citizen's organization trying to clean up the town. *NOTES:* Based on true events that occurred in Portland, Oregon.

310. Portrait of Clare (6/24/51) B&W – 98 mins. (Drama). *DIR:* Lance Comfort. *PRO:* Leslie L. Landau. *SP:* Leslie L. Landau, Adrian Arlington. Based on the book by Francis Brett Young. An Associated British Picture Production. A Stratford Picture Presentation. *CAST:* Margaret Johnston, Richard Todd, Robin Bailey, Ronald Howard, Mary Clare, Marjorie Fielding, Anthony Nicholls, Lloyd Pearson, Bruce Seton, Jeremy Spenser, Campbell Copelin. *SYN:* Told in flashback, an old woman (Johnson) tells her granddaughter the story of her love life to save the girl from making a mistake in marrying the wrong man. *NOTES:* Released in Great Britain in 1950.

311. Portraits of Women (12/70) Eastmancolor – 90 mins. (Comedy). *DIR/SP:* Jorn Donner. *PRO:* Arno Carlstedt. An FJ-Filmi-Jorn Donner Production. *CAST:* Ritva Vepsa, Kirsti Wallasvaara, Marianne Holmstrom, Jorn Donner, Aarre Elo, Henrik Grano, Jaakko Talaskivi, Lennart Laurama, Helena Makela, Jukka Sipila, Heli Sakki, Hannu Oravisto. *SYN:* A pornographic film director (Donner) returns home to his native Finland and while there is persuaded to make a Finnish pornographic film. When he learns that a warrant has been issued for his arrest on obscenity charges, he flees Finland, pursued by his lover (Vepsa). *NOTES:* Limited theatrical

Huntz Hall, Joyce Holden and Leo Gorcey in *Private Eyes* (1953). (Photo courtesy of Scott MacGillivray.)

release. Released in Finland in early 1970. Another of the "soft core" X-rated features distributed by Allied Artists in the seventies. [Original Finnish title: *Naisenkuvia*.]

312. Pride of the Blue Grass (4/4/54) Color—71 mins. (Drama). *DIR:* William Beaudine. *PRO:* Hayes Goetz. *SP:* Harold Shumate. *CAST:* Lloyd Bridges, Vera Miles, Margaret Sheridan, Arthur Shields, Michael Chapin, Harry Cheshire, Cecil Weston, Emory Parnell, Joan Shawlee, Ray Walker. *SYN:* A woman (Miles) refuses to let her horse be destroyed after it breaks a leg. She nurses the horse back to health and eventually enters it in the championship race, which it wins. *NOTES:* Filmed in color by Color Corp. of America. [British title: *Prince of the Blue Grass*.]

Prisoner of the Skull see **Who?**

313. Private Eyes (12/6/53) B&W —64 mins. (Comedy). *DIR:* Edward Bernds. *PRO:* Ben Schwalb. *SP:* Elwood Ullman, Edward Bernds. *CAST:* Leo Gorcey, Huntz Hall, David Condon, Bennie Bartlett, Bernard Gorcey, Rudy Lee, Joyce Holden, Robert Osterloh, William Forrest, Peter Mamakos, Myron Healey, Tim Ryan, Lou Lubin, Emil Sitka, William "Bill" Phillips, Gil Perkins, Edith Leslie, Chick Chandler, Lee Van Cleef. *SYN:* The Bowery Boys open a detective agency when it is learned that after a punch in the nose, Sach (Hall) can read minds. They get involved in a mink coat theft racket when a woman (Holden) gives them evidence against the gang. *NOTES:* Working title was *Bowery Bloodhounds*.

Feature Films 107

Advertisement for *Quantrill's Raiders* (1958).

314. The Purple Gang (1/5/60) B&W −85 mins. (Crime). *DIR:* Frank McDonald. *PRO:* Lindsley Parsons. *SP:* Jack DeWitt. *CAST:* Barry Sullivan, Robert Blake, Elaine Edwards, Marc Cavell, Jody Lawrance, Susy Marquette, Joseph Turkel, Victor Creatore, Paul Dubov, Kathleen Lockhart, Nestor Paiva, Lou Krugman, Mauritz Hugo, Norman Nazarr, John Indrisano, Dirk London, Don Haggerty, George Baxter, Michael Vallon, Ella Ethridge, Craig Fox, Allen Windsor, Ralph Sanford, Walter Maslow, Cecil Watson, Paul McGuire, David Tomack, Dan Easton, John Close. Prologue narrated by Congressman James Roosevelt. *SYN:* In Detroit during the Prohibition, a policeman (Sullivan), who has had enough of juvenile delinquents, goes after the leader (Blake) of the "Purple Gang," a group of young murderous bootleggers. *NOTES:* Loosely based on events surrounding the activities of the real "Purple Gang" that plagued Detroit during the Prohibition.

315. Quantrill's Raiders (4/27/58) DeLuxe Color/Scope −71 mins. (Western). *DIR:* Edward Bernds. *PRO:* Ben Schwalb. *SP:* Polly James. *CAST:* Steve Cochran, Diane Brewster, Leo Gordon, Gale Robbins, Will Wright, Kim Charney, Myron Healey, Robert Foulk, Glenn Strange, Lane Chandler, Guy Prescott, Thomas Browne Henry, Dan M. White, Robert Colbert. *SYN:* A Confederate officer (Cochran) enlists the aid of Quantrill (Gordon) to raid the Union arsenal at Lawrence, Kansas, for the ammunition store there. When the Union Army moves the ammunition from the arsenal, the officer tries to stop Quantrill by alerting the townspeople, and in the ensuing raid, Quantrill is killed. *NOTES:* This film is historically inaccurate in every detail. Quantrill was denounced by the South long before the Lawrence raid and they would not have enlisted his aid. Quantrill did not lead a small band of men as depicted in the film, but led a band of 450 men and destroyed the town of Lawrence. He did not die in the raid but lived to carry on similar activities before his death in 1865.

Advertisement for *Queen of Outer Space* (1958).

Queen of the Gorillas see **The Bride and the Beast**

316. Queen of Outer Space (9/7/58) DeLuxe Color/Scope—80 mins. (Science Fiction). *DIR:* Edward Bernds. *PRO:* Ben Schwalb. *SP:* Charles Beaumont. Story by Ben Hecht. *CAST:* Zsa Zsa Gabor, Eric Fleming, Laurie Mitchell, Paul Birch, Patrick Waltz, Dave Willock, Barbara Darrow, Lisa Davis, Marilyn Buferd, Guy Prescott, Marjorie Durant, Marya Stevens, Colleen Drake, Mary Ford, Brandy Ryan, Lynn Cartwright, Laura Mason, Cathy Marlowe, Tania Velia, Gerry Gaylor, Ralph Gamble, Joi Lansing, John Bleifer, Ruth Lewis, June McCall. *SYN:* Three astronauts (Fleming, Waltz, Willock) and a scientist (Birch), investigating the destruction of several space bases, are transported to Venus where they meet the Queen (Mitchell) of Venus, who wants to destroy Earth. Helped by one of the women (Gabor) who wants peace, the astronauts escape but promise to return. *NOTES:* Sets, costumes, and some of the special effects were from a combination of three films: MGM's *Forbidden Planet*—ray guns, costumes, and forest setting; Monogram's *Flight to Mars*—rocketship; and Allied Artists' *World Without End*—giant spider and sets. Working title was *Queen of the Universe*. Double billed in some areas with *Frankenstein—1970.*

317. The Queen of Spades (9/15/50) B&W—95 mins. (Fantasy-Drama). *DIR:* Thorold Dickenson. *PRO:* Anatole de Grunwald. *SP:* Rodney Ackland, Arthur Boys. Based on the short story by Alexander Pushkin. An Associated British Picture–World Screenplays Production. A Stratford Picture Presentation. *CAST:* Anton Walbrook, Edith Evans, Ronald Howard, Yvonne Mitchell, Anthony Dawson, Pauline Tennant, Miles Malleson, Athene Seyler, Michael Medwin, Ivor Barnard, Yusef Ramart, Valentine Dyall, Gibb McLaughlin. *SYN:* An impoverished Russian officer (Walbrook) tries to wrest from an aging countess (Evans) the secret of winning at cards, a secret for which she had sold her soul. He eventually sneaks into her house one night and accidently frightens her to death. That night he dreams he has the secret of winning. When he goes to gamble with his chief rival, he waits for the winning card, an ace, but when he turns it over, it is the Queen of Spades with the face of the countess grinning at him. *NOTES:* Released in Great Britain in 1948. This story has been filmed a number of times, including at least eight silent versions, this version, a French version, and a Russian operatic version.

Advertisement for *Racing Fever* (1964).

318. Racing Fever (10/30/64) Eastmancolor—80 mins. (Action). *DIR/PRO/SP:* William Grefe. A Racing Fever Production. *CAST:* Joe Morrison, Charles G. Martin, Barbara Biggart, Maxine Carroll, Dave Blanchard, Ruth Nadel, John Vella, Martha Coastworth, Ross Stone, Ben Hawkins, Perry Mavrelis, Patty Morrison. *SYN:* A hydroplane racer (Morrison) sees his father killed by a rival racer (Martin), a millionaire playboy. Learning from his sister (Carroll) who is the playboy's mistress and where he lives, he goes to confront him, and while there, meets the daughter (Biggart) and they fall in love. Later, when he saves the millionaire's life in another racing accident, the sister shoots him because of his unfaithfulness. *NOTES:* Premiered in Miami, Florida, in October 1964, at a running time of 90 mins.

319. Rampart of Desire (1/74) Eastmancolor—90 mins. (Drama). *DIR:* Guy Casaril. *PRO:* Robert Hakim, Raymond Hakim. *SP:* Guy Casaril, Françoise Mallet-Joris. Based on *Le Rempart des Béguines* by Françoise Mallet-Joris. A Paris Film Production. *CAST:* Nicole Courcel, Anicee Alvina, Vanentino Venantini, Jean Martin, Harry-Max, Ginette Leclerc, Yvonne Clech. *SYN:* A lonely young girl (Alvina), neglected by her father (Venantini), seeks solace and love from her new stepmother (Courcel). *NOTES:* Limited theatrical release. Released in France in 1972. Another of the "soft core" X-rated features distributed by Allied Artists in the seventies. Also released in 1973 under the titles *Their Gentle Sex* and *The Wild Girl*. [Original French title: *Le Rempart des Béguines*.]

320. The Rawhide Trail (1/26/58) B&W—67 mins. (Western). *DIR:* Robert Gordon. *PRO:* Earle Lyon. *SP:* Alexander J. Wells. A Terry and Lyon Production. *CAST:* Rex (Rhodes) Reason, Nancy Gates, Richard Erdman, Rusty Lane, Frank Chase, Ann Doran, Robert Knapp, Sam Buffington, Jana Davi, Richard Warren, William Murphy, Al Wyatt, John Dierkes, Richard Geary, Chet Sampson. *SYN:* Two men (Reason, Erdman) suspected of leading settlers into an Indian ambush await hanging at a fort under attack by Indians.

321. Raymie (7/5/60) B&W—72 mins. (Drama). *DIR:* Frank McDonald. *PRO:* A.C. Lyles. *SP:* Mark Hanna. *CAST:* David Ladd, Julie Adams, John Agar, Charles Winninger, Richard Arlen, Frank Ferguson, Ray Kellogg, John Damler, Jester Hairston, Vincent Padula, Ida Smeraldo, Christy Lynn, Brent Wolfson, Shirley Garner, Marianne Gaba, Leslie Glenn, Doak Roberts, Vance Skarstedt. *SYN:* A young boy (Ladd) competes with seasoned veteran fishermen to catch a legendary giant barracuda. *NOTES:* David Ladd is the son of Alan Ladd. Jerry Lewis sings the title song.

322. Rebel City (5/10/53) Sepiatone —62 mins. (Western). *DIR:* Thomas Carr. *PRO:* Vincent M. Fennelly. *SP:* Sid Theil. A Silvermine Production. *CAST:* "Wild" Bill Elliott, Marjorie Lord, Robert E. Kent, Ray Walker, Henry Rowland, Keith Richards, I. Stanford Jolley, Denver Pyle, Otto Waldis, John Crawford, Stanley Price, Michael Vallon, Bill Walker, Pierce Lyden, Gregg Barton. *SYN:* In 1864, a professional gambler (Elliott) returns to the town of Junction City, Kansas, to locate the murderer of his father. He learns that the Copperheads were responsible for his father's death and that a Union captain is their leader.

323. The Rebel Set (6/28/59) B&W—72 mins. (Crime). *DIR:* Gene Fowler, Jr. *PRO:* Earle Lyon. *SP:* Lou Vittes, Bernard Girard. An E. and L. Production. *CAST:* Gregg Palmer, Kathleen Crowley, Edward Platt, John Lupton, Ned Glass, Don Sullivan, Vikki Dougan, I. Stanford Jolley, Robert Shayne, Colette Lyons, Joe "Tiger" Marsh, Gloria Moreland. *SYN:* A coffeehouse owner (Platt) enlists the aid of three cohorts (Palmer, Lupton, Sullivan) when he comes up with a scheme to rob an armored car. *NOTES:* Vikki Dougan became famous in the late fifties for her famous daring, backless dresses; she was known as Vikki "The

John Ericson teaches Mari Blanchard how to shoot in *The Return of Jack Slade* (1955).

Back" Dougan. Double billed in some areas with *Speed Crazy*.

324. The Red Cloak (10/4/61) Eastmancolor–95 mins. (Historical-Drama). *DIR:* Giuseppe Maria Scotese. *PRO:* Elios Vercelloni. *SP:* Giuseppe Maria Scotese, Riccardo Pazzaglia, Albino Principe, Jacopo Corsi, France Roche, Pierre Kast. Story by Albino Principe. A Franca-Centra-Trio-Sefo International Production. *CAST:* Patricia Medina, Bruce Cabot, Fausto Tozzi, Guy Mairesse, Domenico Modugno, Lyla Rocco, Jean Murat, Nyta Dover, Jean François Calve, Jeanne Fusier-Gil. *SYN:* In 1500 Italy, a murdered banker's son (Tozzi) poses as an artist during the day and by night dons a mask and red cloak seeking revenge against the Captain (Cabot) and his men who murdered his father. *NOTES:* Originally filmed in 1955. Released in Italy in 1955 and Paris in 1956 at running times of 102 mins. Limited theatrical release. [Original Italian title: *Il Mantello Rosso.*] [Original French title: *Les Révoltes.*] [Alternate French title: *Le Manteau Rouge.*]

325. Return from the Sea (7/25/54) B&W–79 mins. (War-Drama). *DIR:* Lesley Selander. *PRO:* Scott R. Dunlap. *SP:* George Waggner. Based on *No Home of His Own* by Jacland Marmur. *CAST:* Jan Sterling, Neville Brand, John Doucette, Paul Langton, John Pickard, Don Haggerty, Alvy Moore, Robert Arthur, Lloyd Corrigan, Lee Roberts, Robert Wood, Robert Patten, James Best, John Tarangelo, Bill Gentry, Walter Reed, Harry Landers, Bert Arnold, Nick Stewart, Don MacShane. *SYN:* A sailor (Brand) on leave in San Diego falls in love with a waitress (Sterling). Their wedding plans are put on hold when he returns to action in Korea, but soon they are back together.

326. The Return of Jack Slade (10/9/55) B&W/Scope–79 mins. (Western). *DIR:* Harold Schuster. *PRO:* Lindsley Parsons. *SP:* Warren Douglas. *CAST:* John Ericson, Mari Blanchard, Neville Brand, Casey Adams, Jon Shepodd, Howard Petrie, John Dennis, Angie Dickinson, Donna Drew, Michael Ross, Lyla Graham, Alan Wells, Raymond Bailey. *SYN:* The son (Ericson) of famed gunfighter Jack Slade becomes a lawman to redeem his family name and goes after a gang of outlaws. [British title: *Texas Rose.*]

327. Revolt in the Big House (12/21/58) B&W – 80 mins. (Crime-Drama). *DIR:* R.G. Springsteen. *PRO:* David Diamond. *SP:* Daniel Hyatt, Eugene Lourie. *CAST:* Gene Evans, Robert Blake, Timothy Carey, John Qualen, Sam Edwards, John Dennis, Walter Barnes, Frank Richards, Emile Meyer, Francis De Sales, Ed Gelb. *SYN:* Told in flashback, a hardened criminal, Gannon (Evans), is sent to prison for a long term and he forms an alliance with several other prisoners as they plan a prison break. Gannon then plans to doublecross the other men and escape over the back wall as they stage a riot in front of the prison. He knifes another convict (Blake)

Advertisement for *Revolt in the Big House* (1958).

who intends to inform the other prisoners of his plan. After his escape, Gannon is pursued and eventually gunned down in the subway by police. *NOTES:* This film was shot on location at California's Folsom Prison and uses stock footage from the 1954 Allied Artists film, *Riot in Cell Block 11*; Emile Meyer played a warden in this film and also in *Riot in Cell Block 11*.

328. Rider on a Dead Horse (5/27/62) B&W – 72 mins. (Western). *DIR:* Herbert L. Strock. *PRO:* Kenneth Altrose. *SP:* Stephen Longstreet. Story by James Edmiston. A Phoenix Films Studio Production. *CAST:* John Vivyan, Bruce Gordon, Kevin Hagen, Lisa Lu, Charles Lampkin. *SYN:* A gold prospector (Gordon) kills one of his partners (Lampkin) and leaves the other (Vivyan) wounded and framed for the murder. He is nursed back to health by a Chinese girl (Lu) and is later pursued by a bounty hunter (Hagen), determined to get the gold.

329. Riot in Cell Block 11 (2/28/54) B&W – 80 mins. (Prison-Drama). *DIR:* Don Siegel. *PRO:* Walter Wanger. *SP:* Richard Collins. *CAST:* Neville Brand, Emile Meyer, Frank Faylen, Leo Gordon, Robert Osterloh, Paul Frees, Don Keefer, Alvy Moore, Dabbs Greer, Whit Bissell, James Anderson, Carleton Young, Harold J. Kennedy, William Schallert, Jonathan Hale, William Phipps, Joel Fluellen, Roy Glenn, Joe Kerr, John Tarangelo, Robert Angelo, Frank Hagney. *SYN:* A multiple-sentenced prisoner (Brand) and his psychotic lieutenant (Gordon) lead a group of prisoners as they take eight guards hostage and seize control of a cell block, demanding better prison conditions. *NOTES:* This film was shot on location at California's Folsom Prison.

330. Roar of the Crowd (5/31/53) CineColor – 71 mins. (Action). *DIR:* William Beaudine. *PRO:* Richard Heermance. *SP:* Charles R. Marion. Story by Robert Abel, Charles R. Marion. *CAST:* Howard Duff, Helene Stanley, Dave Willock, Louise Arthur, Harry Shannon, Minor Watson, Don Haggerty, Edna Holland, Ray Walker, Paul Bryar, Duke Nalon, Johnnie Parsons, Henry Banks, Manuel Ayulo, Lucien Littlefield. *SYN:* An auto racing driver (Duff), injured in a racing accident, promises his wife (Stanley) to quit racing after he has one chance at the big race, the Indianapolis 500.

331. Romance of a Horse Thief (8/71) Technicolor – 101 mins. (Drama). *DIR:* Abraham Polonsky. *PRO:* Gene Gutowski. *SP:* David Opatoshu. Story by Joseph Opatoshu. *CAST:* Yul Brynner, Eli Wallach, Jane Birkin, Oliver Tobias, Lainie Kazan, David Opatoshu, Serge Gainsbourg, Henri Sera, Linda Veras, Branko Plesa, Vladimir Bacic, Alenka Rancic, Branko Spolijar, Dina Rutic, Marilu Tolo, Mile Sosa. *SYN:* In 1904, Jewish peasants in a Polish village are ruled by a Cossack captain (Brynner). When an order comes to confiscate all the horses in the village, a young girl (Birkin), who has just returned from France where she learned the politics of revolution, leads the villagers in opposing the Cossacks.

332. Royal African Rifles (9/27/53) CineColor – 75 mins. (Spy-Adventure). *DIR:* Lesley Selander. *PRO:* Richard Heermance. *SP:* Daniel B. Ullman. *CAST:* Louis Hayward, Veronica Hurst, Michael Pate, Angela Greene, Steven Geray, Roy Glenn, Bruce Lester, Barry Bernard, Robert Osterloh, John Warburton, Pat Aherne. *SYN:* During World War I in East Africa, a British naval officer (Hayward) trails a shipment of rifles and machine guns stolen from his ship. [British title: *Storm Over Africa*.]

The Royal Game *see* **Brainwashed**

333. Run for Your Wife (11/15/66) Technicolor/Scope – 97 mins. (Comedy). *DIR:* Gian Luigi Polidoro. *PRO:* Enrico Chroscicki, Alfonso Sansone. *SP:* Rafael Azcona, Ennio Flajano, Gian Luigi Polidoro. Story by Rodolfo Sonego. A Sancro Film–Les Films Borderie Production. *CAST:* Ugo Tognazzi,

Marina Vlady, Rhonda Fleming, Juliet Prowse, Graziella Granata, Carlo Mazzone, Ruth Laney, Sharon Obeck, Robert Hulsh, Gigette Reiner, George Clow, Deanna Lund, Alex Johnson, Soni Compagna, Jamie Wyatt, Nancy McCarter, Michele Weigand. *SYN:* While on a business trip to America, an Italian businessman (Tognazzi) decides to become an American citizen so that he can marry a rich widow and then divorce her for a younger woman. After many escapades and disappointments, he returns to Italy to his fiancée and angry boss. *NOTES:* Released in Italy in 1965 at a running time of 115 mins. Released in France in 1966 at a running time of 90 mins. Filmed on location in Miami, New Orleans, Texas and Cape Kennedy. [Original Italian title: *Una Moglie Americana.*] [Original French title: *Mes Femmes Americaines.*]

334. Sabu and the Magic Ring (11/24/57) DeLuxe Color—61 mins. (Adventure). *DIR:* George Blair. *PRO:* Maurice Duke. *SP:* Sam Roeca, Benedict Freedman, John Fenton Murray. Based on stories from *The Arabian Nights*. *CAST:* Sabu, Daria Massey, Robert Shafto, Peter Mamakos, John Doucette, William Marshall, George Khoury, Vladimir Sokoloff, Robin Morse, Bernard Rich, Kenneth Terrell, John Lomma, Cyril Delevanti. *SYN:* Sabu, with the help of a genie (Marshall) and a magic ring, seeks to rescue an abducted princess (Massey). *NOTES:* Originally an unsold television pilot, this film was re-edited and released to theatres. Television prints are B&W. Sabu's full name was Sabu Dastagir.

335. Safari Drums (6/21/53) B&W —71 mins. (Adventure). *DIR/PRO/SP:* Ford Beebe. Based on characters in the *Bomba* books by Roy Rockwood. *CAST:* Johnny Sheffield, Barbara Bestar, Emory Parnell, Paul Marion, Douglas Kennedy, Leonard Mudie, Robert "Smoki" Whitfield, James Adamson, Carleton Young, Rory Mallinson, Jack Williams, Russ Conway. *SYN:* Bomba (Sheffield) helps to find a murderer among a film crew who has come to Africa to make a wildlife film. [British title: *Bomba and the Safari Drums.*]

336. Screaming Eagles (5/27/56) B&W—80 mins. (War). *DIR:* Charles Haas. *PRO:* Samuel Bischoff, David Diamond. *SP:* David Lang, Robert Presnell, Jr. Story by Virginia Kellogg. *CAST:* Tom Tryon, Jan Merlin, Alvy Moore, Martin Milner, Jacqueline Beer, Joe di Reda, Mark Damon, Paul Burke, Pat Conway, Edward G. Robinson, Jr., Ralph Votrian, Paul Smith, Robert Blake, Robert Roark, Robert Dix, Wayne Taylor, Robert Boon, Peter Michaels. *SYN:* A group of American soldiers parachutes into France in preparation for D-Day and run into resistance fighters and Nazi troops.

337. The Secret Door (3/4/64) B&W—72 mins. (War-Spy). *DIR:* Gilbert L. Kay. *PRO:* Charles Baldour. *SP:* Charles Martin. Based on *Paper Door* by Stephen Longstreet. A Dorton-Fifeshire Production. *CAST:* Robert Hutton, Sandra Dorne, Peter Illing, Peter Allenby, George Pastell, Shirley Lawrence, Bob Gallico, Peter Elliott, Tony Arpino, James Dyrenforth, Chris Lawrence, Martin Benson. Narrated by Joel Aldred. *SYN:* Following the attack on Pearl Harbor, two safecrackers (Hutton, Allenby) are sent to Lisbon by Navy Intelligence to photograph secret documents in the Japanese Embassy. *NOTES:* Working title was *Now It Can Be Told.*

338. Secret of Outlaw Flats (11/15/53) B&W—54 mins. (Western). *DIR:* Frank McDonald. *PRO:* Wesley E. Barry. *SP:* William Raynor. A Newhall Production. *CAST:* Guy Madison, Andy Devine, Kristine Miller, Richard Avonde, Jane Adams, Bobby Jordan, Tristram Coffin, Wade Crosby, John

Feature Films 115

Advertisement for *Serengeti* (1960), also released as *Serengeti Shall Not Die*.

Crawford, Bill Hale, Edward Clark, William Haade, Len Green, Reed Howes. *SYN:* Compiled from two episodes of the *Wild Bill Hickok* television series: "Outlaw Flats" and "Silver Stage Holdup."

Secrets of a Soul *see* **Confessions of an Opium Eater**

339. Security Risk (8/8/54) B&W —69 mins. (Spy-Drama). *DIR:* Harold Schuster. *PRO:* William F. Broidy. *SP:* John Rich, Jo Pagano, Frank McDonald. Story by John Rich. *CAST:* John Ireland, Dorothy Malone, Keith Larsen, Dolores Donlon, John Craven, Suzanne Ta Fel, Joe Bassett, Burt Wenland, Steve Clark, Murray Alper, Harold J. Kennedy. *SYN:* A Federal agent (Ireland), on vacation at Big Bear resort, tracks down Communist spies (Larsen, Donlon) who have murdered an atomic scientist (Craven) and stolen his secret papers.

340. Serengeti (10/12/60) Eastmancolor—84 mins. (Documentary). *DIR:* Michael Grzimek. *PRO/SP:* Michael Grzimek, Dr. Bernhard Grzimek. Based on the book by Michael Grzimek and Dr. Bernhard Grzimek. An Okapia Production. An Asta Motion Picture Presentation. *CAST:* Michael Grzimek, Dr. Bernhard Grzimek. Narrated by Holger Hagen. *SYN:* A documentary showing the great Serengeti Stepps of Africa and the vast roaming herd of wild animals. *NOTES:* Director/producer Michael Grzimek was killed on the final day of production when a vulture flew into his plane, causing it to crash. [Original German title: *Serengeti Darf Nicht Sterben.*]

Serengeti Shall Not Die *see* **Serengeti**

341. The Servant (3/6/64) B&W – 115 mins. (Drama). *DIR:* Joseph Losey. *PRO:* Joseph Losey, Norman Priggen. *SP:* Harold Pinter. Based on the book by Robin Maugham. A Springbok Films Production. A Landau/Unger Releasing Organization Presentation. *CAST:* Dirk Bogarde, Sarah Miles, Wendy Craig, James Fox, Catherine Lacey, Richard Vernon, Ann Firbank, Doris Knox, Patrick Magee, Jill Melford, Alun Owen, Harold Pinter. *SYN:* A manservant (Bogarde), hired by a wealthy, class conscious man (Fox) to take care of his house, uses his dominance to slowly take complete control of his master and the house. *NOTES:* Released in Great Britain in 1963.

342. Seven Angry Men (3/27/55) B&W – 90 mins. (Western). *DIR:* Charles Marquis Warren. *PRO:* Vincent M. Fennelly. *SP:* Daniel B. Ullman. *CAST:* Raymond Massey, Debra Paget, Jeffrey Hunter, Larry Pennell, Leo Gordon, John Smith, James Best, Dennis Weaver, Guy Williams, Tom Irish, James Anderson, James Edwards, John Pickard, Robert "Smoki" Whitfield, Jack Lomas, Robert F. Simon, Dabbs Greer, Robert Osterloh, Ann Tyrrell, Jack Perrin, I. Stanford Jolley, Lane Bradford, Don C. Harvey, Kenneth MacDonald, Carleton Young. *SYN:* John Brown (Massey) and his sons become hunted men as they lead the fight to free the slaves. *NOTES:* Raymond Massey also played the role of "John Brown" in the 1940 Warner Bros. film *Santa Fe Trail*.

343. Seven Guns to Mesa (3/16/58) B&W – 69 mins. (Western). *DIR:* Edward Dein. *PRO:* William F. Broidy. *SP:* Myles Wilder, Edward Dein, Mildred Dein. Story by Myles Wilder. *CAST:* Charles Quinlivan, Lola Albright, James Griffith, Jay Adler, John Cliff, Burt Nelson, John Merrick, Charles Keane, Jack Carr, Don Sullivan, Rush Williams, Neil Grant, Reed Howes, Mauritz Hugo, Gerald Frank, Harvey Russell. *SYN:* Stagecoach passengers are taken prisoner and held hostage by an outlaw gang planning a gold robbery. *NOTES:* Working title was *Seven Guns to Sin Mesa*.

344. Sex Kittens Go to College (8/24/60) B&W – 94 mins. (Comedy). *DIR/PRO:* Albert Zugsmith. *SP:* Robert Hill. Story by Albert Zugsmith. A Photoplay Associates Inc. Production. *CAST:* Mamie Van Doren, Tuesday Weld, Mijanou Bardot, Mickey Shaughnessy, Martin Milner, Pamela Mason, Conway Twitty, Jackie Coogan, Louis Nye, John Carradine, Vampira (Maila Nurmi), Allan Drake, Norman "Woo Woo" Grabowski, Irwin Berke, Babe London, Arlene Hunter, Jody Fair, Buni Bacon, Charles Chaplin, Jr., Harold Lloyd, Jr., Barbara Pepper, Cheerio Meredith, Jose Gonzales-Gonzales, Jack Carr, Noel de Souza, Buddy Douglas, Edwin Randolph, Beverly Englander. *SYN:* Dr. Mathilda West (Van Doren) is selected by the Collins College computerized robot, SAM (Sequential Auxiliary Modulator) THINKO, to head the college science department because of her high I.Q. *NOTES:* Working titles were *Sexpots Go to College* and *Teacher Was a Sexpot*. A special edition of this film was released to theatres specializing in "Adults Only" fare. This version contained nine minutes of extra footage – a dream sequence by the robot involving topless dancers. This sequence was not in the majority of release prints nor the TV version. [TV *titles: The Beauty and the Robot; The Beauty and the Brain.*]

345. Shack Out on 101 (12/4/55) B&W – 80 mins. (Spy-Drama). *DIR:* Edward Dein. *PRO:* Mort Millman. *SP:* Edward Dein, Mildred Dein. A William F. Broidy Pictures Corporation Production.

Martin Milner and Mamie Van Doren in *Sex Kittens Go to College* (1960), released to TV under the titles *Beauty and the Robot* and *Beauty and the Brain*.

CAST: Terry Moore, Frank Lovejoy, Keenan Wynn, Lee Marvin, Whit Bissell, Jess Barker, Donald Murphy, Frank DeKova, Len Lesser, Fred Grabourie. *SYN:* A government agent (Lovejoy), working undercover to crack a spy ring, stops at a roadside diner and learns that one of the people there may be the spy he is after.

346. shinbone alley (3/71) Eastmancolor—86 mins. (Musical-Animated). *DIR:* John D. Wilson. *PRO:* Preston M. Fleet. *SP:* Joe Darion. Based on the *archy and mehitabel* stories by Don Marquis and the musical *shinbone alley* by Joe Darion, Mel Brooks. A Fine Arts Film Production. *CAST:* Voices of Eddie Bracken, Carol Channing, John Carradine, Alan Reed, Ken Sansom, Hal Smith, Joan Gerber, Sal Delano, Jackie Ward Singers. *SYN:* A despondent poet who has committed suicide is reincarnated as archy the cockroach (Bracken). He composes letters and poems on the typewriter (everything is in lower case letters since he cannot use the shift/lock key) of a newspaper columnist to his unrequited love, mehitabel the cat (Channing). *NOTES:* This film was aimed more at adults than at children.

347. Shock Corridor (9/18/63) B&W/Technicolor—100 mins. (Drama). *DIR/PRO/SP:* Samuel Fuller. Based on the scenario *Straitjacket* by Samuel Fuller. A Leon Fromkess–Sam Firks Production. *CAST:* Peter Breck, Constance Towers, Gene Evans, James Best, Hari Rhodes, Larry Tucker, William Zuckert, Philip Ahn, Neyle Morrow, John Matthews, Chuck Roberson, John Craig, Frank Gerstle, Paul Dubov, Rachel

Romen, Linda Randolph, Harry Fleer, Wally Campo, Linda Barnett, Ray Baxter, Barbara Perry, Marlene Manners, Lucille Curtis, Jeanette Dana, Marie Devereux, Karen Conrad, Allyson Daniell, Chuck Hicks. *SYN:* A reporter (Breck) sets out to write the story of his life by solving the killing of an inmate in an insane asylum. With the help of his girl (Towers), he has himself committed in order to interview the three inmates (Evans, Best, Rhodes) who witnessed the killing. He finally learns who the killer is, but with disastrous results. *NOTES:* Working title was *Straitjacket.* Pre-release title was *Long Corridor.* This film has recently been restored with the dream sequences that were edited out on general release.

348. Short Grass (12/24/50) B&W −82 mins. (Western). *DIR:* Lesley Selander. *PRO:* Scott R. Dunlap. *SP:* Tom W. Blackburn. Based on *Range War* by Tom W. Blackburn. *CAST:* Rod Cameron, Cathy Downs, Johnny Mack Brown, Raymond Walburn, Alan Hale, Jr., Morris Ankrum, Jonathan Hale, Harry Woods, Marlo Dwyer, Riley Hill, Jeff York, Stanley Andrews, Jack Ingram, Myron Healey, Tristram Coffin, Rory Mallinson, Felipe Turich, George J. Lewis, Kermit Maynard, Lee Tung Foo. *SYN:* After being forced off his land by a greedy rancher (Ankrum), a drifter (Cameron) returns home after five years and joins forces with the sheriff (Brown) to fight the rancher.

349. Shotgun (4/24/55) Technicolor −81 mins. (Western). *DIR:* Lesley Selander. *PRO:* John C. Champion. *SP:* Clark E. Reynolds, John C. Champion, Rory Calhoun. *CAST:* Sterling Hayden, Yvonne De Carlo, Zachary Scott, Guy Prescott, Robert J. Wilke, Angela Greene, Paul Marion, John Pickard, Ralph Sanford, Rory Mallinson, Fiona Hale, Ward Wood, Lane Chandler, Al Wyatt, Harry Harvey, Robert E. Griffin, Francis McDonald, Peter Coe, Charles Morton, James Parnell, Richard Cutting, Bob Morgan. *SYN:* A sheriff (Hayden), bounty hunter (Scott), and half-breed girl (De Carlo) track a killer (Prescott) and find themselves stalked by Apaches. *NOTES:* Rory Calhoun, who co-wrote the script, was scheduled to star in this film.

350. Silent Dust (1/22/50) B&W − 82 mins. (Crime). *DIR:* Lance Comfort. *PRO:* Nat A. Bronsten. *SP:* Michael Pertwee. Based on the play *The Paragon* by Roland Pertwee and Michael Pertwee. An Associated British Pathé–Independent Sovereign Production. A Stratford Picture Presentation. *CAST:* Sally Gray, Stephen Murray, Derek Farr, Nigel Patrick, Beatrice Campbell, Seymour Hicks, Marie Lohr, Yvonne Owen, James Hayter, Maria Var, Irene Handl. *SYN:* A father (Murray) plans a memorial to his son whom he believes was killed in the war. Before the unveiling is to take place, the son (Patrick) shows up and admits he was a deserter and is involved in blackmail and murder. *NOTES:* Released in Great Britain in 1949.

351. Six-Gun Decision (11/15/53) B&W − 54 mins. (Western). *DIR:* Frank McDonald. *PRO:* Wesley E. Barry. *SP:* William Raynor. A Newhall Production. *CAST:* Guy Madison, Andy Devine, Don Haydon, Gloria Saunders, Peggy Stewart, Fred Kohler, Jr., Lyle Talbot, Zon Murray, Michael Vallon, Parke MacGregor, Fred Hoose, Robert Bice, Tom Steele. *SYN:* Compiled from two episodes of the *Wild Bill Hickok* television series: "Border City Election" and "Pony Express vs. Telegraph."

352. Skabenga (5/29/55) Eastmancolor−61 mins. (Documentary). *DIR:* George Michael. *PRO:* George Michael, Lester A. Sansom. *SP:* Narration written by Edward Bernds. Based on *African Fury* by George Michael. *CAST:* Narrated by Michael Pate. *SYN:* Big game hunter

Feature Films 119

Advertisement for *Ski Fever* (1969).

George Michael encounters the dangers of Africa as he hunts elephants. *NOTES:* Title translates to "Killer Leopard."

353. Ski Fever (3/69) Eastmancolor—98 mins. (Romance-Comedy). *DIR:* Curt Siodmak. *PRO:* Wolfgang Schmidt, Mark Cooper. *SP:* Curt Siodmak, Richard L. Joseph. Story by Frank Agrama, Edward Zatlyn. A Gaumont International–Parnass Film–Ceskoslovensky Film Production. *CAST:* Martin Milner, Claudia Martin, Vivi Bach, Dietmar Schonherr, Toni Sailor, Dorith Dom, Helena Dubova, Lenka Feserova, Rajmund Gabriel, Jana Novakova, Kurt Grosskurth, Curt Bock. *SYN:* An American music student (Milner) in Austria works his way through a European university by teaching skiing at an Austrian resort. He competes with the head instructor (Schonherr) for the affections of an American tourist (Martin) and eventually wins her. *NOTES:* Filmed on location in Austria and released there in 1967 at a running time of 87 mins. Claudia Martin is the daughter of Dean Martin. [Original Austrian title: *Liebesspiele im Schnee.*]

354. Smart Woman (4/30/48) B&W—93 mins. (Drama). *DIR:* Edward A. Blatt. *PRO:* Hal E. Chester. *SP:* Alvah Bessie, Louis Morheim, Herbert Margolis. Adapted by Adela Rogers St. Johns. Story by Leon Gutterman, Edwin V. Westrate. *CAST:* Brian Aherne, Constance Bennett, Barry Sullivan, Michael

O'Shea, James Gleason, Otto Kruger, Isobel Elsom, Richard Lyon, Selena Royle, Taylor Holmes, John Litel, Nita Hunter, Lee Bonnell, Willie Best, Horace McMahon, Benny Baker, Al Bridge, Larry Gaze, Robert Riordan, Phyllis Kennedy, Netta Packer, John Phillips, George Carleton, Paul Bryar, Ralph Sanford, Doris Kemper, Milton Parsons, Margaret Tracy, Iris Adrian, Houseley Stevenson, Joseph Fields, John Eldredge, Frank Mayo, Paul Maxey, Lois Austin, Jimmy Conlin, Edward Gargan, Harry Strang, Charles Lane, Peter Virgo, Stanley Blystone, Cliff Clark. *SYN:* A female lawyer (Bennett) is forced to defend her former husband (Sullivan) when he threatens to harm their child (Lyon), while a special prosecutor (Aherne) attempts to prosecute a corrupt D.A. (Kruger).

355. Snow Treasure (10/4/68) Eastmancolor – 95 mins. (War-Adventure). *DIR/PRO:* Irving Jacoby. *SP:* Irving Jacoby, Peter Hanson. Based on the book by Marie McSwigan. A Sagittarius Production. *CAST:* James Franciscus, Ilona Rodgers, Paul Austad, Raoul Oyen, Randi Borch, Tor Stockke, Wilfred Breistrand. *SYN:* In 1940 Norway, a fourteen-year-old boy (Austad) and his friends, with the help of a sympathetic German officer (Franciscus), plan to smuggle a Nazi hoard of gold out of the country. *NOTES:* Filmed on location in Norway in 1967.

356. Snowfire (7/6/58) Eastmancolor – 73 mins. (Western-Drama). *DIR/PRO/SP:* Dorrell McGowan, Stuart E. McGowan. A Snowfire Production. *CAST:* Don Megowan, Molly McGowan, Claire Kelly, John Cason, Michael Vallon, Melody McGowan, Rusty Westcoatt, Bill Hale, Paul Keast, "Snowfire," the horse. *SYN:* When her father (Megowan) captures a wild stallion, his daughter (Molly McGowan) befriends the horse and persuades her father to let her keep him.

357. Soldier in the Rain (11/27/63) B&W – 87 mins. (Drama-Comedy). *DIR:* Ralph Nelson. *PRO:* Martin Jurow. *SP:* Maurice Richlin, Blake Edwards. Based on the book by William Goldman. A Cedar-Solar Film Production. *CAST:* Steve McQueen, Jackie Gleason, Tuesday Weld, Tony Bill, Tom Poston, Chris Noel, Ed Nelson, Lew Gallo, Rockne Tarkington, Lewis Charles, Sam Flint, Paul Hartman, Adam West, John Hubbard. *SYN:* Supply Sgt. Eustice Clay (McQueen) wants to get out of the Army and start a business enterprise with his friend and role model, M/Sgt. Maxwell Slaughter (Gleason). However, Slaughter is content to stay in the Army since he is living the good life. Later, Slaughter collapses as he saves Clay from being beaten to death by two MPs (Nelson, Gallo). He dies the next day and Clay re-enlists in the Army, possibly as a tribute to his friend.

358. Son of Belle Starr (6/28/53) CineColor – 70 mins. (Western). *DIR:* Frank McDonald. *PRO:* Peter Scully. *SP:* D.D. Beauchamp, William Raynor. Story by Jack DeWitt. *CAST:* Keith Larsen, Dona Drake, Peggie Castle, Regis Toomey, James Seay, Myron Healey, Frank Puglia, Robert Keys, I. Stanford Jolley, Paul McGuire, Lane Bradford, Mike Ragan (Holly Bane), Joe Dominguez, Alex Montoya. *SYN:* Belle Starr's son (Larsen) known as "The Kid," joins in with a crooked sheriff (Healey) to hijack a shipment of gold in order to find the person responsible for setting him up for a crime the year before. In the end, he finally locates him, but his reputation as an outlaw proves his undoing and he is killed while proving his innocence.

359. Song of My Heart (1/31/48) B&W – 85 mins. (Musical). *DIR:* Benjamin Glazer. *PRO:* Nathaniel Finston, J. Theodore Reed. *SP:* Benjamin Glazer, Bernard Schubert. A Symphony Films Incorporated Production. *CAST:* Frank

Sundstrom, Audrey Long, Sir Cedric Hardwicke, Mikhail Rasumny, Gale Sherwood, Serge Krizman, Charles Trowbridge, Kate Lawson, Lester Sharpe, Drew Allen, Scott Elliott, Gordon Clark, Jimmie Dodd, David Leonard, John Hamilton, William Ruhl, Steve Darrell, Robert Barron, Maurice Cass, Elvira Curci, Grandon Rhodes, William Newell, Leonard Mudie, Lane Chandler, Leonid Snegoff, Lewis Howard, Stan Johnson, Leo Kaye, Jack George, Vernon Cansino, Nina Hansen. *SYN:* A fictionalized account of the life of Peter Ilich Tchaikovsky (Sundstrom) as told in flashback. *NOTES:* Pianist Jose Iturbi, who dubbed the piano works, was uncredited.

360. The Sorcerers (1/2/68) Eastmancolor—87 mins. (Horror). *DIR:* Michael Reeves. *PRO:* Patrick Curtis, Tony Tenser. *SP:* Michael Reeves, Tom Baker. Based on an idea by John Burke. A Tigon—Curtwel—Global Production. *CAST:* Boris Karloff, Catherine Lacey, Ian Ogilvy, Elizabeth Ercy, Victor Henry, Susan George, Dani Sheridan, Ivor Dean, Peter Fraser, Meier Tzelniker, Bill Barnsley, Martin Terry, Gerald Champion, Alf Joint. *SYN:* An old couple, Professor Monserrat (Karloff), a retired stage hypnotist, and his wife (Lacey), have created an apparatus producing "psychedelic" light and sound which dominates a person's mind from a distance. They find an irresponsible young man (Ogilvy) to be their subject. As he experiences their commands from a distance, the couple also experience the same sensations as the young man. Eventually the wife takes control from her husband and commands the young man to kill, but the husband manages to gain control of the man's mind and causes him to crash the car he is driving; all three perish in the impact and flames of the crash. *NOTES:* Released in Great Britain in 1967 at a running time of 85 mins.

Souls for Sale *see* **Confessions of an Opium Eater**

361. Southside 1-1000 (11/16/50) B&W—73 mins. (Crime-Drama). *DIR:* Boris Ingster. *PRO:* Maurice King, Frank King. *SP:* Leo Townsend, Boris Ingster. Story by Milton Raison, Bert C. Brown. *CAST:* Don DeFore, Andrea King, George Tobias, Barry Kelley, Morris Ankrum, Robert Osterloh, Charles Cane, Douglas Spencer, William Forrest, Ray Teal, Don Beddoe, Pierre Watkin, Bill Henry, Joseph Turkel, Mickey Simpson, G. Pat Collins, John Harmon, Joseph Crehan, Clancy Cooper, Joan Miller, Paul Bryar, Bennie Bartlett, George J. Lewis, Kippee Valez. *SYN:* When a convict (Ankrum) smuggles counterfeit plates out of prison to a gang of counterfeiters, a treasury agent (DeFore) gets a lead on one of the gang members (Kelley) and trails him until he is murdered by his own gang. The agent then poses as an Eastern kingpin hoping to infiltrate the gang and expose its leader (King). [British title: *Forgery.*]

Space Station X-14 *see* **Mutiny in Outer Space**

362. Speed Crazy (6/28/59) B&W —75 mins. (Crime). *DIR:* William Hole, Jr. *PRO:* Richard Bernstein. *SP:* Richard Bernstein, George Waters. A Viscount Films Production. *CAST:* Brett Halsey, Yvonne Lime, Charles Wilcox, Slick Slavin, Jacqueline Ravell, Keith Byron, Charlotte Fletcher, Jackie Joseph, Vic Marlo, Robert Swan, Mark Sheeler, Troy Patterson, Baynes Barron, Regina Gleason. *SYN:* A murderer and hot rodder (Halsey) gets a job as a mechanic in a small town and becomes involved with the racetrack crowd. *NOTES:* Yvonne Lime's last screen role. Double billed in some areas with *The Rebel Set.*

Spell of the Hypnotist *see* **Fright** (141)

363. Spook Chasers (6/2/57) B&W—62 mins. (Comedy). *DIR:* George Blair. *PRO:* Ben Schwalb. *SP:* Elwood Ullman. *CAST:* Huntz Hall, Stanley Clements, David Gorcey, Jimmy Murphy, Eddie LeRoy, Percy Helton, Darlene Fields, Bill Henry, Peter Mamakos, Ben Welden, Robert Christopher, Robert Shayne, Pierre Watkin, Audrey Conti, Anne Fleming, Bill Cassidy. *SYN:* The Bowery Boys get involved with gangsters and a shady real estate agent (Henry) when they go with Mike Clancy (Helton) to a mountain house he has bought and find a stash of money hidden there.

364. Spy Chasers (7/31/55) B&W—61 mins. (Spy-Comedy). *DIR:* Edward Bernds. *PRO:* Ben Schwalb. *SP:* Bert Lawrence, Jerome S. Gottler. *CAST:* Leo Gorcey, Huntz Hall, David Condon, Bennie Bartlett, Bernard Gorcey, Leon Askin, Veola Vonn, Sig Rumann, Lisa Davis, Frank Richards, Paul Burke, Richard Benedict, Linda Bennett, Mel Welles, John Bleifer. *SYN:* The Bowery Boys help an exiled king (Rumann) and his daughter (Davis) while exposing a couple of traitors (Askin, Vonn).

Advertisement for *Spy Chasers* (1955).

365. Spy in the Sky! (7/20/58) B&W—75 mins. (Spy-Drama). *DIR/PRO:* W. Lee Wilder. *SP:* Myles Wilder. Based on *Counterspy Express* by A.S. Fleischmann. *CAST:* Steve Brodie, Sandra Francis, Andrea Domburg, George Coulouris, Bob DeLange, Hans Tiemeyer, Herbert Curiel, Dity Oorthuis, Leon Dorian, A.E. Collin, E.F. Beavis,

Feature Films 123

Carroll Baker in *Station Six-Sahara* (1963).

Alex Sweers, Harold Horsten, Rob Milton. *SYN:* A U.S. Intelligence agent (Brodie), posing as a newspaperman, helps a German scientist (Tiemeyer) involved in the Russian satellite program escape to the West. *NOTES:* Filmed in Holland.

366. Stampede (8/28/49) Sepiatone-78 mins. (Western). *DIR:* Lesley Selander. *PRO:* Scott R. Dunlap, John C. Champion, Blake Edwards. *SP:* John C. Champion, Blake Edwards. Based on the book by Edward Beverly Mann. *CAST:* Rod Cameron, Johnny Mack Brown, Gale Storm, Don Castle, Donald Curtis, John Miljan, Jonathan Hale, John Eldredge, James Harrison, Ted Elliott, Jack Parker, Chuck Roberson, Carol Henry, Adrian Wood, I. Stanford Jolley, Marshall Reed, Philo McCullough, Charles King, Kenne Duncan, Tim Ryan, Steve Clark, Bob Woodward, Duke York, Artie Artego, Neal Hart, Bud Osborne, Henry Hall, Boyd Stockman, Wes Christenson. *SYN:* Two cattle baron brothers (Cameron, Castle) become involved with homesteaders who are being cheated out of their water rights by two crooks (Curtis, Eldredge).

367. Star of Texas (1/11/53) B&W -68 mins. (Western). *DIR:* Thomas Carr. *PRO:* Vincent M. Fennelly. *SP:* Daniel B. Ullman. Story by Daniel B. Ullman. A Westwood Production. *CAST:* Wayne Morris, Paul Fix, Frank Ferguson, Rick Vallin, Jack Larson, James Flavin, William Fawcett, Robert Bice, Mickey Simpson, George Wallace, John Crawford, Stanley Price, Lyle Talbot, Ray Jones, Jack O'Shea, Pierce Lyden, Frank Ellis. *SYN:* A Texas Ranger (Morris) pretends to be an escaped convict to infiltrate a gang of outlaws who pose as respectable townspeople and free prisoners from jail and then kill them for the reward money. *NOTES:* Remade by Allied Artists in 1957 as *Last of the Badmen* and in 1963 as *Gunfight at Comanche Creek*. Wayne Morris's first B western series entry for Allied Artists. Western sources and film historians credit this film as the first entry in the last B Western series.

368. Station Six-Sahara (8/10/63) B&W-99 mins. (Drama). *DIR:* Seth Holt.

PRO: Victor Lyndon. *SP:* Bryan Forbes, Brian Clemens. Based on the play *Men Without a Past* by Jacques Maret. A CCC-Filmkunst Production. *CAST:* Carroll Baker, Peter Van Eyck, Ian Bannen, Denholm Elliott, Mario Adorf, Biff McGuire, Hansjorg Felmy, Harry Baird. *SYN:* Five love-starved men (Van Eyck, Bannen, Elliott, Adorf, Felmy) working at an isolated oil drilling station in the Sahara Desert suffer from the heat, mutual contempt for each other, and the desire for a woman. Into their lives, via an automobile accident, comes a beautiful woman (Baker) and her ex-husband (McGuire), creating an explosive situation. *NOTES:* Released in Great Britain at a running time of 100 mins. Released in Germany at a running time of 101 mins. A nude sequence of Carroll Baker was cut for U.S. release. [Original German title: *Endstation 13 Sahara.*]

369. Stop Train 349 (7/15/64) B&W – 95 mins. (Drama). *DIR:* Rolf Haedrich. *PRO:* Hans Oppenheimer, Ray Ventura. *SP:* Victor Vicas, Jim Henaghan, Norman Borisoff. Story by Will Tremper. A Da.Ma. Film–Hoche–Hans Oppenheimer–PCM Production. *CAST:* Jose Ferrer, Sean Flynn, Nicole Courcel, Jess Hahn, Joseph Yadin, Hans Joachim Schmiedel, Christiane Schmidtmer, Joy Aston, Art Brauss, Fred Durr, Wolfgang Georgi, Anne Gorassini, Charles Hickman, Carlo Hintermann, Hjordis Hume, Margaret Jahnen, Maria Pia Luzi, Edward Meeks, Robert Shankland, Lothar Mann, Antonella Murgia. *SYN:* An East German (Schmiedel) refugee sneaks aboard an American military train headed from Berlin to Frankfurt in the West zone. When it is learned he is aboard, an international incident seems inevitable as the Americans and Russians demand that the commanding officer (Flynn) of the train turn him over to the Germans. *NOTES:* Working title was *Train 349 from Berlin.* Released in France at a running time of 92 mins. Released in Germany at a running time of 105 mins. Sean Flynn was the son of Errol Flynn. He was declared Missing in Action in Vietnam in 1970 while on a photographic assignment. [Original German title: *Verspatung In Marienborn.*] [Original French title: *Le Train de Berlin Est Arrête.*] [Original Italian Title: *Un Treno e Fermo a Berlino.*] [British title: *Delay in Marienborn.*]

370. The Story of O (11/75) Eastmancolor – 97 mins. (Drama-Romance). *DIR:* Just Jaeckin. *PRO:* Roger Fleytoux. *SP:* Sebastien Japrisot. Based on the book by Pauline Reage. *CAST:* Corrine Clery, Udo Kier, Anthony Steel, Jean Gaven, Christiane Minazzoli, Martin Kelly, Jean Pierre Andreani, Gabriel Cartand, Li Sellgren, Albane Navizet, Henry Piegay, Alain Noury. *SYN:* A young woman (Clery) submits to degrading and humiliating treatment to demonstrate her obedience to her lovers (Steel, Kier, Gaven). *NOTES:* One of the "soft core" X-rated features distributed by Allied Artists in the seventies. "Pauline Reage" was an alleged pseudonym of a male member of the French Academy. [Original French title: *Historie d'O.*]

371. Strange Intruder (9/2/56) B&W – 82 mins. (Drama). *DIR:* Irving Rapper. *PRO:* Lindsley Parsons. *SP:* David Evans, Warren Douglas. Based on *The Intruder* by Helen Fowler. *CAST:* Edmund Purdom, Ida Lupino, Ann Harding, Jacques Bergerac, Gloria Talbott, Carl Benton Reid, Douglas Kennedy, Donald Murphy, Ruby Goodwin, Mimi Gibson, Eric Anderson, Marjorie Bennett. *SYN:* A soldier (Purdom) agrees to honor a war buddy's final request to visit the man's family and kill his two children so that his widow (Lupino) and her lover (Bergerac) cannot raise them.

372. The Strangler (4/30/64) B&W – 89 mns. (Horror). *DIR:* Burt Topper.

Advertisement for *The Strangler* (1964).

PRO: Samuel Bischoff, David Diamond. *SP:* Bill S. Ballinger. *CAST:* Victor Buono, David McLean, Diane Sayer, Davey Davidson, Ellen Corby, Michael Ryan, Baynes Barron, Russ Bender, Jeanne Bates, Wally Campo, Mimi Dillard, Byron Morrow, John Yates, James B. Sikking, Selette Cole, Robert Cranford, Victor Masi. *SYN:* A laboratory technician (Buono), dominated and warped by his invalid mother (Corby), is in reality the strangler of women. *NOTES:*

Bonita Granville and Rod Cameron in *Strike It Rich* (1949). (Photo courtesy of Scott MacGillivray.)

The film debut of James B. Sikking. This film was possibly released as an exploitation film to capitalize on the "Boston Strangler" murders.

373. Strike It Rich (1/1/49) B&W—81 mins. (Comedy). *DIR:* Lesley Selander. *PRO:* Jack Wrather. *SP:* Francis Rosenwald. *CAST:* Rod Cameron, Bonita Granville, Don Castle, Stuart Erwin, Lloyd Corrigan, Ellen Corby, Emory Parnell, Harry Tyler, Virginia Dale, William Haade, Edward Gargan, Robert Dudley. *SYN:* Set in the late 1920s and early 1930s. When a man (Cameron) learns that his two wildcat partners (Castle, Erwin) have struck oil, he resorts to underhanded maneuvering to demand his share of the strike. *NOTES:* Release date is also given as 11/26/48.

374. Sudden Danger (12/14/55) B&W—65 mins. (Crime-Mystery). *DIR:* Hubert Cornfield. *PRO:* Ben Schwalb. *SP:* Daniel B. Ullman, Elwood Ullman. Story by Daniel B. Ullman. *CAST:* Bill Elliott, Tom Drake, Beverly Garland, Dayton Lummis, Helene Stanton, Lucien Littlefield, Minerva Urecal, Lyle Talbot, Frank Jenks, Pierre Watkin, John Close, Ralph Gamble, Barbara Woodell, Edward Andrews, Cathy Marlowe, Wilbur Mack, Jack Sparks. *SYN:* Lt. Doyle (Elliott) suspects a blind man (Drake) of the murder of his mother. Later, when the man has a successful eye operation and proves his innocence, he assists Lt. Doyle as they search out his mother's killer.

375. Superbug (11/76) Technicolor —83 mins. (Comedy-Adventure). *DIR/*

Feature Films

Advertisement for *The Tall Stranger* (1957).

PRO: Rudolf Zehetgruber. *SP:* Rudolf Zehetgruber, G. von Nazzani. A Scorpio–Barbara Film Production. *Cast:* Robert Mark (Rudolf Zehetgruber), Sal Bogese, Kathrin Oginski (Kathrin Ogen), Evelyne Kraft, Heidi Hansen, George Goodman, Walter Giller, Walter Roderer, Ruth Jecklin, Gerhard Frickhoefer, Walter Feuchtenberg. *SYN:* A Volkswagen Beetle and its owner (Mark) try to outwit a gang of counterfeiters, led by an international money man (Goodman). They return the counterfeit plates to their owner, with the help of the car's inventor (Oginski). *NOTES:* A German version of Walt Disney's popular movie, *The Love Bug*. Filmed in Portugal. Released in West Germany in 1974 at a running time of 93 mins.

Superbug, Super Agent see **Superbug**

376. Surrender—Hell! (7/26/59) B&W – 85 mins. (War). *DIR/SP:* John Barnwell. *PRO:* Edmund Goldman. Based on *Blackburn's Headhunters* by Philip Harkins, from the diaries of Col. Donald D. Blackburn. A Corey Film Corporation Production. *CAST:* Keith Andes, Susan Cabot, Nestor De Villa, Paraluman. *SYN:* During World War II, Col. Blackburn (Andes) organizes Filipino headhunters into a guerrilla force to fight the Japanese. *NOTES:* Double billed in some areas with *Battle Flame*.

377. Taffy and the Jungle Hunter (3/31/65) Technicolor – 87 mins. (Comedy- Adventure). *DIR:* Terry O. Morse. *PRO:* William Faris. *SP:* Arthur Hoerl, Alfred Zimbalist. Story by Donald Zimbalist. A Zimbalist Co. Production. *CAST:* Jacques Bergerac, Manuel Padilla, Shary Marshall, Hari Rhodes, Robert DoQui, "Taffy," the elephant, "Margo," the chimp. *SYN:* The eight-year-old son (Padilla) of an African jungle hunter (Bergerac), upset over being separated from his pet elephant, runs away into the jungle with the elephant and a chimp. *NOTES:* Associate producer was Jack Warner, Jr.

378. The Tall Stranger (11/17/57) DeLuxe Color/Scope – 83 mins. (Western). *DIR:* Thomas Carr. *PRO:* Walter Mirisch. *SP:* Christopher Knopf. Based on *Plunder* by Louis L'Amour. *CAST:*

Joel McCrea, Virginia Mayo, Barry Kelley, Michael Ansara, Whit Bissell, James Dobson, George Neise, Adam Kennedy, Michael Pate, Leo Gordon, Ray Teal, Philip Phillips, Robert Foulk, Jennifer Lea, George J. Lewis, Guy Prescott, Ralph Reed, Mauritz Hugo, Ann Morrison, Tom London, Len Geer, Don McGuire, Danny Sands. *SYN:* Shot and left for dead, a man (McCrea) is nursed back to health by a wagon train of settlers and in gratitude agrees to help them as they settle their new land.

379, The Tall Women (3/1/67) Eastmancolor/Scope – 101 mins. (Western). *DIR:* Rudolf Zehetgruber. *PRO:* Zeliko Kunkera. *SP:* Mino Roli, Jim Henaghan. Story by Mike Ashley. A Danubia Films–Danny Films–L.M. Films Production. English version produced and presented by Sidney Pink. *CAST:* Anne Baxter, Maria Perschy, Gustavo Rojo, Rossella Como, Adriana Ambesi, Perla Cristal, Maria Mahor, Christa Linder, Luis Prendes, Mara Cruz, Fernando Hilbeck, Alejandra Nilo, John Clarke, Jorge Rigaud. *SYN:* Seven women survive a wagon train massacre and struggle to make their way across the desert to Fort Lafayette. As they are about to be ambushed again by the Apaches, an Army patrol and scout (Rojo) come to their rescue. Although the patrol is wiped out, the Indians grant the women and scout safe passage because of their bravery. *NOTES:* Released in Spain and Italy in 1966 at a running time of 92 mins. Released in Austria in 1967 at a running time of 94 mins. [Original Spanish title: *Las Siete Magníficas.*] [Original Italian title: *Donne alla Frontiera.*] [Original Austrian title: *Frauen, die Durch die Holle Gehen.*]

380. Tangier Incident (2/1/53) B&W – 77 mins. (Spy-Drama). *DIR:* Lew Landers. *PRO:* Lindsley Parsons. *SP:* George Bricker. *CAST:* George Brent, Mari Aldon, Dorothy Patrick, Bert Freed, Dan Seymour, Dayton Lummis, Alix Talton, John Harmon, Richard Karlan, Shepard Menken, Benny Rubin, Michael Ross. *SYN:* A government agent (Brent) poses as a black marketeer in North Africa to find the spies who are selling atomic secrets to the Russians.

381. Target Earth! (11/7/54) B&W – 75 mins. (Science Fiction). *DIR:* Sherman A. Rose. *PRO:* Herman Cohen. *SP:* William Raynor. Based on *Deadly City* by Ivar Jorgenson (Paul W. Fairman). An Abtcon Picture Production. *CAST:* Richard Denning, Kathleen Crowley, Richard Reeves, Virginia Grey, Robert Roark, Mort Marshall, Arthur Space, Whit Bissell, Jim Drake, Steve Pendleton, House Peters, Jr. *SYN:* A robot invasion of Earth from the planet Venus wipes out the city of Chicago, leaving only a handful of survivors to battle the robots. *NOTES:* The science fiction gangster theme would show up again in the American International films *The Astounding She-Monster* (1954) and *The Day the World Ended* (1956), and would continue into the 1960s. The debut of producer Herman Cohen.

382. Teenage Doll! (9/22/57) B&W/Scope – 68 mins. (Crime-Drama). *DIR/PRO:* Roger Corman. *SP:* Charles B. Griffith. A Woolner Bros. Production. *CAST:* June Kenney, Fay Spain, John Brinkley, Collette Jackson, Barbara Wilson, Ziva Rodann, Sandy Smith, Barboura Morris, Dorothy Neumann, Ed Nelson, Bruno Ve Sota. *SYN:* When a teenage gang member (Kenney) of the Vandalettes knifes a girl from a rival gang, the Black Widows, she finds herself the target of revenge. This leads to an all out rumble between the male and female rival gangs, the Vandals and Vandalettes versus the Tarantulas and the Black Widows. *NOTES:* Released in varying lengths, 68 mins. and 71 mins., due to the violence being cut for various showings. Double billed in some areas with *Undersea Girl.*

Double feature advertisement for *Teenage Doll* and *Undersea Girl* (1957).

383. Teenage Graffiti (5/77) Eastmancolor—90 mins. (Drama). *DIR/SP:* Christopher G. Casler. *PRO:* Sheldon Tromberg, Stephen M. Trattner. *CAST:* Michael R. Driscoll, Jeanetta Arnette, Alden Sherry, Brian Donohue, August Bayard, James Devney, Robert Lamar. *SYN:* During the summer following his graduation from high school, a young man (Driscoll) experiences romance with his girl (Arnette) and an older woman (Sherry), along with family conflicts involving his father (Donohue) and brothers (Bayard, Devney). *NOTES:* Cast and crew were recruited from the Washington, D.C. area. This film had the working title *Country Dreamin'* when it was shot in North Carolina in 1975. Distribution was delayed when Universal, producer of *American Graffiti*, took offense at the title change and tried to prevent Allied Artists from releasing the film. As far as the author can determine, this film has been shown in the Washington, D.C. area only.

384. Terror in the City (6/24/66) B&W—90 mins. (Drama). *DIR/SP:* Allen Baron. *PRO:* Merrill Brody, Allen Baron, Dorothy E. Reed. A Barbro Production. A Bischoff-Diamond Corp. Presentation. *CAST:* Lee Grant, Richard Bray, Michael Higgins, Roberto Marsach, Robert Allen, Sylvia Miles, Ruth Attaway, Robert Earl Jones, Jaime Charlamagne, Charles Jordan, Roscoe Lee Browne, Rick Colitti, Monroe Arnold, Boris Marshalov, Spencer Davis, Fred Feldt, Danny Dresser, Milton Luchan, Mel Brown, Muriel Franklin, Debby Bliss, Susie Dresser. *SYN:* A young farm boy (Bray) runs away from his Pennsylvania home to make his fortune in New York. He falls in with a gang of shoeshine boys and paper carriers who pay protection money to a young hood (Charlamagne). He is beaten up by the hood's gang for taking their money and is rescued by a prostitute (Grant) who takes him home. When he sees her arrested he becomes disillusioned and heads back home, sadder but wiser. *NOTES:* Filmed in 1963. Working title was *The Truant.* Pre-released in 1965 by Allied Artists as *Pie in the Sky.* Neither the pre-release title nor the release title seemed to fit this film and it lost money all around.

385. Texas Bad Man (12/20/53) B&W—62 mins. (Western). *DIR:* Lewis D. Collins. *PRO:* Vincent M. Fennelly. *SP:* Joseph F. Poland. A Westwood Production. *CAST:* Wayne Morris, Frank Ferguson, Elaine Riley, Sheb Wooley, Denver Pyle, Myron Healey, Mort Mills, Nelson Leigh. *SYN:* A lawman (Morris) sets out to stop his outlaw father (Ferguson) and his gang from robbing a gold shipment.

386. That Lucky Touch (12/75) Technicolor—93 mins. (Comedy). *DIR:* Christopher Miles. *PRO:* Dimitri de Grunwald. *SP:* John Briley. From an idea by Moss Hart. A Gloria-RANK Production. *CAST:* Roger Moore, Susannah York, Shelley Winters, Lee J. Cobb, Raf Vallone, Jean-Pierre Cassel, Sydne Rome, Donald Sinden, Michael Shannon, Alfred Hoffman, Aubrey Woods, Timothy Carlton, Fabian Cevellos, Vincent Hall, Julie Dawn Cole, Merelina Kendall, Michael Green, Linda Gray, David Enders, Marianne Stone, Taki Emmanuel. *SYN:* A pacifist journalist (York) covering NATO war games tries to stop a playboy arms dealer (Moore) from selling weapons to the NATO forces during the war games.

387. That Man George! (9/15/67) Eastmancolor — 90 mins. (Crime-Adventure). *DIR:* Jacques Deray. *PRO:* Claude Giroux. *SP:* Henri Lanoe, Jose Giovanni, Jacques Deray, Suzanne Arduini. Based on *Les Pilleurs de Demanche (The Heisters)* by Robert Page-Jones. A Europazur–Benito Perojo–Atlantis–Jolly Production. *CAST:* George Hamilton, Claudine Auger, Alberto de Mendoza, Daniel Ivernel, Tiberio Murgia, Jorge Rigaud, Giacomo Furia, Renato Baldini, Roberto Camardeil. *SYN:* After a successful gold robbery, two gang members (Hamilton, Auger) flee with the gold after trouble brews between the gang, and two of the gang are left for dead. However, one member (Ivernel) survives and trails the two, hoping to get revenge and the gold. *NOTES:* Released in France and Italy in 1966. Released in Spain in 1968 at a running time of 98 minutes. [Original French title: *L'Homme de Marrakech.*] [Original Italian title: *L'Uomo di Casablanca.*] [Original Spanish title: *Hombre de Marrakech.*] [Alternate Spanish title: *Los Saqueadores del Domingo.*]

388. There's a Girl in My Heart (1/11/49) B&W—79 mins. (Musical). *DIR/PRO:* Arthur Dreifuss. *SP:* Arthur Hoerl, John Eugene Hasty. *CAST:* Lee Bowman, Elyse Knox, Gloria Jean, Peggy Ryan, Lon Chaney, Jr., Ludwig Donath, Ray McDonald, Joel Marston, Richard Lane, Irene Ryan, Lanny Simpson, Paul Guilfoyle, Iris Adrian, Kay Anne Nelson, Martin Garralaga, Robert Emmett Keane, Lee Tong Foo. *SYN:* In the 1890s, a successful property developer (Bowman) tries to swindle a widow (Knox) out of her property since it sits next to his partner's (Chaney) music hall. He eventually falls in love with her and gives up his scheme. *NOTES:* Release date is also given as 1/6/50.

They Shall Not Die *see* **Serengeti Shall Not Die**

Thin Air *see* **The Body Stealers**

389. The Thin Red Line (5/2/64) B&W/Scope—99 mins. (War). *DIR:*

Advertisement for *The Thin Red Line* (1964).

Andrew Marton. *PRO:* Sidney Harmon. *SP:* Bernard Gordon. Based on the book by James Jones. A Philip Yordan–Security–A.C.E. Production. *CAST:* Keir Dullea, Jack Warden, James Philbrook, Ray Daley, Bob Kanter, Merlyn Yordan, Kieron Moore, Jim Gillen, Steve Rowland, Stephen Levy, Mark Johnson, Edward King, Jack Gaskins, Graham Sumner, Charles Stalnaker, Gary Lasdun, Jeffrey O'Kelly, Joe Collins, Thomas Freeman, Ted Macauley, Howard Hagen, Bill Barrett, Francis Deale, Russ Stoddard, John Clarke, Stan Nelson. *SYN:* During World War II on the island of Guadalcanal, a young private (Dullea) is at odds with his first sergeant (Warden) when he becomes a killing machine instead of a soldier.

390. This Man Must Die (10/70) Eastmancolor – 115 mins. (Drama-Suspense). *DIR:* Claude Chabrol. *PRO:* Andre Genoves. *SP:* Paul Gegauff, Claude Chabrol. Based on *The Beast Must Die* by Nicholas Blake. A Les Films La Boetie–Rozzoli Films Production. *CAST:* Michael Duchaussoy, Caroline Cellier, Jean Yanne, Anouk Ferjac, Marc Di Napoli, Maurice Pialat, Guy Marly, Lorraine Rainer, Stephane Di Napoli, Louise Chevalier, Dominique Zardi, Jean-Louis Maury, Michel Charrel, France Girard, Bernard Papineau, George Charrier. *SYN:* When a man (Duchaussoy), a famous author of children's books, learns that his son was killed by a hit and run driver, he swears revenge and sets out to find the driver of the car. Learning that a woman (Cellier) was a passenger in the car, he seeks her out and becomes friends with her, hoping she will lead him to the driver. *NOTES:* Released in France in 1969 and in Italy in 1970. Released in both subtitled and dubbed versions by Allied Artists. [Original French title: *Que la Bête Meure.*] [Original Italian title: *Uccidero un Uomo.*] [British title: *Killer!*]

391. Three for Jamie Dawn (7/8/56) B&W – 82 mins. (Crime-Drama). *DIR:* Thomas Carr. *PRO:* Hayes Goetz. *SP:* John Klempner. *CAST:* Laraine Day, Ricardo Montalban, Richard Carlson, June Havoc, Maria Palmer, Eduard Franz, Regis Toomey, Scotty Beckett, Herb Vigran, Marilyn Simms, Dorothy Adams. *SYN:* When a wealthy socialite (Simms) is put on trial for killing her boyfriend, a shady lawyer (Carlson) buys off three jurors to insure a verdict of "not guilty."

392. Three the Hard Way (6/74) DeLuxe Color – 93 mins. (Crime). *DIR:* Gordon Parks, Jr. *PRO:* Harry Bernsen. *SP:* Eric Bercovici, Jerry Ludwig. A Three C's Service Production. *CAST:* Jim Brown, Fred Williamson, Jim Kelly, Sheila Frazier, Jay Robinson, Charles McGregor, Howard Platt, Richard Angarola, David Chow, Marian Collier, Junero Jennings, Alex Rocco, Corbin Bernsen, Jeanie Bell, Renie Radich, Janice Carroll. *SYN:* Three friends (Brown, Williamson, Kelly) set out to stop a white supremist (Robinson) from destroying the black population of Los Angeles, Detroit, and Washington by introducing a serum in the water supply that only affects blacks. *NOTES:* The film debut of Corbin Bernsen; Harry Bernsen is the father of Corbin Bernsen. One of the many "blaxploitation" pictures of the seventies.

393. Thunderstorm (5/6/56) B&W – 81 mins. (Drama). *DIR:* John Guillermin. *PRO:* Binnie Barnes. *SP:* Daniel Mainwaring. Story by George St. George. A Hemisphere Films Limited Production. *CAST:* Carlos Thompson, Linda Christian, Charles Korvin, Gary Thorne, Tito Junco, Erica Vaal, Catherine Ferraz, Marco Davo, Fleixes De Pomes, Nestor M. Neana, Carlos Diaz Mendoza, Julia Cabe Alba, Isabel De Pomes, Conchita Bautista, Amalia Iglesias, Manuel San Roman. *SYN:* In a small fishing village on the coast of Spain, a fisherman (Thompson) saves a woman (Christian) from drowning and falls in love with her. Trouble soon develops as the village mayor (Korvin) and his son (Thorne) also fall in love with the woman. *NOTES:* Producer Binnie Barnes was a former actress.

394. Tickle Me (6/24/65) DeLuxe Color/Panavision—90 mins. (Western-Musical). *DIR:* Norman Taurog. *PRO:* Ben Schwalb. *SP:* Elwood Ullman, Edward Bernds. *CAST:* Elvis Presley, Jocelyn Lane, Julie Adams, Jack Mullaney, Merry Anders, Connie Gilchrist, Edward Faulkner, Bill Williams, Barbara Werle, John Dennis, Grady Sutton, Allison Hayes, Angela Greene, Louie Elias, Robert Hoy, Dorothy Konrad, Linda Rogers, Ann Morrell, Laurie Burton, Jean Ingram, Lilyan Chauvin, Francine York, Eve Bruce, Jackie Russell, Peggy Ward, Dorian Brown, Inez Pedroza. *SYN:* A crooning rodeo rider (Presley) seeks work at a dude ranch for women as a handyman, falls in love with one of the guests (Lane), and when she goes to a ghost town in search of gold and ends up being captured by a bunch of crooks also searching for the gold, he comes to her rescue, captures the crooks, and finds the gold. *NOTES:* Filmed on the Paramount sound stages.

395. Timber Country Trouble (5/8/55) B&W—54 mins. (Western). *DIR:* Frank McDonald. *PRO:* Wesley E. Barry. *SP:* Maurice Tombragel. A Newhall Production. *CAST:* Guy Madison, Andy Devine, Frances Charles, Kenne Duncan, George Barrows. *SYN:* Compiled from two episodes of the *Wild Bill Hickok* television series: titles unknown.

396. Time Bomb (4/23/61) B&W—92 mins. (Drama). *DIR:* Yves Ciampi. *PRO:* Raymond Froment. *SP:* Yves Ciampi, Henri-François Rey, Jacques-Laurent Bost. Story by Jean-Charles Tacchella. A Le Groupe des Quatre–Da. Ma. Production. *CAST:* Curt Jurgens, Mylene Demeongeot, Alain Saury, Paul Mercey, Robert Porte, Daniel Sorano, Jean Daurand, Gabriel Gobin, Andre Dalibert, Jess Hahn, Raymond Loyer, Jim Gerald, Pierre Collet, Guy Daker, Jean-Jacques Lecot, Henri Maik, Pierre Paulet, Jean Murat, Claire Guibert. *SYN:* A sea captain (Jurgens) gets involved in a scheme with his lover (Demongeot) and her brother (Saury) to blow up his freighter to collect the insurance money. *NOTES:* Released in France at a running time of 90 mins. Released in Italy at a running time of 95 mins. [Original French title: *Le Vent se Leve.*] [Original Italian title: *Il Vento si Alza.*] [British title: *Operation Time Bomb.*]

397. The Titled Tenderfoot (5/8/55) B&W—54 mins. (Western). *DIR:* Frank McDonald. *PRO:* Wesley E. Barry. *SP:* Maurice Tombragel. A Newhall Production. *CAST:* Guy Madison, Andy Devine, Jeanne Cagney, Clayton Moore, Hal Gerard, James Bell, Jack Reynolds, Dick Cavendish, Dick Elliott, Gerald Smith, Parke MacGregor, Russ Whiteman, I. Stanford Jolley, Guy Teague, Marshall Reed. *SYN:* Compiled from two episodes of the *Wild Bill Hickok* television series: "The Trapper Story" and "A Joke on Sir Anthony."

398. Tonight's the Night (12/19/54) Technicolor—88 mins. (Comedy). *DIR/PRO:* Mario Zampi. *SP:* Jack Davies, Michael Pertwee, L.A.G. Strong. Story by Jack Davies, Michael Pertwee. An Associated British Picture Production. *CAST:* David Niven, Yvonne De Carlo, Barry Fitzgerald, George Cole, A.E. Matthews, Noelle Middleton, Robert Urquhart, Michael Shepley, Eddie Byrne, Joseph Tomelty, Liam Redmond, Anthony Nicholls, James Mageean, Patrick McAlinney, Brian O'Higgins,

134   The Allied Artists Checklist

Advertisement for *Tormented* (1960).

Patrick Westwood, Fred Johnson, Ronan O'Casey, Michael Martin-Harvey, Denis Martin, Bill Shine, Harry Hutchinson, Tommy Dugan. *SYN:* When an Irish squire (Matthews) is killed in a fall from a horse, his nephew (Niven) arrives from England and takes over the estate. He begins to make enemies of the villagers by collecting debts, evicting tenants, persecuting poachers, and even refusing to buy rounds at the local pub. The villagers then decide to get rid of the new squire. *NOTES:* Released in Great Britain in June, 1954. [British title: *Happy Ever After.*]

399. Topeka (8/9/53) Sepiatone—69 mins. (Western). *DIR:* Thomas Carr. *PRO:* Vincent M. Fennelly. *SP:* Milton Raison. A Westwood Production. *CAST:* "Wild" Bill Elliott, Phyllis Coates, Fuzzy Knight, Rick Vallin, John James, Denver Pyle, Dick Crockett, Harry Lauter, Dale Van Sickel, Ted Mapes, Henry Rowland, Edward Clark, I. Stanford Jolley, Michael Vallon, Michael Colgan, Stanley Price. *SYN:* An outlaw leader (Elliott) and his gang hole up in Deer Creek. They plan to take over the town and run the leader (Lauter) of a protection racket and his men out of town. The townspeople make the outlaw leader sheriff and his pal (Vallin) joins him while his gang sides with the other faction. Going into action, the gang members are killed or jailed. The townspeople then petition the governor for a full pardon for both men.

400. Tormented (9/22/60) B&W—75 mins. (Horror). *DIR:* Bert I. Gordon. *PRO:* Bert I. Gordon, Joe Steinberg. *SP:* George Worthing Yates. Story by Bert I. Gordon. A Cheviot Production. *CAST:* Richard Carlson, Susan Gordon, Juli Reding, Lugene Sanders, Joseph Turkel, Lillian Adams, Gene Roth, Vera Marshe, Harry Fleer, Merritt Stone. *SYN:* A pianist (Carlson) pushes his mistress (Reding) from the top of his lighthouse so he can marry his fiancée (Sander). Later the mistress turns up as a ghost to haunt him and ruin his impending marriage. *NOTES:* Susan Gordon is the daughter of Bert I. Gordon. Lugene Sanders played the role of "Babs Riley" in television's "The Life of Riley." Double billed

Dorothy Malone and Mark Stevens in *Torpedo Alley* (1953).

in some areas with *Caltiki, the Immortal Monster*.

401. Torpedo Alley (1/25/53) B&W —84 mins. (War). *DIR:* Lew Landers. *PRO:* Lindsley Parsons. *SP:* Warren Douglas, Sam Roeca. *SYN:* Mark Stevens, Dorothy Malone, Charles Winninger, Bill Williams, Douglas Kennedy, James Millican, Bill Henry, Robert Rose, John Alvin, James Seay, John Close, Carl Christian, Ralph Reed, Carleton Young, Ralph Sanford, William Schallert, Richard Garland, Ross Thompson, Jean Willes. *SYN:* Near the end of World War II, a pilot (Stevens) loses his plane and two crewmen. Unable to adjust to civilian life, he enlists in the submarine service where he sees action during the Korean War. *NOTES:* Charles Bronson has an uncredited bit part as a sailor.

402. Toughest Man Alive (11/6/55) B&W—72 mins. (Spy-Action-Drama). *DIR:* Sidney Salkow. *PRO:* William F. Broidy. *SP:* Steve Fisher. *CAST:* Dane Clark, Lita Milan, Anthony Caruso, Ross Elliott, Myrna Dell, Thomas Browne Henry, Paul Levitt, John Eldredge, Dehl Berti, Richard Karlan, Syd Saylor, Jonathan Seymour, Don Maters. *SYN:* A U.S. government agent (Clark) goes undercover to break up a gun smuggling ring that is supplying arms to Central American revolutionaries.

403. The Trail Blazers (4/19/53) B&W—69 mins. (Action). *DIR:* Wesley E. Barry. *PRO:* William F. Broidy. *SP:* Sam Roeca, John Marks. A Newhall Production. *CAST:* Alan Hale, Jr., Richard Tyler, Barney McCormack, Jim Flowers, Henry Blair, Danny Welton, Mickey Colpack, Duke York, Bobby Hyatt, Ted Hecht, Lyle Talbot, Rick Vallin. *SYN:* A compilation of two episodes of *The Trail Blazers* unsold TV pilot show, "The

Fugitive" and one other, with possible additional footage. NOTES: Limited theatrical release. This film possibly played on a double bill with another feature.

404. Treasure of Ruby Hills (1/23/55) B&W – 71 mins. (Western). DIR: Frank McDonald. PRO: William F. Broidy. SP: Thomas G. Hubbard, Fred Eggers. Story by Louis L'Amour. CAST: Zachary Scott, Carole Mathews, Barton MacLane, Dick Foran, Lola Albright, Lee Van Cleef, Raymond Hatton, Gordon Jones, Steve Darrell, Charles Fredericks, Stanley Andrews, Jim Alexander, Rick Vallin, Glenn Strange, John Cason, Ray Jones, Carl Mathews. SYN: A rancher (Scott) tries to stop two groups of crooked cattlemen from getting control of range land.

405. Trilogy (12/69) Eastmancolor – 100 mins. (Drama). DIR/PRO: Frank Perry. SP: Truman Capote, Eleanor Perry. Based on stories by Truman Capote. CAST: *Miriam* – Mildred Natwick, Susan Dunfee, Carol Gustafson, Robin Ponterio, Beverly Ballard, Jane Connell, Frederic Morton, Richard Hamilton, Phyllis Eldridge, Brooks Rogers. *Among the Paths to Eden* – Maureen Stapleton, Martin Balsam. *A Christmas Memory* – Geraldine Page, Donnie Melvin, Lavinia Cassels, Christine Marler, Josip Elric, Lynn Forman, Win Forman. Narrated by Truman Capote. SYN: *Miriam* – A nanny (Natwick) slowly loses her mind. *Among the Paths to Eden* – A spinster (Stapleton) looks for a husband amongst widowers visiting their wives' graves. *A Christmas Memory* – A young child (Melvin) watches a loved one (Page) slowly lose her memory as years go by. NOTES: Originally intended as three different television specials, the stories were re-edited into a theatrical feature that was given limited distribution. Only one of the stories, *A Christmas Memory*, was broadcast on television, winning both an Emmy and a Peabody Award.

406. Trouble on the Trail (12/26/54) B&W – 54 mins. (Western). DIR: Frank McDonald. PRO: Wesley E. Barry. SP: Maurice Tombragel. A Newhall Production. CAST: Guy Madison, Andy Devine. SYN: Compiled from two episodes of the *Wild Bill Hickok* television series: titles unknown.

Truman Capote's Trilogy *see* **Trilogy**

407. Twenty Plus Two (8/13/61) B&W – 102 mins. (Mystery-Drama). DIR: Joseph M. Newman. PRO/SP: Frank Gruber. Based on the book by Frank Gruber. CAST: David Janssen, Jeanne Crain, Dina Merrill, Jacques Aubuchon, William Demarest, Agnes Moorehead, Brad Dexter, Robert Strauss, Fredd Wayne, George Neise, Mort Mills, Robert Gruber, Will Wright, Teri Janssen, Carleton Young, Robert H. Harris, Ellie Kent, Billy Varga. SYN: A private detective (David Janssen), specializing in missing person cases, is out to find a missing heiress who vanished after a scandal. During his search, he is approached by a man (Aubuchon) to find his missing brother and is also approached by a movie star (Dexter) to solve the murder of his secretary. He later links all three cases to an old flame (Merrill) he met in Tokyo during the Korean War. NOTES: Executive producer was Scott R. Dunlap. [British title: *It Started in Tokyo*.]

408. Twilight's Last Gleaming (2/77) Technicolor – 146 mins. (Drama). DIR: Robert Aldrich. PRO: Merv Adelson. SP: Ronald M. Cohen, Edward Huebsch. Based on *Viper Three* by Walter Wager. A Geria–Lorimar–Bavaria Production. CAST: Burt Lancaster, Richard Widmark, Charles Durning, Melvyn Douglas, Paul Winfield, Burt Young, Joseph Cotten, Roscoe Lee

Advertisement for *Twenty Plus Two* (1961).

Browne, Gerald S. O'Loughlin, Richard Jaeckel, William Marshall, Charles Aidman, Leif Erickson, Charles McGraw, Simon Scott, Morgan Paull, William Smith, Bill Walker, Roy Glenn, David Baxt, Glenn Beck, Ed Bishop, Phil Brown, Gary Cockrell, Don Fellows, Werton Gavin, Garrick Hagon, David Healy, Bill Hootkins, Ray Jewers, Ron Lee, Robert Sherman, John Ratzenberger, Robert MacLeod, Lionel Murton, Shane Rimmer, Robert O'Neil, Vera Miles. *SYN:* A former Air Force general (Lancaster) and his men (Young, Winfield, Smith), all prison escapees, take over a SAC base that they helped design.

The general demands that the president (Durning) reveal to the American people the truth about the Vietnam War by reading National Security Council document No. 9759 on national television. If these demands are not met, the general and his men will send nine Titan missiles to their targets in the Soviet Union. *NOTES:* The scenes with Vera Miles as the president's wife were cut from the final print. This film uses split-screen technique in the telling of the story. Filmed in West Germany.

409. Two-Gun Marshal (11/15/53) B&W – 52 mins. (Western). *DIR:* Frank McDonald. *PRO:* Wesley E. Barry. *SP:* William Raynor, Maurice Tombragel. A Newhall Production. *CAST:* Guy Madison, Andy Devine, Carole Mathews, Frankie Darro, Raymond Hatton, Sara Hayden, Pamela Duncan, Minerva Urecal, Michael Vallon, Richard Tyler, Alan Foster, Francis McDonald, Elizabeth Harrower, Irene Martin, George Meader. *SYN:* Compiled from two episodes of the *Wild Bill Hickok* television series: "Papa Antinelli" and "The Slocum Family."

410. The Two Gun Teacher (12/26/54) B&W – 52 mins. (Western). *DIR:* Frank McDonald. *PRO:* Wesley E. Barry. *SP:* Maurice Tombragel. A Newhall Production. *CAST:* Guy Madison, Andy Devine. *SYN:* Compiled from two episodes of the *Wild Bill Hickok* television series: titles unknown.

411. Two Guns and a Badge (9/12/54) B&W – 69 mins. (Western). *DIR:* Lewis D. Collins. *PRO:* Vincent M. Fennelly. *SP:* Daniel B. Ullman. A Silvermine Production. *CAST:* Wayne Morris, Morris Ankrum, Beverly Garland, Roy Barcroft, William Phipps, Damian O'Flynn, I. Stanford Jolley, Robert J. Wilke, Chuck Courtney, John Pickard, Henry Rowland, Gregg Barton, William Fawcett, Lyle Talbot, Stanley Price, Ted Mapes, Mike Ragan (Holly Bane). *SYN:* An ex-convict (Morris) is mistaken for a deputy sheriff when he arrives in a small town and must fight the corrupt rancher (Barcroft) while romancing his daughter (Garland). *NOTES:* Western and film historians credit this film as being the last entry in a B Western series.

412. The Umbrellas of Cherbourg (12/16/64) Eastmancolor – 92 mins. (Musical-Drama). *DIR/SP:* Jacques Demy. *PRO:* Mag Bodard. A Madeline–Parc–Beta Production. A Landau/Unger Releasing Organization Presentation. *CAST:* Catherine Deneuve, Nino Castelnuovo, Anne Vernon, Ellen Farner, Marc Michel, Mirelle Perrey, Jean Champion, Harald Wolff, Dorothee Blank. *SYN:* A young girl (Deneuve) lives with her mother (Vernon) and works in her umbrella shop in Cherbourg. She becomes pregnant by her fiancé (Castelnuovo) before he leaves for military service. Later, when she has not heard from him, she marries a wealthy diamond merchant (Michel) who promises to raise her child as his own. When her fiancé returns and learns of the marriage, he marries his mother's nurse (Farner) and the former lovers go their separate ways. *NOTES:* Released in 1964 by Allied Artists with subtitles. Released by American-International in 1965. Released in Paris in 1964 at a running time of 95 mins. and released in West Germany in 1965 at a running time of 95 mins. Warner Bros. released a sequel in 1967, *Young Girls of Rochefort*. [Original French title: *Les Parapluies de Cherbourg*.] [Original West German title: *Die Regenschirme von Cherbourg*.]

413. Undersea Girl (9/22/57) B&W – 74 mins. (Action-Adventure.) *DIR:* John Peyser. *PRO:* Norman T. Herman. *SP:* Arthur V. Jones. A Nacirema Production. *CAST:* Mara Corday, Pat Conway, Florence Marley, Dan Seymour, Ralph Clanton, Myron Healey,

Lewis Charles, Jerry Eskow, Dehl Berti, Sue George, Mickey Simpson, Mike Mason, Brick Sullivan, Don Warren, Jess Kirkpatrick, Russell Thorsen, Corrine Laine, William Kendis, Mack Chandler. *SYN:* When a cruiser is sunk with $2 million in Navy money and a newspaper reporter (Corday) finds the body of a tuna fisherman with $1,800 of the missing money, she and her Navy boyfriend (Conway) set out to solve the murder and locate the missing money. *NOTES:* Working title was *Crime Beneath the Sea*. Double billed in some areas with *Teenage Doll!*

414. The Unfaithfuls (11/28/60) B&W – 89 mins. (Comedy). *DIR:* Stefano Steno, Mario Monicelli. *PRO:* Dino De Laurentiis, Carlo Ponti. *SP:* Ivo Perilli, Franco Brusati, Mario Monicelli, Stefano Steno. Story by Ivo Perilli. *CAST:* May Britt, Gina Lollobrigida, Pierre Cressoy, Marina Vlady, Anna Maria Ferrero, Tina Lattanzi, Carlo Romano, Charles Fawcett, Irene Pappas, Franco Rossi, Paolo Ferrera, Barnardo Tafuri, Carlo Lampas, Giulio Cali, Margherita Bagni, Tania Weber. *SYN:* A blackmailer (Cressoy) brings into the open the adulterous activities of several married couples. *NOTES:* Released in Italy in 1953

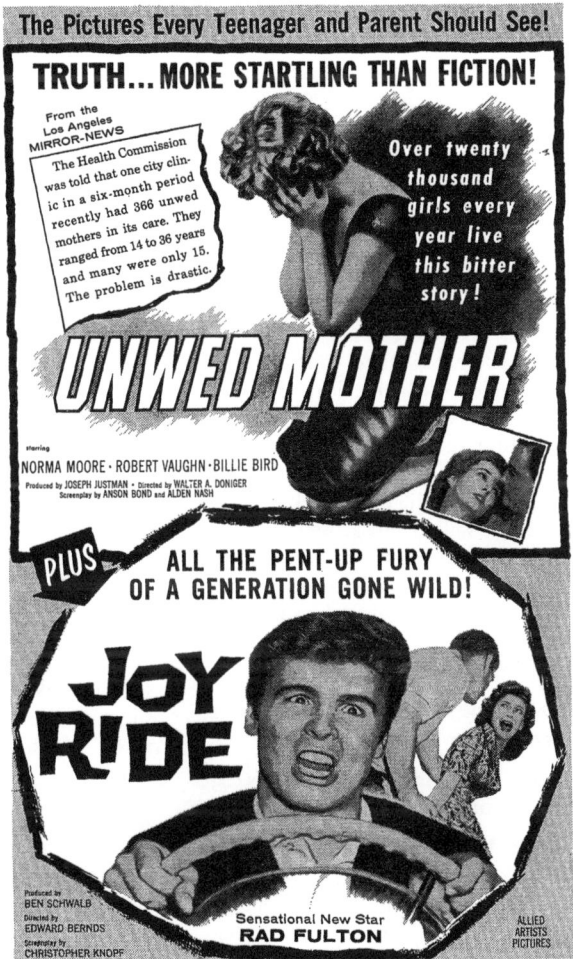

Double feature advertisement for *Unwed Mother* and *Joy Ride* (1958).

at a running time of 97 mins. [Original Italian title: *Le Infedeli*.]

415. Unwed Mother (11/23/58) B&W – 74 mins. (Drama). *DIR:* Walter A. Doniger. *PRO:* Joseph Justman. *SP:* Anson Bond, Alden Nash. Story by Anson Bond. *CAST:* Norma Moore, Robert Vaughn, Diana Darrin, Billie Bird, Jeanne Cooper, Ron Hargrave, Kathleen Hughes, Sam Buffington, Claire Carleton, Collette

Jackson, Ken Lynch, Dorothy Adams, Ralph Gamble, Timothy Carey. *SYN:* A country girl (Moore) arrives in Los Angeles in a family way. She gives her baby up for adoption but has a change of heart and chases down the foster parents to get her baby back. *NOTES:* Double billed in some areas with *Joy Ride.*

416. Up in Smoke (12/22/57) B&W – 61 mins. (Comedy). *DIR:* William Beaudine. *PRO:* Richard Heermance. *SP:* Jack Townley. Story by Elwood Ullman, Bert Lawrence. *CAST:* Huntz Hall, Stanley Clements, David Gorcey, Eddie LeRoy, Byron Foulger, Dick Elliott, Judy Bamber, Ric Roman, Ralph Sanford, Joe Devlin, James Flavin, Earle Hodgins, John Mitchum, Jack Mulhall, Fritz Feld, Wilbur Mack, Benny Rubin. *SYN:* Sach (Hall) makes a deal with the devil (Foulger) for horseracing tips, but on the last day of his deal, he substitutes for the jockey and tries to make the winning horse lose.

Valley of the White Wolves see **Mara of the Wilderness**

The Venetian Anonymous see **The Anonymous Venetian**

417. Vigilante Terror (11/15/53) B&W – 70 mins. (Western). *DIR:* Lewis D. Collins. *PRO:* Vincent M. Fennelly. *SP:* Sid Theil. A Westwood Production. *CAST:* "Wild" Bill Elliott, Mary Ellen Kay, Myron Healey, Fuzzy Knight, Henry Rowland, I. Stanford Jolley, George Wallace, Zon Murray, Richard Avonde, Michael Colgan, Denver Pyle, Robert Bray, Al Haskell, John James, Lee Roberts, Stanley Price, Ted Mapes, Ray Jones. *SYN:* Riding into Pinetop, a man (Elliott) stops a lynching and is appointed sheriff. The leader (Healey) of the masked vigilantes plants evidence falsely accusing the new sheriff of gold robbery. As he is about to be lynched by the vigilantes, he is saved by a storekeeper's daughter (Kay). They ride out of town after the real gold robbers, pursued by the vigilantes and townspeople. A gun battle ensues with the leader of the outlaws and the vigilante leader being killed.

A Violent Journey see **The Fool Killer**

418. War Is Hell! (10/23/63) B&W – 81 mins. (War). *DIR/SP:* Burt Topper. *PRO:* Burt Topper, Ross Hahn. *CAST:* Tony Russel, Baynes Barron, Burt Topper, Judy Dan, Tony Rich, J.J. Dahner, Wally Campo, Bobby Byles, Michael Bell, Russ Prescott, Robert Howard, Paul Sherriff, Kei Chung. Narrated by Audie Murphy. *SYN:* During the Korean War, a cowardly sergeant (Russel) stays behind as his men storm a Communist bunker. Most of his men are killed, but the rest succeed in taking the bunker. The sergeant then takes credit for the attack, expecting a medal, and denounces his men as cowards in the attack. He later resorts to killing a fellow officer who suspects the truth. Eventually he is killed as he attacks unarmed Chinese troops who have surrendered. *NOTES:* Working title was *War Hero.* Pre-release title was *War Madness.*

419. War of the Satellites (5/18/58) B&W – 66 mins. (Science Fiction). *DIR:* Roger Corman. *PRO:* Roger Corman, Jack Rabin, Irving Block. *SP:* Lawrence L. Goldman. Story by Jack Rabin, Irving Block. A Santa Cruz Production. *CAST:* Dick Miller, Susan Cabot, Richard Devon, Eric Sinclair, Michael Fox, Robert Shayne, Bruno Ve Sota, Jerry Barclay, Jay Sayer, Mitzi McCall, John Brinkley, Beech Dickerson, Roger Corman, Roy Gordan, James Knight. *SYN:* A scientist (Miller) suspects that a fellow scientist (Devon), who supposedly has died in an auto accident, but then reappears, has been taken over by aliens to prevent the Earth from launching its first manned spaceflight. *NOTES:* Shot and

Feature Films 141

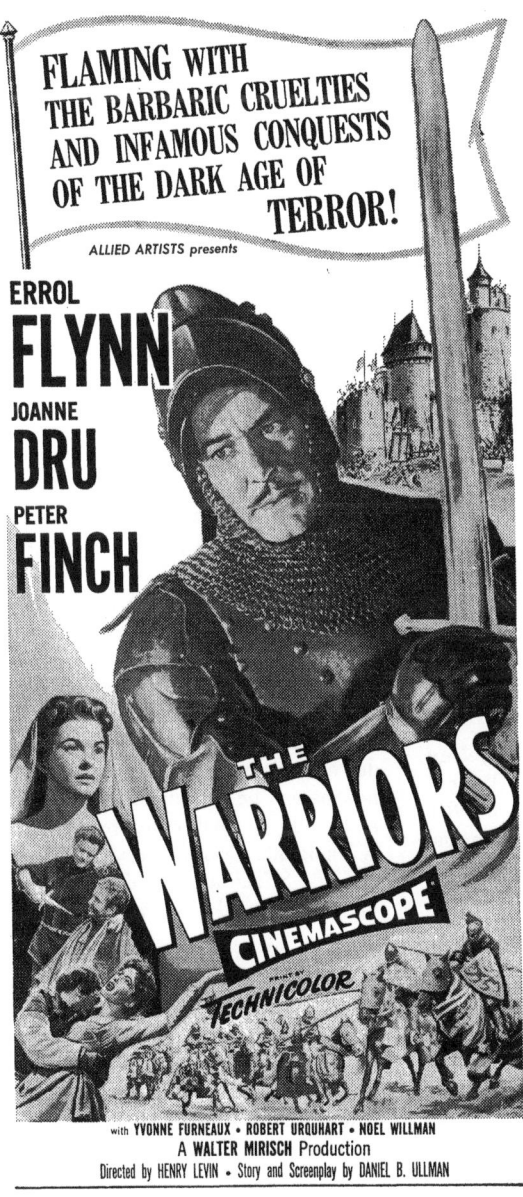

Advertisement for *The Warriors* (1955).

released in eight weeks by Roger Corman to capitalize on the Sputnik launch by Russia. Double billed in some areas with *Attack of the 50 Ft. Woman*.

420. The Warriors (9/11/55) Technicolor/Scope – 85 mins. (Historical). *DIR:* Henry Levin. *PRO:* Walter Mirisch. *SP:* Daniel B. Ullman. *CAST:* Errol Flynn, Joanne Dru, Peter Finch, Yvonne Furneaux, Patrick Holt, Michael Hordern, Moultrie Kelsall, Robert Urquhart, Vincent Winter, Noel Willman, Frances Rowe, Alastair Hunter, Rupert Davies, Ewen Solon, Richard O'Sullivan, Jack Lambert, John Welsh, Harold Kasket, Leslie Linder, Robert Brown, John Phillips, Sam Kydd, Christopher Lee. *SYN:* Following the Hundred Years' War, in 1358, King Edward III (Hordern) returns to England after vanquishing the French, and he leaves his son, Prince Edward (Flynn), in command of Aquitaine. Two French lords, de Ville (Finch), and Du Gueselin (Willman), determined to drive the remaining British out of France, kidnap a British noblewoman (Dru) and keep her as a hostage. Edward poses as a knight in de Ville's army to learn his weaknesses to defeat him in battle. *NOTES:* Working title was *The Black Prince*. Errol Flynn's final swashbuckler film. Screenwriter

Phil Park was uncredited. The castle used in this film was the same one used for the 1952 MGM film *Ivanhoe*. [British title: *The Dark Avenger*.]

421. The Wasp Woman (3/14/60) B&W – 73 mins. (Horror). *DIR/PRO:* Roger Corman. *SP:* Leo Gordon. Story by Kinta Zertuche, A Filmgroup–Santa Clara Production. *CAST:* Susan Cabot, Fred (Anthony) Eisley, Michael Mark, Barboura Morris, William Roerick, Frank Gerstle, Bruno Ve Sota, Roy Gordon, Frank Wolff, Carolyn Hughes, Lynn Cartwright, Lani Mars, Philip Barry, Roger Corman. *SYN:* The head of a cosmetics firm (Cabot) hires a scientist (Mark) who can make women younger using queen wasp jelly. When she demands that she be a test subject, she becomes younger. But as she takes more of the jelly, she is transformed into a giant wasp. *NOTES:* Released in 1959 by Filmgroup. Picked up for distribution by Allied Artists in 1960. Double billed in some areas with *Beast from Haunted Cave*.

422. The Weak and the Wicked (7/18/54) B&W – 81 mins. (Prison-Drama). *DIR:* J. Lee Thompson. *PRO:* Victor Skutezky. *SP:* J. Lee Thompson, Anne Burnaby, Joan Henry. Based on *Who Lie in Gaol* by Joan Henry. A Marble Arch–Associated British Pictures Production. *CAST:* Glynis Johns, John Gregson, Jane Hylton, Diana Dors, Sidney James, A.E. Matthews, Anthony Nicholls, Athene Seyler, Olive Sloane, Sybil Thorndike, Barbara Couper, Joyce Heron, Ursula Howells, Mary Merrall, Rachel Roberts, Marjorie Rhodes, Josephine Griffin, Simone Silva, Josephine Stuart, Edwin Styles, Cecil Trouncer, Paul Carpenter, Elliot Makeham, Jean Taylor Smith, Sandra Dorne, Bessie Love, Irene Handl, Joan Haythorne, Thea Gregory, Tom Gill, Marjorie Stewart, Margaret Diamond, Ruth Denning. *SYN:* In this glorified depiction of prison life, Jean Raymond (Johns) is sent to prison for a year when she cannot pay her gambling debts. While there she befriends several inmates; Betty (Dors), who is "taking the rap" for her boyfriend; Babs (Hylton), who caused the needless death of her child; Nellie (Stone), a shoplifter; and Millie (Seyler), an old woman framed on a blackmail charge. *NOTES:* Based on the real life prison stay of author Joan Henry. Released in Great Britain at a running time of 88 mins.

423. Web of Evidence (10/18/59) B&W – 88 mins. (Mystery). *DIR:* Jack Cardiff. *PRO:* John R. Sloan, Maxwell Seton. *SP:* Kenneth Taylor. Based on *Beyond This Place* by A.J. Cronin. A Georgefield Production. *CAST:* Van Johnson, Vera Miles, Emlyn Williams, Bernard Lee, Jean Kent, Leo McKern, Rosalie Crutchley, Vincent Winter, Moultrie Kelsall, Ralph Truman, Geoffrey Keen, Jameson Clark, Joyce Heron, Henry Oscar. *SYN:* When a man (Johnson) returns to England to find his father (Lee), he is informed that his father has been imprisoned since 1940 for the murder of a young girl. With the help of a newspaper, he sets about to clear him and find the real murderer. *NOTES:* Working title was *P.O. Box 33*. Released in Great Britain at a running time of 90 mins. [British title: *Beyond This Place*.]

424. While the Sun Shines (6/20/50) B&W – 81 mins. (Comedy). *DIR:* Anatole de Grunwald. *PRO:* Anthony Asquith. *SP:* Terence Rattigan, Anatole de Grunwald. Based on the play by Terence Rattigan. An Associated British Picture–International Screenplays Production. A Stratford Picture Presentation. *CAST:* Barbara White, Ronald Squire, Ronald Howard, Brenda Bruce, Bonar Colleano, Margaret Rutherford, Cyril Maude, Michael Allan, Miles Malleson, Garry Marsh, Joyce Grenfall, Charles Victor, Wilfrid Hyde-White, Geoffrey Sumner, O.B. Clarence, Gordon Begg. *SYN:* An American soldier (Col-

Feature Films 143

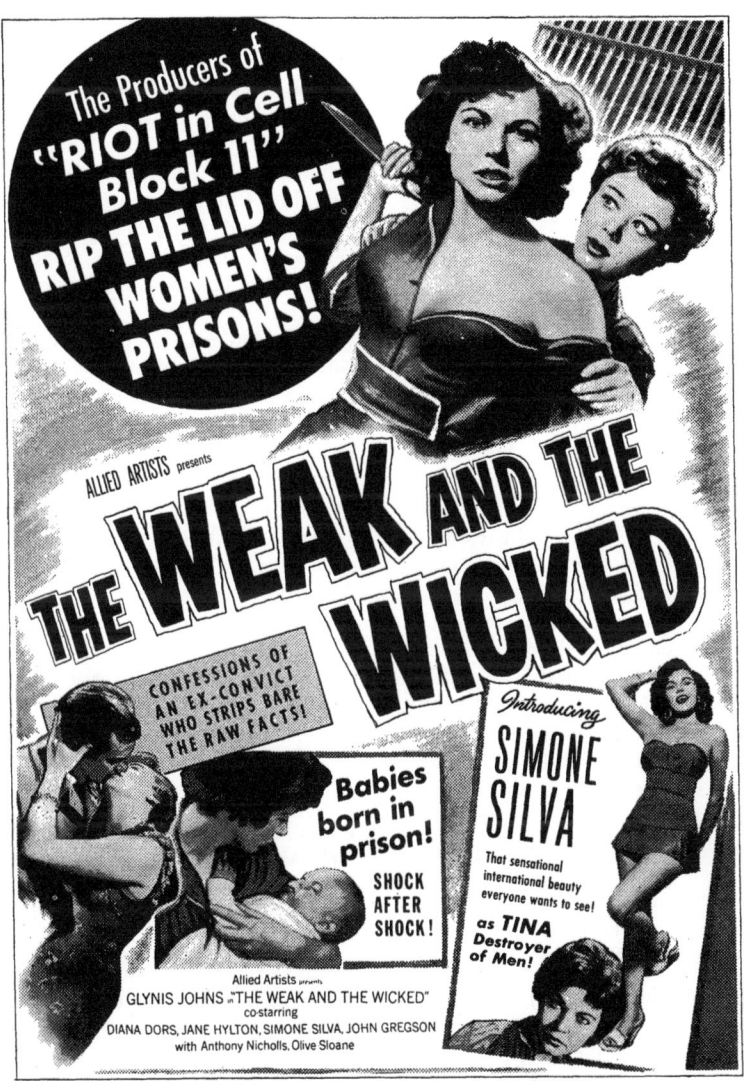

The Weak and the Wicked (1954): Bad Girls + Prison = Grand Entertainment. (Photo courtesy of Ted Okuda.)

leano) and a Frenchman (Allan) vie for the affections of a young woman (White), unaware that she is engaged to a British seaman (Howard), who happens to be a wealthy earl. NOTES: Released in Great Britain in 1947.

425. White Lightning (3/8/53) B&W – 61 mins. (Crime-Sports). *DIR:* Edward Bernds. *PRO:* Ben Schwalb. *SP:* Charles R. Marion. *CAST:* Stanley Clements, Steve Brodie, Gloria Blondell, Barbara Bestar, Lyle Talbot, Frank Jenks,

Paul Bryar, Lee Van Cleef, Myron Healey, Riley Hill, Tom Hanlon, Jane Easton, John Bleifer, Duncan Richardson, Joel Marston. *SYN:* A hotshot egotist (Clements) joins the Red Devils hockey team, and because of his talent on the ice, the players and coaches overlook his personality. When mobsters try to bribe him to throw the big game, honesty triumphs, and he leads the team to victory.

426. Who? (8/75) Eastmancolor – 93 mins. (Spy–Science Fiction). *DIR:* Jack Gold. *PRO:* Barry Levinson. *SP:* John Gould (Jack Gold). Based on the book by Algis Budrys. A Lion International–Hemisphere–MacLean Production. A Lorimar Pictures release. *CAST:* Elliott Gould, Trevor Howard, Joseph Bova, Ed Grover, John Lehne, James Noble, Kay Tornburg, Lyndon Brook, Joy Garrett, Ivan Desny, Alexander Allerton, Michael Lombard, John Stewart, Bruce Boa, Fred Vincent, Dan Sazarino, Craig McConnel. *SYN:* An American scientist (Bova), injured in an auto accident along the Russian border, is saved by Russian doctors who reconstruct his face and make him half man–half machine. When he returns to his top secret work, an American official (Gould) must determine whether he is working for the Russians or the Americans. [British title: *Man Without a Face.*]

427. Wichita (7/3/55) Technicolor/Scope – 81 mins. (Western). *DIR:* Jacques Tourneur. *PRO:* Walter Mirisch, Richard Heermance. *SP:* Daniel B. Ullman. *CAST:* Joel McCrea, Vera Miles, Lloyd Bridges, Wallace Ford, Edgar Buchanan, Peter Graves, Keith Larsen, Carl Benton Reid, John Smith, Walter Coy, Walter Sande, Robert J. Wilke, Rayford Barnes, Jack Elam, Mae Clark, Gene Wesson, I. Stanford Jolley, Kermit Maynard, voice of Tex Ritter. *SYN:* In 1874, Wyatt Earp (McCrea) agrees to take the job of sheriff in the wide, open cowtown of, Wichita, Kansas. *NOTES:* Allied Artists' first Cinemascope release.

428. Wicked Wife (10/25/55) B&W – 75 mins. (Crime). *DIR:* Bob McNaught. *PRO:* Phil C. Samuel. *SP:* Bob McNaught, Val Valentine. Based on the play *Grand National Night* by Dorothy and Campbell Christie. A Talisman–George Minter Production. *CAST:* Nigel Patrick, Moira Lister, Beatrice Campbell, Betty Ann Davies, Michael Hordern, Noel Purcell, Leslie Mitchell, Barry MacKay, Colin Gordon, Gibb McLaughlin, Richard Grayden, May Hallatt, George Sequira, Ernest Jay, Russell Waters, George Rose, Harold Goodwin, Arthur Howard, Edward Evans, Maria Mercedes. *SYN:* A horse owner (Patrick) accidently kills his wife (Lister) and, in a panic, hides the body in the trunk of the car of another man. When the police come to investigate he denies any knowledge of the crime. *NOTES:* Release date is also given as 5/8/56. Released in Great Britain in 1953 at a running time of 81 mins. [British title: *Grand National Night.*]

429. The Wild Geese (11/78) Eastmancolor/Panavision – 132 mins. (War). *DIR:* Andrew V. McLaglan. *PRO:* Euan Lloyd. *SP:* Reginald Rose. Based on the book by Daniel Carney. *CAST:* Richard Burton, Roger Moore, Richard Harris, Hardy Kruger, Stewart Granger, Jack Watson, Winston Ntshona, John Kani, Frank Finlay, Kenneth Griffith, Barry Foster, Jeff Corey, Ronald Fraser, Ian Yule, Brock Williams, Percy Herbert, Patrick Allen, Glyn Baker, Rosalind Lloyd, Joe Cole, David Ladd, Ken Gampu, Graham Clarke, Gordon Steel. *SYN:* Sir Edward Matherson (Granger), a London businessman, hires Col. Allen Faulkner (Burton), a mercenary, to rescue a former African president (Ntshona) and put him back in office. Faulkner recruits an army, trains them, and then leaves for Africa. They rescue the former president, but are double crossed by Matherson who makes a deal with the present government. They have to make their way across Africa to freedom, pursued by the Army of the present government. *NOTES:* After 31 years, this was the last film released by Allied Artists before declaring bankruptcy. A sequel, *Wild Geese II*, was released in 1985 by Universal Pictures and carried a dedication to Richard Burton, who was to have starred in it before his untimely death.

430. Will Any Gentleman? (9/27/55) Technicolor—84 mins. (Comedy). *DIR:* Michael Anderson. *PRO:* Hamilton G. Inglis. *SP:* Vernon Sylvaine. Based on the play by Vernon Sylvaine. An Associated British Picture Production. A Stratford Picture Presentation. *CAST:* George Cole, Veronica Hurst, Jon Pertwee, Heather Thatcher, James Hayter, William Hartnell, Diana Decker, Joan Sims, Alan Badel, Sidney James, Brian Oulton, Alexander Gauge, Josephine Douglas, Peter Butterworth, Wally Patch, Lionel Jeffries, Richard Massingham. *SYN:* A timid bank clerk (Cole) leads a frivolous life after he takes part in a hypnotist's show and is hypnotized. Before the spell can be broken, he cheats on his wife, spends his bank's money, and makes a fool of himself. *NOTES:* Released in Great Britain in 1953.

431. Wolf Larsen (10/26/58) B&W—83 mins. (Adventure-Drama). *DIR:* Harmon C. Jones. *PRO:* Lindsley Parsons. *SP:* Jack DeWitt, Turnley Walker. Based on *The Sea Wolf* by Jack London. *CAST:* Barry Sullivan, Peter Graves, Gita Hall, Thayer David, John Alderson, Rico Alaniz, Robert Gist, Jack Grinnage, Jack Orrison, Henry Rowland. *SYN:* Tyrannical sea captain Wolf Larsen (Sullivan) sadistically abuses his crew and the survivors (Graves, Hall) he saves. *NOTES:* Jack London's story has been filmed many times: as *The Sea Wolf* by Bosworth Films in 1913, Paramount in 1920, Producers Distributors Corp. in 1926, Fox in 1930, and Warner Bros. in 1941. It was also filmed by Warner Bros. in 1950 as a western, *Barricade*, by Cougar Films in 1975 as *Wolf Larsen—Legend of the Sea Wolf,* and by Turner Films in 1993.

432. The Woman's Angle (8/25/54) B&W—86 mins. (Romance). *DIR:* Leslie Arliss. *PRO:* Walter C. Mycroft. *SP:* Leslie Arliss, Mabbie Poole. Based on *Three Cups of Coffee* by Ruth Feiner. An Associated British Picture–Bow Bells Production. A Stratford Picture Presentation. *CAST:* Edward Underdown, Cathy O'Donnell, Lois Maxwell, Claude Farell, Peter Reynolds, Marjorie Fielding, Anthony Nicholls, Isabel Dean, John Bentley, Olaf Pooley, Ernest Thesiger, Eric Pohlmann, Joan Collins, Dagmar Wynter, Geoffrey Toone, Anton Diffring, Miles Malleson. *SYN:* A musical director (Underdown) finds true love with a music critic (O'Donnell). *NOTES:* Released in Great Britain in 1952.

Women of Nazi Germany see **Hitler**

433. World for Ransom (1/31/54) B&W—82 mins. (Spy-Drama). *DIR:* Robert Aldrich. *PRO:* Robert Aldrich, Bernard Tabakin. *SP:* Lindsay Hardy. A Plaza Production. *CAST:* Dan Duryea, Gene Lockhart, Patric Knowles, Reginald Denny, Nigel Bruce, Marian Carr, Douglass Dumbrille, Keye Luke, Clarence Lung, Lou Nova, Arthur Shields, Carmen D'Antonio. *SYN:* In Singapore, a World War II veteran (Duryea) turned private eye, is hired by an ex-girlfriend (Carr) to free her husband (Knowles) from the criminal activities in which he has become embroiled. He learns that the husband and a notorious black marketeer (Lockhart) have kidnapped an English nuclear scientist (Shields) and are holding him for ransom for the highest

Advertisement for *World Without End (1956)*.

bidding country. *NOTES:* The film debut of Marian Carr. Screenwriter Hugo Butler was uncredited. Loosely based on the *China Smith* television series.

434. World Without End (3/25/56) Technicolor/Scope – 80 mins. (Science Fiction). *DIR/SP:* Edward Bernds. *PRO:* Richard Heermance. *CAST:* Hugh Marlowe, Nancy Gates, Nelson Leigh, Booth Coleman, Rod Taylor, Christopher Dark, Shawn Smith, Lisa Montell, Everett Glass, Stanley Fraser, William Vedder, Rankin Mansfield, Paul Brineger, Mickey Simpson. *SYN:* Four astronauts (Marlowe, Leigh, Taylor, Dark) returning to Earth after orbiting Mars, encounter a time warp and land on earth in the year 2508, which has been devastated by nuclear war. *NOTES:* Costume designer for this film was Alberto Vargas, the famous pinup illustrator. Double billed in some areas with *The Indestructible Man.*

The Worst Secret Agents see **Oh! Those Most Secret Agents**

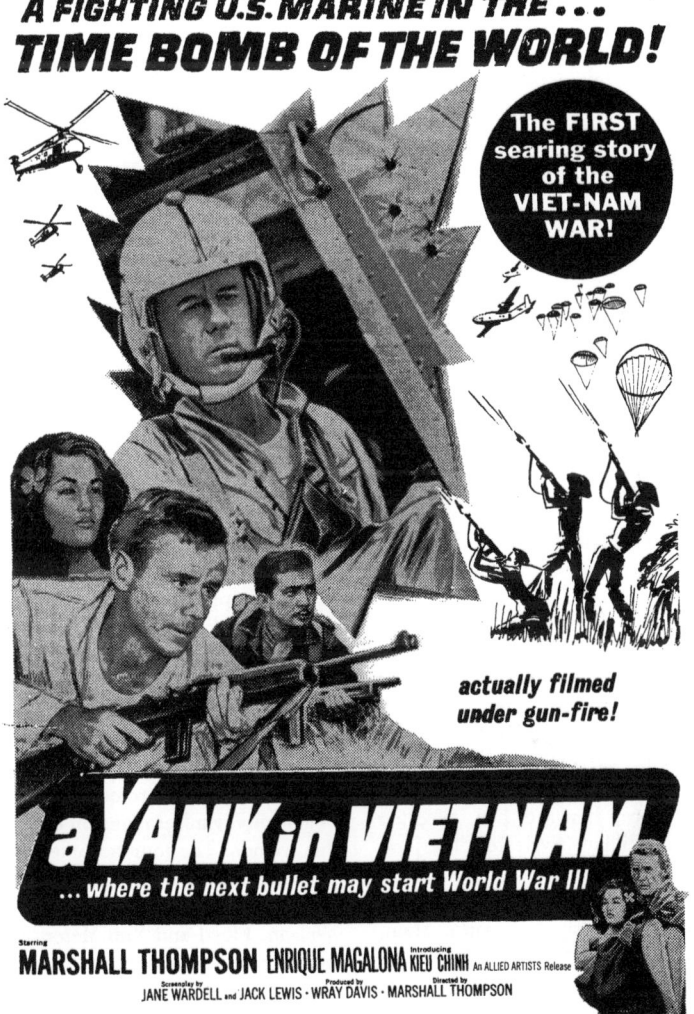

Advertisement for *A Yank in Viet-Nam* (1964). (Photo courtesy of Ted Okuda.)

435. A Yank in Viet-Nam (12/26/64) B&W – 80 mins. (War). *DIR:* Marshall Thompson. *PRO:* Wray Davis. *SP:* Jane Wardell, Jack Lewis. Story by Jack Lewis. A Kingman Production. *CAST:* Marshall Thompson, Enrique Magalona, Mario Barri, Kieu Chinh, Urban Drew, Donald Seely, Hoang Vinh Loc, Mi Tin, Rene Laporte, Doan Chau Mau, Pham Phouc Chi, Nam Chau, Kieu Nanh, Nam Luong, Le Van. *SYN:* A Marine pilot (Thompson) is captured by the Viet Cong when his helicopter crashes. He is saved by a group of guerrillas out to rescue an important doctor (Chau) and his daughter (Chinh), and they eventually make it back to the American lines. *NOTES:* Released 2/5/64 as *The*

Year of the Tiger. Re-released by Allied Artists on the above release date with the above title change. One of the few films released during this period that glorified the Americans' activities in Vietnam.

436. Yaqui Drums (10/12/56) B&W—71 mins. (Western). *DIR:* Jean Yarbrough. *PRO:* William F. Broidy. *SP:* Jo Pagano, D.D. Beauchamp. Story by Paul Leslie Peil. *CAST:* Rod Cameron, Mary Castle, J. Carrol Naish, Roy Roberts, Robert Hutton, Denver Pyle, Keith Richards, Ray Walker, Donald Kerr, G. Pat Collins, John Merrick, Paul Fierro, Fred Gabourie, Saul Gorss. *SYN:* A rancher (Cameron) fights a corrupt saloon owner (Naish) with the help of a Mexican outlaw gang.

The Year of the Tiger *see* **A Yank in Viet-Nam**

437. The Yellow Balloon (10/4/53) B&W—80 mins. (Crime). *DIR:* J. Lee Thompson. *PRO:* Victor Skutezky. *SP:* Anne Burnaby, J. Lee Thompson. Story by Anne Burnaby. A Marble Arch–Associated British Pictures Production. *CAST:* Andrew Ray, Kathleen Ryan, Kenneth More, Bernard Lee, Stephen Fenemore, William Sylvester, Marjorie Rhodes, Peter Jones, Elliot Makeham, Sidney James, Veronica Hurst, Sandra Dorne, Campbell Singer, Laurie Main, Hy Hazell. *SYN:* A crook (Sylvester) forces a boy (Ray) to steal for him and to be a decoy in bigger crimes by making the boy believe that he accidentally killed his friend over a yellow balloon. *NOTES:* Released in Great Britain in 1952.

438. You Can't Beat the Irish (4/30/52) B&W—78 mins. (Comedy). *DIR:* John Paddy Carstairs. *PRO:* Alex Boyd. *SP:* Frederic Gotfurt. Based on the play *They Got What They Wanted* by Louis d'Alton. An Associated British Picture Production. A Stratford Picture Presentation. *CAST:* Jack Warner, Barbara Mullen, Noel Purcell, Ronan O'Casey, Michael Dolan, Niall McGinnis, Vincent Ball, Joan Kenney, Elizabeth Erskine, Sidney James, Alfie Bass, Milo O'Shea. *SYN:* A lazy Irishman (Warner) poses as a royal heir to impress his English neighbors. *NOTES:* Released in Great Britain in 1951. [British title: *Talk of a Million.*]

439. Young Dillinger (4/28/65) B&W—102 mins. (Crime). *DIR:* Terry O. Morse. *PRO:* Alfred Zimbalist. *SP:* Donald Zimbalist, Arthur Hoerl. Story by Donald Zimbalist. A Zimbalist Co. Production. *CAST:* Nick Adams, Robert Conrad, John Ashley, Mary Ann Mobley, Victor Buono, Dan Terranova, John Hoyt, Reed Hadley, Robert Osterloh, Anthony Caruso, Art Baker, Gene Roth, Emile Meyer, Walter Sande, Ted Knight, Mike Masters, Aylene Gibbons, Frank Gerstle, Beverly Hills, Harvey Gardner, Helen Stephens, Joy Harmon, Robin Raymond, Sol Gorse, Charles Sloan, Wally Rose. *SYN:* In this Hollywood version, John Dillinger (Adams), in prison for robbery, becomes friends with Pretty Boy Floyd (Conrad), Baby Face Nelson (Ashley), and Homer Van Meter (Terranova). He is released from prison and soon organizes a prison break to free his friends. The four become bank robbers and, after many crimes, are eventually cornered by the FBI. In the end, Nelson, Floyd and Van Meter are killed as Dillinger makes good his escape to continue his life of crime, leaving behind his girl (Mobley). *NOTES:* The film debut of Mary Ann Mobley. Filmed in black and white, film processing was by Technicolor labs. Once deemed "too violent" for television by CBS, the film is now shown regularly on television. Double billed in some areas in 1967 with the Warner Bros. film *Bonnie and Clyde.*

440. The Young Guns (9/12/56) B&W—84 mins. (Western). *DIR:* Albert Band. *PRO:* Richard Heermance. *SP:* Louis Garfinkle. *CAST:* Russ Tamblyn,

Feature Films

Advertisement for *Young Dillinger* (1965).

Advertisement for *The Young Guns* (1956). (Photo courtesy of Ted Okuda.)

Gloria Talbott, Perry Lopez, Scott Marlowe, Wright King, Walter Coy, Chubby Johnson, Myron Healey, James Goodwin, Rayford Barnes, I. Stanford Jolley. *SYN:* The son (Tamblyn) of a famous gunman tries to live a peaceful life in a small town, but his father's reputation makes his life difficult.

The Young Rebels see **Teenage Doll!**

441. Young Wives' Tale (6/9/52) B&W – 78 mins. (Comedy). *DIR:* Henry Cass. *PRO:* Victor Skutezky. *SP:* Anne Burnaby. Based on the play by Ronald Jeans. An Associated British Picture

Production. A Stratford Picture Presentation. *CAST:* Joan Greenwood, Nigel Patrick, Derek Farr, Guy Middleton, Athene Seyler, Helen Cherry, Audrey Hepburn, Fabia Drake, Irene Handl, Joan Sanderson, Jack McNaughton, Brian Oulton, Carol James, Selma Vaz Dias. *SYN:* Mixups abound as a playwright (Patrick) and his wife (Greenwood) share their house with another couple (Farr, Cherry), a boarder (Hepburn) and assorted loonies. *NOTES:* Released in Great Britain in 1951. Re-released under the Allied Artists logo in 1954.

442. Yukon Vengeance (1/17/54) B&W – 68 mins. (Western). *DIR:* William Beaudine. *PRO:* William F. Broidy. *SP:* William Raynor. Based on a story by James Oliver Curwood. *CAST:* Kirby Grant, Monte Hale, Mary Ellen Kay, Henry Kulky, Carol Thurston, Parke MacGregor, Fred Gabourie, Billy Wilkerson, Marshall Bradford, "Chinook," the dog. *SYN:* A Mountie (Grant) travels to Bear Creek to track down the murderer of three mail carriers.

00-2 Most Secret Agents *see* **Oh! Those Most Secret Agents**

443. Zorro (6/76) Eastmancolor – 100 mins. (Western-Adventure). *DIR/PRO:* Duccio Tessari. *SP:* Giorgio Arlorio. A Titanus Production. *CAST:* Alain Delon, Stanley Baker, Ottavia Piccolo, Moustache, Adriana Asti, Enzo Cerusico, Jack Stuart (Giacomo Rossi Stuart), Giampiero Albertini, Duccio Tessari. *SYN:* Don Diego (Delon), also known as Zorro, becomes governor of a South American country and must pretend to be afraid of his military chief (Baker) while righting wrongs in the guise of Zorro. *NOTES:* Originally released in France in 1975 at a running time of 125 mins. Running times vary from 89 mins. to 100 mins.

Problem Films

The following features were scheduled by Allied Artists for theatrical distribution. Whether or not they did receive theatrical distribution is uncertain. Although no formal reviews have been given these features, they are listed here for the sake of completeness.

444. And Millions Will Die! (1974) Eastmancolor—96 mins. (Crime-Drama.) *DIR:* Leslie Martinson. *PRO:* Not given. *SP:* Not given. *CAST:* Richard Basehart, Susan Strasberg, Leslie Nielsen, Peter Sumner, Tony Wager, Joseph Furst, Alwyn Kurts, George Assang, Jack Allen, Rowena Wallace, Les Foxcroft, Willie Fennell, Carmen Duncan, Russell Waters, Gary Mullay, Bill Jarvis, James Ho. *SYN:* A scientist (Basehart) searches for a time bomb hidden beneath the streets of Hong Kong. *NOTES:* Release dates vary between 1972 and 1974, and running times vary between 96 mins. and 104 mins.

445. The Human Vapor (1964) Eastmancolor/Scope—80 mins. (Science Fiction). *DIR:* Inoshiro Honda. *PRO:* Tomoyuki Tanaka. *SP:* Takeshi Kimura. A Toho Production. A Brenco Film Presentation. *CAST:* Yoshio Tsuchiya, Kaoru Yachigusa, Tatsuya Mihashi, Keiko Sata, Bokuzen Hidari. *SYN:* An ex-convict (Tsuchiya), who as a result of his participation in prison experiments, is able to transform himself into a gaseous vapor. *NOTES:* Released in Japan in 1960. Possibly released by Allied Artists in Southern California only. Released elsewhere by Brenco Pictures. [Original Japanese title: *Gasu Ningen Daiichigo.*]

446. Seven Times Seven (1969) Eastmancolor/Scope—92 mins. (Crime-Comedy). *DIR:* Michele Lupo. *PRO:* Marco Vicario. *SP:* Lorenzo Ruffino. Story by Walter Patriarca, Gianfranco Clerici. A Euroatlantica Production. *CAST:* Lionel Stander, Gastone Moschin, Gordon Mitchell, Paul Stevens, Adolfo Celi, Raimondo Vianello, Nino Zamperla, Theodor Corra, Erika Blane, Turi Terro, Terry-Thomas, Neil McCarthy, Christopher Benjamin, David Lodge, Gladys Dawson, Lionel Murton. *SYN:* Seven convicts break out of prison to break into the Royal Mint in order to print their own batch of money. They then break back into prison. *NOTES:* Filmed and released in Italy in 1968. This film may have had a limited theatrical release. [Original Italian title: *Sette Volte Sette.*]

447. Ways of Women (1971) Eastmancolor/B&W—90 mins. *DIR/PRO/SP:* Gabriel Axel. Story by Gabriel Axel. An Axel-Merry Film Production in association with Les Films La Boetie of Paris. *CAST:* Dirch Passer, Ghita Norby, Svend Johansen, Ole Guldbrandsen, Morten Grunwald. *SYN:* None available. *NOTES:* Completed in Denmark in October, 1969. Also known as *Three Kinds of Love.* The first two-thirds of the film were in color and the last third was a black and white French sex spoof added to the film.

448. The World of Sportfishing (1972) Eastmancolor—107 mins. (Documentary). *DIR:* Bud Morgan. *PRO:* Leonard Gruenberg. *CAST:* Bing Crosby, Van Heflin, Ernest Borgnine, Phil Harris. *SYN:* Compilaton from eight years of TV's *American Sportsman* series, centering around fishing in various parts of the world.

Short Subjects
(1947–1978)

Following is a known list of live action and animated short subjects distributed by Allied Artists Pictures Corporation. They are listed here for reference as no formal reviews could be found for these shorts.

449. The Mighty Fortress (6/26/54). (Documentary). *PRO:* Paul Short. *SYN:* A religious documentary centering on the Reverend Billy Graham and his crusade.

450. Paris, City of Fashion (11/11/51). (Documentary). A Stratford Picture Presentation. *SYN:* A tour of Paris, France.

451. The Thieving Magpie (10/21/65). (Animated). *PRO:* Emanuele Luzzati. *SYN:* An animated short based on the Rossini overture.

452. World Championship Fight (9/27/62) (Sports). *SYN:* Filmed heavyweight fight between Charles "Sonny" Liston and Floyd Patterson on September 25, 1962, which ended in a one round TKO by "Sonny" Liston.

Appendix A: Film Titles by Release Date

The number after each film title and release date (month/day or month) refers to the entry number, not the page number.

1947

It Happened on Fifth Avenue (4/19) 200
Black Gold (9/16) 41
The Gangster (11/22) 145

1948

Song of My Heart (1/31) 359
Panhandle (2/22) 295
The Hunted (4/3) 189
Smart Woman (4/30) 354
The Dude Goes West (5/30) 116
The Babe Ruth Story (9/6) 18

1949

Strike It Rich (1/1) 373
There's a Girl in My Heart (1/11) 388
Bad Boy (1/22) 19
Bad Men of Tombstone (2/22) 20
Massacre River (6/26) 251
My Brother Jonathan (6/29) 267
Stampede (8/28) 366
The Golden Madonna (9/15) 151

1950

No Room at the Inn (1/10) 282
Silent Dust (1/22) 350
Bond Street (3/29) 53
Mrs. Fitzherbert (5/10) 262
While the Sun Shines (6/20) 424
For Them That Trespass (7/6) 134
Dancing Years (8/23) 94
The Queen of Spades (9/15) 317
Last Holiday (11/13) 219
Southside 1-1000 (11/16) 361
Short Grass (12/24) 348

1951

No Place for Jennifer (3/30) 280
I Was an American Spy (4/14) 192
Murder Without Crime (4/27) 264
Portrait of Claire (6/24) 310
Guilt Is My Shadow (7/8) 154
Her Panelled Door (7/30) 164
The Highwayman (8/12) 171
Man on the Run (8/29) 244
Disc Jockey (9/30) 108
The Lucky Mascot (10/11) 238
Double Confession (11/4) 112
Laughter in Paradise (11/11) 222
Paris, City of Fashion (11/11) 450

1952

The Franchise Affair (4/28) 137
You Can't Beat the Irish (4/30) 438
Young Wives' Tale (6/9) 441
Battle Zone (10/26) 26
Flat Top (10/26) 131
The Maverick (12/14) 254
Castle in the Air (12/26) 70
Hiawatha (12/28) 167

1953

Star of Texas (1/11) 367
Fangs of the Arctic (1/18) 122
Torpedo Alley (1/25) 401
Tangier Incident (2/1) 380
Jalopy (2/15) 204
Kansas Pacific (2/22) 209
White Lightning (3/8) 425
The Homesteaders (3/22) 175
Fort Vengeance (3/29) 135
The Marksman (4/12) 248
The Trail Blazers (4/19) 403
Father's Doing Fine (4/22) 153
Cow Country (4/26) 84
Rebel City (5/10) 322
Landfall (5/11) 253
Loose in London (5/24) 234
Roar of the Crowd (5/31) 330
Murder Without Tears (6/14) 265
Safari Drums (6/21) 335
Son of Belle Star (6/28) 358
Northern Patrol (7/12) 283
The Maze (7/26) 255
Topeka (8/9) 399
Affair in Monte Carlo (8/14) 3
Clipped Wings (8/14) 73
Mr. Potts Goes to Moscow (9/3) 259
Mexican Manhunt (9/13) 257
The Fighting Lawman (9/20) 126
The Royal African Rifles (9/27) 332
The Yellow Balloon (10/4) 437
Hot News (10/11) 179
Jennifer (10/25) 205
Jack Slade (11/8) 202
Border City Rustlers (11/15) 54
Secret of Outlaw Flats (11/15) 338
Six-Gun Decision (11/15) 351
Two-Gun Marshal (11/15) 409
Vigilante Terror (11/15) 417
Fighter Attack (11/29) 125
Private Eyes (12/6) 313
Texas Bad Man (12/20) 385

1954

The Golden Idol (1/10) 150
Yukon Vengeance (1/17) 442
World for Ransom (1/31) 433
Highway Dragnet (2/7) 170
Bitter Creek (2/21) 39
Riot in Cell Block 11 (2/28) 329
Paris Playboys (3/7) 298
Dragonfly Squadron (3/21) 114
Loophole (3/28) 233
Pride of the Blue Grass (4/4) 312
Arrow in the Dust (4/25) 11
Angels One Five (4/30) 7
The Forty-Niners (5/4) 136
The Bowery Boys Meet the Monsters (6/6) 55
The Desperado (6/20) 101
Men Are Children Twice (6/26) 256
The Mighty Fortress (6/26) 449
The Weak and the Wicked (7/18) 422
Return from the Sea (7/25) 325
The House of the Arrow (8/1) 184
Security Risk (8/8) 339
Killer Leopard (8/22) 211
The Woman's Angle (8/25) 432
Jungle Gents (9/5) 208
Two Guns and a Badge (9/12) 411
The Human Jungle (10/3) 187
The Bob Mathias Story (10/24) 50
Target Earth! (11/7) 381
Isn't Life Wonderful (11/10) 199
Cry Vengeance (11/21) 91
The Good Beginning (11/28) 152
Port of Hell (12/5) 308
Tonight's the Night (12/19) 398
Marshals in Disguise (12/26) 250
Outlaw's Son (12/26) 292
Trouble on the Trail (12/26) 406
The Two Gun Teacher (12/26) 410

1955

Bowery to Baghdad (1/2) 56
Treasure of Ruby Hills (1/23) 404
The Big Combo (2/13) 34
Murder Is My Beat (2/27) 263
Dial Red "O" (3/13) 103
The Big Tip Off (3/20) 35
Seven Angry Men (3/27) 342
An Annapolis Story (4/10) 8
High Society (4/17) 168
Shotgun (4/24) 349
The Match-Making Marshal (5/8) 253
Phantom Trails (5/8) 304

Timber Country Trouble (5/8) 395
The Titled Tenderfoot (5/8) 397
Las Vegas Shakedown (5/15) 218
Skabenga (5/29) 352
Lord of the Jungle (6/12) 235
Case of the Red Monkey (6/19) 69
Fingerman (6/19) 129
Cocktails in the Kitchen (6/20) 74
Wichita (7/13) 427
Betrayed Women (7/17) 30
Spy Chasers (7/31) 364
The Phenix City Story (8/14) 305
Night Freight (8/28) 278
The Warriors (9//11) 420
Jail Busters (9/18) 203
Will Any Gentleman? (9/27) 430
The Return of Jack Slade (10/9) 326
Bobby Ware Is Missing (10/23) 51
Wicked Wife (10/25) 428
Toughest Man Alive (11/6) 402
Paris Follies of 1956 (11/27) 297
Shack Out on 101 (12/4) 345
Sudden Danger (12/14) 374
At Gunpoint (12/25) 13

1956

Dig That Uranium (1/8) 105
The Deadliest Sin (1/29) 98
Invasion of the Body Snatchers (2/5) 197
The Atomic Man (3/4) 14
The Indestructible Man (3/25) 195
World Without End (3/25) 434
The Come-On (4/16) 76
Crashing Las Vegas (4/22) 85
Thunderstorm (5/6) 393
Navy Wife (5/20) 272
Screaming Eagles (5/27) 336
Crime in the Streets (6/10) 87
The Naked Hills (6/17) 269
King of the Coral Sea (6/24) 213
The First Texan (6/29) 130
Fright (6/30) 141
Three for Jamie Dawn (7/8) 391
Magnificent Roughnecks (7/22) 241
Hold Back the Night (7/29) 173
Canyon River (8/5) 68
No Place to Hide (8/28) 281

Strange Intruder (9/2) 371
The Young Guns (9/12) 440
Fighting Trouble (9/16) 127
Calling Homicide (9/30) 64
Yaqui Drums (10/12) 436
The Cruel Tower (10/28) 88
Blonde Sinner (11/18) 44
Friendly Persuasion (11/25) 140
The High Terrace (12/9) 169
Hot Shots (12/23) 182

1957

Chain of Evidence (1/6) 71
Attack of the Crab Monsters (2/10) 16
Not of This Earth (2/10) 284
Last of the Badmen (2/17) 220
Hold That Hypnotist (3/10) 174
The Badge of Marshal Brennan (4/14) 21
Footsteps in the Night (4/14) 133
Dragoon Wells Massacre (4/28) 115
The Persuader (5/5) 303
Destination 60,000 (5/12) 102
The Oklahoman (5/19) 287
Let's Be Happy (5/26) 226
Spook Chasers (6/2) 363
Calypso Joe (6/9) 66
Hot Rod Rumble (6/9) 181
Love in the Afternoon (6/30) 237
Dino (7/21) 106
The Constant Husband (7/25) 80
The Cyclops (7/28) 93
Daughter of Dr. Jekyll (7/28) 95
Portland Exposé (8/11) 309
The Disembodied (8/25) 109
From Hell It Came (8/25) 144
Death in Small Doses (9/15) 99
Teenage Doll! (9/22) 382
Undersea Girl (9/22) 413
Naked in the Sun (9/29) 270
Affair in Havana (10/1) 2
Looking for Danger (10/6) 232
Gun Battle at Monterey (10/27) 155
The Hunchback of Notre Dame (11/3) 188
The Tall Stranger (11/17) 378
Sabu and the Magic Ring (11/24) 334
Up in Smoke (12/22) 416
Oregon Passage (12/29) 291

1958

Blonde Blackmailer (1/19) 43
The Rawhide Trail (1/26) 320
Man from God's Country (2/9) 243
In the Money (2/16) 193
The Beast of Budapest (2/23) 28
The Bride and the Beast (2/23) 58
Macabre (3/9) 239
Seven Guns to Mesa (3/16) 343
Cole Younger, Gunfighter (3/30) 75
Contraband Spain (4/10) 81
Hell's Five Hours (4/13) 163
Quantrill's Raiders (4/27) 315
Good Companions (5/1) 153
Hong Kong Affair (5/11) 176
Attack of the 50 Ft. Woman (5/18) 17
War of the Satellites (5/18) 419
Bullwhip (5/25) 62
The Pagans (6/1) 294
New Orleans After Dark (6/15) 275
Now and Forever (6/21) 285
Never Love a Stranger (6/22) 273
The Littlest Hobo (7/6) 230
Snowfire (7/6) 356
The Accursed (7/13) 1
Frankenstein–1970 (7/20) 139
Spy in the Sky! (7/20) 365
The Inbetween Age (8/3) 194
Cry Baby Killer (8/17) 89
Hot Car Girl (8/17) 178
It's Never Too Late (9/2) 201
Queen of Outer Space (9/7) 316
Legion of the Doomed (9/21) 224
Wolf Larsen (10/26) 431
Joy Ride (11/23) 207
Unwed Mother (11/23) 415
Gunsmoke in Tucson (12/7) 159
Johnny Rocco (12/21) 206
Revolt in the Big House (12/21) 327

1959

The Cosmic Man (2/17) 83
House on Haunted Hill (2/17) 185
Arson for Hire (3/1) 12
The Giant Behemoth (3/1) 148
Al Capone (4/5) 4
King of the Wild Stallions (5/17) 215/216

The Rebel Set (6/28) 323
Speed Crazy (6/28) 362
The Big Circus (7/5) 33
Battle Flame (7/26) 24
Surrender–Hell! (7/26) 376
The Bat (8/9) 23
Face of Fire (8/9) 121
Web of Evidence (10/18) 423
Crime and Punishment, U.S.A. (11/1) 86
House of Intrigue (11/15) 183
The Atomic Submarine (11/29) 15

1960

The Purple Gang (1/5) 314
The Hypnotic Eye (2/27) 190
Beast from Haunted Cave (3/14) 27
The Wasp Woman (3/14) 421
I Passed for White (3/18) 191
Bluebeard's Ten Honeymoons (4/2) 49
Heroes Die Young (5/22) 166
Raymie (7/5) 321
Pay or Die (7/27) 301
Sex Kittens Go to College (8/24) 344
Caltiki, the Immortal Monster (9/20) 65
Tormented (9/22) 400
Hell to Eternity (9/30) 162
Serengeti Shall Not Die (10/12) 340
The Bloody Brood (10/22) 48
The Plunderers (11/5) 307
The Unfaithfuls (11/28) 414
Herod the Great (12/5) 165

1961

Look in Any Window (1/29) 231
Operation Eichmann (3/15) 290
Dondi (3/26) 111
Time Bomb (4/23) 396
The Bridge (5/1) 59
Angel Baby (5/14) 6
David and Goliath (5/28) 96
King of the Roaring 20s–The Arnold Rothstein Story (6/11) 214
Brainwashed (6/25) 57
Armored Command (7/9) 10
Karate, the Hand of Death (8/9) 210
Twenty Plus Two (8/13) 407
The Red Cloak (10/4) 324

Appendix A

The George Raft Story (11/22) 147
El Cid (12/15) 117

1962

The Bashful Elephant (2/4) 22
Hitler (3/21) 172
Hands of a Stranger (4/22) 160
The Big Wave (4/29) 36
Payroll (5/20) 302
Rider on a Dead Horse (5/27) 328
Confessions of an Opium Eater (6/20) 79
The Frightened City (7/20) 143
Convicts Four (9/15) 82
World Championship Fight (9/27) 452
Billy Budd (11/12) 38
Night Encounter (12/28) 277

1963

The Day of the Triffids (4/27) 97
Black Zoo (5/15) 42
Play It Cool (5/29) 306
55 Days at Peking (6/26) 124
The Gun Hawk (8/28) 156
Shock Corridor (9/18) 347
Cry of Battle (10/9) 90
War Is Hell! (10/23) 418
Gunfight at Comanche Creek (11/6) 157
Soldier in the Rain (11/27) 357

1964

Life in Danger (2/1) 228
The Servant (3/16) 341
Never Put It in Writing (4/28) 274
The Strangler (4/30) 372
The Thin Red Line (5/2) 389
The Secret Door (6/4) 337
Stop Train 349 (7/5) 369
Station-Six Sahara (8/10) 368
Master Spy (8/19) 252
Escape by Night (8/29) 120
Blood on the Arrow (10/11) 46
The Naked Kiss (10/29) 271
Racing Fever (10/30) 318
The Umbrellas of Cherbourg (12/16) 412

A Yank in Viet-Nam (12/26) 435
The Human Vapor (?) 445

1965

Mara of the Wilderness (1/20) 247
The Human Duplicators (3/3) 186
Mutiny in Outer Space (3/3) 266
Taffy and the Jungle Hunter (3/31) 377
Blood and Black Lace (4/7) 45
The Pawnbroker (4/20) 300
The Fool Killer (4/28) 132
Young Dillinger (4/28) 439
Finger on the Trigger (5/26) 128
Gunmen of the Rio Grande (6/23) 158
Tickle Me (6/24) 394
Life Upside Down (8/17) 229
City of Fear (9/8) 72
Operation C.I.A. (9/8) 289
Curse of the Voodoo (9/22) 92
Frankenstein Meets the Space Monster (9/22) 138
The Magic Weaver (9/22) 240
The Thieving Magpie (10/21) 451
The Desert Raven (10/27) 100
The Eleanor Roosevelt Story (11/8) 118
The Leather Boys (11/8) 223
King and Country (11/30) 212

1966

The Gentle Rain (2/10) 146
The Party's Over (3/23) 299
Oh! Those Most Secret Agents (3/25) 286
Moonwolf (5/11) 261
Disk-O-Tek Holiday (6/1) 110
Once Upon an Island (6/15) 288
Terror in the City (6/24) 384
Nightmare Castle (7/5) 279
A Man and a Woman (8/5) 242
Hot Rod Hullabaloo (11/1) 180
Run for Your Wife (11/15) 333

1967

The Tall Women (3/1) 379
Bikini Paradise (5/3) 37
That Man George! (9/15) 387

Battle of Algiers (9/21) 25
Island of the Doomed (11/15) 198
Lemonade Joe (11/25) 225

1968

The Sorcerers (1/2) 360
Belle de Jour (4/10) 29
The Man Outside (6/20) 245
Mission Mars (7/26) 258
Snow Treasure (10/4) 355
The Hooked Generation (11/13) 177

1969

The Man Outside (3) 245
Ski Fever (3) 353
The Body Stealers (4) 52
The Candy Man (7) 67
Last Summer (10) 221
La Femme Infidele (11) 123a
Marry Me! Marry Me! (11) 249
Trilogy (12) 405
Seven Times Seven (?) 446

1970

End of the Road (2) 119
Diary of a Schizophrenic Girl (4) 104
Paddy (4) 293
Head of the Family (7) 161
The Blood Rose (10) 47
This Man Must Die (10) 390
Portraits of Women (12) 311

1971

Beyond Love and Evil (3) 32
shinbone alley (3) 346
Love in a Four-Letter World (3) 236
Romance of a Horse Thief (8) 331
The Anonymous Venetian (9) 9
Cometogether (9) 77
Ways of Women (?) 447

1972

Cabaret (2) 63
Fright (5) 142
The World of Sport Fishing (?) 448

1973

Papillon (12) 296

1974

Rampart of Desire (1) 319
Three the Hard Way (6) 392
The Internecine Project (9) 196
Gold (10) 149
And Millions Will Die (?) 444

1975

A Brief Vacation (2) 60
The Dragon Dies Hard (4) 113
Mitchell (6) 260
Conduct Unbecoming (8) 78
Who? (8) 426
The Story of O (11) 370
The Man Who Would Be King (12) 246
That Lucky Touch (12) 386

1976

Zorro (6) 443
Bruce Lee—Superdragon (7) 61
My Friends (7) 268
Let's Talk About Men (8) 227
The Next Man (11) 276
Superbug (11) 375

1977

Dirty Money (1) 107
Twilight's Last Gleaming (2) 408
Black and White in Color (4) 40
Teenage Graffiti (5) 383

1978

The Betsy (2) 31
Alice, Sweet Alice (5) 5
The Wild Geese (11) 429

Appendix B: The Monogram/Allied Artists Movie Series

*Films marked with * were continued through Allied Artists.*

Bomba, the Jungle Boy

Bomba, the Jungle Boy (1949)
Bomba on Panther Island (1949)
The Lost Volcano (1950)
Bomba and the Hidden City (1950)
The Lion Hunters (1951)
Elephant Stampede (1951)
African Treasure (1952)
Bomba and the Jungle Girl (1952)
*Safari Drums (1953)
The Golden Idol (1954)
Killer Leopard (1954)
Lord of the Jungle (1955)

The East Side Kids

East Side Kids (1940)
Boys of the City (1940)
That Gang of Mine (1940)
Pride of the Bowery (1941)
Flying Wild (1941)
Bowery Blitzkrieg (1941)
Spooks Run Wild (1941)
Mr. Wise Guy (1942)
Let's Get Tough (1942)
Smart Alecks (1942)
'Neath Brooklyn Bridge (1942)
Kid Dynamite (1943)
Clancy Street Boys (1943)
Ghosts on the Loose (1943)
Mr. Muggs Steps Out (1943)
Million Dollar Kid (1944)
Follow the Leader (1944)
Block Busters (1944)
Bowery Champs (1944)
Docks of New York (1945)
Mr. Muggs Rides Out (1945)
Come Out Fighting (1945)

The Bowery Boys

Live Wires (1946)
In Fast Company (1946)
Bowery Bombshell (1946)
Spook Busters (1946)
Mr. Hex (1946)
Hard Boiled Mahoney (1947)
News Hounds (1947)
Bowery Buckaroos (1947)
Angels' Alley (1948)
Jinx Money (1948)
Smugglers' Cove (1948)
Trouble Makers (1948)
Fighting Fools (1949)
Hold That Baby! (1949)
Angels in Disguise (1949)
Master Minds (1949)
Blonde Dynamite (1950)
Lucky Losers (1950)
Triple Trouble (1950)

Blues Busters (1950)
Bowery Battalion (1951)
Ghost Chasers (1951)
Let's Go Navy (1951)
Crazy Over Horses (1951)
Hold That Line (1952)
Here Comes the Marines (1952)
Feudin' Fools (1952)
No Holds Barred (1952)
*Jalopy (1953)
Loose in London (1953)
Clipped Wings (1953)
Private Eyes (1953)
Paris Playboys (1954)
The Bowery Boys Meet the Monsters (1954)
Jungle Gents (1954)
Bowery to Baghdad (1955)
High Society (1955)
Spy Chasers (1955)
Jail Busters (1955)
Dig That Uranium (1956)
Crashing Las Vegas (1956)
Fighting Trouble (1956)
Hot Shots (1956)
Hold That Hypnotist (1957)
Spook Chasers (1957)
Looking for Danger (1957)
Up in Smoke (1957)
In the Money (1958)

Charlie Chan
(Sidney Toler)

Charlie Chan in the Secret Service (1944)
The Chinese Cat (1944)
Black Magic (AKA: Meeting at Midnight) (1944)
The Jade Mask (1945)
The Scarlet Clue (1945)
The Shanghai Cobra (1945)
The Red Dragon (1946)
Dark Alibi (1946)
Shadows Over Chinatown (1946)
Dangerous Money (1946)
The Trap (1946)

Charlie Chan
(Roland Winters)

The Chinese Ring (1947)
Docks of New Orleans (1948)
The Shanghai Chest (1948)
The Golden Eye (1948)
The Feathered Serpent (1948)
Sky Dragon (1949)

Snuffy Smith
(Bud Duncan)

Private Snuffy Smith (1942)
Hillbilly Blitzkrieg (1942)

James Lee Wong
(Boris Karloff)

Mr. Wong, Detective (1938)
The Mystery of Mr. Wong (1939)
Mr. Wong in Chinatown (1939)
The Fatal Hour (1940)
Doomed to Die (1940)

James Lee Wong
(Keye Luke)

Phantom of Chinatown (1940)

Tailspin Tommy
(John Trent)

Mystery Plane (1939)
Stunt Pilot (1939)
Sky Patrol (1939)
Danger Flight (1939)

The Shadow
(Kane Richmond)

The Shadow Returns (1946)

Behind the Mask (1946)
The Missing Lady (1946)

Kitty O'Day

Detective Kitty O'Day (1944)
Adventures of Kitty O'Day (1944)
Fashion Model (1945)

The Teen Agers

Junior Prom (1946)
Freddie Steps Out (1946)
High School Hero (1946)
Vacation Days (1947)
Sarge Goes to College (1947)
Smart Politics (1948)
Campus Sleuth (1948)

Henry Latham
(Raymond Walburn)

Henry, the Rainmaker (1949)
Leave It to Henry (1949)
Father Makes Good (1950)
Father's Wild Game (1950)
Father Takes the Air (1951)

Jiggs and Maggie
(Joe Yule, Renie Riano)

Bringing Up Father (1946)
Jiggs and Maggie in Society (1947)
Jiggs and Maggie in Court (1948)
Jiggs and Maggie in Jackpot Jitters (1949)
Jiggs and Maggie Out West (1950)

Joe Palooka
(Joe Kirkwood)

Joe Palooka, Champ (1946)
Gentleman Joe Palooka (1946)
Joe Palooka in the Knockout (1947)
Joe Palooka in Fighting Mad (1948)
Winner Take All (1948)
Joe Palooka in the Big Fight (1949)
Joe Palooka in the Counterpunch (1949)
Joe Palooka Meets Humphrey (1950)
Humphrey Takes a Chance (1950)
Joe Palooka in the Squared Circle (1950)
Triple Cross (1951)

Lt. Doyle
(Bill Elliott)

*Sudden Danger (1955)
Calling Homicide (1956)
Chain of Evidence (1957)
Footsteps in the Night (1957)

Appendix C: Westerns and Players Associated with Monogram/Allied Artists

*Films marked with * were continued through Allied Artists.*

Bill Cody

Dugan of the Badlands (1931)
The Montana Kid (1931)
Oklahoma Jim (1931)
Land of Wanted Men (1931)
Ghost City (1932)
Mason of the Mounted (1932)
Law of the North (1932)
Texas Pioneers (1932)

Tom Tyler

Partners of the Trail (1931)
The Man from Death Valley (1931)
Two-Fisted Justice (1931)
Galloping Thru (1931)
Single-Handed Sanders (1932)
The Man from New Mexico (1932)
Vanishing Men (1932)
Honor of the Mounted (1932)

Rex Bell

From Broadway to Cheyenne (1932)
The Man from Arizona (1932)
Lucky Larrigan (1932)
The Diamond Trail (1932)
Crashing Broadway (1933)
The Fighting Texans (1933)
The Fugitive (1933)
Rainbow Ranch (1933)

Bob Steele

Hidden Valley (1932)
Young Blood (1932)
The Fighting Champ (1932)
Breed of the Border (1933)
The Gallant Fool (1933)
Trailin' North (1933)
Galloping Romeo (1933)
The Ranger's Code (1933)

John Wayne

Riders of Destiny (1933)
The Sagebrush Trail (1933)
The Lucky Texan (1934)
West of the Divide (1934)
Blue Steel (1934)
The Man from Utah (1934)
Randy Rides Alone (1934)
The Star Packer (1934)
The Trail Beyond (1934)
The Lawless Frontier (1934)
'Neath Arizona Skies (1934)
Texas Terror (1935)
Rainbow Valley (1935)
The Desert Trail (1935)
The Dawn Rider (1935)
Paradise Canyon (1935)

Appendix C

Jack Randall

Riders of the Dawn (1937)
Stars Over Arizona (1937)
Danger Valley (1937)
Where the West Began (1938)
Land of Fighting Men (1938)
Gunsmoke Trail (1938)
Man's Country (1938)
Mexicali Kid (1938)
Gun Packer (1938)
Wild Horse Canyon (1938)
Drifting Westward (1939)
Trigger Smith (1939)
Across the Plains (1939)
Oklahoma Terror (1939)
Overland Mail (1939)
Pioneer Days (1940)
The Cheyenne Kid (1940)
Covered Wagon Trails (1940)
Land of the Six Guns (1940)
The Kid from Santa Fe (1940)
Riders from Nowhere (1940)
Wild Horse Range (1940)

Tex Ritter

Starlight Over Texas (1938)
Where the Buffalo Roam (1938)
Song of the Buckaroo (1939)
Sundown on the Prairie (1939)
Rollin' Westward (1939)
Man from Texas (1939)
Down the Wyoming Trail (1939)
Riders of the Frontier (1939)
Roll, Wagons, Roll (1939)
Westbound Stage (1939)
Rhythm of the Rio Grande (1940)
Pals of the Silver Sage (1940)
Cowboy from Sundown (1940)
The Golden Trail (1940)
Rainbow Over the Range (1940)
Arizona Frontier (1940)
Take Me Back to Oklahoma (1940)
Rollin' Home to Texas (1940)

Ridin' the Cherokee Trail (1941)
The Pioneers (1941)

Tim McCoy

West of Rainbow's End (1938)
Code of the Rangers (1938)
Two Gun Justice (1938)
Phantom Ranger (1938)

Renfrew of the Mounties
(James Newill)

Fighting Mad (1939)
Crashing Thru (1939)
Yukon Flight (1940)
Danger Ahead (1940)
Murder on the Yukon (1940)
Sky Bandits (1940)

Tom Keene

God's Country and the Man (1937)
Where Trails Divide (1937)
Romance of the Rockies (1937)
The Painted Trail (1938)
Wanderers of the West (1941)
Dynamite Canyon (1941)
The Driftin' Kid (1941)
Riding the Sunset Trail (1941)
Lone Star Law Men (1941)
Western Mail (1942)
Arizona Roundup (1942)
Where Trails End (1942)

The Rough Riders
(Buck Jones, Tim McCoy, Raymond Hatton)

Arizona Bound (1941)
The Gunman from Bodie (1941)
Forbidden Trails (1941)
Below the Border (1942)
Ghost Town Law (1942)
Down Texas Way (1942)

Riders of the West (1942)
West of the Law (1942)

The Rough Riders
(Buck Jones, Rex Bell, Raymond Hatton)

Dawn on the Great Divide (1942)

The Range Busters
(John King, Ray Corrigan, Max Terhune)

The Range Busters (1940)
Trailing Double Trouble (1940)
West of Pinto Basin (1940)
Trail of the Silver Spurs (1941)
The Kid's Last Ride (1941)
Tumbledown Ranch in Arizona (1941)
Wrangler's Roost (1941)
Fugitive Valley (1941)
Saddle Mountain Roundup (1941)
Tonto Basin Outlaws (1941)
Underground Rustlers (1941)
Thunder River Feud (1942)
Rock River Renegades (1942)
Boot Hill Bandits (1942)
Texas Trouble Shooters (1942)
Arizona Stagecoach (1942)

The Range Busters
(John King, David Sharpe, Max Terhune)

Texas to Bataan (1942)
Trail Riders (1942)
Two-Fisted Justice (1943)
Haunted Ranch (1943)

The Range Busters
(Ray Corrigan, Dennis Moore, Max Terhune)

Land of Hunted Men (1943)

Cowboy Commandos (1943)
Black Market Rustlers (1943)
Bullets and Saddles (1943)

Johnny Mack Brown, Raymond Hatton

The Ghost Rider (1943)
The Stranger from Pecos (1943)
Six-Gun Gospel (1943)
Outlaws of Stampede Pass (1943)
The Texas Kid (1943)
Raiders of the Border (1944)
Partners of the Trail (1944)
Law Men (1944)
Range Law (1944)
West of the Rio Grande (1944)
Land of the Outlaws (1944)
Law of the Valley (1944)
Ghost Guns (1944)
The Navajo Trail (1945)
Gun Smoke (1945)
Stranger from Santa Fe (1945)
Flame of the West (1945)
The Lost Trail (1945)
Frontier Feud (1945)
Drifting Along (1945)
Border Bandits (1946)
The Haunted Mine (1946)
Under Arizona Skies (1946)
The Gentleman from Texas (1946)
Trigger Fingers (1946)
Shadows on the Range (1946)
Silver Range (1946)
Raiders of the South (1947)
Valley of Fear (1947)
Trailing Danger (1947)
Land of the Lawless (1947)
The Law Comes to Gunsight (1947)
Code of the Saddle (1947)
Flashing Guns (1947)
Prairie Express (1947)
Gun Talk (1947)
Overland Trails (1948)
Crossed Trails (1948)

Frontier Agent (1948)
Triggerman (1948)
Back Trail (1948)
The Fighting Ranger (1948)
The Sheriff of Medicine Bow (1948)
Gunning for Justice (1948)
Hidden Danger (1948)

*Johnny Mack Brown,
Max Terhune*

Law of the West (1949)
Trail's End (1949)
West of Eldorado (1949)
Range Justice (1949)
Western Renegades (1949)

Johnny Mack Brown

West of Wyoming (1950)
Over the Border (1950)
Six Gun Mesa (1950)
Law of the Panhandle (1950)
Outlaw Gold (1950)
Colorado Ambush (1951)
Man from Sonora (1951)
Blazing Bullets (1951)
Montana Desperado (1951)
Canyon Ambush (1952)

*Johnny Mack Brown,
Jimmy Ellison*

Oklahoma Justice (1951)
Whistling Hills (1951)
Texas Lawmen (1951)
Texas City (1952)
Man from Black Hills (1952)
Dead Man's Trail (1952)

Johnny Mack Brown
(as costar)

*Stampede (1949)
 Short Grass (1950)

The Trail Blazers
(Ken Maynard, Hoot Gibson)

Wild Horse Stampede (1943)
The Law Rides Again (1943)
Blazing Guns (1943)

The Trail Blazers
(Ken Maynard, Hoot Gibson,
Bob Steele)

Death Valley Rangers (1943)
Western Bound (1944)
Arizona Whirlwind (1944)

The Trail Blazers
(Hoot Gibson, Bob Steele,
Chief Thunder Cloud)

Outlaw Trail (1944)
Sonora Stagecoach (1944)

Hoot Gibson, Bob Steele

Marked Trails (1944)
The Utah Kid (1944)
Trigger Law (1944)

*Jimmy Wakely,
Lee "Lasses" White*

Song of the Range (1944)
Springtime in Texas (1945)
Saddle Serenade (1945)
Riders of the Dawn (1945)
Lonesome Trail (1945)
Moon Over Montana (1946)
West of the Alamo (1946)
Trail to Mexico (1946)
Song of the Sierras (1946)
Rainbow Over the Rockies (1947)
Six Gun Serenade (1947)
Song of the Wasteland (1947)

Jimmy Wakely, Dub "Cannonball" Taylor

Ridin' Down the Trail (1947)
Song of the Drifter (1948)
Oklahoma Blues (1948)
Partners of the Sunset (1948)
Range Renegades (1948)
Cowboy Cavalier (1948)
Silver Trails (1948)
The Rangers Ride (1948)
Outlaw Brand (1948)
Courtin' Trouble (1948)
Gun Runner (1949)
Gun Law Justice (1949)
Across the Rio Grande (1949)
Brand of Fear (1949)
Roaring Westward (1949)
Lawless Code (1949)

The Cisco Kid
(Duncan Renaldo)

The Cisco Kid Returns (1945)
In Old New Mexico (1945)
South of the Rio Grande (1945)

The Cisco Kid
(Gilbert Roland)

The Gay Cavalier (1946)
South of Monterey (1946)
Beauty and the Bandit (1946)
Riding the California Trail (1947)
Robin Hood of Monterey (1947)
King of the Bandits (1947)

Whip Wilson, Andy Clyde

Crashing Thru (1949)
Shadows of the West (1949)
Haunted Trails (1949)
Riders of the Dusk (1949)
Range Land (1949)
Fence Riders (1950)
Gunslingers (1950)
Arizona Territory (1950)
Silver Raiders (1950)
Cherokee Uprising (1950)
Outlaws of Texas (1950)
Abilene Trail (1951)

Whip Wilson, Fuzzy Knight, Jim Bannon

Canyon Raiders (1951)
Nevada Badmen (1951)
Stagecoach Driver (1951)
Wanted: Dead or Alive (1951)
Lawless Cowboys (1951)

Whip Wilson, Fuzzy Knight

Stage to Blue River (1951)
Night Raiders (1952)
The Gunman (1952)

Whip Wilson

Montana Incident (1952)
Wyoming Roundup (1952)

Wild Bill Hickok
(Guy Madison)

Behind Southern Lines (1952)
The Ghost of Crossbones Canyon (1952)
Trail of the Arrow (1952)
The Yellow-Haired Kid (1952)
*Border City Rustlers (1953)
Secret of Outlaw Flats (1953)
Six-Gun Decision (1953)
Two-Gun Marshal (1953)
Marshals in Disguise (1954)
Outlaw's Son (1954)
Trouble on the Trail (1954)
The Two Gun Teacher (1954)
The Match-Making Marshal (1955)
Phantom Trails (1955)

Timber Country Trouble (1955)
The Titled Tenderfoot (1955)

Kirby Grant

Trail of the Yukon (1949)
The Wolf Hunters (1949)
Snow Dog (1950)
Call of the Klondike (1950)
Yukon Manhunt (1951)
Northwest Territory (1951)
Yukon Gold (1952)
*Fangs of the Arctic (1953)
Northern Patrol (1953)
Yukon Vengeance (1954)

Wayne Morris

Sierra Passage (1951)
Desert Pursuit (1952)
*Star of Texas (1953)
The Marksman (1953)
The Fighting Lawman (1953)
Texas Bad Man (1953)
The Desperado (1954)
Two Guns and a Badge (1954)

Rod Cameron

*Panhandle (1948)
Stampede (1949)
Short Grass (1950)
Cavalry Scout (1951)
Fort Osage (1952)
Wagons West (1952)
Yaqui Drums (1956)
The Gun Hawk (1963)

Joel McCrea

*Wichita (1955)

The First Texan (1956)
The Oklahoman (1957)
The Tall Stranger (1957)

Wild Bill Elliott

The Longhorn (1951)
Waco (1952)
Kansas Territory (1952)
Fargo (1952)
*The Maverick (1952)
The Homesteaders (1953)
Rebel City (1953)
Topeka (1953)
Vigilante Terror (1953)
Bitter Creek (1954)
The Forty-Niners (1954)

Sterling Hayden

*Kansas Pacific (1953)
Arrow in the Dust (1954)
Shotgun (1955)
Gun Battle at Monterey (1957)

Guy Madison

*Massacre River (1949)
Bullwhip (1958)
Gunmen of the Rio Grande (1965)

George Montgomery

*Canyon River (1956)
Last of the Badmen (1957)
Man from God's Country (1958)
King of the Wild Stallions (1959)

Appendix D: The Monogram/Allied Artists Academy Award Nominations

*Dates marked with * indicate winners for that year.*

Best Picture
1956 Friendly Persuasion
1972 Cabaret

Best Foreign Language Film
1959 The Bridge
1966 The Battle of Algiers
*1966 A Man and a Woman
*1976 Black and White in Color

Best Actor
1965 Rod Steiger—The Pawnbroker

Best Actress
1966 Anouk Aimée—A Man and a Woman
*1972 Liza Minnelli—Cabaret

Best Supporting Actor
1956 Anthony Perkins—Friendly Persuasion
1962 Terence Stamp—Billy Budd
*1972 Joel Gray—Cabaret

Best Supporting Actress
1969 Catherine Burns—Last Summer

Best Director
1956 William Wyler—Friendly Persuasion
1966 Claude Lelouch—A Man and a Woman
1968 Gillo Pontecorvo—The Battle of Algiers
*1972 Bob Fosse—Cabaret

Writing—Adaptation
1956 Michael Wilson—Friendly Persuasion
(Writer was ineligible under Academy By-laws. See #140.)

Writing—Original Story
1947 Roy Del Ruth—It Happened on Fifth Avenue

Writing—Original Screenplay
1944 Philip Yordan—Dillinger (Monogram)

Writing—Motion Picture Story
1956 Edward Bernds, Elwood Ullman—High Society
(Withdrawn from final ballot. See #168.)

Writing—Screenplay—Based on material from another medium

1972 Jay Allen—Cabaret
1975 John Huston, Gladys Hill—The Man Who Would Be King

Writing—Story and Screenplay—Written directly for the screen

*1966 Claude Lelouch, Pierre Uytterhoeven—A Man and a Woman
1968 Franco Solinas, Gillo Pontecorvo—The Battle of Algiers

Cinematography—Color

*1972 Geoffrey Unsworth—Cabaret

Art Direction/Set Decoration—Color

1961 Viniero Colasanti, John Moore—El Cid
*1972 Rolf Zehetbauer, Jurgen Kiebach, Herbert Strabel—Cabaret
1975 Alexander Trauner, Tony Inglis, Peter James—The Man Who Would Be King

Sound

1956 Samuel Goldwyn, Sound Department; Gordon E. Sawyer, Westrex Sound Services, Inc.; Don R. Glennan—Friendly Persuasion
*1972 Robert Knudson, David Hildyard—Cabaret

Costume Design—Color

1975 Edith Head—The Man Who Would Be King

Film Editing

1952 William Austin—Flat Top
*1972 David Bretherton—Cabaret
1975 Russell Lloyd—The Man Who Would Be King

Music Scoring—Original—Drama

1941 Edward J. Kay—King of the Zombies (Monogram)
1942 Edward J. Kay—Klondike Fury (Monogram)
1945 Edward J. Kay—G.I. Honeymoon (Monogram)
1961 Miklos Rozsa—El Cid
1963 Dimitri Tiomkin—55 Days at Peking
1973 Jerry Goldsmith—Papillon

Music Scoring—Original—Musical

1944 Edward J. Kay—Lady Let's Dance (Monogram)
1945 Edward J. Kay—Sunbonnet Sue (Monogram)

Music Scoring—Adaptation

*1972 Ralph Burns—Cabaret

Best Song

1944 "Silver Shadows and Golden Dreams" from *Lady Let's Dance*. Music by Lew Pollack, lyrics by Charles Newman. (Monogram)
1956 "Friendly Persuasion (Thee I Love)" from *Friendly Persuasion*. Music by Dimitri Tiomkin, lyrics by Paul Francis Webster.
1961 "Love Theme from El Cid (The Falcon and the Dove)"

from *El Cid.* Music by Miklos Rozsa, lyrics by Paul Francis Webster.

1963 "So Little Time" from *55 Days at Peking.* Music by Dimitri Tiomkin, lyrics by Paul Francis Webster.

1974 "Wherever Love Takes Me" from *Gold.* Music by Elmer Bernstein, lyrics by Don Black.

Short Films—Two Reelers

*1947 Irving Allen—Climbing the Matterhorn (Monogram)

Short Films—Cartoons

1965 Emanuele Luzzati—The Thieving Magpie (La Gazza Ladra)

Documentary—Features

*1959 Bernhard Grzimek—Serengeti Shall Not Die
*1965 Sidney Glazier—The Eleanor Roosevelt Story

Jean Hersholt Humanitarian Award

*1962 Steve Broidy

Bibliography

Adams, Les, and Buck Rainey. *Shoot-Em-Ups*. New Rochelle, N.Y: Arlington House, 1978.
Alicoate, Jack, ed. *Film Daily Yearbook of Motion Pictures*. New York: Film Daily, 1947–1970.
Baer, Richard D. *The Filmbuff's Checklist of Motion Pictures (1912–1979)*. Hollywood Film Archive, 1979.
Bergan, Ronald, and Robyn Karney. *The Holt Foreign Film Guide*. New York: Henry Holt, 1988.
Bojarski, Richard, and Kenneth Beals. *The Films of Boris Karloff*. Secaucus, N.J.: Citadel, 1976.
Cross, Robin. *2000 Movies: The 1940's*. New York: Arlington House, 1985.
_____. *2000 Movies: The 1950's*. New York: Arlington House, 1988.
Dickens, Homer. *The Films of Gary Cooper*. Secaucus, N.J.: Citadel, 1970.
di Franco, Philip, ed. *The Movie World of Roger Corman*. New York: Chelsea House, 1979.
Dimmitt, Richard B. *A Title Guide to the Talkies (1927–1963)*. New York: Scarecrow, 1965.
Gifford, Denis. *The British Film Catalogue 1895–1985, A Reference Guide*. New York: Facts on File, 1986.
Hayes, David, and Brent Walker. *The Films of the Bowery Boys*. Secaucus, N.J.: Citadel, 1984.
Hayes, R.M. *3-D Movies: A History and Filmography of Stereoscopic Cinema*. Jefferson, N.C.: McFarland, 1989.
Krasfur, Richard P., ed. *American Film Institute Catalog of Motion Pictures: Feature Films 1961–1970*. New York: R.R. Bowker, 1976.
McGee, Mark Thomas. *Beyond Ballyhoo: Motion Picture Promotion and Gimmicks*. Jefferson, N.C.: McFarland, 1989.
Maltin, Leonard. *TV Movies and Video Guide*. New American Library, 1967–1989.
Marrill, Alvin H. *The Films of Anthony Quinn*. Secaucus, N.J.: Citadel, 1975.
Miller, Don. *B Movies*. New York: Ballantine, 1973.
Naha, Ed. *The Films of Roger Corman*. New York: Arco, 1982.
Nash, Jay Robert, and Stanley Ralph Ross. *The Motion Picture Guide: 9 Vols*. Evanston, Il.: Cinebooks, 1986.
The New York Times Directory of the Film. New York: Arno Press/Random House, 1971.
The New York Times Film Reviews 1913–1968: 6 Vols. New York: Arno Press/New York Times, 1970.
Parish, James Robert. *Hollywood Character Actors*. Westport, CT.: Arlington House, 1978.
_____. *The Great Combat Pictures*. Metuchen, N.J.: Scarecrow, 1990.
_____ and Michael R. Pitts. *The Great Science Fiction Pictures*. Metuchen, N.J.: Scarecrow, 1977.

_____, and _____. *The Great Science Fiction Pictures II*. Metuchen, N.J.: Scarecrow, 1990.
_____, and _____. *The Great Western Pictures*. Metuchen, N.J.: Scarecrow, 1976.
_____, and _____. *The Great Western Pictures II*. Metuchen, N.J.: Scarecrow, 1988.
_____, and _____. *The Great Gangster Pictures*. Metuchen, N.J.: Scarecrow, 1976.
_____, and _____. *The Great Gangster Pictures II*. Metuchen, N.J.: Scarecrow, 1987.
_____, and _____. *The Great Spy Pictures*. Metuchen, N.J.: Scarecrow, 1974.
_____, and _____. *The Great Spy Pictures II*. Metuchen, N.J.: Scarecrow, 1986.
_____, and _____. *The Great Detective Pictures*. Metuchen, N.J.: Scarecrow, 1990.
Peary, Danny. *Cult Movies*. New York: Dell, 1981.
Pitts, Michael R. *Western Movies: A TV and Video Guide to 4200 Genre Films*. Jefferson, N.C.: McFarland, 1986.
Quigley, Martin, Jr., ed. *International Motion Picture Almanac*. New York: Quigley, 1959–1967.
Warren, Bill. *Keep Watching the Skies!: 2 Vols*. Jefferson, N.C.: McFarland, 1982–1986.
Weldon, Michael. *The Psychotronic Encyclopedia of Film*. New York: Ballentine, 1983.
Willis, John. *Screen World*. New York: Crown, 1966–1978.

Name Index

Numbers refer to entries, not pages. Alternate names (i.e., Geoffrey Homes [Daniel Mainwaring]) are also given wherever possible.

A

Abbey, Leo 192
Abdullah, Joseph 224
Abel, Robert 148, 330
Ackerman, Bettye 121
Ackerman, Leonard J. 4
Ackland, Rodney 53, 317
Adam, Ronald 7, 194, 222, 259
Adams, Casey 115, 195, 326
Adams, Clifton 75, 101
Adams, Dorothy 391, 415
Adams, Jane 338
Adams, Jill 80
Adams, Joe 108
Adams, Julie 321, 394
Adams, Lillian 400
Adams, Nick 258, 439
Adams, Peter 62
Adams, Phil 181
Adams, Polly 274
Adams, Stanley 64
Adams, Victoria 6
Adamson, James 150, 235, 335
Addams, Dawn 183
Addiss, Jus 89
Adelson, Merv 408
Adler, Allen 148
Adler, Jack 300
Adler, Jay 34, 263, 343

Adley, Ilma 213
Adorf, Mario 57, 368
Adrian, Arnold 43
Adrian, Iris 170, 354, 388
Advincula, Vicenta 281
Agar, John 95, 321
Agrama, Frank 353
Aherne, Brian 354
Aherne, Pat 332
Ahn, Philip 26, 79, 192, 347
Ahn, Ralph 79
Aidman, Charles 408
Aimée, Anouk 81, 242
Ainsworth, Helen 62
Akins, Claude 39, 187
Aladdin, Johnny 275
Alaimo, Steve 177
Alaniz, Rico 431
Alba, Alney 141
Alba, Julia Cabe 393
Alberoni, Sherry 301
Albert, Eddie 116, 299
Albert, Edward, Jr. 132
Albertini, Giampiero 443
Albertson, George 178
Albertson, Jack 82, 147
Albin, Andy 82
Albright, Lola 291, 343, 404
Alcorn, Ron W. 10
Alderson, John 431
Aldon, Mari 380
Aldred, Joel 337

Aldrich, Robert 408, 433
Alexander, Denise 87
Alexander, Jane 31
Alexander, Jim 218, 278, 308, 404
Alexander, Marc 300
Alexander, Robert 87
Alexander, Terence 164, 196
Allan, Michael 424
Alland, William 231
Allen, Adrianne 53
Allen, Barbara 175
Allen, Drew 359
Allen, Gary 5
Allen, Irwin 33
Allen, Jack 228, 444
Allen, Jay 63
Allen, Joel 254
Allen, Mel 18
Allen, Patrick 52, 98, 429
Allen, Robert 384
Allen, Ruth 145
Allen, Sheila 98
Allen, Steve 33
Allenby, Peter 337
Allerton, Alexander 426
Allison, Joe 108
Almoros, Antonio 81
Almquist, Dean L. 141
Alper, Murray 35, 54, 66, 71, 145, 170, 174, 203, 204, 208, 218, 265, 339

Name Index

Altayskaya, Vera 240
Altrose, Kenneth 328
Alvin, John 401
Alvina, Anicee 319
Ambesi, Adriana 379
Ambro, Will 164
Ames, Florenz 187
Ames, Judith 291
Amidou, Souad 242
Anchoriz, Leo 128
Anders, Merry 99, 190, 394
Anders, Rudolph 139, 208
Anderson, Axel 128
Anderson, Chuck 67
Anderson, Eric 371
Anderson, James 13, 329, 342
Anderson, Leona 185
Anderson, Michael 78, 183, 430
Anderson, Michael, Jr. 306
Anderson, Robert 207
Anderson, Rona 69
Anderson, U.S. 170
Anderson, Warner 10
Andes, Keith 376
Andreani, Jean Pierre 370
Andree, Victor 65
Andren, Joan 200
Andrew, Jean 197
Andrews, Edward 305, 374
Andrews, Harry 124, 196
Andrews, Robert D. 19
Andrews, Stanley 295, 348, 404
Andrews, Tod 144
Andronico, Enzo 286
Anet, Claude 237
Angarola, Richard 392
Angelini, Nando 286
Angelo, Robert 329
Angers, Avril 238
Angold, Edith 265

Anka, Paul 231
Ankrum, Morris 20, 135, 167, 257, 348, 361, 411
Annakin, Ken 112, 217
Ansara, Michael 220, 378
Anson, Bill 108
Anstruther, Gerald 252
Anthony, Michael 226
Anthony, Philip 196
Anthony, Tony 77
Antrim, Paul 246
Anwar, Rafiq 78
Appel, Benjamin 90
The Applejacks 110
Arden, Mary 45
Arden, Neal 148
Ardito, Gino 273
Arduini, Suzanne 387
Ari, Ben 4
Arlen, Richard 43, 186, 321
Arlington, Adrian 267, 310
Arliss, Leslie 432
Arlorio, Giorgio 161, 443
Armetta, Sal 301
Armstrong, Bill 270
Armstrong, Paul 245
Armstrong, R.G. 273
Armstrong, Robert 218
Arnatt, John 120
Arnaud, Jean-Jacques 40
Arne, Peter 14
Arnette, Jeanetta 383
Arnold, Bert 325
Arnold, John 180
Arnold, Monroe 384
Arnold, Newton 160
Arnold, Phil 272
Arnoux, Jean-Marie 123a
Arpino, Tony 337
Artego, Artie 366
Arthur, Doug 108
Arthur, Johnny 200
Arthur, Louise 330
Arthur, Richard 212

Arthur, Robert 325
Ashdown, Nadene 192
Asher, Peter 199
Ashley, John 439
Ashley, Mike 379
Ashton, Barry 94
Askin, Leon 364
Aslan, Coco 219
Aslan, Gregoire 249
Asquith, Anthony 424
Assan, Ratna 296
Assang, George 444
Asseyev, Tamara 293
Assumpaco, Roberto 146
Asti, Adriana 60, 443
Aston, Joy 369
Astor, Gertrude 13, 234, 287
Atami, Sachiko 36
Atchori, Memel 40
Attal, Henri 123a
Attaway, Ruth 384
Attenborough, Richard 78, 123
Atterbury, Malcolm 87
Atwater, Barry 86
Aubrey, Daniel 37
Aubry, Danielle 289
Aubuchon, Jacques 407
Audley, Maxine 49
Audran, Stephane 123a
Auer, Florence 19, 200
Auger, Claudine 161, 387
Aurenche, Jean 188
Austad, Paul 355
Austen, Ray 120
Austin, Alan 301
Austin, Charlotte 58, 139
Austin, Lois 354
Avakian, Aram 119
Avery, Tol 147
Avonde, Richard 122, 232, 338, 417
Axel, Gabriel 288, 447
Ayres, Robert 3, 81, 201
Ayulo, Manuel 330
Azcona, Rafael 333

Name Index

B

Babcock, Dwight V. 233
Bach, Vivi 353
The Bachelors 110
Bacic, Vladimir 331
Backus, Jim 239, 269
Bacon, Buni 344
Bacon, Irving 13, 209
Bacon, Max 306
Baddeley, Hermione 282
Badel, Alan 430
Baer, Buddy 22
Baer, John 37
Bagni, Margherita 414
Baguez, Salvador 130
Bailey, Anne Howard 48
Bailey, John 137, 244
Bailey, Raymond 4, 326
Bailey, Rex 122, 257, 283
Bailey, Robin 74, 310
Bain, Conrad 221
Baird, Harry 368
Baird, Jim 214, 290
Bakalyan, Richard 106, 178
Baker, Art 251, 439
Baker, Benny 354
Baker, Carroll 368
Baker, Derek 245
Baker, Doyle 87
Baker, Glyn 429
Baker, Joe Don 260
Baker, Robert S. 169
Baker, Stanley 443
Baker, Tom 360
Bakken, Vicki 224
Balaban, Burt 146
Baldi, Ferdinando 96
Baldi, Gian Vittorio 104
Baldini, Renato 165, 387
Baldour, Charles 337
Balfour, Michael 259
Ball, Vincent 43, 438
Ballantine, Sarah 274
Ballantyne, Lon 191
Ballard, Beverly 405

Ballinger, Bill S. 289, 372
Ballis, Socrates 177
Balsam, Martin 4, 260, 405
Balzer, Karl Michael 59
Bamber, Judy 416
Band, Albert 121, 133, 440
A Band of Angels 110
Banki, Zsu Zsu 72
Banks, Henry 330
Banks, Leslie 262
Bannen, Ian 142, 368
Banner, John 28, 172, 290
Bannon, Jim 202
Barbash, Bob 307
Barber, Elsie Oaks 6
Barbi, Vincent 79, 301
Barbulee, Madeleine 188
Barclay, Jerry 419
Barcroft, Roy 101, 411
Bardette, Trevor 115
Bardot, Mijanou 344
Bardsley, June 164
Barker, Art 258
Barker, Jess 114, 345
Barker, Ronnie 245
Barkworth, Peter 306
Barnard, Ivor 317
Barnes, Binnie 116, 393
Barnes, Rayford 56, 101, 260, 427, 440
Barnes, Walter 291, 327
Barnett, Griff 145
Barnett, Linda 347
Barnsley, Bill 360
Barnwell, John 376
Baron, Allen 384
Barouh, Pierre 242
Barr, Patrick 201
Barrat, Robert 20, 84
Barrere, Michael 271
Barrett, Bill 389
Barrett, Claudia 71
Barri, Mario 435
Barrier, Maurice 40

Barron, Baynes 34, 144, 362, 372, 418
Barron, Robert 359
Barrows, George 395
Barry, Christopher 271
Barry, Dave 168
Barry, Donald "Red" 139
Barry, Philip 421
Barry, Wesley E. 54, 250, 253, 292, 304, 338, 351, 395, 397, 403, 406, 409, 410
Barry, Yane 242
Barrymore, John Drew 273
Barth, John 119
Bartlett, Bennie 55, 56, 73, 105, 168, 203, 204, 208, 234, 298, 313, 361, 364
Bartlett, Richard 167, 192
Bartok, Eva 45
Bartold, Norman 230
Barton, Ann 102
Barton, Gregg 136, 156, 243, 251, 254, 322, 411
Barton, James 269
Barton, Margaret 217
Basehart, Richard 172, 444
Bass, Alfie 438
Bassett, Joe 339
Bast, William 31
Bates, Jeanne 372
Battaglia, Rik 279
Bau, Gene 180
Baucin, Escolastico 192
Bautista, Conchita 393
Bava, Mario 45, 65; see also John Foam
Baxt, David 408
Baxt, George 302
Baxter, Anne 76, 379
Baxter, George 155, 224, 314
Baxter, Ray 347

Name Index

Bay, John 149
Bayard, August 383
Bayldon, Geoffrey 124
Bayley, Hildy 267
Baylor, Hal 179
Beach, Guy 250
Beachie, Ma 305
Beatty, Robert 37
Beauchamp, D.D. 308, 358, 436
Beaudine, William 168, 193, 203, 204, 265, 298, 312, 330, 416, 442
Beaumont, Charles 316
Beaumont, Hugh 186
Beaumont, Victor 252
Beavis, E.F. 365
Beban, George 19
Beck, Glenn 408
Becker, Ken 15
Beckerman, Sidney 221
Beckett, Scotty 179, 287, 391
Beckley, Tony 149
Beckwith, Reginald 274
Beddoe, Don 62, 84, 233, 361
Bedford, Patrick 276
Beebe, Ford 150, 211, 215/216, 235, 335
Beeby, Bruce 302
Beer, Jacqueline 336
Begg, Gordon 424
Behm, Marc 299
Bekassy, Stephen 66
Belasco, Leon 200, 204
Belita 145, 189
Bell, Arnold 81
Bell, Don 108
Bell, James 397
Bell, Jeanie 392
Bell, Michael 418
Bell, Tom 302
Bella, Giuseppe 9
Beller, Kathleen 31
Bellis, Dickie 309
Beltran, Alma 115
Ben Bouih, Karroum 246

Bendandi, Poldo 286
Bender, Russ 372
Bendix, William 18
Benedek, Laslo 2
Benedict, Richard 35, 204, 265, 364
Beniades, Ted 276
Benjamin, Christopher 446
Ben Kassen, Mohamed 25
Bennet, Spencer G. 15
Bennett, Bruce 35, 83, 114
Bennett, Charles 33
Bennett, Constance 354
Bennett, Fran 8
Bennett, Joan 170, 272
Bennett, Kevin 302
Bennett, Linda 364
Bennett, Marjorie 371
Benson, Martin 337
Bentley, John 98, 432
Bento, Serge 123a
Benucci, Pippe 151
Benvenuti, Leo 268
Benz, Inge 59
Bercovici, Eric 392
Beregi, Oscar, Jr. 290
Berenson, Marisa 63
Bergerac, Jacques 190, 371, 377
Berk, Howard 37
Berke, Irwin 139, 344
Berling, Peter 40
Berman, Monty 169
Bernard, Barry 211, 332
Bernard, Carl 169
Bernardi, Herschel 147
Bernds, Edward 55, 56, 64, 73, 105, 157, 168, 179, 207, 208, 232, 234, 272, 298, 313, 315, 316, 352, 364, 394, 425, 434
Bernerd, Jeffrey 41
Bernhard, Jack 189
Bernsen, Corbin 392
Bernsen, Harry 392

Bernstein, Richard 144, 156, 362
Bernstein, Walter 31
Berrell, Lloyd 213
Berri, Claude 249
Berti, Dehl 402, 413
Berto, Giuseppe 9
Bessie, Alvah 354
Bessler, Albert 57
Best, James 64, 75, 220, 325, 342, 347
Best, Willie 354
Bestar, Barbara 335, 425
Betts, Jack 48
Bezencenet, Peter 72
Bice, Robert 54, 56, 103, 167, 248, 351, 367
Bickerton, Derek 302
Bickford, Charles 18
Bigazzi, Gian Paolo 165
Biggart, Barbara 6, 318
Bilboa, Fernando 128
Bilkie, Helen S. 269
Bill, Tony 357
Bilyeu, Chick 166
Binkley, Allan 275
Binns, Edward 309
Birch, Paul 284, 301, 316
Bird, Billie 415
Birdwell, Russell 76
Birkin, Jane 331
Birt, Dan 282
Bischoff, Samuel 214, 290, 305, 336, 372
Bishop, Curtis 84
Bishop, Ed 408
Bishop, Norman 55
Bishop, Terry 228
Bisoglio, Val 180
Bissell, Whit 13, 34, 197, 329, 345, 378, 381
Bissett, Donald 69
Blackburn, Col. Donald D. 376
Blackburn, Tom W. 84, 247, 348

Blackler, Betty 282
Blackman, Honor 142
Blain, Tats 272
Blaine, Frank 210
Blair, Betsy 249
Blair, George 127, 190, 334, 363, 403
Blair, Lionel, and His Dancers 306
Blair, Nicky 85, 162, 173
Blake, Amanda 168
Blake, Grey 94
Blake, Larry 103, 189
Blake, Nicholas 390
Blake, Robert 24, 28, 314, 327, 336
Blake, Whitney 31
Blakely, Colin 274
Blanchard, Dave 318
Blanchard, Mari 88, 326
Blanche, Francis 29
Blanco, Hugo 60
Blanco, Miguel Angel 2
Blane, Erika 446
Blank, Dorothee 412
Blatt, Edward A. 354
Bleifer, John 71, 85, 127, 133, 147, 316, 364, 425
Blier, Bernard 268
Blin, Roger 188
Bliss, Debby 384
Bliss, Lela 35
Bloch, Charles B. 190
Block, Bernice 106
Block, Irving 15, 419
Block, Martin 108
Blondell, Gloria 425
Blondell, Joan 6
Bloom, Claire 57
Blore, Eric 56
Blystone, Stanley 354
Boa, Bruce 426
Bobby Breen Quintet 92
Bock, Curt 353
Bodard, Mag 412
Boddey, Martin 137
Bodeen, DeWitt 38

Bogarde, Dirk 74, 212, 341
Bogese, Sal 375
Bohn, Chris 141
Bohnet, Volker 59
Boignan, Marius Beugre 40
Boisgel, Valerie 47
Boles, Jim 270
Bolkan, Florinda 9, 60
Bonanova, Fortunio 20
Bond, Anson 415
Bond, David 125
Bond, Derek 169
Bond, Julian 245
Bond, Lillian 255
Bond, Ward 50
Bondi, Francesca 151
Bonifas, Paul 188, 237
Bonnell, Lee 354
Boon, Robert 336
Boone, Pat 274
Borch, Randi 355
Borg, Veda Ann 39, 179
Borgnine, Ernest 301, 448
Borilla, Joe 45
Borisoff, Norman 369
Borland, Scott 166
Borsten, Orin 6
Bost, Jacques-Laurent 396
Boswell, Hugh 187
Boucher, Chili 262
Bouchey, Willis 220, 241
Bouillard, Charles 237
Bould, Beckett 226
Boulter, Rosalyn 134
Boulton, Matthew 234
Bouquet, Michel 123a
Bourdin, Lise 237
Bourg, Wilson 275
Bourne, Max 72
Bourne, Peter 224
Bousquet, Robert 229
Boutall, Kathleen 164
Bova, Joseph 426
Bowman, Lee 388

Bowman, Tom 120, 143
Boyd, Alex 438
Boyett, William 127
Boys, Arthur 317
Brack, Claudia 42
Bracken, Eddie (voice of) 346
Bradford, Jack 272
Bradford, Lane 136, 150, 156, 192, 209, 342, 358
Bradford, Marshall 442
Bradford, Sue 195
Bradley, Bart 301
Bradley, Lee 156
Bradley, Leslie 206
Bradley, Mary H. 191
Bradley, Pat 230
Bradshaw, Joan 232
Brady, Leslie 16
Brady, Scott 24
Brand, Neville 51, 147, 325, 326, 329
Brandt, Martin 172
Braun, Pinkas 72, 245
Brauner, Wolf 261
Brauss, Art 369
Bray, Richard 384
Bray, Robert 1, 254, 273, 417
Brazzou, Anna 37
Breck, Peter 347
Bredecka, Jiri 225
Bregman, Martin 276
Breistrand, Wilfred 355
Brendel, Mike 198
Brennan, Michael 142
Brennan, Walter 13
Brenner, Paul 108
Brent, Eve 247
Brent, George 257, 380
Brewster, Diane 215/216, 287, 315
Brian, David 281
Bricker, George 91, 233, 257, 380
Bridge, Al 41, 354
Bridges, Jim 207
Bridges, Lloyd 312, 427

Name Index

Brietschopf, Trudy 59
Briggs, Johnny 223
Briggs, Matt 18
Briley, John 386
Brill, Charles 28
Brineger, Paul 434
Brinkley, John 178, 181, 382, 419
Britt, May 414
Brittain, Ronald 124
Britton, Barbara 114, 278
Brock, Ray 119
Brodie, Steve 12, 88, 251, 365, 425
Brody, Merrill 384
Brogan, Harry 274
Broidy, William F. 12, 30, 35, 62, 66, 170, 218, 224, 265, 278, 308, 339, 343, 345, 402, 403, 404, 436, 442
Bromfield, John 131
Bromley, Sidney 43
Bronson, Betty 271
Bronson, Charles 401
Bronsten, Nat A. 238, 350
Bronston, Samuel 117, 124
Bronte, James 224
Brook, Lyndon 426
Brooke, Hillary 255, 257
Brookes, Olwen 169
Brooks, Conrad 73, 204
Brooks, Dwight 83
Brooks, Mel 346
Brooks, Rand 254
Brooks, Ray 306
Brooks, Thor 12, 224
Brooks, Victor 38, 97, 228
Brophy, Edward 200
Brown, Barbara 8
Brown, Bert C. 361
Brown, Dorian 394
Brown, Harry 251

Brown, J.G. 53
Brown, Jim 392
Brown, John 252
Brown, Johnny Mack 348, 366
Brown, Lew 86
Brown, Mel 384
Brown, Pamela 285
Brown, Phil 408
Brown, Robert 38, 120, 420
Browne, Bill 166
Browne, Roscoe Lee 384, 408
Browning, Maurice 299
Bruce, Brenda 424
Bruce, Eve 394
Bruce, Nigel 433
Brunetti, Argentina 147
Brunius, Jacques 3
Brusati, Franco 414
Bryan, Dora 282
Bryant, John 23
Bryar, Paul 55, 71, 179, 232, 330, 354, 361, 425
Brydon, William 48
Brynner, Yul 331
Buchanan, Edgar 215/216, 427
Buck, Jules 299
Buck, Pearl S. 36
Buckley, Keith 212
Budrys, Algis 426
Buferd, Marilyn 316
Buffington, Adele 62, 84
Buffington, Sam 320, 415
Bufman, Zeev 224
Bugliari, Annamaria 294
Buka, Donald 290
Bulloch, Jeremy 306
Bulmer, Michael 176
Bunuel, Luis 29
Buono, Victor 372, 439
Burbank, Leon 56
Burgess, Jane 232
Burke, Alfred 226
Burke, John 360

Burke, Marie 80
Burke, Paul 109, 336, 364
Burke, Walter 273
Burn, Jonathan 299
Burnaby, Anne 123, 217, 422, 437, 441
Burns, Cathy 221
Burr, Raymond 2
Burridge, Geoffrey 196
Burrows, John H. 4
Burt, Benny 127
Burton, Laurie 394
Burton, Norman 141
Burton, Richard 164, 429
Bush, James 250, 251
Busoni, Manilo 104
Butler, Hugo 433
Butterworth, Peter 430
Buttons, Red 33
Buxton, Sheila 194
Byles, Bobby 418
Byrne, Eddie 398
Byrne, Michael 78
Byron, Keith 362

C

Cabot, Bruce 324
Cabot, Sebastian 115
Cabot, Susan 376, 419, 421
Cacao, Johnny 47
Cadell, Jean 226, 280
Cagney, Jeanne 397
Cahn, Edward L. 30
Caiano, Carlo 279
Caiano, Mario (Allen Grunewald) 279
Caine, Howard 301
Caine, Michael 246
Cal Monte, Toti 9
Calhoun, Rory 128, 156, 251, 349
Cali, Giulio 414
Calihan, William 125
Callaghan, Ray 196

Name Index

Callahan, George 18
Callaway, Cheryl 91
Calo, Carla 286
Calve, Jean François 324
Calvert, Phyllis 151, 164, 201
Calvert, Steve 55, 58
Calvet, Corinne 49
Calvin, Barbara 201
Camardeil, Roberto 387
Cameron, Rod 156, 295, 348, 366, 373, 436
Campa, Miranda 60
Campbell, Beatrice 219, 222, 267, 280, 350, 428
Campbell, Colin 223
Campbell, Murray 194
Campo, Wally 27, 347, 372, 418
Campos, Rafael 106
Cane, Charles 155, 361
Cannon, Debbie 290
Cannon, Esma 112, 154, 219
Cannon, Freddy 110
Cansino, Vernon 359
Capell, Peter 10
Capote, Truman 405
Capuano, Sam 301
Capucci, Fabrizio 96
Carbone, Anthony 12
Card, Jack 166
Cardiff, Jack 423
Cardile, Angela 60
Cardwell, James 200
Carena, Anna 60
Carey, Timothy 71, 82, 129, 327, 415
Carleton, Claire 20, 415
Carleton, George 354
Carlson, Richard 131, 206, 255, 391, 400
Carlstedt, Arno 311
Carlton, Timothy 386
Carmen, Jeanne 309
Carmet, Jean 40
Carminati, Tullio 117, 151
Carney, Daniel 429

Carol, Sheila 27
Caron, Leslie 161
Carotenuto, Mario 161
Carpenter, Paul 217, 422
Carpenter, Richard 120
Carpi, Fabio 104
Carr, Claudia 43
Carr, Jack 62, 343, 344
Carr, Larry 241
Carr, Marian 195, 283, 433
Carr, Mary 140
Carr, Thomas 39, 51, 101, 106, 126, 136, 159, 254, 322, 367, 378, 391, 399
Carradine, John 83, 344; (voice of) 346
Carraher, Robert 35
Carriaga, Jean 47
Carricart, Robert 46
Carriere, Jean-Claude 29
Carroll, Anne 284
Carroll, Janice 392
Carroll, Mary 35
Carroll, Maxine 318
Carroll, Virginia 20, 35
Carroll Levis's Discoveries 238
Carson, Charles 226
Carson, Jack 214, 241
Carson, Jean 305
Carson, John 252
Carson, Kit 122
Carson, Robert 265
Carstairs, John Paddy 438
Cartand, Gabriel 370
Carter, Cathy 189, 200
Carter, Winifred 262
Cartwright, Lynn 89, 316, 421
Caruso, Anthony 125, 203, 224, 287, 402, 439
Carvajal, Alfonzo 281
Carver, Mary 301
Carver, Tina 71, 144
Casaravilla, Carlos 124

Casaril, Guy 319
Case, Gerald 94
Case, Kathleen 64
Casimis, Spiros 224
Casler, Christopher G. 383
Cason, John 356, 404
Cass, Henry 70, 123, 169, 219, 280, 441
Cass, Maurice 359
Cass, Peggy 293
Cassavetes, John 2, 87
Cassel, Jean-Pierre 386
Cassell, Walter (Wally) 76, 297
Cassels, Lavinia 405
Cassidy, Bill 363
Cassidy, Jack 231
Cast, Edward 302
Castelnuovo, Nino 412
Castle, Don 366, 373
Castle, Mary 85, 436
Castle, Peggie 84, 129, 358
Castle, William 185, 190, 239
Catching, William 289
Catlett, Walter 140
Cavalcanti 134
Cavalier, Sebastian 128
Cavan, Barbara 152
Cavanagh, Paul 18, 193
Cave, Des 293
Cavell, Marc 314
Cavendish, Dick 397
Cawdron, Robert 143
Celi, Adolfo 161, 268, 276, 446
Cellier, Caroline 390
Cerchio, Fernando 165
Ceriana, Ludovico 183
Cerio, Ferrucio 294
Cerusico, Enzo 443
Cevellos, Fabian 386
Cey, Jacques 183
Cha, Stanley 173
Chabing 192
Chabrol, Claude 123a, 390

184 Name Index

Challee, William 307
Chalmers, W.G. 194
Chambers, Wheaton 287
Chambers, Whitman 76
Chaminade, Pierre 183
Champion, Gerald 360
Champion, Jean 412
Champion, John C. 114, 295, 349, 366
Chandler, Chick 313
Chandler, Jeff 307
Chandler, John Davis 177
Chandler, Lane 84, 130, 315, 349, 359
Chandler, Mack 413
Chaney, Lon, Jr. 93, 195, 388
Channing, Carol (voice of) 346
Chantler, David 220
Chapin, Michael 312
Chaplin, Charles, Jr. 344
Chaplin, Sydney 98
Chapman, Edward 244
Chapman, Eric 128
Chapman, Robert 38
Charlamagne, Jaime 384
Charles, Frances 395
Charles, Lewis 4, 129, 357, 413
Charles, Theresa 164
Charlton, Fluff 297
Charney, Kim 13, 51, 243, 315
Charrel, Michel 29, 123a, 390
Charriere, Henri 296
Chase, Barrie 147
Chase, Frank 17, 320
Chase, James 223
Chase, Stephen 19, 167
Chau, Nam 435
Chauvin, Lilyan 394
Chefe, Jack 85
Chemin, Henri 242
Chernin, Kayle 236
Cherry, Helen 70, 78, 134, 164, 219, 441

Chesebro, George 20
Cheshire, Harry 312
Chester, Hal E. 171, 354
Chetham-Strode, Warren 3
Chevalier, Louise 123a, 390
Chevalier, Maurice 237
Chi, Pham Phouc 435
The Chiffons 110
Chinh, Kieu 289, 435
"Chinook," the dog 122, 283, 442
Chow, David 392
Chow, Michael 124
Christenson, Wes 366
Christian, Carl 401
Christian, Linda 26, 393
Christie, Campbell 428
Christie, Robert 48
Christine, Virginia 145, 197
Christopher, Robert 82, 99, 109, 163, 290, 363
Chroscicki, Enrico 333
Chuman, Howard 192
Chung, Kei 418
Ciampi, Yves 396
Cicogna, Marina 60
Cioffi, Charles 276
Clanton, Ralph 413
Clare, Mary 262, 267, 310
Clarence, O.B. 424
Clark, Bobby 102, 197
Clark, Cliff 354
Clark, Dane 308, 402
Clark, Dort 273
Clark, Edward 338, 399
Clark, Ernest 252
Clark, Gordon 298, 359
Clark, Jameson 169, 226, 423
Clark, Lon 146
Clark, Mae 427
Clark, Gen. Mark W. 192
Clark, Oliver 119
Clark, Roger 6
Clark, Steve 84, 339, 366

Clarke, Graham 429
Clarke, John 128, 379, 389
Clay, Philippe 188
Clay, Virginia 152
Clayton, Bob 108
Clayton, Ken 83
Cleary, Leo 187
Clech, Yvonne 229, 319
Clemens, Brian 368
Clemens, Pilar 37
Clementi, Pierre 29
Clements, Stanley 18, 19, 127, 174, 179, 182, 193, 232, 363, 416, 425
Clerici, Gianfranco 446
Clery, Corrine 370
Cliff, John 129, 159, 343
Clifford, Jefferson 98
Clift, Lawrence 279
Clinton, Mildred 5
Close, John 71, 82, 122, 129, 133, 314, 374, 401
Clow, George 333
Clute, Chester 200
Clute, Sidney 86, 90, 260
Clyde, June 3
Coastworth, Martha 318
Coates, Phyllis 131, 254, 399
Cobb, Lee J. 386
Coburn, Charles 171
Coburn, James 196
Cochran, Steve 315
Cockrell, Gary 245, 408
Coco, James 119
Cocos, George 237
Codrington, Ann 280
Cody, Iron Eyes 11, 251
Cody, J.W. 62
Coe, Peter 349
Coffin, Tristram 189, 250, 338, 348
Cohen, Herman 42, 241, 381

Name Index

Cohen, Ronald M. 408
Cohn, Arthur 40, 60
Colantuoni, Antonio 286
Colbert, Robert 207, 239, 315
Cole, Mrs. Francis 118
Cole, George 80, 142, 222, 259, 398, 430
Cole, Joe 429
Cole, Julie Dawn 386
Cole, Phyllis 190
Cole, Selette 372
Coleman, Booth 28, 434
Coleman, Bryan 228
Coleman, Caryl 41
Coleman, Edward 21
Coletti, Duilio 183
Colgan, Michael 399, 417
Colin, Jean 219
Colitti, Rick 384
Colleano, Bonar 424
Collet, Pierre 396
Collick, Cyril 289
Collier, Ian 276
Collier, Marian 392
Collin, A.E. 365
Collins, Anne 48
Collins, G. Pat 30, 35, 278, 361, 436
Collins, Joan 432
Collins, Joe 389
Collins, Joel 106
Collins, Lewis D. 175, 248, 385, 411, 417
Collins, Richard 50, 301, 329
Collinson, Peter 142
Collinson, Tara 142
Colpack, Mickey 403
Colpeyn, Louisa 249
Colstan, Rolf 48
Comfort, Lance 310, 350
Comiskey, Pat 155
Como, Rossella 379
Compagna, Soni 333
Compton, Fay 222
Compton, John 140

Compton, Joyce 303
Conchon, Georges 40
Condon, David 55, 56, 73, 85, 105, 168, 203, 204, 208, 234, 298, 313, 364
Conley, Amelia 141
Conlin, Jimmy 354
Connell, Jane 405
Conners, Joan 156
Connery, Neil 52
Connery, Sean 143, 246, 276
Connors, Chuck 99, 114, 173, 187
Conrad, Charles J. 163
Conrad, Karen 271, 347
Conrad, Michael 107
Conrad, Robert 439
Considine, Bob 18
Conte, Richard 34, 35, 69, 170
Conti, Audrey 363
Contreras, Roberto 247
Conway, Pat 8, 102, 336, 413
Conway, Russ 205, 206, 211, 309, 335
Conway, Tom 15
Coogan, Jackie 344
Cook, Clyde 234, 255
Cook, David 212
Cook, Elisha, Jr. 42, 46, 145, 185
Cook, Tommy 19
Cookson, Alma 152
Cooley, Isabelle 191
Coombes, Norman 149
Coontz, Bill 230
Coop, Franco 151
Cooper, Ben 157
Cooper, Betty 256
Cooper, Clancy 145, 361
Cooper, Dorothy 226
Cooper, Gary 140, 237
Cooper, Jeanne 42, 64, 415
Cooper, Mark 353
Cooper, Tamar 284

Coote, Robert 80
Copelan, David 238
Copeland, Jack L. 163
Copelin, Campbell 310
Copley, Lewis 290
Copley, Peter 212
Coppel, Alec 238
Copponex, Kathryn 275
Corby, Ellen 55, 239, 372, 373
Corcoran, Hugh 281
Corday, Mara 413
Corden, Henry 167
Cordet, Louise 110
Cording, Harry 20, 208, 211
Corey, Jeff 145, 429
Corey, Wendell 46
Corman, Gene 27, 178
Corman, Roger 16, 27, 89, 170, 178 198, 284, 382, 419, 421
Cornfield, Hubert 374
Cornish, Richard 196
Cornwell, Judy 293
Corra, Theodor 446
Corrigan, Lloyd 55, 297, 325, 373
Corsaro, Franco 301
Corsi, Jacopo 324
Cortez, Carlos 67
Corwin, Norman 281
Cosme, Eusebia 300
Costa, Joseph 273
Costa, Sam 110
Cotten, Joseph 408
Cottrell, William 234
Coulibaly, Mamadou 40
Coulouris, George 49, 296, 365
Council, Elizabeth 191
Couper, Barbara 422
Courcel, Nicole 319, 369
Court, Hazel 53
Courtemarche, Gerald 20
Courtenay, Tom 212
Courtney, Chuck 84, 411
Coutant, Marc 32

Name Index

Cowan, Ashley 193
Cowan, Jerome 42, 108
Cox, Phyllis 191
Coxe, Louis O. 38
Coy, Walter 131, 427, 440
Craig, Carolyn 185, 309
Craig, James 93, 135, 270, 303
Craig, John 347
Craig, Michael 44, 302
Craig, Wendy 341
Crain, Jeanne 407
Crandall, Eddie 21
Crane, Richard 24
Crane, Stephen 121
Cranford, Robert 372
Crauchet, Paul 107
Craven, John 140, 173, 272, 339
Crawford, Broderick 20, 82
Crawford, Howard Marion 228
Crawford, Jimmy 306
Crawford, John 322, 338, 367
Crean, Robert 146
Creatore, Victor 314
Crehan, Joseph 18, 20, 170, 189, 361
Crenna, Richard 107
Cressoy, Pierre 96, 294, 414
Cresswell, John 44, 270
Cristal, Perla 379
Crockett, Dick 295, 399
Croft, Colin 1
Croft, Leila 237
Croft, Valerie 237
Croft-Cooke, Rupert 120
Cromer, Dean 136
Cronin, A.J. 423
Crosby, Bing 448
Crosby, Wade 338
Cross, Dennis 270
Cross, Larry 245
Crouzet, Roger 277
Crow, Carl 266

Crowley, Kathleen 323, 381
Crown, Alfred W. 221
Cruickshank, Andrew 117
Crutcher, Jack 204
Crutchley, Rosalie 423
Crux, Angel 192
Cruz, Celia 2
Cruz, Mara 379
Cucciolla, Riccardo 107
Culver, Howard 178
Culver, Michael 52, 78
Cummings, Susan 243
Cummins, Ron 180
Cunningham, Beryl 92
Cunningham, Jack 169
Cuny, Alain 188
Curci, Elvira 359
Curiel, Herbert 365
Curram, Roland 152
Curran, Dandy 46
Curran, Pamela 266
Currie, Finlay 267
Curtis, Donald 366
Curtis, Gabriel 266
Curtis, Lucille 347
Curtis, Mickey 36
Curtis, Oren 42
Curtis, Patrick 360
Curtis, Peter 154
Curtis, Richard 87
Curwood, James Oliver 122, 283, 442
Curzon, George 134
Cutell, Lou 138
Cuthbertson, Allan 52
Cutting, Richard 16, 349

D

Dae, Frank 295
Dahan, Armand 276
Dahlke, Paul 261
Dahner, J.J. 418
Dainton, Patricia 70, 94
Daker, Guy 396
Dale, Esther 30, 287
Dale, Michael 278

Dale, Virginia 373
Daley, Ray 389
Dalibert, Andre 396
Dallas, Julian 262
Dalton, Abby 75
Dalton, Audrey 98, 173
d'Alton, Louis 438
Dalz, John 273
Damiani, Damiano 165
Damler, John 30, 71, 155, 192, 220, 224, 321
Damon, Mark 336
Damone, Vic 162
Dan, Judy 418
Dana, Jeanette 347
Dana, Mark 182
Dandrieux, Dominique 29
Dane, Edward 98
Dane, Peter 4
Danelli, Ileana 96
Danet, Jean 188
D'Angelo, Carlo 96
Danielewski, Tad 36
Daniell, Allyson 347
Daniels, Jody 156
Daniely, Lisa 92
Dano, Royal 121
Dante, Michael 271
Dante, Tony 125
Dantes, Claude 45
Danton, Ray 147
D'Antonio, Carmen 433
Darcy, Ita 293
Darion, Joe 346
Dark, Christopher 434
Darrell, Steve 202, 359, 404
Darrin, Diana 88, 415
Darro, Frankie 409
Darrow, Barbara 316
Das Bolas, Xan 158
Daurand, Jean 396
Davi, Jana 320
David, Clifford 31, 299
David, Thayer 431
Davidson, Bruce 221

Davidson, Davey 372
Davies, Betty Ann 164, 428
Davies, David 143
Davies, Jack 222, 259, 398
Davies, Rupert 1, 420
Davis, Arthur L. 99
Davis, Humphrey 141
Davis, Jim 21
Davis, Lisa 316, 364
Davis, Sammy, Jr. 82
Davis, Spencer 384
Davis, Wray 435
Davo, Marco 393
Davys, Carolyn 158
Dawson, Anthony 317
Dawson, Gladys 446
Day, David 202
Day, Laraine 391
Day, Lynda 146
Day, Richard 273
Deacon, Richard 197
de Agostini, Fabio 279
Deale, Francis 389
Dean, Isabel 3, 432
Dean, Ivor 360
Dean, Jeanne 73
Dean, Vaughan M. 184, 256
Deane, Charles 43
Dearing, Peter 270
Deaton, Emil 177
de Barnardi, Pietro 268
De Beausset, Michael 177, 258
De Carlo, Yvonne 349, 398
De Chabanieux, Lucas 32
Decker, Diana 430
Deckers, Eugene 226
de Clara, Patrizia 227
De Concini, Ennio 183
de Corsia, Ted 34, 46, 155, 179
Deeley, Michel 78
Defauce, Felix 124
DeFore, Don 200, 361

De Gooyer, Ryk 57
de Grunwald, Anatole 53, 317, 424
de Grunwald, Dimitri 386
Dehner, John 55
Dein, Edward 66, 343, 345
Dein, Mildred 66, 343, 345
DeKova, Frank 125, 345
De Lane Lea, Jacques 110
De Lange, Bob 365
Delannoy, Jean 188
Delano, Sal (voice of) 346
de Lapparent, Hubert 188
De Laurentiis, Dino 414
de Lavallade, Yvonne 224
Delderfield, R.F. 285
Delevanti, Cyril 334
Dell, Myrna 269, 278, 402
Delon, Alain 107, 443
De Los Arcos, Luis 128
Deloux, Jean Pierre 32
Del Prete, Duilio 268
Del Ruth, Roy 18, 200
Deltgen, Rene 183
de Luna, Alvaro 158
Deman, Robert 296
Demara, Ferdinand W. "Fred" 190
Demarest, William 214, 407
DeMarney, Terence 79
de Mendoza, Alberto 387
Demeongeot, Mylene 396
Demicheli, Tulio 158
DeMille, Katherine 41
Demy, Jacques 412
Dene, Terry 194
de Nesle, Robert 32
Deneuve, Catherine 29, 107, 412

Denham, Christopher 245
Denham, Maurice 217
Denison, Leslie 193
Denison, Michael 7, 81, 137, 217, 267
Denner, Charles 229
Denning, Richard 381
Denning, Ruth 422
Dennis, John 64, 82, 139, 326, 327, 394
Dennis, Matt 205
Denny, Reginald 135, 433
DeNoble, Alphonso 5
De Paolo, Dante 45
De Pomes, Fleixes 393
De Pomes, Isabel 393
DeQuincey, Thomas 79
Deray, Jacques 387
Derek, John 8
deRoseville, D. 29
Desailly, Jean 107
de Sales, Francis 309, 327
De Santis, Joe 4, 106, 147
De Sica, Vittorio 60
DeSimone, Pat 106
Desny, Ivan 426
de Souza, Noel 344
Deus, Beny 128, 158
Devereaux, Ed 274
Devereux, Marie 271, 347
De Villa, Nestor 376
Devine, Andy 54, 250, 253, 292, 304, 338, 351, 395, 397, 406, 409, 410
Devlin, Joe 39, 416
Devney, James 383
Devon, Richard 419
De Vries, George 258
Dewever, Jean 229
DeWitt, Jack 171, 291, 309, 314, 358, 431
DeWitt, Louis 15, 148

Dexter, Brad 147, 287, 407
Dexter, Rosemary 77
Deyl, Rudolf 225
Diamond, Arnold 143
Diamond, David 148, 192, 214, 290, 305, 327, 336, 372
Diamond, I.A.L. 237
Diamond, Jack 55
Diamond, Margaret 422
Dias, Maria Helena 146
Dias, Selma Caz 49
Diaz, Victor 289
Dibbs, Kem 168
Dick, Douglas 133, 287
Dickenson, Thorold 317
Dickerson, Beech 16, 419
Dickerson, Dudley 200
Dickinson, Angie 66, 326
Dierkes, John 30, 95, 101, 320
Dierkop, Charles 300
Dietz, Jack 171
Diffring, Anton 1, 432
Dignam, Basil 252
Dignam, Mark 120
Dillard, Mimi 372
Dillard, R.H.W. 138
Dillman, Bradford 149
DiMario, Tony 35
Di Napoli, Marc 390
Di Napoli, Stephane 123a, 390
Diop, Baye Macoumba 40
di Reda, Joe 336
Dix, Robert 336
Dixon, Paul 108
Dobkin, Lawrence 21, 309
Dobson, James 10, 140, 266, 378
Dodd, Jimmie 359
Dodsworth, John 193, 255
Dolan, Michael 438
Dolenz, George 231

Dolgin, Larry 181
Dolinsky, Meyer 181
Doll, Dora 40
Dom, Dorith 353
Domburg, Andrea 365
Domergue, Faith 14
Domick, Arthur (Arturo Dominci) 65
Dominguez, Joe 358
Don Rendell Six 194
Donahue, Jill 121
Donahue, Patricia 193
Donald, James 78
Donaldson, Bonnie Lou 20
Donally, Andrew 78
Donath, Ludwig 388
Donavan, Gregg 100
Doniger, Walter A. 173, 415
Donlevy, Brian 34
Donlon, Dolores 339
Donnell, Jeff 102, 241
Donner, Jorn 311
Donohue, Brian 383
Donovan, King 197
DoQui, Robert 377
Doran, Ann 50, 207, 320
Dorfmann, Robert 107, 296
Dorian, Leon 365
Dorne, Sandra 337, 422, 437
Dorr, Lester 12
Dors, Diana 44, 214, 422
D'Orsay, Fifi 145
d'Orsay, Ghislaine 104
Dorsey, Tommy 108
Dostoyevsky, Feodor 86
Doucet, Catherine 116
Doucette, John 8, 91, 136, 220, 325, 334
Doud, Gil 162, 308
Dougan, Vikki 323
Douglas, Buddy 344
Douglas, Don 141
Douglas, Felicity 201
Douglas, George 17

Douglas, Jerry 42
Douglas, Josephine 430
Douglas, Katya 97
Douglas, Melvyn 38, 408
Douglas, Scott 130
Douglas, Warren 76, 88, 91, 115, 122, 129, 202, 233, 283, 326, 371, 401
Dover, Nyta 324
Dowling, Joan 3, 53, 134, 217, 264, 282
Down, Lesley-Anne 31
Downing, Joseph 127, 218
Downs, Cathy 35, 251, 295, 348
Doyle, Mimi 301
Drake, Allan 344
Drake, Claudia 66, 283
Drake, Colleen 316
Dranke, Dona 358
Drake, Fabia 153, 199, 441
Drake, Jim 381
Drake, Ken 86
Drake, Oliver 115
Drake, Tom 30, 93, 108, 374
Dreifuss, Arthur 388
Dresdel, Sonia 285
Dresser, Danny 384
Dresser, Susie 384
Drew, Donna 34, 326
Drew, Urban 435
Dreyfus, Jack J., Jr. 132
Driscoll, Michael R. 383
Dru, Joanne 420
Dryer, Bernard Victor 309
Dryhurst, Edward 70, 184, 201
Dubov, Paul 15, 314, 347
Dubova, Helena 353
Duchaussoy, Michel 123a, 390
Duda, Gernot 22
Dudley, Robert 373
Duering, Carl 226

Name Index

Duff, Howard 205, 330
Dufilho, Jacques 40, 188
Dugan, Tommy 398
Dugay, Yvette 167
Duggan, Tom 139
Duke, John 301
Duke, Maurice 108, 334
Duke of Iron 66
Dullea, Keir 389
Dumbrille, Douglass 433
Dumke, Ralph 197
Dumont, Danielle 188
Dunbar, John 43, 274
Duncan, Archie 245
Duncan, Carmen 444
Duncan, Kenne 366, 395
Duncan, Pamela 16, 114, 155, 409
Duncan, Renault (Duncan Renaldo) 171
Dunfee, Susan 405
Dunlap, Scott R. 68, 84, 189, 206, 243, 307, 325, 348, 366, 407
Dunn, Cal 100
Dunn, Geoffrey 223
Dunne, Brendan 293
Dunne, Lee 293
Duperey, Annie 47
duPont, Michael 160
Durant, Marjorie 140, 316
Durant, Ted 186
Durning, Charles 408
Durr, Fred 369
Durrant, Theo 239
Duryea, Dan 433
Duvall, Robert 31
Dvorak, Ann 192
Dwan, Allan 173
Dwyer, Hilary 52
Dwyer, Leslie 53, 112, 222
Dwyer, Marlo 348
Dyall, Valentine 134, 317
Dyneley, Peter 194
Dyrenforth, James 337

E

Easton, Bob 173
Easton, Dan 314
Easton, Jane 39, 204, 425
Eastwood, James 69
The Easy Riders 66
Eaton, Evelynne 129
Eberhardt, Norma 250
Edmiston, James 328
Edson, Gus 111
Edwards, Blake 295, 357, 366
Edwards, David 110
Edwards, Elaine 23, 24, 314
Edwards, Henry 112, 238
Edwards, James 305, 342
Edwards, Sam 327
Edwards, Vince 167
Effa, Karel 225
Efraim, R. Ben 260
Eggers, Fred 170, 224, 308, 404
Eisley, Anthony 271; see also Fred Eisley
Eisley, Fred (Anthony) 421; see also Anthony Eisley
El-Kader, Fawzia 25
Elam, Jack 115, 427
Elcar, Dana 132
Eldredge, George 54, 103
Eldredge, John 233, 254, 354, 366, 402
Eldridge, Phyllis 405
Elias, Louie 394
Elie, Willy P. 128
Elkind, Mort W. 196
Ellenstein, Robert 214, 301
Elliot, Dick 116
Elliott, Bill ("Wild" Bill Elliott) 39, 64, 71, 103, 133, 136, 175, 254, 322, 374, 399, 417

Elliott, Cecil 35
Elliott, Denholm 368
Elliott, Dick 174, 193, 232, 397, 416
Elliott, Peter 337
Elliott, Ross 71, 195, 402
Elliott, Scott 359
Elliott, Ted 366
Ellis, Bobby 18
Ellis, Frank 367
Ellis, Marvin 195
Elo, Aarre 311
Elric, Josip 82, 405
Elsner, Edeltraut 59
Elsom, Isobel 354
Elton, Hugh 245
Elvenspoeck, Hans 59
Emery, Katherine 167, 255
Emilfork, Daniel 188
Emmanuel, Taki 386
Emo, Maria 172
Emory, Richard 26
Enders, David 386
Enders, Robert 78
Engel, Roy 99, 207, 284
England, Barry 78
Englander, Beverly 344
Engle, Paul 159, 303
Ercy, Elizabeth 360
Erdman, Richard 121, 320
Erickson, Leif 145, 408
Ericson, John 88, 291, 326
Erman, John 83
Ermeli, Claudio 151
Erskine, Elizabeth 438
Erwin, Bill 89
Erwin, Stuart 373
Eskow, Jerry 413
Esmond, Carl 172
Estella, Alfonso 81
Esterhazy, Andre 124
Estes, Carole 260
Estes, Frank 289
Etcheverry, Michel 277

Name Index

Ethridge, Ella 307, 314
Eustis, Helen 132
Evans, Claude 275
Evans, Clifford 256
Evans, David 371
Evans, Edith 317
Evans, Edward 256, 428
Evans, Gene 148, 192, 327, 347
Evans, Linda 260
Evans, Maurice 52
Evans, Murray 302
Evans, Rex 234
Everest, Barbara 117
Eyer, Richard 68, 140, 162, 206

F

Fabian, François 29
Fabregas, Manolo 67, 294
Fabrizi, Franco 294
Fadden, Tom 20, 116, 197, 209
Fain, M.G. (Matty) 206, 241
Fair, Jody 344
Fairfax, James 234
Fairman, Paul W. (Ivar Jorgenson) 381
Faith, Dolores 186, 266
Falk, Peter 48
Falkenberg, Kort 309
Fancey, E.J. 1
Farell, Claude 432
Farge, Derek 267
Faris, William 377
Farner, Ellen 412
Farnsworth, Richard 224
Farr, Derek 53, 112, 244, 264, 350, 441
Farr, Felicia 130
Farrar, Stanley 309
Farrell, Paul 267
Farwell, Frances 140
Faulds, Andrew 302

Faulkner, Edward 394
Faulkner, James 78
Faulkner, Keith 302
Faulkner, Sally 52
Faulls, Shirley 37
Fawcett, Charles 414
Fawcett, William 68, 101, 175, 248, 367, 411
Faye, Janina 97
Faylen, Frank 106, 329
Feiner, Ruth 432
Feld, Fritz 203, 298, 416
Feldary, Eric 241
Feldt, Fred 384
Felgate, Jimmy 92
Fellows, Don 408
Felmy, Hansjorg (Jorg) 57, 368
Felton, Verna 287
Fen, Nam Kung 113
Fenemore, Hilda 120
Fenemore, Stephen 437
Fennell, Willie 444
Fennelly, Vincent M. 13, 39, 51, 87, 101, 103, 126, 136, 175, 220, 248, 254, 322, 342, 367, 385, 399, 411, 417
Fenton, Frank 155, 269
Fenton, Shane, and the Fentones 306
Ferguson, Frank 13, 75, 189, 248, 321, 367, 385
Ferjac, Anouk 390
Fernandes, Nadyr 146
Ferraday, Lisa 192
Ferrari, Mario 294
Ferrat, Lupita 67
Ferrau, Alessandro 294
Ferraz, Catherine 393
Ferrel, Ray 163, 307
Ferrer, George 198
Ferrer, Jose 369
Ferrera, Paolo 414
Ferrero, Anna Maria 414

Ferris, James 297
Feserova, Lenka 353
Feuchtenberg, Walter 375
Feuer, Cy 63
Feury, Peggy 276
Feyistan, Nigel 92
Fiala, Eman 225
Fiala, Karel 225
Fialova, Kveta 225
Fiasconaro, Frank 275
Field, Jonathan 123, 169
Field, Martin 263
Fielding, Marjorie 137, 310, 432
Fields, Charlie 31
Fields, Darlene 30, 224, 363
Fields, George 192
Fields, Joseph 354
Fierro, Paul 105, 125, 291, 436
Fillmore, James 89
Fina, Jack 108
Finch, Peter 420
Fine, Harry 142
Fine, Morton 132, 276, 300
Finlay, Frank 429
Finnerty, Warren 300
Finney, Jack 197
Finston, Nathaniel 359
Firbank, Ann 341
Firestone, Eddie 6
Firks, Sam 46, 271, 347
Fischer, Kai 22, 198
Fisher, Steve 26, 30, 35, 131, 189, 218, 278, 402
Fist, Fletcher 271
Fitzgerald, Barry 398
Fitzgerald, Geraldine 300
Fix, Paul 367
Fiz, Umberto 96
Flaherty, Pat 18, 55, 208
Flajano, Ennio 333
Flavin, James 125, 133, 174, 179, 200, 206, 367, 416
"Fleecie," the lamb 230

Name Index

Fleer, Harry 83, 156, 347, 400
Fleet, Preston M. 346
Fleischmann, A.S. 365
Fleming, Anne 363
Fleming, Eric 141, 316
Fleming, Michael 78
Fleming, Rhonda 33, 62, 333
Flemyng, Robert 52, 53, 226
Fletcher, Charlotte 362
Fletcher, Lester 172, 290
Fleytoux, Roger 370
Flint, Sam 35, 84, 278, 357
Flippen, J.C. 307
Flor, Celia 281
Flowers, Jim 403
Fluellen, Joel 140, 208, 235, 329
Flynn, Errol 420
Flynn, Joe 309
Flynn, Pat 284
Flynn, Sean 369
Foam, John 65; see also Mario Bava
Foley, Bill 274
Foley, William 293
Fondat, Marcel 45
Fong, Benson 114
Fong, Harold 284
Fontaine, John 26, 125
Foo, Lee Tong 348, 388
Foote, Dick 20, 85
Foran, Dick 15, 404
Foran, Mary 190
Forbes, Bryan 285, 368
Forbes, Scott 171
Ford, Carole Ann 97, 245
Ford, Mary 316
Ford, Wallace 130, 427
Foreman, John 246
Foreman, L.L. 11
Forest, Michael 27
Forester, William A. 89
Forman, Joey 181

Forman, Lynn 405
Forman, Win 405
Forrest, William 135, 313, 361
Forster, Rudolf 57
Foscari, Carla 96
Fosse, Bob 63
Foster, Alan 409
Foster, Barry 212, 429
Foster, Bill 287
Foster, Bob 110
Foster, Dianne 199, 214
Foster, Pamela 94
Foster, Preston, 102, 189
Foulger, Byron 13, 106, 155, 215/216, 243, 416
Foulk, Robert 163, 174, 220, 315, 378
The Four Gypsies 237
Fowler, Gene, Jr. 323
Fowler, Harry 7, 120, 134
Fowler, Helen 371
Fowley, Douglas 20, 21, 116, 209, 251
Fox, Craig 314
Fox, James 341
Fox, Michael 419
Foxcroft, Les 444
Foxwell, Ivan 3, 154, 282
Franchi, Franco 286
Francis, Derek 252
Francis, Freddie 97
Francis, Linda 271
Francis, Sandra 365
Francisci, Mario 294
Franciscus, James 191, 355
Frank, Fredric M. 117
Frank, Gerald 343
Frank, Pat 173
Franklin, Gretchen 169
Franklin, Muriel 384
Franklin, Sidney A., Jr. 155
Franz, Arthur 15, 51
Franz, Eduard 391
Fraser, Alex 234

Fraser, John 117, 152, 153, 256
Fraser, Peter 360
Fraser, Ronald 429
Fraser, Shelagh 52
Fraser, Stanley 255, 434
Frawley, William 18
Frazer, Moyra 94
Frazier, Sheila 392
Freddie and the Dreamers 110
Fredericks, Charles 218, 278, 308, 404
Fredric, Norman 109
Freed, Bert 380
Freedland, George 261
Freedman, Benedict 334
Freeland, Thornton 238
Freeman, C. Dennis 238
Freeman, Everett 200
Freeman, Gillian 223; see also Eliot George
Freeman, Mona 115, 173
Freeman, Thomas 389
Frees, Paul 329
French, Harold 94, 199, 267
French, Ted 20
French, Valerie 80
Fresson, Bernard 29
Frickhoefer, Gerhard 375
Friedgen, J. Raymond 176
Friedkin, David 132, 300
Friend, Philip 171
Froment, Raymond 396
Fromkess, Leon 46, 271, 347
Frost, Terry 85, 159, 254
Frye, Gil 58
Fuchs, Daniel 145, 187
Fulci, Lucio 286
Fuller, Lance 58
Fuller, Samuel 271, 347
Fulton, Rad 207
Furia, Giacomo 387

Name Index

Furie, Sidney J. 223
Furneaux, Yvonne 3, 184, 420
Furst, Joseph 124, 444
Fury, Billy 306
Fusier-Gil, Jeanne 324

G

Gaba, Marianne 321
Gabor, Zsa Zsa 316
Gabourie, Fred 170, 436, 442
Gabriel, Rajmund 353
Gaffney, Robert 138
Gainsbourg, Serge 331
Galion, Estera 249
Gallagher, Thomas 97
Gallaher, Ed 108
Gallico, Bob 337
Gallo, Lew 357
Gallu, Samuel 245
Galvan, Pedro 67
Gamble, Ralph 71, 193, 316, 374, 415
Gampu, Ken 429
Ganley, Gail 284
Gannaway, Albert C. 21
Garcia, Tito 128
Garden, John 112
Gardett, Robert 141
Gardiner, John 274
Gardner, Ava 124
Gardner, Frank 156
Gardner, Harvey 439
Gardner, Richard 162
Garfinkle, Louis 121, 440
Gargan, Edward 116, 200, 354, 373
Garland, Beverly 39, 101, 211, 284, 374, 411
Garland, Charles 101
Garland, Richard 16, 140, 266, 401
Garner, Shirley 321
Garr, Francis 132
Garralaga, Martin 388
Garret, Stephen 183

Garrett, George 138
Garrett, Joy 426
Gartside, Ernest 70, 81
Gary, Lou 221
Gaskins, Jack 389
Gates, Larry 197
Gates, Nancy 241, 320, 434
Gates, Tudor 142
Gauge, Alexander 430
Gaven, Jean 370
Gavin, Werton 408
Gay, Gregory 172
Gayle, Patricia 271
Gaylor, Anna 229
Gaylor, Gerry 316
Gaze, Larry 354
Gazzara, Ben 82
Gazzoli, Victor 237
Geary, Richard 320
Geer, Len 378
Gegauff, Paul 390
Geiser, Linda 300
Gelb, Ed 327
Gell, William 245
Genn, Leo 3, 124, 280
Genoino, Arnaldo 165
Genoves, Andre 123a, 390
Gentry, Bill 325
George, Christopher 146
George, Eliot 223; see also Gillian Freeman
George, Jack 265, 359
George, Muriel 94, 219
George, Sue 413
George, Susan 142, 360
Georgi, Wolfgang 369
Geraghty, Clive 293
Gerald, Jim 396
Gerard, Hal 224, 265, 397
Geray, Steven 298, 332
Gerber, Joan (voice of) 346
Germaine, Mary 123
Germi, Pietro 268
Germon, Nane 229
Gerry, Alex 76, 295

Gerry, Toni 291
Gerson, Betty Lou 8
Gerson, Jeanne 58
Gerstle, Frank 241, 347, 421, 439
Getz, Robert 166
Gibbons, Aylene 439
Gibbs, Jill 282
Gibson, Gail 119
Gibson, Julie 20
Gibson, Mimi 13, 287, 371
Gielgud, John 149
Gifford, Alan 57
Gilbert, Dick 108
Gilbert, Olive 94
Gilchrist, Connie 394
Gilford, C.B. 207
Gill, Tom 422
Gillat, Sidney 80
Gillen, Jim 389
Giller, Walter 375
Gilling, John 154
Gilmore, Lowell 171
Gilmore, Peter 252
Gilson, Tom 82
Gimpera, Teresa 60
Ginsburg, Arnie 110
Giovanni, Jose 387
Girard, Bernard 323
Girard, France 390
Girotti, Massimo 165
Giroux, Claude 387
Giskes, H.J. 183
Gist, Robert 4, 431
Giustini, Carlo 117
Glass, Everett 140, 197, 434
Glass, Ned 141, 181, 205, 323
Glasser, Bernard 37
Glaubrecht, Frank 59
Glazer, Benjamin 359
Glazier, Sidney 118
Gleason, Jackie 357
Gleason, James 19, 116, 354
Gleason, Regina 103, 218, 362

Name Index 193

Glenn, Leslie 321
Glenn, Roy 150, 208, 211, 329, 332, 408
Glover, Charles 260
Glover, Julian 196
Glynne, Maureen 137
Gobin, Gabriel 396
Godsell, Vanda 120, 302
Goetz, Hayes 11, 173, 187, 312, 391
Gold, Jack 426; see also John Gould
Goldin, Pat 200
Goldman, Edmund 376
Goldman, Lawrence L. 419
Goldman, William 357
Goldner, Charles 53, 259
Goldsmith, Myron B. 192
Goldstone, Richard 2
Gomez, Thomas 218, 278
Gonzales-Gonzales, Jose 344
Gonzalez, Ernesto 221
Gonzalez, Felix 67
Gonzalez, Servando 132
Goodman, George 375
Goodwin, Alan 267
Goodwin, Angela 268
Goodwin, Harold 7, 428
Goodwin, James 440
Goodwin, Ruby 371
Goodwins, Leslie 297
Gorassini, Anne 286, 369
Gorcey, Bernard 55, 56, 73, 105, 168, 203, 204, 208, 234, 298, 313, 364
Gorcey, David 8, 127, 174, 182, 193, 232, 363, 416
Gorcey, Leo 55, 56, 73, 85, 105, 168, 203, 204, 208, 234, 298, 313, 364
Gordan, Roy 419

Gordon, Alex 15
Gordon, Barry 160
Gordon, Bernard 90, 124, 389
Gordon, Bert I. 93, 400
Gordon, Bill 108
Gordon, Bruce 328
Gordon, Cliff 256
Gordon, Colin 69, 428
Gordon, Don 296
Gordon, Gale 111
Gordon, Gavin 23, 168
Gordon, Glenn 129
Gordon, Leo 89, 178, 315, 329, 342, 378, 421
Gordon, Robert 42, 320
Gordon, Roy 17, 34, 122, 263, 421
Gordon, Susan 400
Gorini, Arianna 45
Gorky Film Studio 240
Gorse, Sol 439
Gorshin, Frank 147, 309
Gorss, Saul 62, 224, 436
Gossage, John 7
Gotell, Walter 124
Gotfurt, Frederic 438
Gottler, Jerome S. 168, 364
Gough, Lloyd 18
Gough, Michael 42
Gould, Elliott 426
Gould, John 426; see also Jack Gold
Gould, Rita 34
Grabourie, Fred 345
Grabowski, Norman "Woo Woo" 344
Graham, Fred 209
Graham, Lyla 326
Graham, Tim 62, 157
Grahame, Alec 74
Granata, Graziella 333
Granger, Michael 135, 167, 232
Granger, Stewart 429
Grano, Henrik 311

Granstedt, Greta 145
Grant, Kathryn 33, 305
Grant, Kirby 122, 283, 442
Grant, Lee 196, 384
Grant, Neil 343
Granville, Bonita 373
Grauman, Walter 109
Gravers, Steve 290
Graves, Peter (American actor) 68, 99, 173, 427, 431
Graves, Peter (English actor) 262
Gravesi, Steve 4
Gray, Billy 20, 145
Gray, Charles 245
Gray, Coleen 11, 102, 163, 206, 218
Gray, Donald 14
Gray, Dulcie 7, 137, 267
Gray, Linda 194, 386
Gray, Nadia 259
Gray, Sally 350
Gray, Vernon 285
Gray, Willoughby 164, 245, 259
Grayam, Dan 231
Grayden, Richard 428
Great, Johnny B. 110
Grech, German 128
Green, Austin 290
Green, Garard 169
Green, Janet 2, 152
Green, Len 338
Green, Michael 386
Greenburg, Harry 4
Greene, Angela 83, 234, 332, 349, 394
Greene, Candy 236
Greene, David 151
Greene, Herbert 83
Greene, Otis 109
Greene, Richard 81
Greenway, Tom 220
Greenwood, Joan 441
Greer, Dabbs 39, 71, 101, 197, 329, 342

Name Index

Greeves, Vernon 226
Grefe, William 177, 318
Gregg, Hubert 217
Gregg, Virginia 87, 309
Gregor, Manfred 59
Gregory, James 4
Gregory, Thea 422
Gregson, John 7, 142, 143, 422
Grenfall, Joyce 153, 222
Grey, Joel 63
Grey, Virginia 42, 126, 136, 271, 381
Griem, Helmut 53
Griffin, Frank 62
Griffin, Josephine 184, 422
Griffin, Robert E. 349
Griffith, Ann 127, 133
Griffith, Charles B. 16, 27, 284, 382
Griffith, Hugh 153, 222
Griffith, James 13, 62, 130, 209, 243, 343
Griffith, Kenneth 53, 143, 302, 429
Griffiths, Jane 1
Grimaldi, Hugo 186, 266
Grinfan, Alessandro 9
Grinnage, Jack 85, 431
Groom, Pelham 7
Gross, Jack J. 102
Grosskurth, Kurt 353
Grover, Ed 426
Groves, Fred 267
Gruber, Frank 407
Gruber, Robert 407
Gruel, Maurice 210
Gruenberg, Leonard 448
Grunfeld, Svea 28
Grunwald, Morten 447
Grzimek, Dr. Bernhard 340
Grzimek, Michael 340
Guardino, Harry 35
Gudegast, Hans (Eric Braeden) 290

Guderman, Linda 239
Gueden, Nicole 229
Guerin, Lenmana 144
Guerra, Mario 286
Guerritore, Monica 60
Guibert, Claire 396
Guilfoyle, Paul 150, 388
Guillermin, John 393
Guinness, Alec 219
Gulbranson, Robert 289
Guldbrandsen, Ole 447
Gunn, Gilbert 152, 217, 256
Gurvich, Louis 275
Gustafson, Carol 405
Gutowski, Gene 331
Gutterman, Leon 354
Guy, Darryl 21
Gwynne, Anne 295
Gynt, Greta 49

H

Haade, William 338, 373
Haas, Charles 336
Haddon, Larry 160
Haden, Sara 30
Hadley, Reed 170, 209, 295, 439
Haedrich, Rolf 369
Haerter, Gerald 65
Hafner, Ingrid 49
Hagen, Holger 340
Hagen, Howard 389
Hagen, Kevin 159, 328
Hagen, Paul 288
Haggerty, Don 8, 64, 71, 85, 91, 133, 145, 233, 314, 325, 330
Haggiag, Brahim 25
Hagney, Frank 85, 140, 329
Hagon, Garrick 408
Hahn, Jess 369, 396
Hahn, Ross 418
Hairston, Jester 321

Hakim, Raymond 29, 188, 319
Hakim, Robert 29, 188, 319
Hale, Alan, Jr. 68, 88, 200, 348, 403
Hale, Barbara 287
Hale, Bill 170, 250, 338, 356
Hale, Fiona 349
Hale, Jonathan 41, 209, 329, 348, 366
Hale, Monte 442
Hale, Nancy 235
Hale, Richard 140
Hall, Gita 431
Hall, Grayson 119
Hall, Henry 295, 366
Hall, Huntz 55, 56, 73, 85, 105, 127, 168, 174, 182, 193, 203, 204, 208, 232, 234, 298, 313, 363, 364, 416
Hall, Irlin 164
Hall, Robert 137, 152
Hall, Thurston 41
Hall, Vincent 386
Hallatt, May 428
Haller, Daniel 293
Halliday, Bryant 92
Halloran, John 202
Halsdorf, Serge 32
Halsey, Brett 15, 89, 181, 362
Halton, Charles 140
Hambledon, Phyllis 280
Hambleton, Duffy 260
Hamer, Robert 124
Hamilton, Brett 192
Hamilton, George 6, 86, 387
Hamilton, Guy 299
Hamilton, John 200, 359
Hamilton, Joseph 307
Hamilton, Richard 405
Hammond, Michael 46
Hammond, Peter 98, 123, 201

Name Index 195

Hampton, Orville H. 15
Hamshere, Keith 306
Hampton, Robert (Ricardo Freda) 65
Handl, Irene 134, 201, 259, 350, 422, 441
Hanley, Frank 35, 218
Hanlon, Tom 204, 425
Hanmer, Don 296
Hanna, Mark 17, 46, 284, 321
Hanold, Marilyn 138
Hansard, Paul 149
Hansen, Heidi 375
Hansen, Lorna 122
Hansen, Nina 359
Hanson, Peter 355
Harari, Clement 277
Harding, Ann 200, 371
Harding, John 86
Hardman, Des 48
Hardstack, Michael 5
Hardwicke, Sir Cedric 359
Hardy, Lindsay 433
Hargrave, Ron 202, 415
Harkins, Phillip 376
Harmon, John 39, 68, 202, 203, 208, 232, 361, 380
Harmon, Joy 439
Harmon, Sidney 34, 389
Harmon, Tom 8
Harout, Magda 86
Harper, Kenneth 44, 74
Harries, Ronnie 152
Harrington, Prudence 249
Harris, Holly 190
Harris, Phil 448
Harris, Richard 429
Harris, Robert H. 82, 147, 290, 407
Harris, Stacy 275
Harrison, James 295, 366
Harrison, Kathleen 53, 112, 217
Harrison, Rex 80

Harrison, Richard 24
Harrower, Elizabeth 191, 409
Harry-Max 319
Hart, Buddy 230
Hart, Diane 123
Hart, Dolores 307
Hart, John 103
Hart, Maurice 108
Hart, Moss 386
Hart, Neal 366
Hartleben, Jerry 215/216
Hartley, William B. 88
Hartman, Paul 357
Hartmann, Georg 63
Hartmann, Ronald 48
Hartnell, William 112, 430
Hartunian, Richard 181
Harvye, Clem 10
Harvey, Don C. 105, 106, 150, 342
Harvey, Harry 170, 349
Harvey, Henry A., Sr. 263
Harvey, Joan 160
Harvey, Laurence 217, 244
Harvey, Paul 168
Hasen, Irwin 111
Haskell, Al 417
Haskin, Byron 10, 130
Hasty, John Eugene 388
Hatfield, Hurd 117
Hatton, Raymond 41, 84, 105, 404, 409
Hatton, Temple 191
Hauser, Gilgi 97
Hausmeister, Ruth 59
Haussler, Richard 261
Havoc, June 391
Hawkins, Ben 318
Hawkins, Carol Ann 52
Hawkins, Jack 7, 299
Hawtrey, Charles 14
Hayakawa, Sessue 36, 162
Hayakawa, Tsuru Aoki 162

Hayden, Harry 20, 116
Hayden, Sara 409
Hayden, Sterling 11, 76, 125, 131, 155, 209, 349
Haydon, Don 351
Haye, Helen 262
Hayers, Sidney 302
Hayes, Allison 17, 109, 190, 394
Hayes, Bruce 108
Hayes, Chester 144
Hayter, James 74, 134, 164, 267, 350, 430
Haythorne, Joan 143, 422
Hayward, Jim 39, 269
Hayward, Louis 332
Haze, Jonathan 284
Hazell, Hy 137, 437
Healey, Myron 64, 75, 82, 105, 126, 130, 147, 179, 209, 241, 254, 313, 315, 348, 358, 385, 413, 417, 425, 440
Healey, David 408
Heard, Paul F. 176
Hearne, Reginald 43
Heathcoate, Thomas 38
Hecht, Ben 316
Hecht, Ted 20, 145, 403
Hedloe, John 114
Heermance, Richard 68, 99, 131, 193, 255, 330, 332, 416, 427, 434, 440
Heffley, Wayne 24, 86
Heflin, Van 90, 245, 448
Heiberg, Brigit 72
Heims, Jo 156
Heinz, Gerard 259
Heinz, Michael 59
Heinz, Richard 294
Heisler, Stuart 172
Hellman, Marcel 226
Hellman, Monte 27
Hellmold, Kalus 59

Helpmann, Robert 124
Helton, Percy 203, 363
Henaghan, Jim 369, 379
Henderson, Douglas 42
Henderson, Marcia 68, 190, 269
Hendriks, Jan 57
Hendrix, Wanda 170, 171
Hendry, Ian 196
Henrickson, Lance 276
Henry, Bill 159, 297, 361, 363, 401
Henry, Carol 209, 366
Henry, Gloria 179
Henry, Jack 306
Henry, Joan 44, 422
Henry, Robert "Buzz" 175
Henry, Thomas Browne 64, 127, 157, 191, 315, 402
Henry, Victor 360
Henson, Gladys 223
Hepburn, Audrey 222, 237, 441
Herb Jeffries' Calypsomanics 66
Herbert, Percy 98, 429
Herlie, Eileen 74, 199
Herman, Ace 278
Herman, Gil 192
Herman, Norman T. 181, 413
Hermann, Hans 290
Hernandez, Joe 41
Hernandez, Juano 300
Heron, Joyce 422, 423
Herrmann, Edward 31
Hersent, Philippe 183
Hershey, Barbara 221
Hershey, Burnett 301
Hertz, Lone 288
Hertz, Nathan 17; see also Nathan Juran
Heston, Charlton 117, 124
Hewitt, Celia 228

Hewitt, Heather 258
Hewitt, Henry 259
Heydt, Louis Jean 20, 21
Hickman, Charles 369
Hickman, Darryl 41, 303
Hickok, Douglas 110, 148
Hicks, Chuck 347
Hicks, Russell 189, 254
Hicks, Seymour 350
Hidari, Bokuzen 445
Higa, Reiko 36
Higgins, John C. 173
Higgins, Michael 384
Hilbard, John 288
Hilbeck, Fernando 379
Hill, David 210
Hill, Gladys 246
Hill, Marianna 42
Hill, Riley 192, 209, 348, 425
Hill, Robert 79, 344
Hilling, Jacques 188
Hills, Beverly 439
Hilton, Edward 96
Hinkle, Robert 287
Hintermann, Carlo 369
Hirakawa, Joe 210
Hird, Thora 74, 153
Hirsch, Robert 188
Hittleman, Carl K. 155
Hlinomaz, Josef 225
Ho, Linda 79
Ho, James 444
Hobbes, Peter 267
Hobeaux, Les 194
Hobley, Macdonald 280
Hodgins, Earle 39, 136, 287, 416
Hodgson, J.L. 153
Hodiak, John 26, 114
Hodson, James Lansdale 212
Hoerl, Arthur 377, 388, 439
Hoey, Dennis 20
Hofer, Chris 183
Hoffman, Alfred 386

Hoffman, Dustin 296
Hoffman, Guenther 59
Hoffman, Howard 185, 230, 239
Hohl, Arthur 200
Holden, Joyce 265, 313
Hole, William, Jr. 362
Holland, Edna 189, 330
Holland, John 251
Holliman, Earl 10, 34
Holmes, Taylor 354
Holmstrom, Marianne 311
Holt, Joel 210
Holt, Patrick 143, 154, 420
Holt, Seth 368
Home, William Douglas 134
Homeier, Skip 13, 91
Homes, Geoffrey 8, 101; see also Daniel Mainwaring
Homolka, Oscar 184, 259
Honda, Inoshiro 445
Hoo, Geri 79
Hood, Darla 23
Hooker, Hugh M. 230
Hoose, Fred 351
Hootkins, Bill 408
Hope, Gary 97
Hope, Vida 7, 112, 134
Hopkins, Bob 85
Hopkins, Joan 112, 244
Hopkins, Julie 228
Hopkins, Pixie 67
Hopper, William 130
Hopwood, Avery 23
Hordern, Michael 80, 117, 420, 428
Horsbrugh, Walter 259
Horsfall, Bernard 149
Horsley, John 69
Horsten, Harold 365
Horton, Helen 226
Horton, Louisa 5
Hossein, Robert 277
Hoty, Clegg 127

Name Index

Houston, Brett 84
Houston, Glyn 302
Howard, Arthur 428
Howard, Breena 271
Howard, Joyce 262
Howard, Lewis 359
Howard, Rance 100
Howard, Robert 418
Howard, Ronald 53, 112, 267, 310, 317, 424
Howard, Sandy 72
Howard, Trevor 78, 426
Howells, Ursula 422
Howes, Bobby 153
Howes, Reed 12, 101, 338, 343
Howlin, Olin 20, 116
Hoy, Robert 394
Hoyos, Rodolfo 130, 156, 290
Hoyt, John 28, 34, 76, 289, 439
Hua, Chang Yeuh 61
Huart, Gerard 47
Hubbard, Eddie 108
Hubbard, John 157, 357
Hubbard, Thomas G. 12, 21, 170, 224, 265, 308, 404
Huc, Nicole 32
Hudd, Walter 217
Hudis, Norman 169
Hudson, James 176
Hudson, William 17
Huebel, Klaus 40
Huebsch, Edward 408
Huggett, Richard 98
Hugh, R. John 270
Hughes, Carolyn 421
Hughes, Kathleen 415
Hughes, Ken 14, 69, 98, 196
Hughes, Mary Beth 105, 155, 170, 218, 233
Hughes, Robin 255
Hughes, Tony 170
Hugo, Mauritz 155, 314, 343, 378
Hugo, Victor 188

Hulett, Otto 305
Hulke, Malcolm 228
Hull, Henry 132
Hulsh, Robert 333
Hume, Hjordis 369
Hung, Kong 113
Hunt, Marsha 281, 307
Hunt, Peter 149
Hunt, Ronald Leigh 92
Hunter, Alastair 420
Hunter, Arlene 344
Hunter, Evan 221
Hunter, James 212
Hunter, Jeffrey 162, 342
Hunter, Nita 354
Hunter, Tony 270
Hunter, William 180
Huntington, Lawrence 81, 137, 244
Huntley, Raymond 80
Hurst, David 259
Hurst, Veronica 7, 222, 255, 332, 430, 437
Hussenot, Olivier 158
Hussey, John 149, 246
Huston, Virginia 171
Hutchinson, Harry 398
Hutchinson, June 119
Hutchinson, Leslie "Hutch" 238
Huttinger, Burt 177
Hutton, Robert 337, 436
Hyatt, Bobby 403
Hyatt, Daniel 148, 327
Hyde-White, Wilfrid 219, 259, 267, 424
Hyer, Martha 46, 91, 297
Hyland, Jim 86
Hylton, Jane 422

I

Iglesias, Amalia 393
Iglesias, Eugene 167
Illing, Peter 3, 49, 201, 337

Indrisano, John 186, 314
Infante, Eddie 281
Ingels, Marty 10
Inglis, Hamilton G. 153, 280, 430
Ingram, Jack 84, 135, 348
Ingram, Jean 394
Ingrassia, Ciccio 286
Ingster, Boris 361
Inness, Jean 140
Ireland, John 124, 145, 339
Irish, Tom 342
Irwin, Charles 135
Isherwood, Christopher 63
Ishii, Arnold 272
Itami, Ichizo, 36, 124
Ito, Fujio 210
Iturbi, Jose 359
Ivernel, Daniel 387
Ivo, Tommy 28

J

Jabbour, Gabriel 249
Jackie and the Raindrops 110
Jackie Ward Singers (voice of) 346
Jackson, Calvin 191
Jackson, Collette 28, 382, 415
Jackson, Freda 282
Jackson, George 149
Jackson, Gordon 70, 226
Jackson, Louis H. 262
Jackson, Marty 140
Jackson, Selmer 15
Jackson, Thomas 17, 189
Jacobi, Lou 152
Jacobs, David 194
Jacoby, Irving 355
Jaeckel, Richard 408
Jaeckin, Just 370
Jaffe, Carl 1, 14, 94
Jaffrey, Saeed 246
Jahnen, Margaret 369

Name Index

James, Carol 441
James, John 399, 417
James, Polly 315
James, Sidney 74, 123, 219, 422, 430, 437, 438
Jann, Gerald 79
Janson, Horst 261
Janssen, David 111, 162, 214, 407
Janssen, Eilene 42
Janssen, Teri 214, 407
Japrisot, Sebastien 370
Jara, Maurice 125
Jarlego, Ike, Jr. 281
Jarvis, Bill 444
Jarvis, Graham 119
Jason, Judy 110
Jason, Will 108
Jay, Ernest 259, 428
Jayne, Jennifer 120
Jayston, Michael 196
Jean, Gloria 388
Jeans, Ronald 441
Jecklin, Ruth 375
"Jeffrey," the dog 22
Jeffries, Herb 66, 108
Jeffries, Jan 171
Jeffries, Lionel 169, 430
Jenkins, Megs 280
Jenks, Frank 105, 140, 170, 192, 374, 425
Jenks, Si 116
Jennings, Junero 392
Jennings, Kay 27
Jennings, Talbot 217
Jens, Salome 6, 132
Jergens, Adele 127
Jergens, Diane 50, 140
Jerrold, Mary 53
Jessua, Alain 229
Jewell, Austen 174, 232
Jewers, Ray 408
Jilovec, Jaroslav 225
Johansen, Svend 447
John, Rosamund 280
Johns, Glynis 422
Johns, Mervyn 97, 124, 256

Johnson, Agnes Christine 41
Johnson, Alex 333
Johnson, Brad 248
Johnson, Celia 153
Johnson, Chubby 130, 187, 440
Johnson, Dorothy 230
Johnson, Fred 398
Johnson, Jason 12, 303
Johnson, Lamont 187
Johnson, Mark 389
Johnson, Noel 69
Johnson, Russell 16
Johnson, Stan 359
Johnson, Van 423
Johnston, Margaret 310
Johnston, Oliver 152
Joint, Alf 360
Jolley, I. Stanford 101, 136, 155, 159, 209, 243, 248, 287, 322, 323, 342, 358, 366, 397, 399, 411, 417, 427, 440
Jones, Arthur V. 413
Jones, Carolyn 197
Jones, Charlotte 132
Jones, Evan 212
Jones, G. Stanley 172
Jones, Gordon 24, 404
Jones, Harmon 28, 62, 68, 431
Jones, Henry 6
Jones, James 389
Jones, James Earl 119
Jones, L.Q. 8
Jones, Morgan 272, 284
Jones, Peter 3, 7, 74, 137, 152, 219, 437
Jones, Ray 84, 367, 404, 417
Jones, Robert Earl 384
Jones, Tommy Lee 31
Jordan, Bobby 338
Jordan, Charles 384
Jordan, Joanne 233
Jordan, Patrick 143

Jorgenson, Connie 286
Jory, Victor 171, 296
Joseph, Jackie 362
Joseph, Richard L. 353
Joseph, Robert 159
Joslyn, Donald 166
Jost, Edith 183
Judels, Charles 295
Junco, Tito 393
Jungmeyer, Jack, Jr. 170
Jurado, Katy 115
Juran, Nathan 170; see also Nathan Hertz
Jurgens, Curt 57, 183, 396
Jurow, Martin 357
Just, Philip (Filippano Sanjust) 65
Justice, Barry 212
Justice, James Robertson 267
Justine, William 58
Justman, Joseph 415
Juul, Ole 288

K

Kalmus, Bea 108
Kaltenborn, H.V. 18
Kamb, Karl 19
Kamo, Kyoko 272
Kananagh, John 293
Kandel, Aben 42
Kandel, Stephen 241
Kane, Michael 236
Kani, John 429
Kann, Lily 262
Kanter, Bob 389
Kanter, Marianne 300
Kaplan, Richard 118
Kardell, Lili 232
Karen, James 138
Karlan, Richard 380, 402
Karlatos, Olga 268
Karloff, Boris 139, 360
Karlson, Phil 41, 162, 305

Name Index

Karns, Todd 26, 73, 131
Kasket, Harold 184, 420
Kast, Pierre 324
Kasznar, Kurt 124
Katayama, Julia 272
Katch, Kurt 28
Katcher, Leo 214
Kath, Katherine 226
Kaufman, Herbert 159
Kaufman, Joe 18
Kaufman, Millard 82
Kaufman, Willy 172
Kaufmann, Maurice 142, 148, 306
Kay, Gilbert L. 337
Kay, Mary Ellen 417, 442
Kaye, Leo 359
Kazan, Lainie 331
Keach, Stacy 78, 119
Keane, Charles 234, 343
Keane, Robert Emmett 388
Keans, Charles R. 66
Keast, Paul 356
Keays, Vernon 100
Keefer, Don 187, 329
Keegan, Barry 38, 302
Keel, Howard 10, 97
Keen, Geoffrey 7, 44, 423
Keene, Ralph 112
Keese, Oscar 90
Keiko 79
Keir, David 164
Keith, Brian 106
Keith, Ronald 168
Kellaway, Cecil 171
Kellerman, Sally 160
Kellett, Pete 30, 35
Kelley, Barry 361, 378
Kelley, DeForrest 157
Kellino, Roy 154
Kellogg, John 20, 82, 126, 145
Kellogg, Ray 191, 321
Kellogg, Virginia 336
Kelly, Barbara 70

Kelly, Bill 258
Kelly, Carol 88
Kelly, Claire 356
Kelly, Jack 176
Kelly, Jim 392
Kelly, Karolee 76
Kelly, Martin 370
Kelly, Patsy 271
Kelly, Susan 111
Kelsall, Moultrie 137, 420, 423
Kelsey, Fred 250, 265
Kemmer, Ed 66, 247
Kemmerling, Warren 82
Kemper, Doris 85, 287, 354
Kempf, Nadia 32
Kendall, Kay 80
Kendall, Merelina 386
Kendis, William 413
Kenneally, Philip 141
Kennedy, Adam 378
Kennedy, Don 8
Kennedy, Dorothy 91, 202
Kennedy, Douglas 91, 157, 192, 220, 257, 335, 371, 401
Kennedy, Harold J. 329, 339
Kennedy, Mary Jo 293
Kennedy, Phyllis 354
Kenney, Joan 438
Kenney, June 178, 382
Kenny, Jack 139
Kent, Dorothea 200
Kent, Ellie 407
Kent, Gary 24, 224
Kent, Jean 49, 53, 423
Kent, Lenny 108
Kent, Robert E. 46, 322
Kenyon, Curtis 303
Kenyon, Sandy 4
Kerbash, Samia (Michele) 25
Kerman, David 138
Kerner, Ben 48
Kerr, Donald 436

Kerr, Joe 329
Kerr, Kendra 180
Kerridge, Mary 92
Kerwin, William 177
Kessel, Joseph 29
Kesten, Stephen F. 119
Keymas, George 75, 159
Keys, Robert 209, 358
Khachapuridze, Olya 240
Khambatta, Persis 78
Khan, Iska 29
Khoury, George 232, 334
Khvylya, Aleksandr 240
Kidd, Jonathan 239
Kido, Caroline 79
Kiel, Richard 186
Kier, Udo 370
Kiley, Richard 140, 305
Kim, June 79
Kimbell, Anne 73, 150, 292
Kimbrell, Marketa 300
Kimura, Takeshi 445
King, Andrea 361
King, Charles 366
King, Edward 389
King, Frank 20, 116, 145, 361
King, Kip 106
King, Maurice 20, 116, 145, 361
King, Nicholas 207
King, Wright 181, 440
King-Kelly, John 69
The Kings Men 200
Kingsford, Guy 135, 211
Kingsford, Walter 234
Kipling, Rudyard 246
Kirby, John 8
Kirk, Joe 182, 278
Kirkpatrick, Jess 413
Klaven, Walter 141
Klebb, Helen 140
Klemperer, Werner 290
Klempner, John 391
Kline, Robert 230
Klinger, Michael 149

Name Index

Klunis, Tom 276
Knapp, Robert 178, 320
Knight, Fuzzy 269, 399, 417
Knight, James 419
Knight, Shirley 140
Knight, Ted 172, 439
Knight, Vick 200
Knopf, Christopher 207, 378
Knowles, Patric 433
Knox, Alexander 37
Knox, Doris 341
Knox, Elyse 41, 388
Knox, Mona 204
Knudson, Barbara 89
Knudson, Peggy 30
Kobe, Gail 159
Kobi, Michi 162
Koch, Howard W. 139
Koenig, Mark 18
Kohler, Fred, Jr. 351
Kohler, Walter 172
Kohner, Susan 106
Kokas, Gyula 237
Kokas, Michael 237
Koly, Natou 40
Komuro, Tom 272
Konrad, Dorothy 394
Kooy, Pete 99
Kopecky, Milos 225
Korber, Susanne 57
Korvin, Charles 393
Kory, David 111
Kosleck, Martin 172
Kossoff, David 152, 285
Kouao, Tanoh 40
Kowal, Mitchell 124
Kowalchuk, Billy 48
Kowalski, Bernard L. 178
Kraft, Evelyne 375
Kramarsky, David 89
Kramer, Al 287
Kramer, David 160
Krance, Andrew 221
Krasne, Philip N. 102
Krieger, Lee 82
Krizman, Serge 359
Kroeger, Berry 172

Kronos 96
Krueger, Kurt 224
Kruger, Christiane 196
Kruger, Hardy 429
Kruger, Jacqueline 231
Kruger, Otto 354
Krugher, Lea 45
Krugman, Lou 314
Kruschen, Jack 82, 103
Kubatskiy, Anatoliy 240
Kulky, Henry 73, 129, 203, 442
Kuluva, Will 87
Kunkera, Zeliko 379
Kurlick, Daniel 42
Kurts, Alwyn 444
Kuznetsov, Mikhail 240
Kydd, Sam 420

L

Lablais, Michel 32
Lacey, Catherine 341, 360
Lackteen, Frank 283
Ladd, Alan 321
Ladd, David 321, 429
Lady T 66
Lagrange, Valerie 242
Lahn, Ilse 263
Laine, Corrine 413
Lake, Florence 39, 101, 254
Lamar, Robert 383
Lambert, Jack 13, 68, 147, 178, 420
L'Amoreaux, Paul 100
L'Amour, Louis 378, 404
Lampas, Carlo 414
Lampert, Zohra 301
Lampkin, Charles 328
Lancaster, Burt 408
Lanchbury, Liz 274
Landau, Leslie L. 267, 310
Landau, Richard 139
Landers, Harry 202, 325

Landers, Lew 88, 380, 401
Landis, Carole 238
Landis, Monty 306
Landone, Avice 137, 154, 223, 267
Landres, Paul 71, 206, 220, 243, 291
Landy, Hanna 290
Lane, Burton 2
Lane, Charles 200, 354
Lane, Jocelyn 394
Lane, Lari 12
Lane, Lenita 23
Lane, Mara 3
Lane, Mike 139
Lane, Richard 18, 388
Lane, Rusty 309, 320
Laney, Ruth 333
Lang, David 336
Lang, Howard 43
Langan, Glenn 266
Lange, Burt 82
Langer, Philip 300
Langley, Noel 123
Langova, Sylva 69
Langton, Paul 83, 202, 263, 325
Lanoe, Henri 387
Lansing, Joi 15, 129, 182, 316
Laporte, Rene 435
Larbi, Doghmi 246
Larch, John 39, 162, 305
Lardner, John 129
Larkin, Mary 293
Larsen, Keith 11, 103, 131, 135, 167, 220, 278, 339, 358, 427
Larson, Jack 26, 367
Lasdun, Gary 389
Latell, Lyle 13
LaTorre, Charles 295
Latour, Maria 29
Lattanzi, Tina 414
Laughinghouse, John 289
Launder, Frank 80

Name Index

Laurama, Lennart 311
Lauren, Rod 42, 156
Laurence, Michael 134
Laurie, John 222
Lauter, Harry 13, 21, 89, 99, 105, 114, 125, 126, 136, 235, 287, 399
Lawrance, Jody 314
Lawrence, Andre 236
Lawrence, Bert 105, 168, 204, 364, 416
Lawrence, Chris 337
Lawrence, Delphi 201
Lawrence, Sheldon 49
Lawrence, Shirley 337
Lawson, Kate 359
Lawson, Sarah 201
Lawson, Wilfrid 285
Layde, Pat 293
Lazarus, Miklos 297
Lazo, Lilia 2
Lea, Andrea 184
Lea, Jennifer 287, 378
Leary, Nolan 303
Le Beal, Robert 277
Lebeau, Madeleine 158
Leberman, Joseph 273
LeBlanc, Donal 293
Lechtenbrink, Volker 59
Leclerc, Ginette 319
Lecot, Jean-Jacques 396
Leder, Herbert J. 67
Lee, Alan S. 100
Lee, Bernard 219, 423, 437
Lee, Caroline 110
Lee, Christopher 1, 259, 420
Lee, Georgia 303
Lee, Margaret 227
Lee, Reba 191
Lee, Ron 408
Lee, Rudy 55, 313
Lee, Ruta 156, 290
Leech, Richard 201
Leeds, Peter 51
le Fevre, Pierre 184
Leggatt, Alison 97

Legros, Claude 40
Lehne, John 426
Lehner, Helga 72
Leicester, William 129
Leigh, Constance 43
Leigh, Nelson 130, 140, 173, 202, 385, 434
Leighton, Margaret 80
Leister, Frederick 134, 217, 259, 262
Lelouch, Claude 242
Lemaire, Philippe 47
Le Mesurier, John 153, 274
Lemont, John 143
Lenard, Kay 272
Leonard, David 125, 359
Leonard, Jack 155
Leonard, Sheldon 145
Leonetti, Tommy 186
Leong, James 192
Le Person, Paqul 242
Leplat, Rene 184
Lerner, Irving 90
LeRoy, Eddie 193, 232, 363, 416
Leroy, Philippe 124
Lesley, Carole 238
Leslie, Edith 313
Leslie, William 266
Lesser, Julian 251
Lesser, Len 86, 345
Lester, Bruce 332
Lester, William 19
Lester Horton Dancers 66
Lestocq, Humphrey 7, 152, 228
Letchworth, Eileen 221
Letourneau, Pierre 236
Lettieri, Louis 125
Levene, Sam 18
Levin, Henry 226, 420
Levin, Irving H. 162
Levin, Robert 207
Levinson, Barry 196, 426
Levis, Carroll 238

Levitt, Paul 402
Levy, Gerry 52
Levy, Melvin 89
Levy, Stephen 389
Lewis, George J. 54, 84, 348, 361, 378
Lewis, Herbert Clyde 200
Lewis, Jack 435
Lewis, Jean Ann 58
Lewis, Jerry 321
Lewis, Joseph 34
Lewis, Roger 300
Lewis, Ronald 38
Lewis, Ruth 316
Li, Alicia 79
Lieven, Albert 57, 72, 183
Light, Pamela 193
Lightner, Fred 18
Lilburn, James 13
Lime, Yvonne 362
Linden, Walter 290
Linder, Christa 379
Linder, Leslie 420
Lindman, Ake 261
Lindo, Olga 44
Lindsell, R. Stuart 267
Line, Helga 279
Lionel, Guy 158
Lipsius, Morris 129
Lipsky, Oldrich 225
Lipton, Lawrence 190
Lister, Moira 428
Lit, Hy 110
Litel, John 156, 202, 354
Littlefield, Lucien 20, 330, 374
Liuzzi, Giuseppe 104
Lloyd, Bill 100
Lloyd, Euan 429
Lloyd, George 200
Lloyd, Harold, Jr. 266, 344
Lloyd, Rosalind 429
Loc, Hoang Vinh 435
Locke, Harry 7, 44, 123
Locke, Joe 241
Lockhart, Gene 433
Lockhart, Kathleen 314

Lockwood, Roy 235
Lodge, Andrew 78
Lodge, David 446
Lodge, Jean 92
Lodge, Ruth 184
Loftin, Harry 206
Logan, James 234
Lohr, Marie 350
Lollobrigida, Gina 188, 414
Lom, Herbert 117, 143, 238
Lomas, Jack 342
Lombard, Michael 426
Lombard, Robert 188
Lomma, John 334
"London," the dog 230
London, Babe 344
London, Dirk 314
London, Jack 431
London, Julie 147
London, Tom 378
Long, Audrey 359
Long, Richard 185
Longdon, Terence 120
Longfellow, Henry Wadsworth 167
Longstreet, Stephen 328, 337
Lontac, Leon 192
Loo, Richard 79, 176, 192
Loos, Mary 116
Lopez, Perry 440
Lopez, Sylvia 165
Lord, Barbara 48
Lord, Marjorie 257, 308, 322
Lord, Steve 275
Lord Flea and His Calypsonians 66
Loren, Sophia 117
Lorre, Peter 33, 112
Lorring, Joan 145
Losey, Joseph 212, 341
Lotis, Dennis 194
Lott, Barbara 299
Louie, Ducky 41
Louise, Tina 10

Lourie, Eugene 148, 327
Love, Bessie 422
Love, Phyllis 140
Lovegrove, Arthur 120
Lovejoy, Frank 75, 129, 345
Lovsky, Celia 172
Low, Martin L. 180
Lowery, Robert 84, 175, 204
Lowry, Jane 5
Loy, Nanni 161
Loyer, Raymond 396
Lozano, Margarita 104
Lu,,Lisa 328
Lubin, A. Ronald 82
Lubin, Lou 313
Lucas, Andres 192
Lucas, Nick 108
Lucas, William 302
Lucerne, Carla 290
Luchan, Milton 384
Luckham, Cyril 38
Ludwig, Edward 156
Ludwig, Jerry 392
Ludwig, Salem 273, 276
Luez, Laurette 208
Luft, Herman G. 176
Lukas, Paul 124
Lukather, Paul 160
Luke, Keye 433
Lukes, Oldrich 225
Lulli, Folco 183
Lumet, Baruch 300
Lumet, Sidney 300
Lummis, Dayton 130, 168, 233, 374, 380
Lund, Deanna 333
Lund, Jana 139, 178
Lung, Charlie 56
Lung, Clarence 433
Luong, Nam 435
Luotto, Gene 158
Lupino, Ida 205, 371
Lupo, Alberto 165
Lupo, Michele 446
Lupton, John 114, 323
Lutz, Ingrid 261
Luzi, Maria Pia 369

Luzzati, Emanuele 451
Lydal, Benita 169
Lyden, Pierce 322, 367
Lydon, James 19, 71, 101, 190, 191
Lye, Reginald 213
Lyel, Viola 199
Lyles, A.C. 321
Lynch, Alfred 124
Lynch, Ken 415
Lynd, Eva 190
Lyndon, Victor 368
Lynn, Ann 299
Lynn, Christy 321
Lynn, Dani 42
Lynn, Diana 8
Lynn, Emmett 175, 283
Lynn, Jonathan 196
Lynn, Marianne 298
Lyon, Earle 320, 323
Lyon, Francis D. 50, 287
Lyon, Richard 354
Lyons, Colette 323
Lytton, Herbert 83

M

McAfee, Mara 218
McAlinney, Patrick 398
McAnally, Ray 38
MacArthur, James 90
Macauley, Ted 389
McCall, June 316
McCall, Mitzi 89, 419
McCalla, Irish 160
McCallum, David 38, 219
McCambridge, Mercedes 6
Maccari, Ruggero 161
McCart, Mollie 95, 106
McCarter, Nancy 333
McCarthy, Clem 41
McCarthy, Kevin 8, 197
McCarthy, Michael 1, 201
McCarthy, Neil 446
McCarty, Robert 138

Name Index

McClory, Sean 247
McConnel, Craig 426
McCormack, Barney 403
McCowen, Alec 153
McCrea, Jody 130
McCrea, Joel 130, 287, 378, 427
McCullough, Philo 366
McCurry, John 300
McDermott, Brian 302
McDonald, Francis 71, 105, 295, 349, 409
McDonald, Frank 35, 54, 157, 247, 250, 253, 292, 304, 314, 321, 338, 339, 351, 358, 395, 397, 404, 406, 409, 410
MacDonald, Ian 167
MacDonald, J. Farrell 295
MacDonald, Kenneth 243, 342
McDonald, Ray 388
McDouglas, John (Giuseppe Addobbati) 279
McFarland, Olive 143
McGavin, Darrin 258
McGinnis, Niall 38, 282, 438
McGiveney, Owen 193, 255
McGiver, John 237
McGovern, Michael 149
McGowan, Dorrell 22, 230, 356
McGowan, Melody 356
McGowan, Molly 356
McGowan, Stuart E. 22, 356
McGowran, Jack 148
McGrath, Pat 98
McGraw, Charles 88, 145, 189, 233, 408
McGreevey, John 28, 99
McGregor, Charles 392
MacGregor, Parke 351, 397, 442

McGuire, Biff 305, 368
McGuire, Dennis 119
McGuire, Don 378
McGuire, Dorothy 140
McGuire, Maeve 119, 221
McGuire, Paul 314, 358
McHugh, Kitty 205
McIntire, John 305
Mack, Brice 247
Mack, Molly 22
Mack, Wilbur 234, 374, 416
Mackay, Barry 14, 428
McKay, Jock 226
McKay, Sheila 178
MacKaye, Norman 141
McKechnie, James 53
KcKenna, Kate 263
McKenna, Virginia 123
McKenzie, Ed 108
Mackenzie, Mary 44
McKern, Leo 212, 423
McLaglen, Andrew W. 209, 260, 429
MacLane, Barton 84, 116, 202, 203, 209, 270, 404
McLaughlin, Gibb 317, 428
McLean, David 372
MacLeish, Archibald 118
MacLeod, Robert 408
McMahon, Horace 354
McMaster, Niles 5
MacMurray, Fred 13
McNally, Stephen 26, 163, 206
McNamara, John 144
McNaught, Bob 428
McNaughton, Gus 238
McNaughton, Jack 238, 441
McNear, Howard 33
McQueen, Steve 273, 296, 357
Macready, George 186
MacShane, Don 325
McSharry, Carmel 228, 245

McSwigan, Marie 355
McVeagh, Eve 86
McVey, Tyler 76, 178
Madamba, Celeste 192
Maddern, Victor 137, 152, 259
Madison, Guy 54, 62, 158, 250, 251, 253, 292, 304, 338, 351, 395, 397, 406, 409, 410
Madison, Leigh 148
Magalona, Enrique 435
Magee, Patrick 341
Mageean, James 398
Maggert, Branden 10
Maggio, Dante 96
Mahaut, Michele 37
Mahor, Maria 379
Maik, Henri 396
Main, Laurie 437
Main, Marjorie 140
Maine, Charles Eric 14
Mainwaring, Daniel 75, 197, 305, 393; see also Geoffrey Homes
Mairesse, Guy 324
Maistre, François 29
Maitland, Marne 252
Majan, Juan 158
Majoney, Louis 92
Makeham, Elliot 422, 437
Makela, Helena 311
Malandrinos, Andrea 43
Malet, Arthur 82
Malleson, Miles 317, 424, 432
Mallet-Joris, Françoise 319
Mallinson, Rory 20, 84, 211, 215/216, 295, 335, 348, 349
Mallory, Wayne 62
Malloy, Les 108
Malone, Dorothy 13, 202, 233, 339, 401
Malone, Nancy 141
Maltagliati, Evi 161

Mamakos, Peter 232, 313, 334, 363
Mamo, John 79
Manfredi, Nino 161, 227
Mangean, Teddy 234
Mangini, Gino 96
Mangione, Giuseppe 294
Manku, Vivianne 79
Mann, Anthony 117
Mann, Edward Beverly 366
Mann, Lothar 369
Manners, Marlene 347
Manning, Knox 18
Mansfield, Jayne 147
Mansfield, Michael 59
Mansfield, Monte 271
Mansfield, Rankin 103, 187, 287, 434
Manson, Maurice 163, 272
Mantee, Paul 46
Mapes, Ted 20, 243, 399, 411, 417
Mara, Adele 33
Maranne, Andre 149
Maraschal, Launce 14
March, David 89
Marchal, Georges 29
Marchevsky, Alex 245
Marco, Marya 192
Marcus, Peter 52
Marcuse, Theo 172, 247, 290
Maresch, Harald 57
Maret, Jacques 368
"Margo," the chimp 377
Margolese, E.M. 300
Margolis, Herbert 354
Marion, Charles R. 73, 179, 330, 425
Marion, Paul 56, 135, 335, 349
Mark, Michael 34, 421
Mark, Robert 375; *see also* Rudolf Zehetgruber
Marks, Alfred 143
Marks, John 403
Marks, William 230

Markworth, Bob 210
Marle, Arnold 69
Marler, Christine 405
Marley, Florence 413
Marley, John 301
Marlo, Vic 362
Marlow, Katherine 305
Marlowe, Cathy 316, 374
Marlowe, Don 85, 287
Marlowe, Frank 182
Marlowe, Hugh 434
Marlowe, Linda 245
Marlowe, Scott 440
Marly, Guy 123a, 390
Marmur, Jacland 325
Marn, E. 158
Marquette, Susy 314
Marquis, Don 346
Marr, Eddie 200
Marr, Joe 309
Mars, Lani 421
Marsac, Maurice 10
Marsach, Roberto 384
Marsden, Betty 223
Marsh, Garry 424
Marsh, Joe "Tiger" 323
Marsh, Tani 144
Marshal, Alan 185
Marshall, Mort 381
Marshall, Nancy 138
Marshall, Roger 245
Marshall, Shary 377
Marshall, William 334, 408
Marshall, Zena 133, 226
Marshalov, Boris 384
Marshe, Vera 400
Marston, Joel 109, 125, 388, 425
Marteau, Henri 123a
Martell, Alphonse 298
Marth, Frank 141
Martin, Al 193
Martin, Charles 337
Martin, Charles G. 318
Martin, Claudia 353
Martin, Denis 398
Martin, Don 11, 98
Martin, George 198

Martin, Helen 305
Martin, Ian Kennedy 260
Martin, Irene 409
Martin, Jean 25, 319
Martin, Kreg 82
Martin, Lewis 91, 218, 278
Martin, Louis 277
Martin, Todd 128
Martin, Tony 226
Martin-Harvey, Michael 398
Martinson, Leslie 181, 444
Marton, Andrew 124, 389
Martone, Elaine 160
Marvin, Lee 345
Maschwitz, Eric 69
Mascott, Laurence E. 231
Masi, Victor 372
Maslow, Walter 83, 314
Mason, A.E.W. 184
Mason, Laura 55, 316
Mason, Marsha 180
Mason, Mary 228
Mason, Mike 413
Mason, Pamela 344
Mason, Paul 6
Massey, Daria 334
Massey, Raymond 342
Massingham, Richard 430
Masteroff, Joe 63
Masters, Mike 439
Masterson, Paul 108
Matalon, Vivian 212
Mathers, Don 402
Mathews, Allen 218
Mathews, Carl 404
Mathews, Carole 30, 231, 251, 308, 404, 409
Mathews, Martin 223
Mathews, Walter 271
Mathias, Bob 50
Mathias, Melba 50
Mathis, Alphonse 183
Matsui, George 162

Matthews, A.E. 70, 217, 222, 398, 422
Matthews, Bill 275
Matthews, Geoffrey 97
Matthews, Grace 144
Matthews, John 46, 347
Mature, Victor 33
Matuska, Waldemar 225
Mau, Doan Chau 435
Maude, Beatrice 197
Maude, Cyril 424
Maude-Roxby, Roddy 299
Maugham, Robin 341
Maurey, Nicole 80, 97
Maury, Jean-Louis 390
Mavrelis, Perry 318
Maxey, Paul 354
Maxted, Stanley 201
Maxwell, Charles 129
Maxwell, Edwin 145
Maxwell, Lois 121, 169, 432
Maxwell, Paul 72, 245
May, Jack 246
Maynard, Kermit 243, 251, 287, 348, 427
Mayne, Mildred 299
Mayo, Alfredo 124
Mayo, Archie 28
Mayo, Frank 354
Mayo, Virginia 378
Mazzone, Carlo 333
Meader, George 200, 409
Meadow, Herb 170
Meadows, Stanley 120, 302
Medford, Harold 57
Medin, Harriette White 45
Medina, Patricia 324
Medwin, Michael 134, 259, 317
Meeker, George 116
Meeks, Edward 369
Megowan, Don 356
Meillon, John 38
Melfi, John 111

Melford, Frank 251
Melford, Jack 267
Melford, Jill 341
Mell, Joe 181
Mell, Marisa 72
Mellinger, Max 191
Meltcher, Ira 198
Melton, Sid 15, 145
Melville, Alan 70
Melville, Herman 38
Melville, Jean-Pierre 107
Melvin, Donnie 405
Mendoza, Carlos Diaz 393
Meniconi, Furio 96
Menken, Shepard 380
Menzies, William Cameron 255
Mercedes, Maria 428
Mercein, Tom 108
Mercey, Paul 396
Mercure, Monique 236
Meredith, Cheerio 344
Meredith, Jill 223
Merighi, Augusta 273
Meril, Macha 29
Merivale, John 65
Merlin, Jan 75, 157, 336
Merrall, Mary 134, 422
Merrick, John 12, 343, 436
Merrill, Dina 407
Merrill, Gary 187, 272
Merrill, Stuart 177
Merrill, Toni 86
The Merseybeats 110
Merton, John 250
Messiter, Eric 267
Metz, Vittorio 286
Meunier, Gilbert 229
Meyer, Emile 187, 215/216, 327, 329, 439
Meyer, Wayne 221
Meyers, Andy 92
Meyers, Virginia 205
M'Gobo, Chief 92
Miali, Roberto 96
Michael, George 352

Michaelis, Dario 158, 183
Michaels, Beverly 30
Michaels, Pat 15
Michaels, Peter 336
Michaels, Tony 34
Michel, Albert 188
Michel, Marc 412
Michenaud, Gerald 271
Michon, Pat 191
Mida, Massimo 183
Middleton, Guy 222, 226, 280, 285, 441
Middleton, Noelle 398
Middleton, Robert 34, 140
Mihashi, Tatsuya 445
Mikler, Michael 157
Milan, Lita 270, 273, 402
Milbourne, Olive 81, 164, 194
Miles, Christopher 386
Miles, Sarah 341
Miles, Sylvia 384
Miles, Vera 312, 408, 423, 427
Milford, John 303
Miljan, John 366
Milland, Ray 149
Miller, Colleen 157
Miller, Dick 284, 419
Miller, Eve 209
Miller, Jan 52
Miller, Joan 44, 361
Miller, Ken 24, 106
Miller, Kristine 303, 338
Miller, Linda 5
Miller, Magda 226
Miller, Martin 124
Miller, Martyn 244
Miller, Paul 279
Miller, Peter 87
Miller, Ralph 258
Miller, Seton I. 79
Miller, Tony 16
Milletaire, Carl 179
Millhauser, Bertram 301

Name Index

Millican, James 35, 84, 218, 401
Millman, Mort 345
Mills, Michael 28
Mills, Mort 85, 91, 103, 157, 385, 407
Mills, Sally 271
Millyar, Georgiy 240
Milner, Dan 144
Milner, Jack 144
Milner, Martin 26, 336, 344, 353
Milo, Sandra 165
Milton, Gerald 28, 271
Milton, Rob 365
Minazzoli, Christiane 370
Mineo, Michael 106
Mineo, Sal 87, 106
Minnelli, Liza 63
Mintz, Sheila 271
Mirisch, Walter 8, 130, 131, 167, 255, 287, 378, 420, 427
Mitchel, Bob 206
Mitchell, Cameron 45, 121, 198
Mitchell, Carlyle 230
Mitchell, Carolyn 89
Mitchell, Duke 87
Mitchell, George 305
Mitchell, Gordon 446
Mitchell, Grant 200
Mitchell, Laurie 66, 127, 157, 287, 316
Mitchell, Leslie 428
Mitchell, Pat 250
Mitchell, Stephen 219
Mitchell, Steve 34
Mitchell, Yvonne 44, 317
The Mitchell Boy's Choir 206
Mitchum, John 75, 172, 206, 416
Mitchum, Julie 185
Miya, Jo Anne 79
Mizar, Maria 60
Mobley, Mary Ann 439
Modugno, Domenico 324

Moffitt, Peggy 24
Mohner, Carl 261
Mohr, Gerald 114
Moiselle, Nuala 274
Molinas, Richard 226
Molloy, Dearbhla 293
Molloy, John 293
Molteni, Ambrogio 96
Monaghan, Jay 20
Moncey, Françoise 229
Monicelli, Mario 268, 414
Monkman, Noel 213
Monnet, Jacques 40
Monroe, Tom 175
Montague, Lee 38
Montalban, Ricardo 391
Montell, Lisa 434
Montes, Conchita 124
Montes, Elisa 198
Montgomery, George 68, 215/216, 220, 243
Montinaro, Brizio 9
Montoya, Alex 358
Moon, Lynne Sue 124
Moore, Alvy 8, 303, 325, 329, 336
Moore, Clayton 209, 397
Moore, Dennis 182, 192
Moore, Dickie 19
Moore, Eileen 152
Moore, Ellen 275
Moore, Juanita 235
Moore, Kieron 37, 97, 389
Moore, Margo 147
Moore, Norma 415
Moore, Pauline 230
Moore, Roger 149, 386, 429
Moore, Terry 72, 345
Moore, Tom 210
Moore, Victor 200
Moorehead, Agnes 23, 407
Moorhead, Jean 15
Moray, Yvonne 79
More, Kenneth 137, 244, 437

Morehouse, Ed 300
Moreland, Gloria 323
Morell, Andre 148, 280
Moreno, Liza 90
Moreno, Rita 90, 135
Morey, Edward, Jr. 211
Morgan, Bob 349
Morgan, Bud 448
Morgan, Diana 226
Morgan, Guy 164
Morgan, Henry (Harry) 136, 145, 171
Morgan, Read 31
Morgan, Russ 108
Morheim, Louis 354
Morin, Alberto 257
Moro-Giafferi, François 123a
Morrell, Ann 394
Morris, Barboura 382, 421
Morris, Dorothy 239
Morris, Lana 152, 154
Morris, Phyllis 259
Morris, Tony 270
Morris, Wayne 101, 126, 235, 248, 308, 367, 385, 411
Morrison, Ann 378
Morrison, Barbara 296
Morrison, Chen 158
Morrison, Joe 318
Morrison, Patty 318
Morrison, Quinn 177
Morrison, T.J. 153
Morrow, Byron 42, 372
Morrow, H. 158
Morrow, Jeff 130
Morrow, Neyle 271, 347
Morrow, Scott 83
Morrow, Susan 239
Morrow, Vic 163
Morse, Barry 262
Morse, Robin 334
Morse, Terry O. 377, 439
Morton, Charles 349
Morton, Clive 70
Morton, Frederic 405

Name Index

Morton, Hugh 252, 302
Moschin, Gastone 268, 446
Moses, Albert 246
Moses, Charles A. 139
Moss, Allen 296
Moss, Arnold 132
Moss, Herbert 146
Moss, Lou 45
Moustache 443
Mudie, Leonard 150, 211, 235, 335, 359
Mulachie, Gabriella 104
Mulcaster, G.H. 81
Mulhall, Jack 15, 64, 416
Mulholland, Mark 293
Mullaney, Jack 394
Mullay, Gary 444
Mullen, Barbara 438
Mulot, Claude 47
Mummert, Danny 39
Mumy, Bill 296
Muni, 29
Munoz, Marilou 90
Munroe, Hugh 98
Murat, Jean 324, 396
Murata, Chieko 36
Murgia, Antonella 369
Murgia, Tiberio 387
Murphy, Audie 19, 157, 418
Murphy, Donald 211, 345, 371
Murphy, Fidelma 274
Murphy, Jimmy 85, 174, 182, 232, 363
Murphy, Mary 86
Murphy, William 320
Murray, John Fenton 334
Murray, Paul 265
Murray, Peter 267
Murray, Stephen 3, 134, 252, 267, 350
Murray, Zon 39, 159, 170, 351, 417
Murton, Lionel 408, 446
Musante, Tony 9

Musso, Vito 108
Musu, Antonio 25
Mycroft, Walter C. 432
Myers, Monroe 258
Myers, Peter 74
Myles, Meg 305
Mylong, John 28
Myshkova, Ninel 240

N

Nachama, Estrongo 63
Nadel, Ruth 318
Nader, George 186
Nagy, Bill 245
Naish, J. Carrol 125, 436
Nakamura, Shizue 272
Nakamura, Tetsu 36
Nalder, Reggie 82
Nalon, Duke 330
Nanh, Kieu 435
Napier, Alan 171
Napier, Russell 69
Nash, Alden 415
Natwick, Mildred 405
Naud, William T. 180
Navarro, Ann 202
Navizet, Albane 370
Nazarr, Norman 314
Nazarro, Ray 209
Neana, Nestor M. 393
Nebiolo, Carlo 268
Nehlsen, Hermann 198
Neise, George 378, 407
Nelson, Burt 62, 343
Nelson, David 33
Nelson, Ed 16, 89, 178, 357, 382
Nelson, Gene 14
Nelson, Julia 274
Nelson, Kay Anne 388
Nelson, Ralph 357
Nelson, Stan 389
Neri, Tommaso 25
Nervi, Milarka 32

Nesbitt, Derren 228
Netscher, Robin 282
Neuman, Sam 172
Neumann, Dorothy 287, 382
Neumann, Kurt 19, 20, 116, 167
Neumann-Viertel, Elisabeth 63
Neville, David 78
Neville, John 38
Newell, William 359
Newley, Anthony 153
Newling, Desmond 267
Newman, Joseph M. 33, 99, 147, 187, 214
Newman, Stephen D. 276
Newman, Walter 86
Newsome, Gill 108
Newton, Joel 205
Newton, Mary 20
Newton, Theodore 76, 140
Ney, Marie 44
N'Guessan, Jean-Françoise Eyou 40
Nicholl, Don 194
Nicholl, Gee 194
Nicholls, Anthony 94, 137, 164, 184, 244, 280, 310, 398, 422, 432
Nichols, Barbara 147, 186
Nichols, Dandy 223
Nichols, Red 108
Nichols, Robert 173, 205, 272
Nicholson, Jack 89
Nick, Chung 113
Nicol, Alex 231
Nielsen, Leslie 444
Niesen, Gertrude 18
Nieto, Jose 81, 124
Nigh, Jane 108, 174
Nightingale, Michael 92
Nihonmatsu, Shigeru 36
Nilo, Alejandra 379

Name Index

Niven, David 124, 398
Noble, James 426
Noel, Chris 357
Noiret, Philippe 268
Nolan, Lloyd 19
Nolan, Margaret 37
Nolte, Charles 10
Norby, Ghita 288, 447
Nord, Eric "Big Daddy" 190
Nordman, Marilyn 177
Norman, Gene 108
Norman, Jack (Norman Willis) 41
Norman, Jett (Clint Walker) 208
Norris, Edward 265
Norvo, Red 108
Nosseck, Martin 261
Notorianni, Pietro 227
Nourse, Allen 305
Noury, Alain 370
Nova, Lou 73, 433
Novakova, Jana 353
Novello, Ivor 94
Noyes, Alfred 171
Noyle, Ken 210
Ntshona, Winston 429
Nugent, Judy 272
Nunes, A. Robert 170, 308
Nyby, Christian 289
Nye, Clinton 177
Nye, Louis 344

O

Obeck, Sharon 333
Oberon, Merle 3
O'Brien, Edmond 84
O'Brien, Willis 148
Ocasek, Viktor 225
O'Casey, Ronan 398, 438
O'Connell, Robert 273
O'Dea, Denis 217
Odlum, Jerome 170
O'Donnell, Cathy 432

O'Donnell, Marie 293
O'Dowd, Michael 273
O'Ferrall, George More 7, 164
Offerman, George 224
O'Flynn, Damian 157, 411
Ogg, James 87
Ogg, Sammy 202
Ogilvy, Ian 360
Oginski, Kathrin 375
O'Grady, Tony 92
O'Hanlon, James 206
O'Herlihy, Dan 171, 214
O'Higgins, Brian 398
Ohmart, Carol 185
Okada, Reiko 210
Okawa, Henry 36
Okazaki, Bob 162
O'Keefe, Dennis 115, 218
O'Keefe, Michael 140
O'Kelly, Jeffrey 389
Oliver, Thelma 300
Olivier, Laurence 31
O'Loughlin, Gerald S. 408
Olsen, Chris 269
Olsen, Merlin 260
Olsen, Moroni 41
O'Madden, Lawrence 154, 262
O'Malley, Pat 197
O'Moore, Patrick 193, 208
Onagg, Juddy 36
O'Neil, Robert 408
Onyx, Narda 172
Oorthuis, Dity 365
Opatoshu, David 331
Opatoshu, Joseph 331
Oppenheimer, Edgar 47
Oppenheimer, Hans 369
Oppenheimer, Joel 119
Oppenheimer, Peer J. 289
Oravisto, Hannu 311
The Orchids 110
Orlandi, Felice 273
Orleans, Jenny 229

Orrison, Jack 431
Osborn, Andrew 7, 164
Osborn, Lyn 12, 83
Osborne, Bud 68, 250, 295, 366
Oscar, Henry 423
Oscard, Miko 121
O'Shea, Jack 136, 367
O'Shea, Michael 108, 354
O'Shea, Milo 274, 293, 438
Osterloh, Robert 8, 197, 313, 329, 332, 342, 361, 439
O'Sullivan, Richard 420
Oswald, Gerd 57
Oswald, Marianne 188
Ota, Hiroyuki 36
Otis, Ted 160
Ott, Warene 42
Oulton, Brian 70, 226, 430, 441
Owen, Alun 256, 341
Owen, Garry 200
Owen, Tudor 11
Owen, Yvonne 350
Owens, Patricia 162
Oyen, Raoul 355

P

Pack, Roger Lloyd 142
Packer, Netta 354
Padden, Sarah 116
Padilla, Manuel 377
Padula, Vincent 321
Pagano, Jo 265, 339, 436
Page, Genevieve 29, 117, 405
Page, Joy 125
Page, Patti 111
Page-Jones, Robert 387
Paget, Debra 342
Paget, Robert 180
Paice, Eric 228
Paiva, Nestor 101, 314

Name Index

Paletti, Ugo 25
Pali, Jeanne 184
Palk, Anna 306
Pallans, Art 108
Palmer, Gregg 133, 144, 323
Palmer, Maria 391
Palmer, Robert 266
Paluzzi, Luciana 77, 227
Pani, Corrado 165
Papineau, Bernard 390
Pappas, Irene 414
Paraluman 376
Parfrey, Woodrow 296
Paris, Simone 242
Park, Phil 256, 420
Parker, Cecil 74, 80, 199
Parker, Fess 114
Parker, Frank 297
Parker, Jack 366
Parker, Shirley 258
Parkin, Dean 93
Parkinson, Roy 49
Parks, Gordon, Jr. 392
Parkyn, Leslie 306
Parmentier, Brigitte 29
Parnell, Emory 135, 208, 251, 312, 335, 373
Parnell, James 349
Parrish, Leslie 67
Parry, Gordon 53
Parson, Dete 177
Parsons, Jack 228
Parsons, Johnnie 330
Parsons, Lindsley 76, 88, 91, 115, 122, 129, 202, 233, 247, 257, 283, 291, 309, 314, 326, 371, 380, 401, 431
Parsons, Michael 90
Parsons, Milton 354
Partridge, Derek 212
Passer, Dirch 288, 447
Pastell, George 143, 337
Pastrano, Willie 177
Patch, Wally 430

Pate, Michael 255, 287, 332, 352, 378
Patriarca, Walter 446
Patrick, Dorothy 218, 380
Patrick, Nigel 350, 428, 441
Patridge, Joe 190
Patten, Robert 325
Patterson, Dick 111
Patterson, Elizabeth 218
Patterson, Hank 202
Patterson, Kenneth 197, 307
Patterson, Lee 194
Patterson, Troy 362
Paul, Eugenia 109
Paulet, Pierre 396
Paull, Morgan 260, 408
Paulsen, Albert 276
Pauly, Ursula 32
Pawl, Nick 301
Paxton, Casey 110
Payer, Ivo 96
Payne, John 173
Payton, Barbara 263
Pazzaglia, Riccardo 324
Peacock, William 302
Pearl, Gay 65
Pearson, Lloyd 310
Pearson, Richard 228
Peary, Harold 308
Peckinpah, Sam 103, 197
Pedroza, Inez 394
Peil, Paul Leslie 30, 159, 436
Pelle, Tommy 275
Pena, Julia 60
Pena, Sergio 2
Pendleton, Steve 54, 381
Penman, Lea 309
Penn, Leonard 122, 193, 250, 265
Pennell, Larry 342
Pepper, Barbara 344
Pepper, Dan 174
Peral, Jose Antonio 128
Percival, Robert 143
Perdue, Curtis 177

Perello, Michele 47
Perevalov, Vitya 240
Perilli, Ivo 414
Perkins, Anthony 132, 140
Perkins, Gay 177
Perkins, Gil 313
Perkins, Voltaire 239
Perreau, Gigi 231
Perrey, Mirelle 412
Perrin, Jack 342
Perrin, Jacques 40
Perrins, Leslie 244
Perry, Anthony 299
Perry, Barbara 271, 347
Perry, Desmond 293
Perry, Eleanor 221, 405
Perry, Frank 221, 405
Perry, Vic 14
Perschy, Maria 379
Persoff, Nehemiah 4
Pertwee, Jon 430
Pertwee, Michael 222, 259, 285, 350, 398
Pertwee, Roland 350
Peter and Gordon 110
Peters, A.D. 219
Peters, Brock 300
Peters, Dennis Alaba 92
Peters, Erika 166
Peters, House, Jr. 170, 243, 381
Peters, Vicky 260
Petersen, Hans W. 288
Peterson, Gene 167
Peterson, Lenka 305
Petrie, Daniel 31
Petrie, Howard 50, 326
Petrosino, Lt. Joseph 301
Pettingell, Frank 282
Pevney, Joseph 307
Peynet, Michel 229
Peyser, John 413
Pfitzmann, Gunther 59
Phares, Frank 275
Phil Seamon Jazz Group 194
Philbin, Walter 177
Philbrook, James 128, 389

Name Index

Phillips, Carmen 82
Phillips, Claire 192
Phillips, John 103, 354, 420
Phillips, Leslie 164
Phillips, Philip 182, 378
Phillips, Robert 260
Phillips, Wendell 132
Phillips, William "Bill" 313
Phillpotts, Ambrosine 123, 137
Phipps, William 130, 131, 235, 283, 329, 411
Pialat, Maurice 390
Picchette, John 119
Piccoli, Michel 29
Piccolo, Ottavia 443
Picerni, Paul 51, 76, 103, 235
Pickard, John 11, 13, 39, 126, 287, 325, 342, 349, 411
Piegay, Henri 370
Pieral 188
Pierce, Arthur C. 83, 186, 266
Pierce, Norman 7
Pierlot, Francis 9, 116
Pinelli, Tullio 165, 268
Pink, Sidney 128, 379
Pinter, Harold 341
Pious, Minerva 237
Piper, Frederick 143
Pitani, Daniele 65
Pitcher, George 97, 201
Pithey, Wensley 154
Pizor, William M. 294
Platt, Edward 42, 291, 323
Platt, Howard 392
Plesa, Branko 331
Ploski, Joe 139
Plummer, Christopher 78, 246
Plunkett, Patricia 53, 134, 217, 264
Pohlmann, Eric 80, 124, 169, 432

Poire, Alain 277
Poirier, Rene 184
Poland, Joseph F. 385
Poleri, David (voice of) 301
Polidoro, Gian Luigi 333
Pollack, Ben 108
Pollack, Dee 307
Pollack, Nancy R. 300
Pollard, Snub 193
Pollexfen, Jack 95, 195
Pollock, Ellen 252
Polonsky, Abraham 331
Pontecorvo, Gillo 25
Ponterio, Robin 405
Ponti, Carlo 414
Poole, Bob 108
Poole, Mabbie 432
Poole, Roy 31
Pooley, Olaf 259, 432
Porta, Antonella Della 161
Porte, Robert 396
Portman, Eric 153
Possenbacher, Hans 22
Poston, Tom 357
Pottier, Richard 96
Pousse, Andre 107
Power, Aida 37
Power, Derry 274
Powers, Mala 99
Powers, Richard (Tom Keene) 105
Powers, Tom 248
Prada, Jose Maria 60
Pratt, Mike 299
Prendes, Luis 379
Prescott, Guy 190, 315, 316, 349, 378
Prescott, Norman 108
Prescott, Russ 418
Presley, Elvis 394
Presnell, Robert, Jr. 336
Press, Marvin 257
Preston, Ray 177
Prevert, Jacques 188
Preville, Giselle 94
Prevost, Françoise 302

Price, Dennis 74, 92, 94, 264, 306
Price, Stanley (actor) 39, 101, 136, 175, 248, 322, 367, 399, 411, 417
Price, Stanley (writer) 149
Price, Vincent 23, 33, 79, 82, 185
Prickett, Maudie 272
Priestley, J.B. 153, 219
Priez, Andre 237
Priggen, Norman 212, 302, 341
Prince, William 239
Principe, Albino 324
Prowse, Juliet 333
Pryor, Ainslie 75
Pryse, Hugh 152, 256
Puglia, Frank 130, 358
Purcell, David 78
Purcell, Noel 123, 428, 438
Purdom, Edmund 165, 371
Pushkin, Alexander 317
Pyle, Denver 102, 215/216, 247, 254, 269, 322, 385, 399, 417, 436
Pyott, Keith 184

Q

Qualen, John 13, 327
Quenaud, Daniel 60
Quillan, Eddie 157
Quinlivan, Charles 343
Quinn, Anthony 41, 188
Quinn, Louis 4, 111
Quitak, Oscar 1

R

Rabal, Francisco 29
Rabin, Jack 15, 419
Radich, Renie 392
Raffaelli, Guiliano 45

Name Index

Rafferty, Chips 213
Ragan, Mike (Holly Bane) 39, 103, 358, 411
Raglan, Robert 98, 152
Raho, Umbato 104
Rainer, Lorraine 390
Raison, Milton 175, 361, 399
Ramart, Yusef 317
Ramsing, Robert 288
Rancic, Alenka 331
Randall, Charles 276
Randall, Meg 71, 220
Randall, Stuart 167, 195, 257
Randolph, Edwin 344
Randolph, Isabel 54, 182
Randolph, Linda 347
Rappel, Lillian 293
Rapper, Irving 371
Rasumny, Mikhail 359
Rattigan, Terence 53, 424
Ratzenberger, John 408
Ravell, Jacqueline 362
Rawlins, John 251
Rawlinson, Brian 228
Ray, Andrew 437
Ray, Joey 85
Ray, Nicholas 124
Raymond, Cyril 7
Raymond, Ernest 134
Raymond, Gary 117
Raymond, Paula 187
Raymond, Robin 439
Raymond, Sid 141
Raynor, William 54, 122, 250, 265, 338, 351, 358, 381, 409, 442
Reage, Pauline 370
Reason, Rex (Rhodes) 320
Rebel, Bernard 69
Recco, Mike 270
Reding, Juli 400
Redmond, Liam 44, 398
Reed, Alan (voice of) 346
Reed, Dorothy E. 384
Reed, J. Theodore 359
Reed, Marshall 84, 366, 397
Reed, Oliver 299
Reed, Ralph 89, 284, 378, 401
Reed, Walter 12, 51, 220, 325
Reese, Tom 46
Reeves, Kynaston 259
Reeves, Michael 360
Reeves, Richard 159, 233, 254, 381
Reeves, Robert 202
Regine 249
Regis, Clair 265
Reichow, Otto 172, 232, 290
Reid, Carl Benton 130, 371, 427
Reilly, Robert 138
Reinecker, Herbert 57
Reiner, Gigette 333
Reiner, Thomas 45
Remus, Dudley 6
Remy, Albert 188
Remy, Helene 294
Renard, Maurice 160
Renee, Ricky 63
Rennie, Guy 197, 278
Rennie, Michael 151
Rensing, Violet 28
Resko, John 82
Resner, Lawrence 155
Ressel, Franco 45
Rettig, Tommy 13
Revelala, Freddie 192
Rey, Henri-François 396
Reynolds, Abe 200
Reynolds, Burt 6, 10, 289
Reynolds, Clark E. 108, 349
Reynolds, Harry 112
Reynolds, Jack 62, 192, 397
Reynolds, Marjorie 20
Reynolds, Peter 3, 152, 154, 432
Reynolds, Tom 141
Rhodes, Christopher 117
Rhodes, Grandon 359
Rhodes, Hari 347, 377
Rhodes, Lee 144
Rhodes, Marjorie 44, 285, 422, 437
Riano, Renie 73
Rice, Jack 85, 248
Rice, Joan 302
Rich, Bernard 334
Rich, Dick 126
Rich, John 339
Rich, Tony 418
Richard, Dawn 224
Richards, Addison 168, 220
Richards, Frank 12, 73, 89, 303, 327, 364
Richards, Keith 13, 322, 436
Richards, Sindee Anne 132
Richards, Susan 274
Richardson, Duncan 425
Richlin, Maurice 357
Richman, Mark (Peter) 140
Richmond, Kane 41
Ridgway, Suzanne 144
Ridolfi, Sara 104
Rigaud, Jorge 128, 379, 387
Rigby, Edward 112
Rigg, Carl 52
Righi, Massimo 45
Riley, Elaine 73, 103, 385
Rimmer, Shane 408
Rinehart, Mary Roberts 23
Riordan, Robert 12, 354
Rioton, Louise 123a
Ripper, Michael 44
Risi, Nelo 104
Ritter, Tex (voice of) 427
Ritvo, Rosemary 5

Rive, Kenneth 92
Rivero, Jose Antonio 2
Roark, Robert 336, 381
Robb, David 78
Robbins, Cindy 106
Robbins, Fred 108
Robbins, Gale 159, 315
Robbins, Harold 31, 273
Robbins, Jean 24
Robbins, Marty 21
Roberson, Chuck 84, 347, 366
Roberts, Clete 305
Roberts, Doak 321
Roberts, Ewan 70, 97, 226
Roberts, Lee 68, 84, 103, 209, 325, 417
Roberts, Rachel 153, 256, 422
Roberts, Rosalind C. 100
Roberts, Roy 130, 436
Roberts, Tracey 263
Robertson, Annette 299
Robertson, Dale 46, 169
Robin, Olivia 47
Robinson, Alan 98, 169
Robinson, Betty 271
Robinson, Christopher (Chris) 27
Robinson, Dewey 145
Robinson, Douglas 143
Robinson, Edward G., Jr. 336
Robinson, Jay 392
Robinson, John 80
Robinson, Judy 196
Robinson, Lee 213
Robinson, Patty 271
Robson, Flora 124
Roc, Patricia 49
Rocca, Daniella 65
Rocco, Alex 392
Rocco, Antonino 5
Rocco, Lyla 324
Roche, Dominic 293
Roche, France 324
The Rockin' Ramrods 110

Rockwood, Roy 150, 211, 335
Rodann, Ziva 382
Rodenbeck, John 138
Roderer, Walter 375
Rodgers, Douglas 273
Rodgers, Ilona 355
Rodman, Nancy 67
Roeca, Sam 6, 192, 206, 334, 401, 403
Roehn, Franz 139
Roerick, William 284, 421
Roffman, Julian 48
Rogers, Brooks 405
Rogers, Linda 394
Rogers, Paul 38
Rohm, Marie 72
Rojo, Antonio Molino 128
Rojo, Gustavo 379
Roland, Gilbert 33, 116
Rolfe, Guy 201
Roli, Mino 379
Romain, Yvonne 143
Roman, Ric 416
Roman, Ruth 231
Romanazzi, Allesandro 60
Romand, Gina 67
Romano, Carlo 414
Rome, Sydne 386
Romen, Rachel 100, 347
Roncal, Oscar 90
Rondeau, Charles R. 230
Ronet, Maurice 123a
Rooney, Mickey 214, 241
Rooney, Tim 214
Roope, Fay 73
Roosevelt, Congressman James 314
Rose, George 428
Rose, Reginald 87, 106, 429
Rose, Robert 401
Rose, Sherman A. 241, 381
Rose, Wally 439

Rosenberg, Richard K. 5
Rosenthal, Everett 258
Rosenwald, Francis 373
Ross, Dick 303
Ross, Katherine 31
Ross, Michael 17, 56, 73, 127, 203, 278, 326, 380
Rossen, Robert 38
Rossi, Franco 414
Rossi-Drago, Eleonora 96
Roth, Gene 254, 308, 400, 439
Roth, Johnny 58
Roth, Lillian 5
Rotha, Wanda 262
Rou, Aleksandr 240
Rouvel, Catherine 40
Rowe, Frances 420
Rowland, Henry 182, 232, 322, 399, 411, 417, 431
Rowland, Steve 87, 389
Royce, Riza 23
Royle, Selena 19, 263, 354
Rubin, Benny 380, 416
Rubini, Giulia 96
Rudd, Paul 31
Ruffino, Lorenzo 446
Ruggles, Charlie 200
Ruhl, William 359
Rumann, Sig 364
Ruscio, Al 4
Russel, Tony 418
Russell, Carol 79
Russell, Frank 166
Russell, Harvey 343
Russell, Jackie 394
Russell, Janet 289
Russell, Lewis 269
Russell, Vy 195
Russo, Jackie 290
Rutherford, Margaret 70, 424
Rutic, Dina 331
Ryan, Brandy 316
Ryan, Edward, Jr. 200
Ryan, Irene 388

Ryan, Kathleen 437
Ryan, Michael 372
Ryan, Peggy 388
Ryan, Robert 38
Ryan, Thomas A. 10
Ryan, Tim 127, 204, 248, 313, 366
Rydell, Mark 87
Rye, Michael 160

S

Saadi, Yacef 25
Saan, Miel 79
Sabela, Simon 149
Sabry 32
Sabu (Sabu Dastagir) 334
Sachs, Leonard 148
Sackheim, William 187
Sagigi, Salapata 213
Sailor, Toni 353
St. Angel, Michael 42
St. Clair, Michael 52, 258
St. George, Clive 43
St. George, George 393
St. Jacques, Raymond 300
Saint-James, Fred 32
Saint-Jean, Guy 229
St. John, Marco 276
St. Johns, Adela Rogers 354
Sakki, Heli 311
Salcedo, Leopoldo 90
Sale, Richard 116
Salerno, Enrico Maria 9
Sales, Sammy 48
Salew, John 153, 238, 267
Salkow, Sidney 46, 218, 402
Sallis, Peter 120
Salonika, Patricia 43
Salvador, Lou 281
Salvatori, Renato 60
Salvi, Emimmo 96

Salyin, Vic 90
Sampedro-Munoz, Matilde 198
Sampson, Bill 271
Sampson, Chet 320
Sampson, Robert 231
Samuel, Phil C. 428
Samuels, Bob 275
San Martin, Cornado 81
San Roman, Manuel 393
Sanchez, Jaime 276, 300
Sancho, Fernando 124, 158
Sande, Walter 19, 68, 427, 439
Sanders, Denis 86
Sanders, George 49, 52, 67
Sanders, Gregg 265
Sanders, Hugh 71, 129
Sanders, Lugene 400
Sanders, Terry 86
Sanderson, Joan 441
Sandoz, Maurice 255
Sands, Danny 378
Sands, Johnny 251
Sanford, Ralph 133, 136, 140, 278, 314, 349, 354, 401, 416
Sanipoli, Vittorio 294
Sansom, Ken (voice of) 346
Sansom, Lester A. 24, 37, 352
Sansone, Alfonso 333
Santina, Bruno Della 301
Santon, Penny 106
Sarafian, Richard C. 276
Sargent, Joseph D. 301
Sargent, William 172
Saris, George 86
Sasa, Rumiko 36
Sasso, Ugo 96
Sata, Keiko 445
Sato, Reiko 162
Sattin, Lonnie 186
Saunders, Gloria 351

Saunders, Linda 247
Saury, Alain 396
Savage, Paul 30
Savident, John 196
Saville, Philip 81
Saville, Victor 3
Savo, Ann 261
Sawaya, George 160
Saxon, Al 110
Saxon, John 260, 307
Sayer, Diane 372
Sayer, Jay 419
Sayers, Eric 275
Saylor, Syd 402
Sazarino, Dan 426
Scandelari, Jacques 32
Scannell, Frank 12, 85
Scarpelli, Umberto 96
Scarza, Vince 110
Schaff, Edward 100
Schaffner, Franklin J. 296
Schallert, William 131, 140, 329, 401
Schenck, Aubrey 139
Schidor, Dieter 40
Schildkraut, Joseph 214
Schiller, Frederick 1
Schiller, Norbert 139, 172, 290
Schmid, Helmut 22, 261
Schmidt, Stephen 198
Schmidt, Walter Roeber 162
Schmidt, Wolfgang 353
Schmidtmer, Christiane 369
Schmiedel, Hans Joachim 369
Schneider, Samuel 65
Schneider, Stanley 180
Schoberova, Olga 225
Schoeller, Ingrid 286
Schonherr, Dietmar 57, 353
Schroeder, Arnulf 22
Schubert, Bernard 359
Schulze-Westrum, Edith 59

Schumm, Hans 22
Schurenberg, Siegfried 59
Schuster, Harold 115, 129, 202, 233, 308, 309, 326, 339
Schwalb, Ben 55, 56, 64, 71, 73, 75, 85, 105, 109, 127, 133, 147, 157, 168, 174, 179, 182, 190, 203, 204, 207, 208, 215/ 216, 232, 298, 313, 315, 316, 363, 364, 374, 394, 425
Schwerin, Dr. Herman 59
Schwiner, Michael 289
Scoponi, Giuseppe 183
Scotese, Giuseppe Maria 324
Scott, Bonnie 111
Scott, Harold 164, 280
Scott, Jacqueline 239
Scott, Janette 37, 97, 153, 280, 285
Scott, Kevin 196
Scott, Margaretta 217, 262
Scott, Rod 247
Scott, Simon 408
Scott, Zachary 349, 404
Scotti, Vito 301
Scully, Peter 358
Seaforth, Susan 157
Seay, James 140, 175, 358, 401
Sechehaye, Marguerite Andree 104
Sechehaye, Renee 104
Seebohm, Alison 299
Seely, Donald 435
Sekely, Steve 97
Selander, Lesley 11, 26, 84, 114, 125, 131, 135, 171, 192, 295, 325, 332, 348, 349, 366, 373

Seldes, Marian 86
Selland, Marie 197
Sellars, Elizabeth 124, 154
Sellgren, Li 370
Selwyn, William E. 50
Semple, Lorenzo, Jr. 296
Sengoku, Noriko 36
Sequira, George 428
Sera, Henri 331
Serato, Massimo 96, 117, 124, 158
Serbagi, Roger Omar 276
Sernas, Jacques 124
Sessions, Almira 64
Seton, Bruce 143, 228, 310
Seton, Maxwell 423
Severeid, Eric 118
Seward, Edmond, Jr. 204
Seyler, Athene 44, 74, 137, 317, 422, 441
Seymour, Dan 380, 413
Seymour, James Ed 305
Seymour, Jonah 212
Seymour, Jonathan 402
Shackelton, Richard 101
Shaftel, Josef 269, 281
Shafto, Robert 334
Shaio Lung, Lee 61
Shamsi, Mohammed 246
Shane, Sara 2
Shankland, Robert 369
Shannon, Harry 13, 202, 209, 330
Shannon, Michael 386
Shapiro, Helen 306
Sharp, Don 194
Sharpe, Albert 171
Sharpe, Bruce 34
Sharpe, Cornelia 276
Sharpe, David 250
Sharpe, Edith 280
Sharpe, Karen 257
Sharpe, Lester 359
Shashe, Ed 191
Shaughnessey, Alfred 169

Shaughnessy, Mickey 111, 214, 344
Shaw, Anabel 13
Shaw, Anthony 259
Shaw, Freita 191
Shaw, Sebastian 217
Shaw, Susan 43
Shawlee, Joan 234, 312
Shay, John 89
Shayne, Robert 101, 133, 182, 195, 263, 323, 363, 419
Shearing, George 108
Sheeler, Mark 144, 362
Sheffield, Johnny 150, 211, 235, 335
Shek, Lo Lita 176
Sheldon, Douglas 110
Shelton, Don 62
Shelton, Joy 282
Shepard, Gerald S. 166
Shepley, Michael 398
Shepodd, Jon 115, 291, 326
Sheppard, Paula 5
Sherdeman, Ted 162
Sheridan, Dan 62, 75, 163, 215/216
Sheridan, Dani 360
Sheridan, Margaret 312
Sherman, Fred 155
Sherman, Robert 66, 122, 408
Sherriff, Paul 418
Sherry, Alden 383
Sherwood, Gale 359
Shibata, George 162
Shields, Arthur 95, 312, 433
Shields, Brooke 5
Shiga, Akira 210
Shimada, Teru 272
Shindo, Karie 272
Shine, Bill 398
Shintani, Micko 272
Shipp, Mary 205
Shirreffs, Gordon D. 291
Shitara, Koji 36

Name Index

Shonteff, Lindsay 92
Short, Paul 19, 449
Shumate, Harold 312
Shute, Nevil 217
Shvarts, Yevgeniy 240
Siddons, Althea 43
Siegel, Don 8, 87, 197, 329
Siegfried, John 172
Sierra, Gregory 296
Signorelli, Tom 5
Sikking, James B. 372
Silagni, Giorgio 40
Siletti, Mario 179, 301
Silo, Susan 82
Silos, Manuelk 281
Silva, David 130
Silva, Simone 422
Silvani, Aldo 151
Silvera, Frank 86
Silvern, Bea 100
Silvestre, Armando 167
Sim, Alastair 222
Simms, Ginny 108
Simms, Marilyn 391
Simon, Abe 273
Simon, Ernie 108
Simon, Robert 121, 301, 342
Simonell, Giovanni 158
Simpson, John 97
Simpson, Lanny 388
Simpson, Mickey 361, 367, 413, 434
Simpson, Norman 119
Simpson, Ronald 219
Simpson, Russell 140
Sims, Joan 430
Sinatra, Richard 27
Sinclair, Eric 419
Sinclair, Peter 226
Sinden, Donald 386
Singer, Campbell 437
Singh, Bhogwan 58
Siodmak, Curt 353
Sipila, Jukka 311
Sire, Antoine 242
Sire, Gerard 242
Sirgo, Capt. Louis 275

Sitka, Emil 85, 203, 208, 313
Skarstedt, Vance 321
Skinner, Edna 140
Skutezky, Victor 123, 134, 217, 264, 422, 437, 441
Slate, Jeremy 177
Slattery, Joe 100
Slaughter, Frank G. 270
Slavin, Slick 58. 362
Slavin, Susan 42
Slay, Frank C. 110
Sledge, John 275
Sloan, Charles 439
Sloan, John R. 423
Sloane, Olive 422
Small, Millie 110
Smeraldo, Ida 321
Smith, Brian 280
Smith, Carl 21
Smith, Constance 35
Smith, Cyril 282
Smith, Gerald 397
Smith, Hal 178; (voice of) 346
Smith, Howard 121
Smith, Jean Taylor 201, 422
Smith, Jim B. 260
Smith, John 140, 342, 427
Smith, La Vergne 275
Smith, Malcolm 166
Smith, Marc 149
Smith, Milton 177
Smith, Paul 336
Smith, Queenie 127, 174, 182, 251
Smith, Sandy 382
Smith, Shawn 434
Smith, Terry 177
Smith, Truman 305
Smith, Vincent 293
Smith, Wilbur 149
Smith, William 408
Smithers, William 296
Snegoff, Leonid 359

Snowden, Alec C. 14, 69, 98
Snowden, Eric 208
Snowden, Leigh 181
"Snowfire," the horse 356
Snyder, Arlen Dean 180
Soble, Ron 4
Sofaer, Abraham 130
Sohnker, Hans 57
Sokoloff, Vladimir 334
Solar, Silvia 128
Sole, Alfred 5
Solinas, Franco 25
Solinas, Marisa 161
Sollazzo, Amedeo 286
Solomon, Linda Lee 200
Solon, Ewen 420
Sone, Roy 110
Sonego, Rodolfo 60, 333
Sonny Stewart's Skiffle Kings 194
Soon, Francis Chin 213
Sorano, Daniel 396
Sorel, Jean 29
Sorel, Louise 299
Sorenson, Leilani 303
Sorente, Sylvia 37
Sosa, Mile 331
Souchka 32
Southern, Terry 119
Space, Arthur 73, 381
Spain, Fay 4, 146, 382
Sparks, Jack 64, 374
Spell, George 271
Spencer, Douglas 75, 361
Spencer, Jessica 267
Spencer, Marian 53
Spenser, Jeremy 94, 212, 310
Sperdakos, George 48
Spiesser, Jacques 40
Spikings, Barry 78
Spinola, Matteo 183
Spolijar, Branko 331
Sportelli, Luca 286
The Sportsmen 297

Name Index

Springsteen, R.G. 24, 75, 215/216, 290, 327
Squire, Ronald 285, 424
Stackleborg, Gene 245
Stafford, Eddie 98
Stafford, John 151, 164
Staley, Joan 111
Stalnaker, Charles 389
Stamp, Terence 38
Stander, Lionel 446
Stang, Arnold 111
Stanley, Helene 103, 330
Stanton, Helene 34, 374
Stanton, Philip 7
Stapleton, James 160
Stapleton, Maureen 405
Starkman, Carol 48
Steeber, Max 156
Steel, Anthony 222, 370
Steel, Gordon 429
Steele, Barbara 279
Steele, Bob 15
Steele, Mary 194
Steele, Mike 23
Steele, Tom 351
Steen, Bodil 288
Steffen, Sirry 172
Stegger, Karl 288
Steiger, Rod 4, 82, 300
Steimar, Jiri 225
Steinberg, Joe 90, 400
Steloff, Arthur 72
Steno, Stefano 414
Stensel, Glenn 156
Stepanek, Karel 1, 57
Stephan, Aram 124
Stephani, Frederick 200
Stephen, Susan 74, 123, 201
Stephens, Ann 137, 152, 282
Stephens, Harvey 23, 291, 307
Stephens, Helen 439
Sterland, John 245
Sterling, Jan 187, 325
Stevens, Charles 211
Stevens, Craig 265
Stevens, Dodie 82
Stevens, Dorinda 98
Stevens, Eileen 17, 197
Stevens, Louis 28, 251
Stevens, Mark 91, 159, 202, 401
Stevens, Marya 316
Stevens, Naomi 82
Stevens, Paul 446
Stevens, Robert 273
Stevens, Ronnie 259
Stevens, Vi 164
Stevenson, Houseley 354
Stevlingson, Ed 221
Stewart, Jack 143
Stewart, John 426
Stewart, Marjorie 422
Stewart, Nick 325
Stewart, Peggy 351
Stockke, Tor 355
Stockman, Boyd 366
Stoddard, Russ 389
Stokes, Ron 266
Stolnay, Akos 151
Stone, Andrew L. 274
Stone, Cece 177
Stone, Eric 42
Stone, Genie 66
Stone, Harold J. 260
Stone, John 143, 236
Stone, Marianne 143, 169, 194, 386
Stone, Merritt 400
Stone, Paddy 153
Stone, Ross 318
Stone, Roy 245
Stone, Virginia 274
Storm, Gale 116, 200, 366
Storm, Michael 276
Strang, Harry 13, 64, 232, 354
Strange, Glenn 315, 404
Stranges, Judy 115, 301
Strasberg, Susan 444
Stratford Pictures 7, 53, 70, 74, 80, 81, 94, 112, 123, 134, 137, 151, 152, 153, 154, 164, 184, 199, 201, 217, 219, 222, 244, 256, 259, 260, 264, 280, 282, 285, 310, 317, 350, 424, 430, 432, 438, 441, 450
Stratton, Gil, Jr. 26
Straus, E. Charles 172
Strauss, Robert 111, 147, 407
Strawn, Arthur 20, 167
Stricklyn, Ray 87, 307
Strock, Herbert L. 328
Strode, Woody 208
Strong, L.A.G. 398
Stross, Raymond 223
Strother, James 166
Stroud, Claude 89
Stuart, Aimee 226
Stuart, G.R. 65; see also Jack Stuart
Stuart, Jack (Giacomo Rossi Stuart) 183, 443; see also G.R. Stuart
Stuart, Jean 32
Stuart, John 244, 262
Stuart, Josephine 267, 422
Stuart, Randy 243
Stuart, Wendy 230, 303
Stumph, Wolfgang 59
Style, Michael 142
Styles, Edwin 74, 199, 259, 422
Sullivan, Barry 20, 115, 145, 233, 314, 354, 431
Sullivan, Bill 260
Sullivan, Brick 413
Sullivan, Didi (Didi Perego) 65
Sullivan, Don 323, 343
Sully, Frank 243, 283
Summer, Graham 37

Summerfield, Eleanor 199, 222, 244, 259
Sumner, Geoffrey 259, 424
Sumner, Graham 389
Sumner, Peter 444
Sundstrom, Frank 359
Sury, Bernard 229
Sutton, Dudley 223
Sutton, Grady 394
Sutton, John 23
Swan, Robert 144, 362
Swann, Francis 67
Swanson, Maureen 256
Swanson, Ruth 89
Swanwick, Peter 228
Swarttz, Berman 205
Swawlee, Joan 56
Sweers, Alex 365
Swenson, Inga 31
Swerling, Jo 214
Swift, David 196
Swimmer, Saul 77
Swinburne, Nora 217
Switzer, Carl "Alfalfa" 105
Swoger, Harry 6
Sydes, Anthony 159, 200, 250
Sylvaine, Vernon 430
Sylvester, William 437
Szabo, Albert 172

T

Ta Fel, Suzanne 339
Tabakin, Bernard 297, 433
Tacchella, Jean-Charles 396
"Taffy," the elephant 377
Tafler, Sydney 282
Tafuri, Barnardo 414
Taka, Miiko 162
Takacs, Maria 72
Takahashi, Tauenko 272
Takai, George 162
Talaskivi, Jaakko 311

Talbot, Brad 128
Talbot, Lyle 64, 73, 101, 203, 351, 367, 374, 403, 411, 425
Talbott, Gloria (Gloria Talbot) 54, 93, 95, 283, 287, 371, 440
Tallas, Gregg 37
Talman, William 303
Talton, Alix 380
Tamblyn, Russ 440
Tamiroff, Akim 145
Tanaka, Tomoyuki 445
Tanin, Eleanore 133
Tannen, William 103, 130, 150, 192
Tapley, Colin 7, 69
Tarangelo, John 325, 329
Tarkington, Rockne 357
Tate, Dale 17
Taurog, Norman 394
Tayback, Vic 296
Taylor, Forrest 39, 133
Taylor, Holland 276
Taylor, Kenneth 423
Taylor, Larry 212
Taylor, Rod 213, 434
Taylor, Ronald 48
Taylor, Tony 18
Taylor, Vaughn 159, 307
Taylor, Wayne 336
Tayman, Robert 196
Tead, Phil 122
Teague, Guy 397
Teal, Ray 287, 361, 378
Teddy Kennedy Group 194
Temple, Joan 282
Templeton, William 112
Tenkai, Ziro 272
Tennant, Pauline 317
Tennen, Arthur 166
Tenser, Tony 52, 360
Terra, Renato 96
Terrace, Linda 66
Terranova, Dan 87, 439
Terrell, Kenneth 17,

195, 334
Terrell, Steve 269
Terri, Pia 74
Terro, Turi 446
Terry, Al 62
Terry, Martin 360
Terry, Philip 243
Terry, Robert A. 83, 100
Terry-Thomas 238, 446
Tessari, Duccio 443
Tessier, Elisabeth 47
Tessier, Valentine 188
Tevlin, C.J. 23
Thatcher, Heather 123, 430
Thawnton, Tony 92
Thayer, Lorna 205
Theil, Sid 254, 322, 417
Theil, Sol 175
Thesiger, Ernest 219, 222, 238, 432
Thierry, Paul 290
Thomas, Dylan 282
Thomas, Jeanine 275
Thomas, Lyn 12
Thomas, Rachel 256
Thomas, Richard 221
Thompson, Carlos 393
Thompson, J. Lee 44, 74, 134, 153, 264, 280, 422, 437
Thompson, Marshall 308, 435
Thompson, Paul 109
Thompson, Ross 401
Thomson, Marsh 289
Thon, Dorsi 32
Thor, Jerome 124
Thor, Larry 230, 309
Thorburn, June 252
Thorent, Andre 229
Thorndike, Sybil 422
Thorne, Gary 393
Thorp, Nola 111
Thorpe, George 123
Thorsen, Duane 202
Thorsen, Russell 102, 413
Thring, Frank 117

Name Index

Thurston, Carol 190, 442
Thyssen, Greta 28
Tichy, Gerard 117, 158
Tiemeyer, Hans 365
Tieri, Aroldo 286
Tin, My 435
Tingwell, Charles 213
Tinti, Gabriele 96
Tipping, Brian 212
Toal, Maureen 293
Tobey, Kenneth 125
Tobias, George 361
Tobias, Oliver 331
Tocinowsky, Marija 104
Todd, Richard 3, 134, 310
Tofano, Sergio 161
Tognazzi, Ugo 161, 268, 333
Tokunaga, Frank 36
Tolan, Michael 167
Tolo, Marilu 331
Tomack, David 314
Tombragel, Maurice 250, 292, 395, 397, 406, 409, 410
Tomelty, Joseph 14, 398
Tomlinson, David 70, 217
Tonge, Philip 239
Toomey, Regis 187, 207, 214, 358, 391
Toone, Geoffrey 432
Topper, Burt 372, 418
Torey, Hal 83
Tornburg, Kay 426
Torrey, Roger 307
Torrisi, Francesco 286
Tosi, Luigi 96, 294
Tottenham, Merle 267
Toure, Aboutbaker 40
Tourjansky, W. 165
Tourneur, Jacques 427
Towers, Constance 271, 347
Towers, Harry Alan 72; *see also* Peter Welbeck
Townley, Jack 85, 109, 182, 416

Townsend, Leo 361
Tozzi, Fausto 117, 324
Tracy, Margaret 354
Traeger, Rick 172
Trantow, Cordula 59, 172
Trattner, Stephen M. 383
Treen, Mary 73, 174
Tremper, Will 369
Treves, Frederick 169
Trevor, Claire 18
Tricoli, Carlo 301
Trintignant, Jean-Louis 242
Tristan, Dorothy 119
Troitskiy, L. 240
Tromberg, Sheldon 383
Troughton, Patrick 137, 164
Trouncer, Cecil 199, 422
Trowbridge, Charles 19, 41, 359
Truman, Ralph 117, 262, 423
Trumbo, Dalton 296
Trustman, Alan 276
Tryon, Tom 336
Tsiang, H.T. 41
Tsuchiya, Yoshio 445
Tucker, Forrest 129, 159, 278, 297
Tucker, Larry 347
Tully, Montgomery 120, 252, 262
Tully, Tom 11
Turgeon, Peter 221
Turich, Felipe 348
Turkel, Joseph 28, 314, 361, 400
Turnbull, Lee 76
Turner, Barbara 290
Turner, Don 54, 250
Turner, Helene 176
Turner, John 148
Turner, Richard 194
Turner, Tim 259
Turri, Donatella 123a
Tushingham, Rita 223

Twist, Derek 7
Twitty, Conway 344
Tyler, Harry 133, 373
Tyler, Henry 203
Tyler, Richard 15, 272, 408, 409
Tyler, Tom 84, 116
Tyrrell, Ann 342
Tzeiniker, Meier 219, 360

U

Ukonu, A.E. 109
Ullman, Daniel B. 8, 13, 51, 68, 103, 126, 130, 135, 136, 167, 209, 220, 248, 255, 287, 332, 342, 367, 374, 411, 420, 427
Ullman, Elwood 24, 48, 55, 56, 71, 73, 105, 127, 133, 168, 179, 182, 193, 203, 208, 232, 234, 298, 313, 363, 374, 394, 416
Ulmer, Edgar G. 95, 263
Underdown, Edward 164, 238, 244, 432
Urecal, Minerva 85, 133, 374, 409
Uriani, Adriano 183
Urquhart, Molly 44
Urquhart, Robert 124, 184, 199, 398, 420
Ustinov, Peter 38
Uytterhoeven, Pierre 242

V

Vaal, Erica 393
The Vagrants 110
Vailati, Bruno 65
Vaitl, Eva 59
Vajda, Ladislas 151, 164
Valenska, Paula 53
Valentine, Val 80, 428

Name Index

Valere, Simone 107
Valery, Olga 237
Valez, Kippee 361
Valk, Frederick 259, 262
"Valle," the elephant 22
Valle, Ricardo 198
Vallin, Rick 13, 21, 56, 62, 103, 126, 127, 150, 224, 248, 367, 399, 403, 404
Vallon, Michael 145, 155, 232, 314, 322, 351, 356, 399, 409
Vallon, Rick 250
Vallone, Raf 117, 386
Vampira (Maila Nurmi) 344
Van, Le 435
Vance, Leigh 92, 143
Van Cleef, Lee 11, 21, 34, 101, 155, 202, 313, 404, 425
Vandis, Titos 31
Van Doren, Mamie 344
Van Druten, John 63
Van Eyck, Peter 368
Van Eyssen, John 1
Vanni, Renata 301
Van Rooten, Luis 290
Van Sickel, Dale 283, 399
Van Zandt, Philip 34, 73
Var, Maria 350
Varconi, Victor 15
Varden, Norma 193, 234
Varga, Billy 82, 407
Vargas, Alberto 434
Variety Clubs International 19
Varley, Beatrice 153, 267, 282
Varnam, Valerie 223
Vasile, Turi 9, 161
Vaughn, Gwyneth 238
Vaughn, Peter 245
Vaughn, Robert 415

Vaughn, Sarah 108
Vaz Dias, Selma 441
Vazzoler, Elsa 161
Veazie, Carol 272
Vedder, William 434
Vee, Bobby 306
Vejar, Harry J. 197
Velia, Tania 316
Vella, John 318
Venantini, Vanentino 319
Veness, Amy 7, 164
Ventura, Ray 369
Venture, Richard 31
Venuti, Joe 108
Vepsa, Ritva 311
Vera-Ellen 226
Veras, Linda 331
Vercelloni, Elios 324
Verdugo, Elena 248
Vernon, Anne 412
Vernon, Howard 47
Vernon, Richard 341
Ve Sota, Bruno 178, 382, 419, 421
Vespermann, Gerd 63
Vian, Boris 188
Vianello, Raimondo 446
Vicario, Marco 446
Vicas, Victor 369
Vickers, Martha 19
Vickers, Yvette 17
Victor, Charles 74, 217, 265, 285, 424
Vidal, Pianing 281
Vidon, Henry 148
Vighi, Vittorio 286
Vigran, Herb 64, 391
Villiers, James 212
Vincent, Fred 426
Vincent, June 73
Virgo, Peter 354
Vita, Helen 63
Vitaly, Georges 277
Vitch, Eddie 152
Vitina, Dolores 273
Vittes, Lou 323
Vivian, Sidney 97
Vivier, Karl-Wilhelm 59
Vivyan, John 328

Vlady, Marina 277, 333, 414
Vohs, Joan 91
Vonn, Veola 298, 364
von Naukoff, Rolf 198
von Nazzani, G. 375
Von Richthofen, Sigrid 63
von Theumer, Ernst Ritter 198
Voronka, Arthur 236
Votrian, Peter 87, 287
Votrian, Ralph 336
Vukotic, Milena 227, 268
Vye, Murvyn 4, 147, 214

W

Wagenheim, Charles 234
Wager, Tony 444
Wager, Walter 408
Waggner, George 39, 102, 243, 325
Wahl, Wolfgang 57
Wainscott, Leland 46
Waite, Ralph 221
Wakely, Jimmy 11
Walbrook, Anton 317
Walburn, Raymond 348
Walcott, Gregory 303
Wald, Marvin 4
Waldis, Otto 17, 308, 322
Waldleitner, Luggi 57
Walker, Bill 19, 211, 322, 408
Walker, Helen 34
Walker, Ray 73, 175, 182, 312, 322, 330, 436
Walker, Turnley 431
Wallace, George 175, 187, 367, 417
Wallace, Irving 33
Wallace, Jean 34
Wallace, Rowena 444
Wallach, Eli 331

Wallant, Edward Lewis 300
Wallasvaara, Kirsti 311
Waller, Eddy 251
Walsh, Arthur 24
Walsh, Kay 37, 219, 285
Walsh, Lelia 247
Walsh, M. Emmet 119
Walsh, Richard 283
Walsh, Stuart 100, 247
Walston, Ray 82
Waltz, Patrick 187, 316
Wanger, Walter 26, 135, 197, 209, 272, 329
War Eagle, John 115
Warburton, John 332
Ward, Albert 238
Ward, David 267
Ward, Georgina 148
Ward, John 159
Ward, Les 238
Ward, Patrick 199
Ward, Peggy 394
Ward, Robert 100
Ward, Warwick 94, 267
Warde, Harlan 220
Wardell, Jane 435
Warden, Jack 389
Wark, Robert 270
Warner, Jack 285, 438
Warner, Jack, Jr. 377
Warren, Charles Marquis 342
Warren, Don 413
Warren, Lee 177
Warren, Richard 320
The Warriors 110
Warwick, John 81, 137
Washbourne, Mona 112, 153
Waterman, Dennis 142
Waters, George 362
Waters, Russell 70, 199, 226, 428, 444
Watkin, Pierre 189, 361, 363, 374
Watkins, Frank 15

Watkins, Linda 144
Watkyn, Arthur 74
Watling, Jack 123
Watson, Cecil 314
Watson, Jack 252, 429
Watson, Minor 330
Watson, Wylie 267, 282
Wattis, Richard 259, 306
Watts, Charles 33
Watts, Elizabeth 141
Wau, Shau Pau 113
Way, Gay 197
Wayne, David 269
Wayne, Fredd 407
Wayne, Naunton 112
Weaver, Dennis 342
The Weavers 108
Weber, Tania 414
Webster, Chuck 181
Webster, Nicholas 258
Weed, John 89
Weigand, Michele 333
Weiner, Joe 294
Weir, Molly 226
Weis, Heidelinde 245
Weisman, A.T. 169
Weiss, Adrian 58
Weiss, Fritz 22
Weiss, Louis 58
Welbeck, Peter 72; see also Harry Alan Towers
Welch, Francine 37
Weld, Tuesday 344, 357
Welden, Ben 116, 363
Welles, Mel 16, 174, 198, 364
Welles, Orson 96
Wellman, William, Jr. 111, 157
Wells, Alan 35, 83, 241, 326
Wells, Alexander J. 320
Welsh, John 98, 420
Welton, Danny 127, 403
Wendkos, Paul 6

Wengraf, John E. 109, 172, 298
Wenland, Burt 30, 265, 339
Wentworth, Martha 95
Wepper, Fritz 59, 63
Werker, Alfred L. 13
Werle, Barbara 394
Wertmuller, Lina 227
Wessel, Dick 20, 56
Wesson, Dick 297
Wesson, Gene 114, 427
West, Adam 247, 357
West, Jessamyn 140
West, Lockwood 223
Westcoatt, Rusty 356
Westcott, Helen 84
Westerfield, James 187, 307
Weston, Cecil 312
Weston, Leslie 267
Weston, Robert 31
Westrate, Edwin V. 354
Westwood, Patrick 398
Wexler, Paul 55
Wheatley, Alan 120, 252
Whelan, Arleen 21
Whelan, Ron 156
Whiskey, Nancy 194
White, Barbara 424
White, Christine 239
White, Dan M. 315
White, Jesse 76
White, Lee "Lasses" 116
White, Paul 252
White, Robb 185, 239
White, Will J. 163
Whitelaw, Billie 302
Whiteman, Russ 248, 397
Whitfield, Jordan "Smoki" 89; see also Robert "Smoki" Whitfield
Whitfield, Robert "Smoki" 150, 211, 235, 335, 342; see also Jordan "Smoki" Whitfield
Whitfield, Rosemary 152
Whiting, Barbara 297

Name Index

Whiting, John 153
Whiting, Margaret 297
Whitman, Stuart 82
Whitman, Thorpe 51
Whitmore, James 87, 121
Whitney, Peter 88, 145
Whyte, Helen 236
Whyte, Patrick 135
Wickes, Kenneth 48
Wicki, Bernhard 59
Widmark, Richard 408
Wieck, Dorothea 57
Wiener, Elisabeth 249
Wilbur, Crane 23, 147, 305
Wilcox, Charles 362
Wilcox, Frank 206, 243
Wilcox, Fred M. 191
Wilde, Colette 97, 184
Wilde, Cornel 34
Wilde, Lorna 52
Wilde, Sonya 191
Wilde, Wendy 12
Wilder, Audrey 237
Wilder, Billy 237
Wilder, John 173
Wilder, Myles 49, 141, 343, 365
Wilder, W. Lee 49, 141, 365
Wiles, Gordon 145
Wilke, Robert J. 68, 84, 156, 254, 349, 411, 427
Wilkerson, Billy 442
Willenz, Max 200
Willes, Jean 51, 56, 197, 401
Williams, Adam 82, 114, 157, 287
Williams, Barbara 146
Williams, Bill 162, 224, 394, 401
Williams, Brock 169, 199, 429
Williams, Charles 116, 127
Williams, Danny 306
Williams, David 194
Williams, Edy 271
Williams, Emlyn 423
Williams, Guinn "Big Boy" 20
Williams, Guy 342
Williams, Harcourt 134, 282
Williams, Jack 335
Williams, Kenneth 256
Williams, Rhoda 303
Williams, Rhys 19, 62
Williams, Robert B. 23, 99
Williams, Rush 224, 343
Williamson, Fred 392
Williard, Carol 31
Willing, Foy, and the Riders of the Purple Sage 108
Willman, Noel 420
Willock, Dave 26, 131, 316, 330
Willrich, Rudolph 5
Wilmer, Douglas 117
Wilson, Barbara 382
Wilson, Claude 90
Wilson, Douglas 270
Wilson, John (writer) 212
Wilson, John D. (director) 346
Wilson, Larry 108
Wilson, Maurice J. 120, 252
Wilson, Michael 140
Wilson, Richard 4, 301
Wincelberg, Simon 125
Winchell, Walter 111
Windsor, Allen 314
Winfield, Paul 408
Winner, Michael 306
Winninger, Charles 218, 321, 401
Winston, Norman 231
Winter, Vincent 420, 423
Winters, Bernie 306
Winters, Shelley 145, 386
Wintle, Julian 306
Wisberg, Aubrey 258, 363
Wiseman, Joseph 31
Wismer, Harry 18
Wittingham, Jack 94
Witty, Christopher 228
Wolf, David M. 276
Wolfe, Betty 98
Wolfe, Bud 224
Wolfe, Digby 74
Wolfe, Joel 119
Wolff, Frank 27, 421
Wolff, Harald 412
Wolfit, Donald 1, 199
Wolfson, Brent 321
Wolter, Ralf 63
Wong, Arthur 79
Wood, Adrian 366
Wood, Edward D., Jr. 58
Wood, Harry 275
Wood, Mary Laura 169
Wood, Milton 211
Wood, Robert 325
Wood, Ward 349
Woodbridge, George 74, 112, 267
Woodell, Barbara 13, 19, 62, 175, 374
Woodfield, Gitta 190
Woodfield, William Read 190
Woods, Aubrey 386
Woods, Harry 348
Woods, Thomas F. 6
Woodville, Catherine 299
Woodward, Bob 366
Woodward, Morgan 156
Wooley, Sheb 11, 287, 385
Woolner, Bernard 17
Wootten, Stephen 13
Worden, Hank 62, 115
Worth, Brian 123, 219
Wrather, Jack 373
Wright, Barbara Bel 88
Wright, Bloyce 46
Wright, Harold Bell 251
Wright, Will 315, 407

Name Index

Wyatt, Al 243, 320, 349
Wyatt, Jamie 333
Wyatt, Jane 19
Wyldeck, Martin 14
Wyler, William 140
Wynant, H.M. 291
Wyndham, John 97
Wynn, Keenan 196, 214, 269, 345
Wynn, May 176
Wynter, Dagmar 432
Wynter, Dana 197
Wynter, Mark 110

Y

Yachigusa, Kaoru 445
Yaconelli, Frank 116
Yadin, Joseph 369
Yamaguchi, Shirley 272
Yanne, Jean 229, 390
Yarbrough, Jean 85, 133, 182, 278, 436
Yates, George Worthing 139, 400
Yates, John 372
Yip, William 20
Yordan, Merlyn 389
Yordan, Philip 20, 34, 37, 97, 117, 124, 389

York, Duke 366, 403
York, Francine 394
York, Jeff 295, 348
York, Michael 63, 78
York, Susannah 78, 149, 386
Young, Arthur 199, 267
Young, Buck 260
Young, Burt 408
Young, Carleton 10, 11, 26, 39, 257, 329, 335, 342, 401, 407
Young, Felicity 306
Young, Francis Brett 267, 310
Young, Gerald 176
Young, Muriel 80
Young, Paul 226
Young, Roland 53
Yowlachie, Chief 116
Yu, Jimmy Wang 61
Yule, Ian 429
Yulin, Harris 119
Yung, Victor Sen 79, 308

Z

Zahorsky, Bohus 225
Zampi, Mario 222, 259, 285, 398

Zamperla, Nino 446
Zangarelli, Italo 158; see also Ike Zingarmann
Zardi, Dominique 123a, 390
Zardi, Federico 165
Zareschi, Elena 165
Zaro, Natividad 158
Zatlyn, Edward 353
Zavattini, Cesare 60
Zehetgruber, Rudolf 375, 379; see also Robert Mark
Zenon, Michael 48
Zerbe, Anthony 296
Zertuche, Kinta 421
Zimbalist, Alfred 377, 439
Zimbalist, Donald 377, 439
Zimm, Maurice 2
Zingarmann, Ike 158; see also Italo Zangarelli
Zink, Chuck 258
Zinser, Leo 275
Zuber, Marc 40
Zuckert, William 347
Zugsmith, Albert 79, 111, 344
Zweig, Stefan 3, 57

www.ingramcontent.com/pod-product-compliance
Ingram Content Group UK Ltd.
Pitfield, Milton Keynes, MK11 3LW, UK
UKHW041950140426
5217IPUK00014B/729